AN OVID READER

Cover Photo: istockphoto © Andy Hutchinson

ISBN 10: 1-58510-149-4
ISBN 13: 978-1-58510-149-8

10 9 8 7 6 5 4 3 2 1

0109W

AN OVID READER

Ed DeHoratius

QUAE SEMPER HORTATUR UXORI

Table of Contents

Acknowledgments

I want to offer my heartfelt thanks to the following people for their support, encouragement, and assistance in the completion of this project.

First and foremost, my colleagues and students. This project had its (indirect) genesis seven years ago, when I started piloting the notes format with my sophomore classes. The students in my Honors Latin 3 classes between the years of 2000 and 2004 were instrumental in the refinement of this style. The students in my Honors Latin 3 class in 2005-2006 were the first to pilot this book; I thank them for their patience, and for their assistance in identifying both typographical errors and omissions. The students in my Latin 3 class in 2006-2007 used the final manuscript, identifying errors and offering helpful suggestions for the refinement of its details. Finally, my students this year, 2007-2008, are helping me finalize details and catch lingering errors and inconsistencies

I can't thank enough my colleagues in the language department at Wayland High School for their understanding and patience. The Latin teachers deserve special recognition: Lee Krasnoo whose integrity, whose attention to detail, and whose constant flexibility in the face of my ever-changing projects are beyond admirable; Tim Casey (now of Westford Academy), for being a sounding board for ideas; and Helene Lerner, now retired (*miserabile dictu*), whose mentoring and guidance have made me the teacher I am today. There is more of you in this book, Helene, than you will know.

The Classics Department at Boston College played an essential role in the genesis and development of this project; I thank them for both their financial and academic support. Chris McDonough, now of The University of the South, planted the initial seeds for this project, while David Gill helped develop it further. Charles Ahern was instrumental in critiquing and finalizing formatting and approach issues, and he has served as an invaluable resource for final Ovid questions during the manuscript's completion.

I also want to thank the following individuals and institutions: the College of the Holy Cross for the use of its library; Stephen Wheeler of Penn State University for his generous correspondence regarding Tarrant's new OCT; Kate Rabiteau of the College Board, Barbara Boyd of Bowdoin College, John Sarkessian of Youngstown State University, and Mary Pendergraft of Wake Forest University for their assistance with questions about the AP exam; Charles Kling, of St. Joseph's Preparatory School in Philadelphia (retired) for assistance with the glossary; Shirley Lowe of Wayland Middle School (retired) for reading the manuscript and offerring valuable suggestions; and the Classical Association of New England for funding much of the research for this project.

Finally, I want to thank Ron Pullins and Focus Publishing. His constant encouragement, and especially his foresight and the latitude he has given me to write the book that I want to write has been invaluable. This project never would have been finished without his involvement.

Many have read this manuscript, but only one has written it. While I thank everyone for their help, I take full responsibility for any errors that remain.

I cannot close here without thanking my family, Liz, Will, and Matt, the Kennedys, and my parents, whose patience before the constant presence of my laptop has been Herculean. I love you all and I thank you for your support.

Preface

For the Student

The use of this book is relatively simple. It requires you to know some Latin (not all) and, most important, it requires you to think. All that stands between you and a solid understanding of Latin is a few extra minutes of patience and reflection. When I tell my students this, they laugh or roll their eyes. But these same students can recite endings and the meanings of vocabulary, yet they still lack the confidence, despite demonstrated knowledge, to read Latin successfully. It is my hope that this book will help bridge that gap between knowledge and understanding.

The difficulties you face reading Latin are many:

- multiple definitions of words with different meanings
- understanding words with a wide range of meanings in a specific context
- grammatical rules that don't seem to apply as neatly or consistently as you were taught they would
- putting aside your natural inclination to think in English when it counters what you know (but may initially forget) about the Latin

The best way to address these difficulties is to spend time with the Latin in an active, constructive, and meaningful way. It is essential that you deal with the Latin as it is written and as it is intended to be read. Make certain to read the notes carefully when you no longer understand the flow of the Latin; if your confidence in reading is lower, read the notes for a sentence before going to the Latin to alert you to troublespots in the sentence. The notes in general will not give you explicit answers; particularly difficult phrases or constructions will indeed be translated. But the assumption of this book is that you have a solid foundation in forms and grammatical constructions; that it is not necessarily Latin itself but rather the particular Latin of, in the case of this book, Ovid that will cause difficulty. The book will supply, it is hoped, the context and clues you need to understand the specific Latin of Ovid.

The following summaries will introduce you to specific aspects of the book.

Content. The book contains six poems from Ovid's *Amores* and five stories from Ovid's epic poem, *The Metamorphoses*, the former written in elegiac couplets, the latter in dactylic hexameter. These eleven selections represent the entirety of the Advanced Placement Latin Literature Ovid syllabus. They are grouped into four themes: *Amor Vincit Omnia, Benevolentia Deorum, Difficilia Amoris*, and *Ars Latet Arte Sua*. Each chapter contains anywhere between two and four selections. Each chapter begins with an introduction to the theme, followed by unannotated clean or display copies of the Latin of the texts. Following these clean texts are annotated texts with vocabulary, grammar, and other aids. The annotated versions of each text are preceded by a short introduction to the themes and context of that particular text. In addition to the four chapters are a general Introduction, which includes an introduction to Ovid and his life, a timeline of important dates and a glossary of his works and of important people; an appendix, which includes a vocabulary frequency list for all of the texts, a summary of rhetorical figures included on the

AP syllabus and a summary of terminology and rules for scansion; and a glossary, which includes all words in the text with all not-obvious long syllables marked with macrons.

Clean Copy of Text. At the beginning of each chapter (after the introduction to the theme) is an unbroken, unannotated copy of each text. It is imperative that these texts remain unmarked; when you are reading at home, make any notes you need on the annotated text. The clean texts should be left in reserve for studying for your classroom tests (and the AP exam if you are preparing for it). Studying from an annotated text makes it difficult to interact with unannotated Latin; you become accustomed to having notes nearby when you read, and so, when faced with the unannotated Latin of a test, you find the lack of those notes detrimental to your understanding of the Latin.

General Layout of the Page. Starting from the upper left and moving clockwise around the page: notes, text, prose summary, vocabulary, visual, sentence structure diagram, discussion questions. Few pages will contain all of these, and the last three (visual, sentence structure diagram, and discussion questions) can shuffle their position on the page depending on the specific page layout.

Notes. The notes have been written to assist you with difficult aspects of a given passage. This assistance will take two primary forms: one, leading questions, which are designed to prompt you to think about Latin issues relevant to a particular passage; two, notes of negation, which predict how you might incorrectly interpret the Latin and negate that incorrect assumption to elicit the correct response. These notes promote the flexibility and skills that are essential to becoming better readers of Latin.

Prose Summary. A Latin prose summary (taken from an 1821 edition of Ovid) is included as a potentially easier version of Ovid's Latin. Often, the prose summary uses easier vocabulary and sentence structure, and should prove a useful reference when Ovid's Latin becomes confusing. The prose summary is intended to be read without any aids. While some spellings have been updated to make them more recognizable

to the student of classical Latin, and punctuation has been modernized, the text appears largely as it did in its original printing.

Vocabulary. There are two types of vocabulary in the book: running vocabulary below the text of a given page, and a glossary at the back of the book. The running vocabulary is a selective vocabulary, i.e. not every word will be defined there. The glossary does contain every word that appears in the book. In addition, the glossary contains macrons for every word for assistance with scansion, includes brief grammatical explanations for certain words, and brief explanatory notes for proper nouns or other words that might require further description than the definition alone provides.

Visuals. Visuals should not be considered extra or superfluous. They are included to illustrate specific aspects of the text. Often, visuals will include labels or diagrams that correspond directly to Ovid's text. When they do not, they encompass too much of the Latin to be labeled concisely. If the Latin does not make sense, use the visual as an aid to provide context and to better understand the narrative.

Sentence Structure Diagrams. Sentence structure diagrams do not follow a fixed visual pattern. Each diagram uses a system unique to the sentence it illustrates. Nonetheless, all diagrams render a non-linear sentence into some sort of linear format. The diagrams should be read top to bottom and/or left to right, depending on the specific format. Some explanation of each diagram will be included with it.

Discussion Questions. The discussion questions are designed to be used when reading and not necessarily as an activity separate from or in addition to in-class or nightly reading assignments. Discussion questions should be used as preparation for reading the text; the questions will point out broader themes and more specific points of interpretation for the text. Even if you do not answer the questions explicitly, you should keep them in mind when reading. It is from these questions that preparation for any essay portions of tests administered by your teacher (and for the essay portion of the AP exam if you are preparing for it) should come.

Terms to Know. The following terms are used throughout the text; you should make certain that they are familiar to you if they are not already. (It is assumed that you have an understanding of basic grammatical terminology; these are terms with which you might not be familiar.)

- **substantive**: the use of an adjective without a stated noun to modify; the noun must be supplied in English, and the gender of the adjective will determine the gender of the noun supplied

- **parallelism**: the use of phrases or clauses of similar structure and vocabulary, often with shared words omitted

- **idiom**: an expression whose words carry different meanings in isolation than as a unit, i.e. "raining cats and dogs" parsed individually would be nonsense, but understood idiomatically makes sense

- **apposition/appositive**: a noun connected to another noun by an understood verb "to be," e.g. "Latin, the language of the Romans,..." can be understood as "Latin, (which is) the language of the Romans,..." with the "(which is)" being the understood verb "to be"

- **periphrasis**: literally a "speaking around"; an unnecessarily elaborate way of describing something, e.g. in Ovid's Pygmalion story when, instead of Ovid saying "nine months," he says, "when the crescent of the moon grows into a full circle nine times"

- **temporal clause**: a clause often introduced by *ut* or *cum* with an indicative verb that indicates time; it is important to distinguish temporal clauses, especially those introduced by *ut*, from other clauses that use a subjunctive verb

- **concessive / concession**: a clause that shows concession is introduced by the English word "although"; Latin commonly expresses concession with either an ablative absolute or a *cum* clause; Ovid also uses the impersonal verb *licet* to express concession

- **framing**: a feature of word order whereby a noun and its modifier are separated, and words or phrases, often genitives, ablatives, or prepositional phrases, are written in between the separated noun and modifier to indicate a single unit of meaning; although chiasmus can often act as framing, not every instance of framing is a chiasmus

- **connective relative**: a relative pronoun used at the beginning of a sentence to indicate a close connection between the content of the relative clause and its antecedent in the preceding sentence; the nuance of the connective relative is similar to the difference in English between using a semicolon and a period; it is best to translate a connective relative not as a relative but rather as a demonstrative

- **antecedent**: literally a "falling before"; the noun that a pronoun replaces

- **patronymic**: the identification of someone through the use of their father's, or an ancestor's, name

- **predicative(ly)**: when an adjective or participle is used with modifying clauses or words; the non-predicative adjective or participle will be translated before its noun, e.g. "the running man," while the predicative adjective or participle will be translated after its noun to accomodate the modifying phrases or words, e.g. "the man, running quickly to the store"

For the Teacher

Philosophy and Approach

The fundamental purpose behind this book is to help students become better readers and understanders of Latin. To that end every effort has been made to position students to understand the Latin without providing unnecessary or superfluous information that they should know or can figure out themselves. The primary vehicle for this is the notes. They are designed to present to the student the inherent difficulties of a given passage while still letting students come to some understanding of that passage on their own. Thus, the notes ask leading questions about potentially troublesome passages, or they anticipate incorrect student assumptions so that they might be avoided. While perhaps initially frustrating for students, especially those suckled by more generous texts, the mental process of grappling with Latin's difficulties on their own, rather than being sped through them, is essential for the development of students' reading skills.

On the other hand, there are certainly difficulties through which students should be led with more explicit guidance. Such difficulties often involve agreement and antecedents. In terms of the latter, it tends to be very difficult for students to keep track of antecedents and referents both because of the speed (or lack thereof) with which many of them read Latin and, more important, because of Latin's use and English's lack of use of grammatical gender, which only adds a further layer of complexity to an already difficult task. Agreement also proves difficult, especially in the more convoluted word order of poetry, because of its reliance on careful and exact knowledge of full vocabulary information. While the notes will often encourage students to understand on their own what noun an adjective describes, sometimes the time that that process might take is not worth any potential learning that might occur. In extended passages of particular difficulty, the poetic passage is rewritten in a more easily understood word order or a visual diagram of the structure is provided independent of the notes. Only in rare cases is a sentence or clause translated

outright because it is deemed too complex to explain adequately without translating it.

The AP student is an advanced reader, but certainly not an accomplished or experienced reader. The most advanced AP students will have only two years of reading behind them before the present syllabus, and so will still be developing reading and comprehension skills on, if not a basic level, then certainly not a proficient level. While there are many strengths to the AP student, there remain many weaknesses, and too often AP books present a frustrating combination of advanced and basic information: they will offer plenty of insightful interpretation but identify every subjunctive form outright (how frustrating for the teacher when she thinks that a student has understood the text only to realize, by the smirk on the student's face, that he has simply read the notes). Thus, the notes are focused primarily on increasing reading skills and sharpening comprehension skills. They dispense information outright only in what has been deemed the most nececssary instances. They focus on both difficulties in the grammar of the Latin and difficulties in reading Latin. In the latter category would fall confusing or overlapping forms (e.g. *virum* = genitive plural of *vir, viris* or the accusative singular of *vir, viri*), word choice and lexical range, sentence structure anomalies, etc.; while students may know forms and grammar rules, the notes are intended to allow them to use such rules in a more predictable circumstance. When Ovid renders the Latin unpredictable, the notes will hopefully make it more predictable without providing the answer outright.

I suspect that the students who will benefit most from this book are the ones in the middle range of the class, who understand the basics of Latin but perhaps have not yet put all the pieces together. Our top students can, I suspect, succeed with any book. Unfortunately, our struggling students often have difficulties that stretch too far back in their Latin training for us to remedy them with any long-term success. The students in the middle of our range, however, who need that discipline of remembering what they know, especially when they are working at home, and who need the confidence that Latin is an accessible language given their training, should, I hope, benefit from the pedagogy of this book, which focuses less on dispensing information and more on prompting students to understand how both Ovid and Latin in a more general sense convey meaning.

Translation has in some circles become a dirty word. It is viewed by some as an artificial process, and one that both obscures and hinders true understanding of the text. While I still rely primarily on translation in my own classes, I understand the argument of the anti-translators (I might suggest that there is not as great a distinction made between translation and understanding as many would have us believe). The notes then are designed to facilitate understanding; if the teacher wants to use them to generate a translation, she is welcome to do so. On the other hand, because this is a book that can be used with an Advanced Placement syllabus, translation (and literal translation at that) must be a part of it because of the reliance of the Advanced Placement exam on literal translation. Thus, when an issue of understanding becomes an issue of translation (e.g. a difficult or obscure use of a word) I will in fact translate for the student, or prompt them in terms of a translation.

Clean Texts

At the beginning of each chapter are unmarked, full texts. It is suggested that these be used in the following ways: 1. make overheads of them for focused and annotated reading in class; 2. have students not mark them up as part of their daily work, to keep them in reserve for studying (also explained in the Student section); 3. make these the in-class reading texts: students can make notes on their annotated text, but then cannot use these notes to read in class; they must be prepared enough to read from unmarked Latin (this can be difficult, but is imperative for preparing for the AP exam and its reliance on reading and understanding Latin, both sight and prepared).

Prose Summary

The prose summary is included to allow students to encounter and interact with a Latin that is not intended to be analyzed, but rather could be read (though certainly not in every instance) as we might read English. The summary, taken from an 1821 edition of Ovid, is provided to allow the student another Latin version if Ovid's original proves too difficult. For the most part, the prose has been left as it was found. Spelling and punctuation has been updated (e.g. *ejus* becomes *eius*; *coeli* becomes *caeli*; *arundines* becomes *harundines*; quotation marks have been added) but the language of the prose summary has been neither changed nor glossed. The prose summary often will use more prosaic language and/or words with recognizable cognates: Apollo and Daphne 495, the idiom *deus in flammas abiit* becomes *deus conflagravit*. The prose summary renders an otherwise idiomatic expression into a simple verb with a clear, if difficult, English cognate. Even if students don't know the English "conflagration" (as often mine don't), at least a brief discussion of derivatives can be had. On the other hand, the prose summary can indeed use more abstruse vocabulary that the student (or the teacher) might not recognize: *Baucis and Philemon* 632-3, *illa consenuere casa* becomes *illo tugurio senectutem contraxerant*. In this case, the *casa* of the original is vastly more recognizable than the *tugurio* of the summary, and, while the *consenuere* of the original may not be a recognizable verb, its stem may help students understand its meaning more than they might understand the idiomatic use of *contraxerant* with *senectutem*. Additionally, the prose summary may not always match up with Ovid's text. I have not compensated in these instances for any textual inconsistencies.

Visual Aids

Visual aids are intended to be connected very directly to the understanding of the text. Diagrammed images are included to provide students not only a visual reference for the narrative but also a keyed visual guide to specific phrases or words in the Latin. Thus, when the construction of Daedalus' wing is compared to the gradually lengthening reeds of a pan-pipe, an image of both a pipe and a wing are included to illustrate this somewhat abstruse description.

Sentence Diagrams

The sentence diagrams are intended to break down visually into more easily digestible chunks complex Latin sentences. There is no set format for the diagrams; each will use a format specifically relevant to a particular sentence. To maximize the effectiveness of the sentence diagrams, however, it will likely be necessary for the teacher to offer a brief introduction to them. Some description has been provided with each, but often a written description of a diagram becomes as complex as the sentence itself.

Running Vocabulary

I have eschewed a statistical approach to the running vocabulary. While Pharr's method is certainly valid and popular, its reliance on frequency instead of context renders it somewhat restrictive. Thus, while the running vocabulary is not overly generous, there are certain instances when context might make a word difficult enough to understand that words that would otherwise not be glossed are indeed glossed. For instance, in *Amores* 1.9, *bellum, -i* is used in line 3, while *bellus, -a, -um* is used in line 6 (in the form *bella*). Because of the overlapping nature of these forms, both words are glossed in the running vocabulary to allow students to see the two possible words next to each other. To leave the more common word *bellum* out of the running vocabulary might lead students erroneously to assume that the word in line 3 is a form of *bellus, -a, -um*. In other instances, however, the relatively common *bellum* would not be glossed in the running vocabulary. Similarly, at *Amores* 1.11.13, the verb *ago, -ere* is glossed in the running vocabulary where it normally would not have been because it appears in the text as *agam*, both an uncommon form and one that might be confused with the accusative feminine singular of a first declension noun. As with the notes, I have tried with the running vocabulary to anticipate student difficulties based on individual contexts, and gloss words accordingly.

Conclusion

Encourage your students to make liberal use of the aids that accompany the text. We know all too well how many of our students read Latin: they look up some words, they string together some meanings in a more or less cohesive way, and they largely ignore the endings that they know will convey the meaning of the passage. The aids are designed specifically to slow them down and to encourage them to remember what they know, and apply it judiciously to a given passage. The notes will ask more questions than they answer; I leave it to you to provide the answers.

A Word on The Texts

The Advanced Placement Latin Literature exam quotes Latin from the most recently published Oxford Classical Texts (referred to throughout this volume as OCT): for the *Amores* Kenney's 1995, and for the *Metamorphoses* Tarrant's 2004. Whenever possible texts that reflect Tarrant's new reading have been used; if a new reading is not included in the text proper, it will be included in the notes.

I have left the texts relatively untouched, only updating them to reflect common usage (both Latin and English): words that begin sentences have been capitalized, single quotes have been made double where appropriate, and consonantal "u" has been made "v" (consonantal "i" has been left "i" because students seem more accustomed to this variation than the former); these are changes also made on the AP exam. In 2004 the AP exam stopped glossing the assimilation of prefixes, "easily recognizable" [from the Acorn Book] alternations in spelling, and words that can be written as one or multiple words (e.g. *quemadmodum* vs. *quem ad modum*).

Ovid's frame narrative proved problematic when deciding when to include quotation marks. Both the stories of Pyramus and Thisbe and the story of Pygmalion are entirely narrated by another character; Baucis and Philemon is mostly narrated by another character (Baucis and Philemon is the only story in this volume whose narrator and the transition into the narrative are described). The quotation marks that, because of punctuation rules, begin new paragraphs in Pyramus and Thisbe and Pygmalion have proved consistently problematic for students; because both stories are excerpted without their context, it is difficult to remember that such context exists, and that it necessitates quotation marks. It also means that quotations within the stories, because the story itself is being quoted, use single rather than the more customary double quotation marks. Thus, I have for Pyramus and Thisbe and Pygmalion eliminated the quotation marks of the otherwise invisible narrator. For Baucis and Philemon, because of the introduction of the narrator Lelex and his story, I have included the quotation marks, but made them single quotation marks so that the dialogue of the Baucis and Philemon story can remain in double quotation marks. I leave it up to you to agree or disagree with this editorial decision.

The adoption of Tarrant's new text of the *Metamorphoses* could conceivably impact the text available for the AP exam because of Tarrant's admission of alternate readings commonly not included in previously published texts of the *Metamorphoses*. At *Metamorphoses* 8.184 (Daedalus and Icarus), Tarrant admits *soli* while many previous editions have admitted *loci*. Also, Tarrant's text includes bracketed lines that indicate either alternate readings or additions to the previously accepted text, and these bracketed lines could at least in theory appear on the AP exam. (Informal discussions with John Sarkissian of Youngstown State University, chief reader for the AP Latin Literature exam, indicate that it has not yet been decided how Tarrant's new readings will impact the exam.) These bracketed lines also have traditionally not appeared in texts commonly used for the teaching of the AP Ovid syllabus. On the following page I include a list of such readings, collated against common texts of the *Metamorphoses*.

Bracketed Text in Tarrant's *Metamorphoses* OCT AP selections

Line #s	Text in Question	Tarrant's Reading	Lafleur's Reading	Jestin / Katz Reading
1.477	vitta coercebat positos sine lege capillos	bracketed	included with no brackets	included with no brackets
1.544–545	victa labore fugae "Tellus" ait, "hisce, vela istam, quae facit ut laedar, mutando perde figuram."	bracketed, with the more common *spectans Peneidas undas* made line 544a	not included	not included, with no line 546 included because of "uncertainties and inaccuracies in the ancient texts" (from the notes)
8.190	a minima coeptas, longam breviore sequente	bracketed	included with no brackets	included with no brackets
8.216	et movet ipse suas et nati respicit alas	bracketed	included with no brackets	included with no brackets
8.655–656	concutiuntque torum de molli fluminis ulva impositum lecto sponda pedibusque salignis	bracketed, with *accipit. In medio torus est de mollibus ulvis / impositus lecto sponda pedibus salignis* as lines 655a & 656a	included with no brackets, with 655a & 656a not included	included with no brackets, with lines 652–654 not included because "four lines [652-655a] are of questionable authenticity and are omitted" (from the notes)
8.693a–694b	ite simul." parent et dis praeeuntibus ambo membra levant baculis tardique senilibus annis	bracketed	not included	not included
10.256	oscula dat reddique putat loquiturque tenetque	bracketed	included with no brackets	included with no brackets

Introduction to Ovid

Perdiderint [cum] me duo crimina, carmen et error,
                                   - Ovid, Tristia, *2.207*

Carmen et error. These are the tantalizingly ambiguous causes for Ovid's exile. Ovid himself is our only source for them, and neither is specified further. Both, however, have largely accepted plausible explanations: the *carmen* is generally taken to be Ovid's *Ars Amatoria*, his *Art of Love*, while the error is likely some indirect involvement in a love affair of Augustus' granddaughter Julia. Both were antithetical to the reforms of the emperor Augustus.

The Rome that Augustus officially inherited in 27 BCE was emerging from an era of crisis: over a half-century of civil war had plagued Rome, as varying factions and individuals vied for power. Julius Caesar's adopted nephew, Octavian, only eighteen years old when Caesar was assassinated, eventually emerged victorious with his victory over Marc Antony and the Egyptian queen Cleopatra at Actium in 31 BCE. By 27 BCE, he was officially recognized by the Roman Senate as ruler of Rome and was given the name Augustus to reflect this position.

To heal the wounds of civil war, Augustus looked to Rome's distant past, the monarchy and the early republic, as an example of the virtues that would lift Rome out of its Civil War-induced malaise. The Roman historian Livy, whose overwhelmingly large *Ab urbe condita* (*A History from the City's Founding*) charted Rome's history from its Trojan roots to Livy's contemporary Rome, told stories that extolled the Roman values of courage, dedication, and self-sacrifice. Figures such as Lucretia, Scaevola, and the triplet Horatii

brothers came to represent these virtues. Even if such stories are legendary at best, Livy presents them as history and writes them with an emphasis on the advantages of such virtues for Rome. The Roman poet Vergil creates the character of Aeneas with similar virtues in mind. Although Aeneas is a more complex character than many of Livy's historical figures, nonetheless his foresaking of Dido and his love for her so that he might realize his destiny and the founding of Rome represent exactly the kind of self-sacrifice that Augustus wanted to promote.

You can imagine then how frustrating it was for Augustus when he discovered that his own daughter was leading her life in a way that flaunted the very values that he was promoting, and even violated a law that he himself had enacted. In 18 BCE, Augustus passed legislation that encouraged aristocrats to marry and to have children; the same law made adultery a crime. (It should be noted also that Augustus himself did not quite live up to his own standards.) That his daughter's affairs became public knowledge forced him to address them, and he eventually exiled her to an island barely one mile square off the coast of Italy midway between Rome and Naples. His granddaughter behaved similarly, and it is her profligacy that seems to have indirectly ensnared Ovid. The *error*, though by no means certain, has been plausibly identified as some complicity in one of Augustus' granddaughter's love affairs. Ovid himself was not involved with her; such direct involvement surely would have meant a harsher punishment than he received. But whether Ovid knew of her affairs and did not tell Augustus or whether a close friend of Ovid was one of her lovers, some indirect involvement in her affairs is our best guest for the *error* that led to Ovid's exile.

The identification of the *carmen* is perhaps a bit more straightforward. Although there are some who would argue for the *Metamorphoses* and its potentially anti-Augustan sub-text (based largely on the identification of Augustus with Ovid's Jupiter and the subsequent boorish behavior of Ovid's Jupiter), it seems relatively certain that Ovid's *Ars Amatoria* is the *carmen* that led to his exile. While Augustus was trying to promote better morals and an increased participation in religion, Ovid flaunted such values by writing a step-by-step manual on how to engage in illicit love affairs. It should be noted, however, that the *Ars Amatoria* was published nine years prior to Ovid's exile. So while the *carmen* (or *carmina* as the case may have been) didn't help Ovid's standing with Augustus, it seems certain that the *error* was the direct impetus behind his exile. (That the *Metamorphoses* was published in 8 AD, the same year as Ovid's exile, might be compelling support for it as the *carmen*.)

Even Ovid's exile, however, was lenient: rather than full exile, which would have entailed a loss of citizenship and all property, he was sent away but retained his citizenship and his property. Nonetheless, Ovid's literary output from exile reveals the deep pain that being away from Rome caused him. Tomis, the town on the west coast of the Black Sea to which Ovid was exiled, was hardly the metropolis that Rome was. Ovid himself describes his new situation: *Barbarus hic ego sum, qui non intellegor ulli, / et rident stolidi uerba Latina Getae* (*Tristia* 5.10.37-38). Ovid and his adherents in Rome campaigned tirelessly for his restoration, but to no avail. Ovid died ten years into his exile in 18 AD.

Every age has its artistic renegades: artists who create controversy, artists who invite criticism, artists that entertain as much as they annoy, artists who, rather than create within established definitions, establish definitions for others to follow. Ovid, to some extent, was this sort of artist. He was the quintessential poet. He was not an epic poet. He was not an elegiac poet. He was a poet who loved poetry and language. He was a poet who reveled in the possibility and potential of words and the poetic form. He was a poet who defies definition. He worked in a plurality of poetic genres and, in most cases, did so expressly to expand, lampoon, or change the definition of such genres. This is his legacy. And, because of this legacy, Ovid has had a polarizing effect on his readers. Successive ages have thrilled to his artistic subtlety, his biting wit, his sophisticated perspective on life and the erudition of his mythology. By the same token, successive ages have dismissed him as unserious, have derided him for being sensationalistic, and have ignored him for being scandalous. But if for no other reason, Ovid is a seminal author because of his canonization of many of the myths with which we are most familiar today: in most cases, the myths we know are Ovid's versions of them.

So, why are you reading Ovid? Simple. Ovid tells a great story, Ovid is an unsurpassed poet and writer, and Ovid is irrepresibly witty (so much so, in fact, that it likely contributed to his exile from Rome). A word about wit: Ovid doesn't go for the belly laughs. He's not looking for the obvious (and simple) joke. Ovid's humor is sophisticated. The Irish writer Oscar Wilde ("The Importance of Being Earnest") might best approximate the sort of humor that Ovid achieves. It is wry, it is sophisticated, it is intelligent, and it is biting. And if you take the time to understand it, it is also very rewarding. So enjoy Ovid. That, if nothing else, is what he would have wanted.

An Ovidian Chronology

Dates relevant to Ovid appear in the left column; to Ovid's influences and contemporary history in the right.

84 BCE	Catullus possibly born (exact date unknown)	
70 BCE	Vergil born	
65 BCE	Horace born	
63 BCE	Octavian (Augustus) born	
58-51 BCE	Caesar conquers Gaul	
54 BCE	Catullus' death (exact date unknown)	
44 BCE	Caesar's death	
42 BCE	Battle of Philippi: Octavian and Antony victorious over Caesar's killers Brutus and Cassius	
42 BCE	Vergil begins work on his *Eclogues*	
	43 BCE	born at Sulmo (modern Sulmona), 80 miles east of Rome in the Abruzzi
37 BCE	Vergil publishes his *Eclogues*	
36 BCE	Vergil begins work on his *Georgics*	
31 BCE	Battle of Actium: Octavian defeats Antony and Cleopatra, removing the final obstacle to his acquisition of power	
29 BCE	Vergil publishes his *Georgics* and begins work on the *Aeneid*	
27 BCE	Octavian is granted the name "Augustus" and assumes official control of Rome	
	25 BCE	possible beginning of work on the *Amores*
23 BCE	Horace publishes Books 1-3 of his *Odes*	
19 BCE	Vergil's death, leaving the *Aeneid* incomplete; although Vergil wished the manuscript to be destroyed, Augustus ensured its survival; it was finished and published by 17 BCE	
18 BCE	Julian Marriage Laws passed	
	16 BCE	first edition of the *Amores* published in five books
	?	*Heroides* published (date unknown, but after the *Amores* and before the *DMFF*)
13 BCE	Horace publishes Book 4 of his *Odes*	
	?	*De medicamine faciei femineae* published (date unknown, but after the *Heroides* and before the second edition of the *Amores*)
8 BCE	Horace's death	
	?	second edition of the *Amores* published in three books (date unknown, but just before the *Ars*)
2 BCE	Augustus' daughter Julia exiled for committing adultery	
	1 BCE	*Ars Amatoria* published
	2 AD	*Remedia Amoris* published
	8 AD	*Metamorphoses* and *Fasti* published
	8 AD	Exiled to Tomis, a town in the northeast corner of the Black Sea
8 AD	Augustus' granddaughter Julia exiled for committing adultery	
	9-12 AD	*Tristia* and *Ibis* published
	12-16 AD	*Epistulae ex Ponto* published
	17 or 18 AD	death in Tomis

Ovid's Works

Amores = "Loves." Three books of elegiac love poetry, written in elegiac couplets, that focus on Ovid's relationship with an otherwise unknown woman named Corinna. Originally published in five books, the three-book arrangment is a second edition.

Heroides = "Heroines." Fourteen fictional letters, written in elegiac couplets, from mythological "heroines" to their "heroes" or male counterparts. The women have been abandoned or jilted in love and are expressing their resentment toward their men in the letters. Eight other letters exist, whose attribution to Ovid (with the exception of number 15 to Sappho, whose Ovidian attribution is still questioned) has been doubted but seems now to be accepted. (Letters sixteen to twenty-one are correspondence pairs: the man writes to the woman in one letter, and the woman responds to the man's letter in the next.)

Medicamina Faciei Femineae = "Cosmetics for a Woman's Face." Only 100 lines of this didactic poem, written in elegiac couplets, survive.

Ars Amatoria = "Art of Love." Two books of pseudo-didactic or farcical-didactic poetry, written in elegiac couplets, that provide instructions for men on how to meet and win over women. The third book, written later, apparently as a sequel, advises women in a similar way on men.

Remedia Amoris = "Cure for Love." The "antidote" to the *Ars Amatoria*. One book of elegiac couplets on how to leave or end a relationship.

Metamorphoses = "Changes." Fifteen books of epic, written in dactylic hexameter, that use the concept of change to chart a complex mythological narrative that encompasses the history of the universe, beginning with its creation in Book 1 and ending with Ovid's contemporary Rome in Book 15.

Fasti = "Festivals." Twelve intended books of elegiac couplets that chart the history of the Roman calendar. Ovid describes the history and origin of the festival days of the Roman calendar, and in the process covers a good deal of Roman history and mythology. The work was left incomplete because of Ovid's exile. Only books 1-4, which cover from January to June, survive.

Tristia = "Sorrows." Four books of elegiac couplets, written from Tomis where Ovid was exiled, detailing the past, present, and anticipated regrets and pain of Ovid's life. It is from the autobiographical content of the *Tristia* that much of Ovid's biography is taken.

Epistulae ex Ponto = "Letters from the Black Sea." Four books of literary epistles, written in elegiac couplets, that continue the themes of the *Tristia*. The *epistulae*, by their very nature as letters, are addressed to specific recipients, while the *Tristia* reflect a more general approach.

Ibis. A curse poem whose attribution to Ovid has been continuously debated. Ibis is the name of a bird who represents an enemy of Ovid.

Medea. A tragic play written by Ovid that is now lost.

Glossary of Names

Callimachus. A Greek poet who lived in Alexandria from the late 4th c. BCE to the middle of the 3rd c. BCE (c.310-c.264). Callimachus and his particular brand of poetry exerted a profound influence on Roman poets of the 1st c. BCE who sought to emulate his eschewing of epic conventions and his focus on more personal, individualized, emotional poetry. He advocated a "slender" approach to poetry, forsaking the scope and bombast of Homeric epic, and an erudite approach to mythology.

Catullus. A Roman poet of the first century BCE (c.84 to 54 BCE), and the first and best known of the poets whom Cicero deridingly called the *poetae novi* or "neoterics." Catullus revolutionized Roman poetry by introducing specific, particular, emotional, and individualized poetry that was presented as autobiographical. Much of his poetry centers on his torturous relationship with a married woman whom he calls Lesbia; she is commonly identified as the Clodia whom Cicero lambasts in his *Pro Caelio.*

Corinna. The name of the woman around whom Ovid centers his love poetry. No identification of Corinna with an historical personage has been made.

Gallus. The most elusive of the elegiac poets, Cornelius Gallus (69-26 BCE) is praised by his contemporaries as the best of them; Vergil dedicated his tenth *Eclogue* to Gallus and his poetry. Very little of his poetry has survived: until 1979 only a single pentameter line had survived through quotation. In 1979, a papyrus fragment containing ten verses was discovered.

Horace. A Roman poet who lived from 65 to 8 BCE. Wrote four books of *Odes* that cover a variety of subjects, from love to philosophy; among them, *Ode* 1.11 is the famous *Carpe diem* poem.

Octavian / Augustus. The adopted son of Julius Caesar, he along with Marc Antony vied for the power left available after Caesar's death. Octavian defeated Antony and the Egyptian queen Cleopatra at the Battle of Actium in 31 BCE. By 27 BCE he was given the title "Augustus," which consolidated his power over Rome. Augustus was a patron of the arts and, through his cultural minister Maecenas, sponsored the poetry of Vergil, Horace, and to some extent Ovid, though Ovid would eventually be exiled by the emperor for his probably indirect role in an illicit relationship of Augustus' granddaughter.

Propertius. A Roman elegiac poet who lived in the second half of the 1st c. BCE (his specific dates are unknown: 50ish BCE to post-16 BCE). Propertius too was associated with the literary circle of Maecenas and Augustus. He wrote four books of elegiac poetry centered around a woman whom Propertius calls Cynthia and their tumultuous love affair. Propertius' love poetry, in its conventional nature and its unabashed intensity of emotion, heavily influenced Ovid's *Amores*, even if Ovid would frequently negate the conventions exemplified by Propertius.

Tibullus. A Roman elegiac poet who lived from 54 to 19 BCE. Like Propertius, Tibullus is credited with canonizing many of the conventions associated with elegiac love poetry. The name of his romantic focus was Delia; another love interest, Nemesis, appears also.

Introduction to the Amores

When I first put a tablet on my knees, the Wolf-God
Apollo appeared and said:
"Fatten your animal for sacrifice, poet,
but keep your muse slender." [Callimachus, *Aetia*, Prologue]

To understand the *Amores*, it is perhaps important to understand their genre and literary precedents. A Greek poet of the 4th c. BCE, Callimachus, made it his literary mission to not write epic. He criticized epic for being ponderous, overblown, detached, and over-serious. Rather, he preferred what he called "slender" poetry, i.e. poetry that is characterized by moderation, conciseness, imagery, and erudition. Callimachus found avid followers in Roman poets of the 1st c. BCE. Catullus is perhaps the most famous of these followers, but other poets, such as Propertius, Tibullus, and the elusive Cornelius Gallus, also wrote love elegy and predated Ovid. It is within the literay tradition begun by the Greek poet Callimachus, and adapted to Latin poetry by Catullus, Propertius, Tibullus, and Gallus that Ovid is writing the *Amores*.

Ovid, however, as the last in this long line of poets, cannot simply continue writing the poetry of his predecessors. Catullus, Propetius, Tibullus, and, to the extent we know, Gallus, while writing their own distinctive love poetry, still wrote poetry that followed similar conventions. These poets created for themselves an ostensibly autobiographical *poetic persona*, i.e. they wrote poetry in the first person that apparently reflected their lives. Their poetry was centered around a woman, an object for their love poetry. This woman is either married or prefers other men to the poet; she occasionally returns his affections,

but only enough to keep him interested. The poet is constantly being kept from her by other men, physical obstacles (her door, her maid, etc.), or his own insecurities. This is the poetic tradition that Ovid inherited.

Ovid declares his departure from his elegiac predecessors with the first word of the first poem of the *Amores*: *arma*. Ovid begins his love poetry with the same word with which Vergil begins his epic the *Aeneid*. Ovid writes in the elegiac couplet that characterizes elegiac poetry but begins by unequivocally recalling the subject matter of epic. Ovid communicates immediately that these will not be the elegies of his predecessors. Ovid will go on to write love poetry that eschews the gravity and seriousness of his predecessors; their love-troubles apparently caused them significant pain and hurt them deeply. Ovid, however, will remain more emotionally detached. While Ovid will experience hurt and frustration because of the failures of his relationship, he will remain circumspect; he will not convey the sense of tragedy that is often felt in the poetry of his predecessors. On the countrary, it often seems as if Ovid is quite enjoying the process, even the painful parts of it. His more upbeat and carefree approach to the travails of love are what set him apart as an elegist.

The first five poems of Ovid's *Amores* (two of which are included in the present volume) form an extended introduction to the approach and the themes of the collection. In *Amores* 1.1, Ovid declares not that he is in love (as Propertius did; he began his collection with the name of his love, Cynthia) but rather that Cupid is forcing him to write love poetry when he is in fact not in love at all. *Amores* 1.2 focuses on Ovid's final surrender to Cupid and his mandate to write love poetry (with no hint yet at the identity of his lover; Ovid has not yet even specified whether it is a man or a woman). *Amores* 1.3 finally identifies Ovid's lover as a woman, but provides no further details of her identity. *Amores* 1.4 reveals that Ovid's chance of success with her (still unnamed) is slim: she is married, and there are other impediments to their relationship. And finally in *Amores* 1.5 Ovid identifies the name of his lover: Corinna. Ovid's opening sequence in the *Amores* typifies his approach to writing poetry: he will write something that violates all of his reader's expectations: where they expect love poetry, he suggests epic; where they expect a lover to be named quickly, he waits for five poems to identify her; where they expect fervent emotion, he evinces detached rationalism.

Ovid recast the genre of elegy in that he shifted from an almost exclusive focus on the woman to a more complex focus that is shared in turn by the woman, the poet (not the poet-lover), and the genre itself. Ovid is a self-conscious poet, meaning that he was constantly aware and inclusive in his poetry of observations of the artistic process. The *Amores*, even as Ovid's first published work, is no different. Ovid takes the fervent, desperate, fawning lover of his poetic predecessors and, at least at the outset of the *Amores*, makes that lover coolly detached, and even resistant to his elegiac emotions. Ovid's predecessors observed their love affairs from the eye of the storm: they were passionate, angry, resentful, joyful, and they allowed their readers a first-person perspective of the range of their emotional spectrum. Ovid prefers more of a bird's eye view. While still affording the reader an intimate window into his emotions and relationship, Ovid also forces the reader to consider the nature of such a relationship. Ovid forces the reader to question the validity of his emotions: Are they real and raw or are they merely constructed as part of a poetic persona that demands such rawness? These are the questions that Ovid raises with his *Amores*.

For the modern (and especially younger) reader, The *Amores* are more difficult to access than the *Metamorphoses*. They are certainly not as familiar as Ovid's myths, and they blend affection and erudition in a sophisticated form that requires attention and reflection to understand. Nonetheless, the universality of the emotions of the *Amores* (we have all loved and not been loved in return) renders Ovid's wit personal in a way that is more difficult to accomplish in the extended narrative of the *Metamorphoses*.

The *Amores* At-A-Glance

Number of Books	3 (according to Ovid, 5 in a first edition but shrunk to 3 in a second)
Total Number of Lines	2,460
Genre	elegy
Meter	elegiac couplet or distych
Date Published	last years of the 1st c. BCE (second edition; first edition published in 16 BCE; the specific differences between the two editions are unknown: whether Ovid edited poems or eliminated poems from the first edition, or simply reorganized it)

Introduction to the Metamorphoses

In nova fert animus mutatas dicere formas corpora.
- Metamorphoses 1.1-2

Change. No discussion of the *Metamorphoses* should begin without some understanding of change. If Ovid is writing an epic of changes, what then, we must ask, is changing? The obvious answer is the consistent transformation that defines many of the myths recounted in the *Metamorphoses*. Some of these transformations are seminal to the story, e.g. Daphne's transformation into the laurel tree serves both as narrative conclusion and aetiological (having to do with the origins of something) explanation. On the other hand, the transformation of the mulberry in the Pyramus and Thisbe story, from its original white color to its now deep red, is an aetiology incidental to the narrative of the story.

Ovid's epic ranges over the entirety of history: from the creation of the universe up to his contemporary Rome. He begins with the amorphous chaos rearragning itself into the cosmos and the successive ages of man, and ends with the apotheosis of Caesar and praise of Augustus. The chronological range of the *Metamorphoses* sets it apart from other epics. While the Homeric epics and the *Aeneid* are indeed broad in scope, none range as far back or as far forward in history as Ovid's does; they are limited in chronological scope. But the chronology of the *Metamorphoses* is as deceptive as it is different: while Ovid ostensibly organizes his epic from the very beginning of time to the

very end of time, in the process forsaking the technique common to epic of telling a story *in medias res,* he nonetheless does not organize all of the individual stories in the *Metamorphoses* in chronological order. In fact, he will often use characters and their stories to incorporate other stories into the epic. The Baucis and Philemon tale in this book is one such story: a man named Lelex tells the story to friends at a dinner party as they argue the power of the gods. And Orpheus, the heroic poet who journeyed to the underworld to recover his wife who died young, is given by Ovid almost an entire book of the *Metamorphoses* in which he narrates seven different stories. Within this framework, Ovid includes over two hundred stories, some as short as a few lines, some longer than entire books of the epic (though these longer ones, such as the Orpheus story, are broken up by other stories embedded in them).

The common element among Ovid's stories is of course transformation. But Ovid is interested in the psychology that transformation often represents as much as the transformation itself; indeed, often the transformation itself reflects the psychology that Ovid is exploring. When Ovid's transformations occur, he forces the reader to ask why his characters turned into what they turned into. Often the transformations will have thematic significance. The most common transformation is one inspired by or contextualized by love; indeed four of the five transformations in this book involve love. The majority of Ovid's pre-exile literary output centers on love, and the *Metamorphoses* incorporates Ovid's interest in love with his interest in psychology and transformation. The *Metamorphoses* then becomes not only a series of mythological transformations but also a series of investigations of how humans function and are affected by love in all of its incarnations: how does one react when they are rejected in love? How does one react in the face of violent love? How does one react to deviant or illicit love? How does one find the ultimate expression of love? It is this variety of emotions and psychologies that Ovid explores in the *Metamorphoses*.

An important distinction that Ovid makes, however, is that between gods and humans: the majority of transformations are human while the majority of agents of those transformations are divine. That is, the gods are often involved in either transforming humans or causing humans to be transformed and are rarely transformed themselves. This distinction reflects a common distinction made between gods and human: their immortality versus our mortality. Their immortality prevents them from experiencing the range of emotions that humans experience; because they cannot die, the immediacy of the prospect of death that so often creates or at least sharpens human emotion is absent from the gods. Thus, the potential for exploring their psychology is much less than the potential for exploring human psychology.

The Apollo and Daphne story, the first story in this book from the *Metamorphoses*, becomes all the more suprising because of its focus on Apollo and his love for a nymph that causes him to lose control of his emotions and his ability to make sound, rational decisions. Apollo is by no means the only god to love, but the male gods usually will play the role of controlling and unbending sexual aggressor; their "love" will not bear any markings

of the attempted courting that Apollo engages in (however farcical it becomes). This story, however, precisely because of its anomalous love and its early positioning in the *Metamorphoses*, about midway through Book I, in many ways sets the tone for the rest of the epic: love in Ovid's hand is so strong that it can affect even the gods. If it can do that to a god, imagine what it can do to lowly humans. The titular theme of the *Metamorphoses* most commonly reflects that change that the extreme emotion of love forces us to undergo. When we experience something as unpredictable and raw as love, change becomes inevitable. The only question that remains is what will the result of that transformation be. The *Metamorphoses* is Ovid's epic attempt to answer that question.

In the context of Ovid's literary *corpus*, the *Metamorphoses* is his *opus magnum*. It is by far his most popular poem, and has been since its publication and remains such today; it has exerted an influence on later art, both literary and visual, perhaps unparalleld by any other text from the ancient world except for the Bible; and it represents the culmination and most sophisticated articulation of many of the liteary themes and approaches that Ovid had explored in previous works. Ovid does for epic with the *Metamorphoses* what he did for elegy with the *Amores*: he expands the definition of the genre by violating many of its cardinal tenets, while still leaving it recognizable enough to be counted as epic. Genre was often identified in the ancient world by meter, and so Ovid writes the *Metamorphoses* in dactylic hexameter, the meter of epic. The changes of the *Metamorphoses* from a literary standpoint represent the generic and formal changes that he brings to all of his poetry; it is only in the *Metamorphoses*, however, that those changes receive their fullest and most nuanced treatment.

The *Metamorphoses* At-A-Glance

Number of Books	15
Total Number of Lines	11,995
Genre	epic
Meter	dactylic hexameter
Date Published	8 AD

Chapter One

Amor Vincit Omnia

Amores 1.1
Apollo and Daphne

Introduction

The power of love—it's transformative. It makes us do things we wouldn't normally do. We write songs, we send flowers, we scream, we laugh out loud, we jump for joy, we weep. It is one of the most profound feelings we are capable of feeling.

Both *Amores* 1.1 and *Apollo and Daphne* assess the chaos associated with love: in the former, it is Ovid himself who grapples with love's chaos, while in the latter, it is Apollo. In both, Cupid is the agent of chaos. In both, Cupid forces his victims to accept that which they had previously refused to accept. In both, Cupid, representing love, proves victorious. And in Cupid's victory is encapsulated one of art's most enduring themes: the rational versus the visceral or, more simply put, the head versus the heart. And Ovid makes it quite clear which he values or at least finds more influential.

Both stories also say as much about Ovid's literary aspirations as they do about love. *Amores* 1.1 is an explicit statement of Ovid's poetics, as he grapples with his desire to write epic and his need to write elegy; *Apollo and Daphne* does not ostensibly treat Ovid's poetics, but can be interpreted as the mythological articulation of his poetics. As Ovid introduces explicitly his conflict between writing epic and writing elegy in *Amores* 1.1, he will, by the time he writes the *Metamorphoses*, resolve that conflict. In *Amores* 1.1, Ovid forsakes epic for elegy; the two cannot be rectified. In the *Metamorphoses*, Ovid combines the two genres. He will use the epic form but write elegiac substance. He will write an epic of love; not a traditional one about two lovers, but rather one that examines love in all of its incarnations, from its most tender to its most twisted. As Ovid surrendered to Cupid and love poetry in *Amores* 1.1, so does Apollo, presented as an epic hero, surrender to Cupid, love, and its elegiac tendencies in *Apollo and Daphne*.

Love has indeed conquered Ovid, but in his own way he too has conquered it. Ovid will attempt to tame the untamable through exploration and understanding. If he surveys every possible manifestation of love, perhaps he can overcome the mystery of love and the power of its effects. That is at least what he attempts not only in the *Amores* and the *Metamorphoses* but also to some extent in his entire *oeuvre*.

Amores 1.1

Arma gravi numero violentaque bella parabam
    edere, materia conveniente modis.
Par erat inferior versus: risisse Cupido
    dicitur atque unum surripuisse pedem.
"Quis tibi, saeve puer, dedit hoc in carmina iuris?   5
    Pieridum vates, non tua, turba sumus.
Quid, si praeripiat flavae Venus arma Minervae,
    ventilet accensas flava Minerva faces?
Quis probet in silvis Cererem regnare iugosis,
    lege pharetratae virginis arva coli?   10
Crinibus insignem quis acuta cuspide Phoebum
    instruat, Aoniam Marte movente lyram?
Sunt tibi magna, puer, nimiumque potentia regna:
    cur opus affectas, ambitiose, novum?
An, quod ubique, tuum est? Tua sunt Heliconia tempe?   15
    Vix etiam Phoebo iam lyra tuta sua est?
Cum bene surrexit versu nova pagina primo,
    attenuat nervos proximus ille meos,
nec mihi materia est numeris levioribus apta,
    aut puer aut longas compta puella comas."   20
Questus eram, pharetra cum protinus ille soluta
    legit in exitium spicula facta meum
lunavitque genu sinuosum fortiter arcum
    "quod"que "canas, vates, accipe," dixit "opus."
Me miserum! Certas habuit puer ille sagittas: 25
    Uror, et in vacuo pectore regnat Amor.
Sex mihi surgat opus numeris, in quinque residat:
    ferrea cum vestris bella valete modis.
Cingere litorea flaventia tempora myrto,
    Musa, per undenos emodulanda pedes.   30

Metamorphoses 4.452-567: Apollo and Daphne

Primus amor Phoebi Daphne Peneia, quem non	452
fors ignara dedit, sed saeva Cupidinis ira.	
Delius hunc, nuper victa serpente superbus,	
viderat adducto flectentem cornua nervo	455
"Quid"que "tibi, lascive puer, cum fortibus armis?"	
dixerat; "Ista decent umeros gestamina nostros,	
qui dare certa ferae, dare vulnera possumus hosti,	
qui modo pestifero tot iugera ventre prementem	
stravimus innumeris tumidum Pythona sagittis.	460
Tu face nescioquos esto contentus amores	
irritare tua, nec laudes assere nostras."	
Filius huic Veneris, "Figat tuus omnia, Phoebe,	
te meus arcus," ait, "quantoque animalia cedunt	
cuncta deo, tanto minor est tua gloria nostra."	465
Dixit et, eliso percussis aere pennis,	
impiger umbrosa Parnasi constitit arce,	
eque sagittifera prompsit duo tela pharetra	
diversorum operum. Fugat hoc, facit illud amorem.	
(Quod facit, auratum est, et cuspide fulget acuta;	470
quod fugat, obtusum est, et habet sub harundine plumbum.)	
Hoc deus in nympha Peneide fixit; at illo	
laesit Apollineas traiecta per ossa medullas.	
Protinus alter amat, fugit altera nomen amantis,	
silvarum latebris captivarumque ferarum	475
exuviis gaudens, innuptaeque aemula Phoebes.	
Vitta coercebat positos sine lege capillos.	
Multi illam petiere: illa aversata petentes	
impatiens expersque viri, nemora avia lustrat,	
nec quid Hymen, quid amor, quid sint conubia curat.	480
Saepe pater dixit, "Generum mihi, filia, debes."	
Saepe pater dixit, "Debes mihi, nata, nepotes."	
Illa velut crimen taedas exosa iugales	
pulchra verecundo suffunditur ora rubore,	
inque patris blandis haerens cervice lacertis,	485
"Da mihi perpetua, genitor carissime," dixit,	
"virginitate frui; dedit hoc pater ante Dianae."	
Ille quidem obsequitur, sed te decor iste quod optas	
esse vetat, votoque tuo tua forma repugnat.	

Phoebus amat, visaeque cupit conubia Daphnes,   490
quodque cupit sperat suaque illum oracula fallunt.
Utque leves stipulae demptis adolentur aristis;
ut facibus saepes ardent, quas forte viator
vel nimis admovit vel iam sub luce reliquit,
sic deus in flammas abiit, sic pectore toto   495
uritur, et sterilem sperando nutrit amorem.
Spectat inornatos collo pendere capillos,
et, "Quid si comantur?" ait. Videt igne micantes
sideribus similes oculos; videt oscula, quae non
est vidisse satis; laudat digitosque manusque   500
bracchiaque et nudos media plus parte lacertos;
si qua latent, meliora putat. Fugit ocior aura
illa levi, neque ad haec revocantis verba resistit:
"Nympha, precor, Penei, mane! Non insequor hostis.
Nympha, mane! Sic agna lupum, sic cerva leonem,   505
sic aquilam penna fugiunt trepidante columbae,
hostes quaeque suos. Amor est mihi causa sequendi.
Me miserum, ne prona cadas indignave laedi
crura notent sentes, et sim tibi causa doloris!
Aspera, qua properas, loca sunt. Moderatius, oro,   510
curre fugamque inhibe; moderatius insequar ipse.
Cui placeas, inquire tamen. Non incola montis,
non ego sum pastor, non hic armenta gregesque
horridus observo. Nescis, temeraria, nescis
quem fugias, ideoque fugis. Mihi Delphica tellus   515
et Claros et Tenedos Pataraeaque regia servit.
Iuppiter est genitor. Per me quod eritque fuitque
estque patet; per me concordant carmina nervis.
Certa quidem nostra est, nostra tamen una sagitta
certior, in vacuo quae vulnera pectore fecit.   520
Inventum medicina meum est opiferque per orbem
dicor et herbarum subiecta potentia nobis.
Ei mihi, quod nullis amor est sanabilis herbis,
nec prosunt domino quae prosunt omnibus artes!"
      Plura locuturum timido Peneia cursu   525
fugit, cumque ipso verba imperfecta reliquit;
tum quoque visa decens. Nudabant corpora venti,
obviaque adversas vibrabant flamina vestes,
et levis impulsos retro dabat aura capillos;

aucta fuga forma est. Sed enim non sustinet ultra   530
perdere blanditias iuvenis deus, utque monebat
ipse Amor, admisso sequitur vestigia passu.
Ut canis in vacuo leporem cum Gallicus arvo
vidit, et hic praedam pedibus petit, ille salutem,
alter inhaesuro similis iam iamque tenere   535
sperat, et extento stringit vestigia rostro,
alter in ambiguo est an sit comprensus et ipsis
morsibus eripitur tangentiaque ora relinquit.
Sic deus et virgo est, hic spe celer, illa timore.
Qui tamen insequitur, pennis adiutus Amoris   540
ocior est requiemque negat tergoque fugacis
imminet et crinem sparsum cervicibus afflat.
Viribus absumptis expalluit illa citaeque   543
victa labore fugae "Tellus," ait, "hisce, vel istam   544a
quae facit ut laedar, mutando perde figuram."   545
Victa labore fugae, spectans Peneidas undas,   544
"Fer, pater," inquit, "opem, si flumina numen habetis;   546
qua nimium placui, mutando perde figuram."   547
Vix prece finita, torpor gravis occupat artus;
mollia cinguntur tenui praecordia libro;
in frondem crines, in ramos bracchia crescunt;   550
pes modo tam velox pigris radicibus haeret;
ora cacumen habet: remanet nitor unus in illa.
      Hanc quoque Phoebus amat, positaque in stipite dextra
sentit adhuc trepidare novo sub cortice pectus,
complexusque suis ramos, ut membra, lacertis,   555
oscula dat ligno; refugit tamen oscula lignum.
Cui deus, "At quoniam coniunx mea non potes esse,
arbor eris certe," dixit, "mea; semper habebunt
te coma, te citharae, te nostrae, laure, pharetrae.
Tu ducibus Latiis aderis, cum laeta Triumphum   560
vox canet et visent longas Capitolia pompas;
postibus Augustis eadem fidissima custos
ante fores stabis mediamque tuebere quercum.
Utque meum intonsis caput est iuvenale capillis,
tu quoque perpetuos semper gere frondis honores."   565
Finierat Paean; factis modo laurea ramis
annuit utque caput visa est agitasse cacumen.   567

Amores 1.1 Introduction

Amores 1.1 presents a complex amalgam of innovation and imitation. On the one hand, *Amores* 1.1 does exactly what it is supposed to do: it serves as an introductory poem to Ovid's corpus of elegies. Like Propertius, Tibullus, and even Catullus before him, Ovid states both his goals and his stance in his opening poem. But Ovid does so with a twist; as he imitates, he innovates. Where Propertius and Tibullus state clearly what they are writing, why they are writing, and for whom they are writing, Ovid's opening poem presents a poet in conflict. Ovid is not equipped, as his predecessors were, to write love poetry: he set out to write epic, not elegy, and he has no concept, poetically at least, of what writing love poetry entails. Cupid, however, is forcing Ovid to forsake epic for elegy and, despite Ovid's protests, he must ultimately acquiesce. But the shift in genre that *Amores* 1.1 illustrates is indicative of Ovid's poetic approach to the *Amores*. While his predecessors laid out in clear terms a general direction for their poetry, Ovid creates a sense of uncertainty about the narrative course of the *Amores*; he is unsure about what he will write and in fact reveals that he has nothing or no one to write about. But in one sense that is exactly Ovid's point: he invites us to explore not only his own love elegy along with him but also love elegy in general. As Ovid "learns" this new genre over the course of writing his poetry, so too will we learn it along with him.

The imagery of *Amores* 1.1 is chaotic. Ovid spends much of the poem establishing incongruent dichotomies (the juxtaposition of epic and elegy in 1-2, and the list of divine reversals from lines 7-12), asking naïve rhetorical questions whose answers both reader and narrator must already know (lines 5 and 15-16), and professing literary impotence as he attempts to convince us that he is unprepared to write elegy. But where Propertius and Tibullus will coöpt emotional chaos to imbue their poetry with anger, frustration and resentment, Ovid will coöpt literary chaos to reflect his exploration of genre: although much of the *Amores* will indeed reflect the elegiac tradition, nonetheless Ovid questions the limitations that the elegiac genre imposes on him.

Ovid will close *Amores* 1.1 by confessing that, even though he has accepted that he will now have to write love poetry, he has no one to write love poetry about. While Propertius and Tibullus each states clearly and unequivocally in their opening poems who his lover is, Ovid not only does not identify her but also confesses that she does not yet exist. In fact, it will not be until *Amores* 1.3 that he confirms that she is indeed a woman, and not until *Amores* 1.5 that he identifies her by name: Corinna. But Corinna is not yet important for the literary Ovid in *Amores* 1.1. In *Amores* 1.1, Ovid is still grappling with his new identity as an elegiac lover instead of an epic narrator. And as Ovid struggles with his new identity, he forces the reader to struggle with the innovative poetry he has written, where the lines between epic and elegy, or at least the lines defining elegy, are no longer as clearly defined.

1-4. The first poem of Ovid's Amores *sets the tone for the entire collection. Ovid is writing love elegy, but here in the first poem cannot help but acknowledge (and poke some Ovidian fun at) the genre of elegy. Ovid creates a self-conscious narrator who wants to write the epics of the great poets but cannot avoid the lure of Cupid and love elegy.*

1. **arma.** This word immediately recalls the first half-line (two and a half feet) of Vergil's *Aeneid*: *arma virumque cano* (Ovid's first two and half feet scan exactly the same; see the box on page 29 for the first seven lines of the *Aeneid*). Ovid, however, will tranform Virgil's *arma* into not a central theme for his poetry, but rather a foil for his satire of literary genre. As in Vergil, the noun *arma* is the object of a first person verb.
    gravi. Here used in its literary context, referring to the seriousness of epic. A modern parallel might be the use of the minor key in music to convey a somber or serious tone. This somber tone is what Ovid wants to write, but will be prevented from writing. (The opposite of *gravis* is *levis*, which refers to the lightheartedness and supposed lack of literary seriousness of elegy.)
    numero. Specifically used here as a metrical term: "meter."

2. **materia.** Referring to the epic poetry Ovid was trying to write. What case is this noun? How is it grammatically connected to *conveniente*? And so, what construction is it?
    modis. Another usage specific to metrics: "verse."

3. **par erat inferior versus.** Referring to dactylic hexameter and its lines of equal metrical length; Ovid was initially writing epic. (See the chart at the bottom of page 29 for a comparison of the meters of epic and elegy.)
    risisse. To be read with *dicitur* in line 4.
    Cupido. Be careful about case here. This is not an ablative.

4. **pedem.** Referring specifically to a metrical "foot." Ovid here describes the tranformation of his poetry from the six foot per line dactylic hexameter of epic to the elegiac couplet, whose first line is a line of dactylic hexameter and whose second line is comprised of not six, but five metrical feet (i.e. a six-foot dactylic hexameter line minus a stolen foot).
    surripuisse. Specifically implies a surreptitious or secretive taking away. The two infinitives reinforce the unexpectedness and the stealth of Cupid's "crime."

Discussion Questions, Lines 1-4

1. Identify the Latin words in the first line that recall aspects of epic poetry. Explain their significance both for epic poetry in general and for how Ovid is comparing epic poetry to love elegy.

2. Explain why the imperfect is the appropriate tense for *parabam* in line 1 (instead of, say, the perfect).

3. How does the enjambment in line 2 reflect the poetic tension that Ovid is describing?

4. How does the second couplet (lines 3-4) set the tone for the *Amores*? How will Ovid treat the subject of love?

5. How does the introduction of Cupid in line 3 signal a change in the poetry that Ovid is writing?

6. Why does Cupid laugh in line 3?

7. What is the effect of saying *Cupido dicitur risisse atque surripuisse* in lines 3 and 4 instead of the more direct *Cupido risit atque surripuit*? Why would Ovid choose such phrasing?

8. Identify specific Latin words or phrases in these introductory couplets that establish the humorous tone of the poem.

Arma gravi numero violentaque bella parabam
edere, materia conveniente modis.
Par erat inferior versus: risisse Cupido
dicitur atque unum surripuisse pedem.

Cogitabam proferre arma et bella saeva metro grandiloquo, materia accommodata modulationibus. Versus posterior erat aequalis: Cupido perhibetur risisse, atque furtim sustulisse unum pedem.

atque (conj.). but, and so, still [*an adversative conjunction that often signals a shift in the story or sense*]

convenio, convenire, conveni, conventus. to be convenient, to be useful

edo, edere, edidi, editus. to say, to narrate, to tell, to give forth, to produce

inferior, inferius (gen.: inferioris). lower, inferior, following, next

surripio, surripere, surripui, surreptus. to steal, to take away

---

Ad Comparanda

Arma virumque cano, Troiae qui primus ab oris
Italiam, fato profugus, Laviniaque venit
litora, multum ille et terris iactatus et alto
vi superum, saevae memorem Iunonis ob iram;
multa quoque et bello passus, dum conderet urbem,   5
inferretque deos Latio, genus unde Latinum,
Albanique patres atque altae moenia Romae.

(*Aeneid* 1.1-7)

The Metrical Comparison in lines 1-4

The opening two lines of Vergil's Aeneid (dactylic hexameter)	*The opening couplet of* Amores *1.1* (elegiac couplet)
Arma virumque cano, Troiae qui primus ab oris Italiam fato profugus Laviniaque venit	Arma gravi numero violentaque bella parabam edere, materia conveniente modis

- the second line in each of the above examples is the *inferior versus* of line 3
- the *par* of line 3 refers to how each line of the epic column has the same number of feet
- the *surripuisse pedem* of the elegiac couplet column refers to the one fewer foot of the second line of the elegiac couplet (indicated visually by its indentation)
- the *surripuisse pedem* indicates elegy because now the second verse (the *inferior versus*) is no longer *par*, as it is in epic, but one foot shorter

Epic	**Elegy**
dactylic hexameter	elegiac couplet
each line = dactylic hexameter	couplets of one line of dactylic hexameter and one of pentameter
dactylic hexameter = 6 feet of dactyls	pentameter = 5 (modified) feet of dactyls

5-6. Ovid here directly addresses Cupid and his threat to Ovid's epic; Ovid thinks that he might still resist Cupid.

5.   **hoc iuris = hoc ius.** *Iuris* is a partitive genitive, literally translated as "this (sort / type) of control." But English renders such partitive genitives better as noun-adjective pairs, i.e. "this control."
        in carmina. To be read with *hoc iuris*. What will *in* mean here to make sense with *hoc iuris*?
6.   **Pieridum…sumus =** (Nos) vates sumus turba Pieridum, non tua (turba)
        Pieridum. To be read with *turba*. In some accounts (Ovid's *Metamorphoses* 5 perhaps being the most prominent) the Muses are the daughters of King Pierus of Emathia in the region of Macedonia in northern Greece. More common is their association with Mt. Pierus, a mountain near Mt. Olympus.
        vates. In apposition to the subject of *sumus*. The term, especially used indirectly with *Pieridum* and its divine implications, reflects a mocking and begrudging resistence to the shift in literary focus that the reader and the writer know is inevitable.
        tua. Still refers to the *saeve puer* of line 5 but agrees with an understood *turba*. Ovid continues to disavow Cupid's poetry, as he tries to associate himself with the Muses and the epic they represent, and detach himself from Cupid and his love elegy.

7-12. The next three couplets see Ovid create reversals of roles for divinities; Ovid plays a brief game of "what if."
First, Venus and Minerva are switched, then Ceres and Diana, and finally Apollo and Mars.

7.   **quid = quid (fiat / putemus).** Stands for the implied apodasis of the protasis introduced by *si*, i.e. stands for the "then"-part of this conditional.
        praeripiat. Recalls the *surripuisse* of line 4 (both are compounds of *rapio*) but creates contrast between the actions of Cupid and Venus. *Praeripio* is a more visible and violent taking away, the prepositional prefix *prae* implying "in front of someone," while *surripio*, because of the prepositional prefix *sub*, is more secretive or understated.
        arma. Recalls the *arma* of line 1 and reinforces the incredulity of the switch Ovid proposes: Ovid writing elegy is akin to Venus taking up Minerva's arms. Neither makes sense.
8.   **ventilet.** Another verb, parallel to the *praeripiat* of 7, in the protasis of the conditional introduced by *si* in line 7.
9.   **probet.** Be careful about the mood here. Is this indicative or subjunctive?
10.   **pharetratae virginis = Diana.** But what is the epithet that Ovid uses for her?
        coli. Parallel to *regnare* (and so dependent too on *probet*), but be careful about its voice.
11-12. **quis instruat.** The same construction as *quis probet* in line 9.
11.   **crinibus insignem.** Apollo does not have "distinguished hair." These words do not agree but *crinibus* is read with *insignem*.
12.   **Aoniam…lyram.** Mars is playing Apollo's lyre. What Latin construction does Ovid use to describe this action?
        Aoniam Marte. The juxtaposition emphasizes the incongruity of Mars playing Apollo's lyre.

Discussion Questions, Lines 5-12

1. What is the effect of the apostrophe in line 5? Why does Ovid address Cupid directly?
2. Why does Ovid refer to Cupid as a *saeve puer*? What does the use of this adjective imply about Cupid?
3. What genre does the mention of the *Pieridum* reflect? What is the significance of this allusion?
4. Why does Ovid describe Minerva as *flava*? How does this accentuate the juxtaposition between her and Venus?
5. Why is Apollo described as *crinibus insignem*? What image of Apollo is Ovid trying to create and how is it meant to heighten the contrast between Apollo and Mars?
6. How does the chiasmus of line 12 reflect Mars' assumption of Apollo's realm, and how does it emphasize the juxtaposition between Mars' old role and new role?

"Quis tibi, saeve puer, dedit hoc in carmina iuris?   5
    Pieridum vates, non tua, turba sumus.
Quid, si praeripiat flavae Venus arma Minervae,
    ventilet accensas flava Minerva faces?
Quis probet in silvis Cererem regnare iugosis,
    lege pharetratae virginis arva coli?   10
Crinibus insignem quis acuta cuspide Phoebum
    instruat, Aoniam Marte movente lyram?

"Quis tibi tribuit hoc imperii in versus, puer crudelis? Nos poetae sumus coetus Musarum, non tuus. Quid, si Venus auferat arma flavae Minerva, Minerva flava agitet taedas inflammatas? Quis laudet Cererem imperare in silvis montosis? Agros subigi lege virginis pharetra instructae? Quis armet Phoebum decorum crinibus mucrone acuto, Marte pulsante lyram Aoniam?

accendo, accendere, accendi, accensus. to burn, to smolder, to kindle, to enflame

acutus, -a, -um. sharp

Aonius, -a, -um. of or belonging to Aonia or Boeotia [*this is the region in Greece where Mt. Helicon is located, a peak sacred to Apollo and the Muses*]

arvum, -i. field, meadow, open expanse of grass

crinis, -is (m.). hair

cuspis, cuspidis (f.). tip, (sharp) point

fax, facis (f.). torch, fire, wedding [*because of the torches that burned at weddings*]

flavus, -a, -um. blonde, yellow

instruo, instruere, instruxi, instructus. to build, to construct; (+ abl.) to equip, to furnish

iugosus, -a, -um. hilly, mountainous

ius, iuris (n.). law, rule, precept, guide, legal saction, legal authority, control [*sometimes used in the ablative to mean "by law," "under the law," or "with legal authority"*]

pharetratus, -a, -um. quiver-bearing, wearing or having a quiver

Pieris, Pieridos. Muse [*a patronymic from the identification of the Muses as the daughters of Pierus*]

praeripio, praeripere, praeripui, praereptus. to take away, to steal, to snatch away

probo, -are, -avi, -atus. to test, to try, to approve, to prove

turba, -ae. crowd, mob

vates, vatis (m.). poet, prophet, seer

ventilo, -are, -avi, -atus. to fan

13-16. Ovid turns his attention back to Cupid, questioning his motivation and the origin of his power.

13.   **tibi.** What kind of dative is often used with *sum, esse*? What does the *puer* (Cupid) have?
        magna. Agrees with *regna* and not *potentia*.

14.   **opus novum.** Here referring to Ovid's new undertaking of elegy instead of epic.
        adfectas. Not a subjunctive.

15.   **An...est = An, est (id), quod (est) ubique, tuum?**
        Heliconia. Referring to Mt. Helicon, the legendary home of the Muses, and a location associated not with Cupid but with Apollo.
        tempe. A Greek neuter nominative plural. Derives its meaning from a specific valley at the base of Mt. Olympus through which runs the Peneus river. Peneus is the river-god father of the nymph Daphne, whose story is included next in this collection.

16.   **Phoebo.** To be read with *tuta*.
        sua. Refers to Apollo.

17-20. Ovid now turns to his own situation, first literary (17-18) and then romantic (19-20).

18.   **proximus ille.** Likely describing the *versu* of line 17, though some read it as potentially continuing Ovid's direct address of Cupid.

19.   **numeris levioribus.** To be read with *apta*. And in direct contrast to the *gravi numero* of line 1.

20.   This line, as an appositive to the *materia* of the previous line, explains what *materia* Ovid does not have.
        aut, aut. Maintain the negative introduced by *nec* in line 19.
        longas comas. An accusative of respect with *compta*.

Discussion Questions, Lines 13-20

1. How does Ovid's argument in lines 13-14 change? What approach does he now take?
2. How does the placement of *novum* in line 16 emphasize the emotion and force of Ovid's question to Cupid?
3. How do Ovid's questions in lines 15 and 16 signal another change in Ovid's mindset toward Cupid?
4. How do lines 17-20 both recall the first couplet and at the same time signal a shift in Ovid's attitude?
5. What is the ambiguity introduced in line 20 with the inclusion of both *puer* and *puella*?

Sunt tibi magna, puer, nimiumque potentia regna:
    cur opus affectas, ambitiose, novum?
An, quod ubique, tuum est? Tua sunt Heliconia tempe?   15
    Vix etiam Phoebo iam lyra tuta sua est?
Cum bene surrexit versu nova pagina primo,
    attenuat nervos proximus ille meos,
nec mihi materia est numeris levioribus apta,
    aut puer aut longas compta puella comas."   20

Obtines magna imperia, puer, et nimium valida. Quamobrem, ambitiose, appetis insolitum opus? An tuum est quodcumque est ubique? Tempe Heliconia suntne tua? Vix etiam sua lyra est iam secura Phoebo? Cum nova pagina bene aucta est versiculo primo, ille statim minuit chordas meas. Nec materiam habeo idoneam modis tenuioribus, seu puerum, seu puellam cuius sint ornati prolixi capilli."

affecto, -are, -avi, -atus. to attempt, to try, to strive (for)

ambitiosus, -a, -um. eager, ambitious, adventurous

an (conj.). whether, if [*used to introduce "yes/no" indirect questions*]

aptus, -a, -um. appropriate, easy, apt

attenuo, -are, -avi, -atus. to make thin, to weaken

coma, -ae. hair

como, comere, compsi, comptus. to make beautiful, to adorn, to arrange attractively

Heliconius, -a, -um. of or belonging to Mt. Helicon [*a mountain in Boeotia, a region of central Greece, that is sacred to Apollo and the Muses*]

nervus, -i. sinew, cord, string (or anything else made out of sinew)

nimium (adv.). too much, excessively

pagina, -ae. page

Phoebus, -i. [name; *epithet for Apollo*]

potentia, -ae. power

proximus, -a, -um. nearest, next

surgo, surgere, surrexi, surrecturus. to rise (up), to get up

tempe (n. pl. nom. *and* acc). valley [*a Greek form*]

tutus, -a, -um. safe

ubique. everywhere

vix (adv.). scarcely, hardly

The vale of Tempe.

21-26. Ovid concludes his complaint but Cupid completes his defeat of Ovid with a shot from his bow.

21.   **questus eram.** The abruptness and succinctness of this verb as it concludes Ovid's apostrophe, further emphasized by its tense, signals a shift in action and tone.
         cum. Here a conjunction that governs the rest of the sentence.
         pharetra soluta. To be read with *legit*. What case are these (they are not nominative)?
         ille. Referring to Cupid and the subject of all three verbs of the *cum* clause.

22.   **in exitium meum.** To be read with *facta*; an accusative of purpose.

24.   **opus quod canas** = "the work which you are supposed to sing / write."
         -que. Connects *dixit* to *lunavit* and is not part of the quotation; a common, if confusing, Ovidian structure.
         canas. Relative clause of purpose.

25.   **me miserum.** Accusative of exclamation.
         certas. Does not here mean "certain." What kind of *sagittas* does Cupid have?

27-30. Ovid concludes by returning to the language of poetics and metrics with which he opened the poem.

27.   **sex.** An indeclinable adjective. What does it agree with? What is the only plural in the clause?
         opus. As in line 24, refers to Ovid's writing of poetry.

27-28.   **numeris, modis.** Here, as at line 2, with their poetic meanings.

27.   **quinque** = quinque (numeris)

28.   **ferrea bella.** The objects of *valete*.
         cum. Here the preposition.

29.   **cingere.** The passive imperative with the sense of the Greek middle voice, i.e. a reflexive instead of passive sense.
         litorea. Be careful about what this modifies (not *flaventia tempora*).
         flaventia tempora. The object of *cingere*: "Gird your golden temples"
         myrto. Recalls Venus and her association with love poetry.

30.   **Musa.** A vocative noun on which this entire line depends.
         emodulanda. Future passive participle of a deponent that expresses necessity: "who must regulate…"

Discussion Questions, Lines 21-30

1. How does the sentence structure of lines 21-24 accentuate Cupid's actions? What is Cupid's attitude toward Ovid and how does the arrangement of clauses emphasize this?

2. What are the different connotations of *exitium* in line 22?

3. How have the implications of *vates* changed here from the word's initial appearance in line 6?

4. What imagery, common to elegiac poetry, does *uror* introduce in line 26?

5. Why is *in vacuo pectore regnat Amor* in line 26 oxymoronic?

6. To what does *vacuo* refer in line 26? What is the range of possibilities for the connotations of this word?

7. What effect does the postponement of *Amor* in line 26 (and its inversion with *regnat*) have on the emphasis of the line?

8. What are the ambiguities of *valete* in line 28?

9. Why does Ovid close with a direct address to the Muse(s)? How has this Muse changed from the reference to the *Pierides* in line 6?

10. To what does the *Musa* in line 30 refer?

11. How does the form of *emodulanda* reinforce Ovid's reluctant agreement to write elegiac poetry?

Questus eram, pharetra cum protinus ille soluta
    legit in exitium spicula facta meum
lunavitque genu sinuosum fortiter arcum
    "quod"que "canas, vates, accipe," dixit, "opus."
Me miserum! Certas habuit puer ille sagittas: 25
    uror, et in vacuo pectore regnat Amor.
Sex mihi surgat opus numeris, in quinque residat:
    ferrea cum vestris bella valete modis.
Cingere litorea flaventia tempora myrto,
    Musa, per undenos emodulanda pedes.   30

Conquestus eram; cum ille continuo expedita pharetra dispexit sagittas paratas in meam ruinam; et genu tetendit strenue arcum curvatum; et inquit: "Tene, poeta, opus quod cantes." Hei mihi! Ille puer habuit spicula certa. Ardeo; et Amor imperat in corde inani. Opus mihi initium ducat sex pedibus, in quinque desinat. Bella dura, discedite cum vestris modis. Musa, fingenda per numeros undenos, redimitor tempora flaventia myrto littorea.

cingo, cingere, cinxi, cinctus. to bind, to gird, to surround

emodulor, -ari, -atus. to measure numerically, to put into meter, to control, to regulate

exitium, -i. outcome, end, death

ferreus, -a, -um. (made of) iron

flavens, flaventis. golden, blonde, yellow

genu, genus (n.). knee

litoreus, -a, -um. of or belonging to the (sea)shore

luno, -are, -avi, -atus. to bend into a curve, to shape, to bend back

myrtus, -i (f.). myrtle tree, myrtle leaf

pharetra, -ae. quiver [*holder for arrows*]

protinus (adv.). immediately, at once

queror, queri, questus. to complain, to protest

resido, risidere, residi, -. to sit down, to go down, to fall

sinuosus, -a, -um. curvy, bent, curved

solvo, solvere, solvi, solutus. to loosen, to open, to unravel, to unbind, to release

spiculum, -i. sharp point, arrow

surgo, surgere, surrexi, surrecturus. to rise (up), to get up

tempus, temporis (n.). time; the side of the head, the temple, the forehead

undeni, -ae, -a. eleven (at a time)

uro, urere, ussi, ustus. to burn, to smolder [*can have both the literal and figurative meaning, i.e. to burn with passion*]

vacuus, -a, -um. empty, hollow; devoid of (+ abl.)

vates, vatis (m.). poet, prophet, seer

Apollo and Daphne Introduction

Ovid's *Metamorphoses* is the anti-epic: where Vergil's *Aeneid* is somber and lofty, Ovid's *Metamorphoses* is wry and irreverent; where Vergil is serious of purpose, Ovid intentionally flaunts tradition; where the *Aeneid* focuses on history, culture, and society, the *Metamorphoses* focuses on transformation, psychology, and their humorous potential.

Epic is a relatively emotionless genre. Description by the narrator of a character's emotions is rare. The characters themselves, while able to verbalize their emotions, e.g. Odysseus on the beach of Calypso's island and Achilles before Agamemnon, more often articulate their emotions through action. Epic creates a narrative psychology in which the inner life of characters is most often revealed in its outer expression. And above all, the narrator remains emotionally detached. Elegy is quite the opposite. Ovid's elegiac predecessors, Catullus being perhaps the best known, wrote raw and emotional poetry (not just about love) that exposed them as in turns sentimental, petty, earnest, scared, angry, and insecure. The elegiac narrator is also often the main character of the narrative; he tells his own story. The elegiac narrator expresses his inner self in its raw reality for the reader to view and, ultimately, judge. The elegiac protagonist possesses little of the awareness of the importance of appearance that the epic character does. What is largely taboo in epic is the requirement of elegy. It is a personal and individual genre which demands that the poet write as if the poetry is autobiographical (even if it may not be).

The epic genre also has a number of common features: dactylic hexameter for its meter, a story important enough to concern and directly involve the gods, a grand and sweeping scope, an epic hero, and the beginning of a story *in medias res*. Ovid, with these features in mind, intentionally violates many of them to establish his poem as the epic that is barely an epic, or only an epic in external form.

The meter of the *Metamorphoses* declares it an epic. But few other aspects of the poem participate in the epic tradition. The *Metamorphoses* has no epic hero; it is a collection of over two hundred stories that not only have shifting characters but also are connected by elaborate, and sometimes artificial, transitions. The *Metamorphoses* does not begin *in medias res*. In fact, it begins at the ultimate beginning: the beginning of time, with the creation of the world and the successive ages of man. It is in the context of the creation of the earth that Ovid locates the Apollo and Daphne story.

After the earth was created, Ovid describes the successively degenerating ages of humans: while man began in a utopian golden age, he soon degenerated into an iron age, characterized by crime, jealousy, and war. The gods, to punish humans, sent a great flood to destroy them. When the earth began fresh, it created every kind of animal, one of which was the monstrous Python. The god Apollo kills the Python, and brags about his prowess with the bow and arrow to Cupid, another bow-wielder. It is the exchange between Apollo and Cupid over their shared use of the bow and arrow that both opens this selection from the *Metamorphoses* and drives the narrative of the Apollo and Daphne story.

As the first poem of Ovid's *Amores* established the literary parameters for that collection, so does the Apollo and Daphne story establish literary parameters for the *Metamorphoses*. It marks a conspicuous shift in the poem, providing a transition between the background established with the creation and flood stories and the marriage of the two primary topics of the *Metamorphoses*: love and change. The god Cupid, included by the Greek epic poet Hesiod as one of the primordial gods in his creation story, is noticeably absent from Ovid's creation story, but appears for the first time in the Apollo and Daphne story. His conflict with Apollo, who in the killing of the Python has become an epic hero (and brags like one), then becomes the mythological equivalent of the literary debate Ovid introduced in *Amores* 1.1. Ovid articulates his own literary conflict through the debate between Cupid and Apollo, although his treatment of that conflict in the *Metamorphoses* has become more nuanced: as Cupid conquered Ovid, the aspiring epic poet, in *Amores* 1.1, so

Cupid conquers Apollo, the aspiring epic hero, in Apollo and Daphne. In the *Metamorphoses*, he will write an epic poem that explores amatory themes on an epic scale with epic scope. Instead of an aspiring epic poet forced to write elegy, Ovid is now an epic poet still exploring elegiac themes. Apollo and Daphne is his first foray into his literary amalgam of epic and *amor*.

Apollo and Daphne At-A-Glance

Book	1
Lines	452-567
Main Characters (in order of appearance)	Apollo: God of music Cupid: son of Venus and god of love Daphne: nymph, daughter of the river-god Peneus
Minor Characters	Peneus: father of Daphne
Context	The creation and subsequent destruction of the earth by Jupiter
Preceeding Story	Deucalion and Pyrrha and the Flood. The gods flood the earth because of the misbehavior of its inhabitants, saving two worthy souls, Deucalion and Pyrrha. After the flood, the earth repopulates itself with various animals, one of which is the monstrous Python. Apollo kills the Python.
Transition	Apollo sees Cupid playing with his bow and arrow and, flush from his victory over the Python, advises Cupid to leave the arrow-shooting to him. Cupid should stick to love.
Subsequent Story	Io. All of the river gods assemble to console Daphne's father Peneus. One, however, is missing: Inachus, the father of Io. Jupiter fell in love with Io, but Juno found them out. To hide Io from Juno's wrath, Jupiter turns her into a heifer. Juno, understanding the ruse, asks for the heifer as a gift, and Jupiter must agree or admit to his transgression.
Primary Topics	order vs. chaos / unnatural vs. natural / rational vs. visceral the capriciousness of the gods

Apollo and Daphne Vocabulary Frequency

13 times
am- [root]
fug- [root]

9 times
amor, -oris

8 times
video, -ere

7 times
dico, -ere
do, dare

6 times
deus, -i
fugio, -ere
sic

5 times
facio, -ere
Pen- [root]

4 times
alter
capillus, -i
certus, -a, -um
fuga, -ae
habeo, -ere
Phoebus, -i

3 times
ait
amo, -are
hostis, -is
iam
insequor, -i
lacertus, -i
laedo, -ere
levis, -e
modo
nympha, -ae
os, oris
osculum, -i

pater, -tris
pectus, -oris
penna, -ae
perdo, -ere
peto, -ere
ramus, -i
relinquo, -ere
spero, -are
tamen
velo, -are
vinco, -ere

*452-453. Ovid's introduction to the setting for the story: the **primus amor Phoebi**, and where this **primus amor** came from.*

452.   **Phoebi.** Not part of *Daphne Peneia* but rather an epithet from a Greek word meaning "resplendent" that refers to Apollo's role as sun god.

Daphne Peneia. Provides Daphne's name and parentage: whose daughter is she?

quem. Can't be read with *Daphne Peneia*. What then is its antecedent?

453.   **sed…ira.** Understand *dedit*.

saeva Cupidinis ira. As he does in *Amores* 1.1, Ovid opens the Apollo and Daphne story with a reference to the *Aeneid* in the identification of divine wrath as the cause for what will become the tragedy of this story.

454-460. Apollo is fresh from killing the Python, about which he brags to Cupid. He tells Cupid to stay away from the bows and arrows that so rightfully belong to him.

454.   **Delius hunc.** Can't be read together.

victa serpente. To be read with *superbus*. Why is Apollo *superbus*?

455.   **viderat…nervo** = (Delius) viderat (hunc) flectentem cornua, adducto nervo

456.   **Quid tibi cum…** = "What are you doing with…" or "Why do you have…"

lascive. Not an ablative; the commas are a clue to its case.

457.   **nostros** = meos

458, 459. **qui.** The antecedent is *umeros* which are then personified in the first person plurals *possumus* and *stravimus* (460). Apollo's shoulders, as the location where the bow and arrows are carried, come to stand through a synecdoche of sorts for Apollo himself.

458.   **certa vulnera.** To be read with both clauses in the line. Latin will tend to distribute a noun and its modifier to each clause in which they are used to avoid having to repeat the entire expression in both clauses.

459-460. See the sentence diagram below for structural assistance.

460.   **Pythona.** A Greek accusative singular.

461-462. Apollo leaves Cupid with some final advice: be happy with what you have and stay out of my way.

461.   **face.** Not from *facio, facere*. What case is this noun?

esto. A future imperative whose nuance is difficult to capture in English; translate it as a present imperative. The future imperative carries a haughty implication (recall *superbus* in 454); Apollo's use of it emphasizes his patronizing tone toward Cupid.

462.   **irritare.** To be read with *contentus*.

tua. Not a nominative singular (but feminine). What can it modify (hint: it's in the line before)?

assere. Not an infinitive. What is the present active infinitive of this verb? And so what is this form? (Hint: its mood is parallel to *esto*.)

Discussion Questions, Lines 452-462

1. How does *superbus* in line 454 establish Apollo's character for the story (beyond the meaning of the word)?
2. The question in line 456 recalls *Amores* 1.1.5. How are these questions similar in context and tone to that one? How are they different?

Sentence Structure Diagram 459-460

qui modo pestifero tot iugera ventre prementem
stravimus innumeris tumidum Pythona sagittis

*   a basic subject-verb-object structure
*   two modifiers of the object *Pythona* that govern everything else
*   modifier #1 governs an object and ablative, #2 an ablative

```
                              qui
                               |
                           stravimus
                               |
                            Pythona
                1. _____/       _____ 2.
              prementem               tumidum
                  |                      |
              tot iugera          innumeris sagittis
                  |
          modo pesitfero ventre
```

Primus amor Phoebi Daphne Peneia, quem non   452
fors ignara dedit, sed saeva Cupidinis ira.
Delius hunc, nuper victa serpente superbus,
viderat adducto flectentem cornua nervo   455
"Quid"que "tibi, lascive puer, cum fortibus armis?"
dixerat; "Ista decent umeros gestamina nostros,
qui dare certa ferae, dare vulnera possumus hosti,
qui modo pestifero tot iugera ventre prementem
stravimus innumeris tumidum Pythona sagittis.   460
Tu face nescioquos esto contentus amores
irritare tua, nec laudes assere nostras."

Daphne Peneia fuit primus amor Apollonis, quem non fortuna inscia, sed atrox ira Cupidinis movit. Apollo elatus superato serpente viderat hunc nuper curvantem arcum nervo adducto, et dixerat: "Quid tibi cum duris armis, puer lascive? Ista gestamina conveniunt nostris umeris, qui possumus certas plagas inferre feris et hostibus; qui nuper occidimus infinitis spiculis Pythonem inflatum, tegentem tot iugera ventre venenato.

adduco, adducere, adduxi, adductus. to lead to, to lead back, to pull back, to pull tight

assero, asserere, asserrui, assertus. to claim, to lay claim to, to identify as one's own, to possess

cornu, -us (n.). horn, ivory, something made of ivory, tip

decet, decere, decuit, - (impers.). it is fitting, it is right, it is appropriate

Delius, -a, -um. Delian, of or belonging to Delos [*an epithet for Apollo because of his close association with this island in the Aegean where supposedly his mother Latona birthed him*]

fax, facis (f.). torch, fire, wedding [*because of the torches that burned at weddings*]

ferus, -a, -um. wild; [*often used substantively as:*] wild beast, wild animal

fors, fortis (f.). chance

gestamen, gestaminis (n.). equipment, implement, something worn

ignarus, -a, -um. ignorant, unaware

irrito, -are, -avi, -atus. to incite, to fire up, to provoke

iugerum, -i. measure of land, acre, acreage

lascivus, -a, -um. naughty, troublesome, playful

laus, laudis (f.). praise, honor, glory

modo (adv.). now...now; at this point...at this point [*shows actions that are happening alternately but at the same time*]

nervus, -i. sinew, cord, string (or anything else made out of sinew)

nescioquis, nescioquid (adj.). some, any; someone, -thing; anyone, -thing [*a combination of the verb* nescio, *"I don't know," and the interrogative, becoming literally "I don't know who" or "I don't know what"*]

nuper. recently

Peneius, -a, -um. of or belonging to Peneus; daughter of Peneus

pestifer, -a, -um. disease-bearing, deadly [*a compound word:* pest- = pestis, *meaning "disease" and* fer- = fero, *meaning "to bear"*]

premo, premere, pressi, pressus. to press down, to compress, to touch

Python, Pythonis (m.; acc. sing. = Pythona). Python [*the legendary snake whom Apollo killed to assume control of the oracle at Delphi*]

sterno, sternere, stravi, stratus. to lay low, to lay out, to kill, to slay

tot (indecl.). so many

tumidus, -a, -um. swollen, grown, expanded

umerus, -i. shoulder

venter, ventris (m.). stomach, belly

463-465. Cupid responds to Apollo's boasting with some boasting of his own about the effectiveness of his power.

463.   **huic.** To whom is this referring? To whom is Cupid responding?

463-4. **Figat...arcus** = Tuus (arcus) figat omnia, Phoebe, (sed) meus arcus (figet) te. The use of the understood *figet* in the second clause reinforces the certainty with which Cupid responds to Apollo.

463.   **figat.** Be careful of mood here. Not an indicative.

464-5. **quanto, tanto.** These words establish parallel clauses of comparison, i.e. by as much [*quanto*] as one thing happens [*animalia cedunt cuncta deo*], by that much [*tanto*] something else happens [*minor est tua gloria nostra*].

464.   **animalia.** Generalizes Apollo's killing of the *Pythona* of 460 to his ability to kill other animals.

465.   **minor est tua gloria nostra** = minor est tua gloria nostra (gloria). One of these word pairs is nominative with *est* and one is ablative: whose glory is less than whose?
        minor. To be read with *tanto*: "by so much less."

466-467. Cupid arrives on Mt. Parnassus, a mountain in central Greece sacred to the Muses and so to Apollo as god of poetry.

466.   **percussis pennis.** To be read with *eliso aere* (not the other way around). How was the *aere eliso*?

467.   **umbrosa.** Not a nominative: where did Cupid *constitit*?

468-473. Cupid's revenge for Apollo's boasting: he draws two arrows, one gold, one lead. He shoots Daphne with the lead, which will prevent her from falling in love, and Apollo with the gold, which will make him fall in love.

468.   **eque** = et e. This is the preposition plus the conjunction.
        tela, pharetra. One of these nouns is accusative, one ablative. Both vocabulary and scansion will identify which is which.

469.   **diversorum operum.** To be read with *tela*.
        fugat. Does not mean "flee" (though related).
        hoc, illud. Each refers to one of the *duo tela* of line 468, i.e. the *duo* is split now into individual *tela*.

470-471. Describes the material composition of the two arrows.

470.   **quod facit** = (telum) quod facit (amorem)

471.   **quod fugat** = (telum) quod fugat (amorem)
        sub harundine plumbum. The exact meaning of this is unclear, specifically where the lead of the arrow was located. However this is interpreted, though, its implication is clear: that this arrow is lead as opposed to the other which is gold.

472.   **hoc, illo.** Refer to the two arrows, but each is a different case.
        hoc deus. Cannot mean "this god."

473.   **medullas.** A word with elegiac connotations, referring to the pervasiveness and totality of love. For the distinction between *medullas* and *ossa*, see the diagram on p. 42.

Discussion Questions, Lines 463-473

1. What is the tone of Cupid's responses to Apollo in lines 463-465? How do they respond directly to Apollo's words?

2. What is the imagery created by *eliso...pennis* in line 466?

3. What is the irony of Cupid alighting on Mt. Parnassus in line 467?

4. How is *sagittafera pharetra* in line 468 an iconic structure?

5. Ovid uses the *cuspide acuta* of line 470 in *Amores* 1.1.11. How is the phrase used similarly? Differently?

6. How do the words of Apollo in lines 472-473 (with special attention paid to *medullas*) signal a transformation in Apollo? How does this compare with the wounding of Ovid by Cupid's arrows in *Amores* 1.1?

Filius huic Veneris, "Figat tuus omnia, Phoebe,
te meus arcus," ait, "quantoque animalia cedunt
cuncta deo, tanto minor est tua gloria nostra."   465
Dixit et, eliso percussis aere pennis,
impiger umbrosa Parnasi constitit arce,
eque sagittifera prompsit duo tela pharetra
diversorum operum. Fugat hoc, facit illud amorem.
(Quod facit, auratum est, et cuspide fulget acuta;   470
quod fugat, obtusum est, et habet sub harundine plumbum.)
Hoc deus in nympha Peneide fixit; at illo
laesit Apollineas traiecta per ossa medullas.

Tibi satis sit incendere nescio quos amores face tua, nec tibi arroga nostram gloriam." Filius Veneris huic respondit: "Apollo, arcus tuus cetera transverberet, meus te figat. Et quanto animalia omnia sunt te minora, tanto minores sunt tuae laudes nostris." Absolverat, et celer, aere percusso alis agitatis, pedem posuit in cacumine umbroso Parnasi, et sumpsit duas sagittas ex pharetra variorum effectuum. Haec excutit, illa inducit amorem. Quae inducit, aurata est, et splendet mucrone acuminato. Quae excutit, est hebes, et habet plumbum sub canna. Deus immisit hanc in Nympham Peneidem. At vulneravit illa medullas Apollonis per ossa transfixa.

acutus, -a, -um. sharp

aer, aeris (m.). air [*a two syllable nominative singular and a three syllable genitive singular*]

Apollineus, -a, -um. of or belonging to Apollo; Apollonean

auratus, -a, -um. golden

cedo, cedere, cessi, cessurus (+ dat.). to yield (to), to proceed

consto, constare, consteti, constaturus. to stand, to stand on, to exist, to establish, to be established

cuspis, cuspidis (f.). tip, (sharp) point

duo, duae, duo. two

elido, elidere, elisi, elisus. to crash, to break through, to shatter

figo, figere, fixi, fixus. to drive in, to insert, to fix, to affix, to attach

fugo, -are, -avi, -atus. to make flee, to put to flight

fulgeo, fulgere, fulsi, fulsurus. to gleam, to shine (brightly), to glow

harundo, harundinis (f.). reed, something made of reed, shaft; long, slender pole [*as in a fishing rod*]

impiger, impigra, impigrum. swift, quick, fast

laedo, laedere, laesi, laesus. to harm, to hurt, to injure, to wound

medulla, -ae. bone, bone marrow, marrow

obtusus, -a, -um. dull, blunt

os, ossis (n.). bone

Parnasus, -i. [name; *a mountain in central Greece, near Delphi, just north of the Gulf of Corinth; it is sacred to Apollo and is associated with him and the Muses as overseers of poetry*]

Peneis, Peneidos (m; abl. sing = Peneide; voc. sing. = Penei; accusative plural = Peneidas.). Daphne [*patronymic; daughter of Peneus, a river god, the father of Daphne*]

percutio, percutere, percussi, percussus. to shake violently, to sratch, to tear at, to strike, to beat, to hit

pharetra, -ae. quiver [*holder for arrows*]

plumbum, -i. lead

promo, promere, prompsi, promptus. to bring forth, to draw, to remove, to pull out

quantus, -a, -um. how much, how many

sagittaferus, -a, -um. arrow-bearing [*a compound of* sagitta, *"arrow" and* fero, *"to bear"*]

traicio, traicere, traieci, traiectus. to throw to, to throw into, to throw across, to strike, to pierce, to transfix

umbrosus, -a, -um. shady

474-480. After a brief mention of the effect of Cupid's arrows on both, Ovid focuses on the character and inclination of Daphne.

474.   **nomen amantis.** Refers to being identified as a lover, wife, or girlfriend.

475.   **silvarum, captivarum ferarum.** To be read with their respective ablatives, *latebris* and *exuviis* (476).

475-476. **latebris, exuviis.** To be read with *gaudens*.

476.   **aemula.** Likely to be read with *gaudens*, i.e. *gaudens* as an *aemula*, but could also be read more directly as an appositive to the *altera* of 474.

       Phoebes. Not a nominative or accusative plural but a Greek genitive, and not a name for Apollo. To whom does this refer?

477.   In Tarrant's new OCT, this line is bracketed, which indicates less certainty about its inclusion because of questions surrounding the complex manuscript tradition of the *Metamorphoses*.

       lege. Does not refer to "law." What is lacking from Daphne's *positos capillos*?

478.   **petiere.** Not an infinitive, but a syncopated form.

       petentes. Agrees with the *multi* from earlier in the line.

479.   **viri.** To be read with *expers*.

480.   **nec.** To be read with *curat*.

       quid Hymen, quid amor. Understand *sit* with both of these clauses.

481-482. Daphne's father demands of her what she does not want to give: a family.

481, 482. **debes.** Does not mean "ought".

Discussion Questions, Lines 474-482

1.   Identify specific Latin words in lines 474-480 that connect Daphne to Diana (beyond, of course, the use of Diana's name in line 476).

2.   How does the description of Daphne's hair in line 477 reflect her character?

3.   How do the anaphoras in lines 480 and 481-482 make more vivid the debate between Daphne and her father?

Line 473: The lexical distinction between *ossa* and *medullas* is represented here. It is meant to be a cross-section of a limb of the body, say the arm.

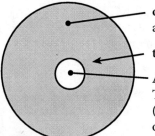

ossa. A general term for the bone or flesh. The marrow (*medulla*) is located at the center of the *ossa*.

traiecta. The *ossa* have been pierced by the *telum* on the way to the *medulla*.

Apollineas medullas. The marrow, or most central part of Apollo's body. The idea is that Cupid's arrow has pierced Apollo as deep as is possible. (Note that if the arrow continues through the center, it gets closer to the outside again, and is not longer as deep.)

> Protinus alter amat, fugit altera nomen amantis,
> silvarum latebris captivarumque ferarum   475
> exuviis gaudens, innuptaeque aemula Phoebes.
> Vitta coercebat positos sine lege capillos.
> Multi illam petiere: illa aversata petentes
> impatiens expersque viri, nemora avia lustrat,
> nec quid Hymen, quid amor, quid sint conubia curat.   480
> Saepe pater dixit, "Generum mihi, filia, debes."
> Saepe pater dixit, "Debes mihi, nata, nepotes."

Continuo alter amat. Altera odit nomen amantis, sese oblectans antris silvarum, et spoliis ferarum captarum, et imitans Dianam virginem. Vitta retinebat comam incomtam. Plurimi illam concupiverunt. Illa exosa ambientes, impatiens et expers mariti, percurrit loca devia et intercepta silvarum. Neque cogitat quid sit Hymen, quid sit Amor, quid sint coniugia. Parens dixit saepe, "Nata, debes mihi generum." Parens dixit saepe, "Nata, debes mihi posteros."

aemula, -ae. (female) rival

aversor, aversari, aversatus. to reject, to spurn

avius, -a, -um. remote, wild, without paths or roads

capillus, -i. hair

coerceo, coercere, coercui, coercitus. to hold in place, to restrain, to bind

conubium, -i. marriage, wedding

expers, expertis (+ gen.). ignorant (of), inexperienced (with)

exuviae, exuviarum (f. pl.). spoils, pelt, skin, hide

ferus, -a, -um. wild; [*often used substantively as...*] wild beast, wild animal

gener, generi. son-in-law

Hymen, Hymenis (m.). [name; *god of marriage*]

impatiens, impatientis (+ gen.). impatient, intolerant (of)

innuptus, -a, -um. unwed, virginal, maiden-like

latebra, -ae. hiding place, lair, refuge, escape

lustro, -are, -avi, -atus. to wander, to roam

nata, -ae. daughter

nec (conj.). and...not [*equivalent to* et...non; *used with another* nec: neither...nor]

nemus, nemoris (n.). grove, forest, woods

nepos, nepotis (m./f.). descendant, grandson / -daughter, grandchild

Phoebe, Phoebes (Gr. f.). [name: *the goddess Diana*]

protinus (adv.). immediately, at once

vitta, -ae. garland, headband, ribbon

477: *Vitta coercebat positos sine lege capillos.*

- Is the woman's hair in the illustration at left *positos sine lege* or not? Explain your answer.

483-487. Daphne, because of her feelings about marriage, cannot agree to her father's request, but presents a counteroffer. Ultimately daddy can't resist his little girl's request.

483.   illa...iugales = illa, exosa iugales taedas velut crimen
484.   **pulchra ora.** An accusative of respect to be read with *suffunditur*.
485.   **in cervice.** Where was Daphne *haerens*?
        patris. To be read with *cervice*: on whose *cervice* was she *haerens*?
        blandis lacertis. With what was Daphne *haerens*?
486.   **da.** From *do, dare*. Its object will be an infinitive.
        perpetua. Agrees with *virginitate* (487).
487.   **virginitate.** Its case is dependent on *frui*. What kind of verb is *frui*?
        hoc. A neuter pronoun referring to Daphne's request of her father.
        ante. Adverbial here.

488-489. Daphne's father Peneus acquiesces, but Ovid interjects a foreboding foreshadowing about the danger of Daphne's beauty.

488.   **Ille =** pater Daphnes
488-489. **sed...vetat =** sed decor iste vetat te esse quod optas
        quod optas te esse. This entire clause is the object of *vetat*.
489.   **voto tuo.** Dative with the compound *repugnat*.
        repugnat. Does not mean "fight back" here.

490-491. Apollo sees Daphne and loves her. Cupid's power proves superior to Apollo's.

490.   **amat =** amat (Daphnen)
        visae Daphnes. To be read with *conubia*. Although it is a genitive, "of" will not work here.
        visae. A temporal clause will capture the meaning here more precisely than the literal participle.
491.   **quod cupit.** The object of *sperat*.
        illum = Apollo
        oracula. Apollo had under his power a number of oracles, religious sites where pilgrims could have their futures predicted. Apollo's love has blinded him such that even his ability to see the future could not prevent him from pursuing what ultimately will be a futile endeavor, his love of Daphne.

Discussion Questions, Lines 483-491

1. How does the juxtaposition of *crimen* and *taedas* in line 483 foreshadow Apollo's role in the story?
2. What is the significance of Daphne's use of Diana as a precedent for her request in line 487?
3. What is the force of the *sed* in line 488? How does it introduce a foreboding tone?
4. How is the placement of *Phoebus* and *Daphnes* in line 490 an iconic structure?
5. How does *sua illum oracula fallunt* in line 491 reflect perhaps most clearly the effect of Cupid's arrows on Apollo?

Illa velut crimen taedas exosa iugales
pulchra verecundo suffunditur ora rubore,
inque patris blandis haerens cervice lacertis,   485
"Da mihi perpetua, genitor carissime," dixit,
"virginitate frui; dedit hoc pater ante Dianae."
Ille quidem obsequitur, sed te decor iste quod optas
esse vetat, votoque tuo tua forma repugnat.
Phoebus amat, visaeque cupit conubia Daphnes,   490
quodque cupit sperat suaque illum oracula fallunt.

Illa aversata faces nuptiales, tamquam flagitium, erubescit venusto ore. Et amplectens collum patris mitibus brachiis dixit, "Concede mihi, pater suavissime, indelibata virginitate frui. Parens istud concessit antea Dianae." Ille equidem annuit. Verum ista elegantia prohibet esse, quod voves, et tua pulchritudo facit contra tuum desiderium. Apollo amat. Et optat coniugia visae Daphnes, et sperat quae optat. Et sua responsa illum decipiunt.

blandus, -a, -um. flattering, encouraging, enticing, inviting
decor, decoris (m.). grace, beauty, charm
exosus, -a, -um (+ acc.). hateful (of), hating, detesting, despising
fallo, fallere, fefelli, falsus. to deceive, to trick
fruor, frui, fructus (+ abl). to enjoy, to take advantage of
genitor, genitoris (m.). father, parent, creator
haereo, haerere, haesi, haesus. to stick, to be stuck, to cling, to be uncertain
iugalis, -e. nuptial, of or belonging to marriage
lacertus, -i. arm, upper part of the arm
obsequor, obsequi, obsecutus. to agree, to comply, to obey
opto, -are, -avi, -atus. to choose, to want
oraculum, -i. oracle, prophet, ability to see the future
os, oris (n.). mouth, face
perpetuus, -a, -um. perpetual, eternal
quidem (adv.). indeed
repugno, -are, -avi, -atus. to fight back, to resist
rubor, ruboris (m.). red coloring, blush
suffundo, suffundere, suffudi, suffusus. to cover, to suffuse, to pour throughout
taeda, -ae. wedding torch, wedding, marriage
velut (conj.). just as [introducing a simile]
verecundus, -a, -um. modest, chaste
veto, vetare, vetui, vetitus. to forbid, to deny
virginitas, virginitatis (f.). maidenhood, virginity, the state of being a maiden or unmarried woman
votum, -i. prayer

492-496. A simile connecting Apollo's new-found love for Daphne to fire, a common image for passion and love.

492. **utque.** Introduces the simile.
       leves. Not necessarily "light" here. What kind of *stipulae* would burn easily?
493. **facibus.** Why do the *saepes ardent*?
       saepes. Not the word for "often" but instead a noun.
       quas. Its antecedent is *facibus.*
494. Explains how the *saepes* might have caught fire.
       nimis admovit. Here refers specifically to why the *facibus* caused the *saepes* to burn.
495. **sic.** Signals the end of the simile and the resumption of the narrative.
496. **sterilem.** Refers to both the emptiness and impossibility of Apollo's love for Daphne.
       sperando. How does Apollo *nutrit* his *amorem*?

497-502. Ovid catalogs the specific aspects of Daphne that Apollo loves. See pg. 48 for an illustration of these lines.

497. **spectat.** Takes the infinitive *pendere* as its object.
       inornatos capillos. Not the object of *spectat.*
       collo. Where do Daphne's *capillos pendere*?
498. **Quid si comantur.** Apollo loves Daphne's wild hair but imagines how much more attractive she would look if it were tamed and arranged.
498-499. **videt…oculos** = (Apollo) videt (Daphnes) oculos, micantes igne, similes sideribus
499-500. **quae…satis** = quae vidisse non est satis. Apollo wants to do more than just look at Daphne's lips.
499. **oscula.** Can mean either "lips," as a diminutive form of *os, oris,* "face," or, by metonymy, "kisses." The relative clause seems to support a reading of "lips," as it draws a distinction between seeing the *oscula* and doing more than seeing them, i.e. kissing them, but reading *oscula* as "kisses" perhaps is the stronger reading, as Ovid has Apollo anticipating the action of kissing before Ovid even describes it.
500. **manus.** Not a nominative; parallel in case, because of the conjunction, to *digitos.*
501. **media plus parte.** To be read with *nudos.*
502. **si…putat.** A universal: if Apollo can't see it, his imagination makes it better than it likely is.

502-503. Daphne reacts imediately and negatively to Apollo's advances.

502. **fugit.** Who *fugit*? The subject is no longer Apollo.
       aura. Not a nominative. How will it be read with *ocior*?
503. **illa levi.** These words do not agree.
       ad. "to" will not work here. How will this be read with the meaning of *resistit*?
       revocantis. A substantive participle. Who is calling Daphne back?

Discussion Questions, Lines 492-503

1. How does the role of the *viator* in the simile in line 493 parallel Cupid's role? How does *forte* reinforce this connection?
2. How can *sterilem* in line 496 be interpreted?
3. What are the implications of *sperando* in line 496? What does it indicate about Apollo?
4. How does the juxtaposition of *inornatos* in line 497 and *comantur* in line 498 reflect Apollo's expectations of Daphne?
5. What is the effect of all of the words of seeing in lines 497-501? How is Apollo conceiving of Daphne by considering her in this way?
6. Identify at least two figures of speech that Ovid uses to emphasize Apollo's emotional state in lines 497-501.
7. What is the effect of Ovid's focusing of Apollo's gaze on very specific physical features of Daphne?
8. How does *Quid si comantur* in line 498 reflect Apollo's personality and intentions toward Daphne?

Utque leves stipulae demptis adolentur aristis;
ut facibus saepes ardent, quas forte viator
vel nimis admovit vel iam sub luce reliquit,
sic deus in flammas abiit, sic pectore toto   495
uritur, et sterilem sperando nutrit amorem.
Spectat inornatos collo pendere capillos,
et, "Quid si comantur?" ait. Videt igne micantes
sideribus similes oculos; videt oscula, quae non
est vidisse satis; laudat digitosque manusque   500
bracchiaque et nudos media plus parte lacertos;
si qua latent, meliora putat. Fugit ocior aura
illa levi, neque ad haec revocantis verba resistit:

Et quemadmodum levis culmus comburitur sublatis aristis, quemadmodum saepes flagrant taedis, quas forte viator vel nimis admovit, vel iam deseruit sub die, sic deus conflagravit. Sic aestuat totis visceribus, et alit sperando vanum amorem. Videt comam incomtam lapsam super collo, et dicit, "Quid, si componatur?" Videt oculos radiantes luce, pares astris. Videt os, quod non est satis vidisse. Probat digitos et manus, et bracchia, et lacertos exertos plus dimidia parte. Si quaedam occultantur, credit formosiora. Illa celerior vento levi dilabitur, neque remoratur ad haec verba revocantis:

adoleo, adolere, adolui, adultus. to burn, to scorch, to set on fire

arista, -ae. grain [*specifically the awn or beard of a stalk of grain, which is the upper part of a stalk of grain that crumbles in the hand*]

bracchium, -i. arm, forearm

collum, -i. neck

como, comere, compsi, comptus. to make beautiful, to adorn, to arrange attractively

demo, demere, dempsi, demptus. to cut (off), to slice, to remove

fax, facis (f.). torch, fire, wedding [*because of the torches that burned at weddings*]

inornatus, -a, -um. unadorned, simple, undecorated, disheveled

lacertus, -i. arm, upper part of the arm

lateo, latere, latui, -. to take shelter, to hide, to lie in hiding, to be hiding

mico, micare, micui, -. to shine, to flash, to gleam

neque (conj.). and...not [*equivalent to et...non; used with another nec: neither...nor*]

nimis (adv.). too much, excessively; too close

nutrio, nutrire, nutrivi, nutritus. to nourish, to cultivate, to feed at the breast

ocior, ocius (comp. adj.; gen. = ocioris). quicker, swifter

oculus, -i. eye

osculum, -i. kiss

resisto, resistere, restiti, -. to stop, to pause, to halt, to cause to stop

revoco, -are, -avi, -atus. to call back, to call out, to summon

saepes, saepis (f.). hedge

satis (adv.). enough

sidus, sideris (n.). star

sterilis, -e. barren, empty, sterile

stipula, -ae. grain, stalk of grain

uro, urere, ussi, ustus. to burn, to smolder [*can have both the literal and figurative meaning, i.e. to burn with passion*]

vel. or; [*when used in conjunction with another vel:*] either... or

viator, viatoris (m.). wanderer, journeyman, traveller

504-505. Apollo beseeches Daphne not to flee.

504. **nympha** = Daphne
      Penei. Vocative with *nympha.*
      hostis. Nominative in apposition to the subject of *insequor.*

505-507. Apollo compares Daphne's flight to that of prey fleeing a predator to reassure her that she is not his prey.

505. **sic…leonem.** Understand the *fugiunt* of 506.
505-506. **sic.** Connects the clauses that follow to the way that Daphne is fleeing Apollo, i.e. as you're fleeing, so
      does the *agna lupum fugit,* etc.
506. **penna trepidante.** How does the *columbae fugiunt?*
507. **hostes quaeque suos.** Understand *fugiunt.*

508-511. Apollo expresses concern that Daphne might injure herself by running too quickly through the dense forest. He promises to run more slowly so that she can run more slowly and avoid injury.

508. **ne.** Negates the three volitives, *cadas, notent,* and *sim.* What does Apollo hope does not happen?
      indigna. Is not a nominative feminine singular; does not agree with Daphne. What else can it agree with
      in this clause?
      laedi. To be read with *indigna.* Be careful of voice here.
509. **sentes.** Not from *sentio.*
510. **aspera…sunt = loca, qua properas, sunt aspera**
      moderatius. How does Apollo want Daphne to *curre?*
511. **fugam.** Not a form of the verb *fugio, -ere.*
      insequar. Not a present tense verb. When will Apollo *insequar?*

Discussion Questions, Lines 504-511

1. What is the irony in Apollo's comparisons of lines 505-506? How does *hostes quaeque suos* reinforce this irony?
2. What is the (wryly humorous) assumption implicit in the *amor est mihi causa sequendi* of line 507?
3. How does the *sim tibi causa doloris* of line 509 capture Apollo's humorous irony?
4. What are the different ways that the *moderatius insequar ipse* of line 511 can be read?
5. Why is the *ipse* of line 511 mocking in tone?

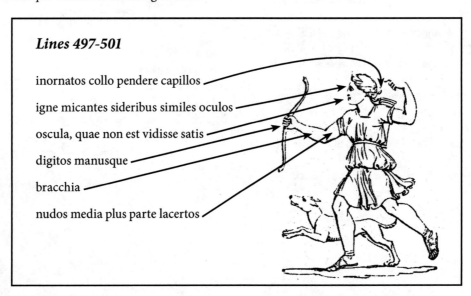

Lines 497-501

inornatos collo pendere capillos

igne micantes sideribus similes oculos

oscula, quae non est vidisse satis

digitos manusque

bracchia

nudos media plus parte lacertos

"Nympha, precor, Penei, mane! Non insequor hostis.
Nympha, mane! Sic agna lupum, sic cerva leonem,   505
sic aquilam penna fugiunt trepidante columbae,
hostes quaeque suos. Amor est mihi causa sequendi.
Me miserum, ne prona cadas indignave laedi
crura notent sentes, et sim tibi causa doloris!
Aspera, qua properas, loca sunt. Moderatius, oro,   510
curre fugamque inhibe; moderatius insequar ipse.

"Nympha Penei, quaeso, exspecta. Non persequor infensus. Nympha, exspecta. Sic agna fugit lupum, sic cerva leonem, sic columbae sese surripiunt aquilae alis timidis. Singulae suos hostes. Amor est mihi causa insequendi. Me infelicem! Ne labaris prona, et vepres lacerent pedes immeritos vulnerari, et sim tibi causa maeroris. Loca, qua festinas, sunt difficilia. Curre, quaeso, lenius, et cohibe fugam. Ipse persequar lenius.

agna, -ae. a young lamb [*specifically a ewe lamb, which is a female sheep under one year of age and/or which has not yet given birth*]

aquila, -ae. eagle, bird of prey

asper, aspera, asperum. rough, harsh, forbidding, dangerous

cerva, -ae. female deer, doe

columba, -ae. dove

crus, cruris (n.). (lower) leg, shin

dolor, doloris (m.). grief, suffering, pain

inhibeo, inhibere, inhibeo, inhibitus. to restrain, to hold back, to inhibit

insequor, insequi, insecutus. to pursue, to follow

laedo, laedere, laesi, laesus. to harm, to hurt, to injure, to wound

lupus, -i. wolf

moderatus, -a, -um. moderated, slow, restrained, held back

noto, -are, -avi, -atus. to note, to mark, to scribe, to mar; to recognize, to know

Peneius, -a, -um. of or belonging to Peneus; daughter of Peneus

precor, precari, precatus. to beg, to pray, to ask for

pronus, -a, -um. prone, face-down

sentes, sentium (m. pl.). thorns, bushes, brambles, shrubbery

trepido, -are, -avi, -atus. to tremble, to quiver, to shiver, to shake

-ve (conj.). and, or

512-518. Apollo now pursues Daphne by offering her his resume, first by telling her what he is not, and then bragging about both his power and his divine family.

512.   **cui placeas.** To be read with *inquire.*
       inquire. The main verb, and not an infinitive. What mood is it? How is Apollo speaking to Daphne?
       non incola montis. Understand the *sum* of 513 here.
513.   **hic.** Does not mean "this" here. What does *hīc* as opposed to *hic* mean?
       armenta gregesque. These are not nominatives.
514.   **nescis, nescis.** Note the change of subject here. The repetition reflects Apollo's desperation.
       temeraria. How is Apollo describing to whom he is speaking?
515.   **quem fugias.** To be read with *nescis.*
515-516. **Mihi…servit.** A simple sentence structure: a series of nominatives, a verb, and *mihi,* which is to be read with the verb.
516.   **servit.** What case does this verb take?
517-518. **quod…estque.** All three of these clauses are the subject of *patet* and refer to Apollo's prophetic ability.
518.   **per me…nervis.** Refers to Apollo's invention and patronage of music.

Discussion Questions, Lines 512-518

1. What aspect of Daphne's initial description do Apollo's negated professions in lines 512-514 recall?
2. What shift in Apollo's tone toward Daphne does the *temeraria* of line 514 signal?
3. What is ironic about *per me…patet* in lines 517-518 (remember the *oracula fallunt* of 491)?

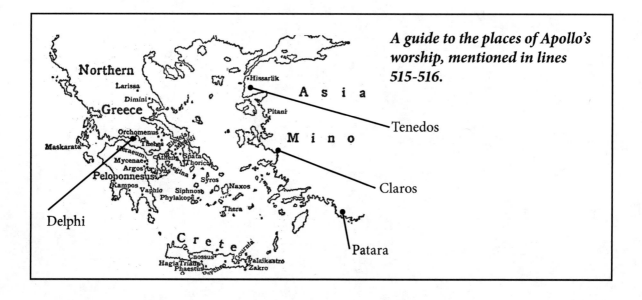

A guide to the places of Apollo's worship, mentioned in lines 515-516.

Cui placeas, inquire tamen. Non incola montis,
non ego sum pastor, non hic armenta gregesque
horridus observo. Nescis, temeraria, nescis
quem fugias, ideoque fugis. Mihi Delphica tellus   515
et Claros et Tenedos Pataraeaque regia servit.
Iuppiter est genitor. Per me quod eritque fuitque
estque patet; per me concordant carmina nervis.

"Pete tamen, cui grata sis. Ego non sum monticola, non sum pastor. Non hic custodio hirsutus armenta vel greges. Nescis, inconsulta, quem vites, ideoque vitas. Terra Delphica, et Claros, et Tenedos, et regia Pataraea mihi paret. Iupiter pater est. Quodcumque fuit, est, et erit, apparet per me. Per me versus consonant chordis.

armentum, -i. herd (of cattle)

Claros, Clari (f.). [name; *a Greek town in Ionia, which is the southwestern coast of modern-day Turkey*]

concordo, -are, -avi, -aturus. to be in synch, to be in harmony, to be in agreement

Delphicus, -a, -um. Delphic, of or belonging to Delphi [*Delphi was a site sacred to Apollo; his oracle, the most famous in the ancient world, was located there*]

ei (interj.). woe, miserable [*an exclamation of grief or sadness*]

genitor, genitoris (m.). father, parent, creator

grex, gregis (m.). herd, flock, group

horridus, -a, -um. horrid, horrible, awful, terrible

ideo (adv.). still, therefore, for that reason

incola, -ae (m.). inhabitant, resident

inquiro, inquirere, inquisivi, inquisitus. to ask, to inquire

Iuppiter, Iovis (m.). [name; *the sky god, the king of the gods*]

nervus, -i. sinew, cord, string (or anything else made out of sinew)

nescio, nescire, nescivi, nescitus. to not know

nullus, -a, -um. none, no

observo, -are, -avi, -atus. to guard, to watch over

pastor, pastoris (m.). shepherd

Patareus, -a, -um. of or belonging to Patara [*Patara is a city on the coast of Lycia, a region on the southern coast of Asia Minor, modern-day Turkey; Apollo had an oracle there*]

pateo, patere, patui, -. to lie open, to be open, to open

regia, -ae. kingdom, palace, shrine

servio, servire, servivi, serviturus (+ dat.). to serve, to be a servant to

tellus, telluris (f.). earth, ground

temerarius, -a, -um. rash, unthinking, impulsive, bold

Tenedos, -i (f). [name; *an island off of the western coast of Asia Minor, modern-day Turkey, where there is located a temple to Apollo*]

519-520. Apollo mentions his power with the bow and arrow, but acknowledges that there is a power greater than his.

519.   **certa, nostra** [1st one]. Both describe *sagitta*.

        nostra [2nd one]. Not a nominative. How will this be read with the *certior* of 520?

520.   **in vacuo…fecit.** A relative clause introduced by *quae*.

        vacuo. Does not modify *quae* or *vulnera*.

521-522. Apollo continues to try to impress Daphne with his accomplishments, specifically here his association with medicine.

521.   **inventum medicina meum est = medicina est meum inventum**

        opifer. To be read as a predicate with the *dicor* of 522.

522.   **dicor.** Does not mean "say" or "speak" or "tell" here.

523-524. Apollo now realizes the powerlessness of his medicinal power before love.

523.   **ei.** Not a form of *is, ea, id.*

        sanabilis. Not an ablative.

524.   **nec…artes = (et) artes, quae prosunt omnibus, (non) prosunt domino**

        prosunt. Takes the dative.

525-530. Daphne does not listen to Apollo and continues to flee, but her flight accentuates her physical attributes and makes her more attractive to Apollo.

525.   **plura.** Does not agree with *Peneia* but is the neuter object of *locuturum*.

        locuturum. Agrees with the object of *fugit* in 526. Whom does Daphne *fugit*?

526.   **cum…reliquit.** Daphne leaves behind both what Apollo says and Apollo himself.

        cum. Not a conjunction here; does not mean "when."

        ipso = (Apolline) ipso

        imperfecta. Refers to the fact that Apollo wanted to say more than he could.

527.   **tum quoque = "even still"**

        visa decens = (Daphne) visa (est) decens.

        visa. What does *video* mean in the passive?

        corpora. Not the subject. Her body was not nude.

529.   **levis.** Not an ablative. What declension is this? What does it modify?

        dabat. "Give" will not work here. What is happening to Daphne's hair?

530.   **fuga.** Not a nominative. What is *aucta est* and by what?

530-532. The tone of Apollo's pursuit changes. He will continue to pursue Daphne even if his more pleasant advances have failed.

530.   **Sed enim = "but still."** Daphne's increased attractiveness will not temper his pursuit.

        sustinet. What will this mean with an infintive (*perdere* in 531)?

531.   **perdere.** To be read with *sustinet*.

        ut. What does *ut* mean with the indicative?

        monebat. *Iuvenis deus* is not the subject of this aside, and "warn" will not quite capture the sense. What is Amor doing to Apollo?

532.   **admisso passu = "with increased pace."**

Discussion Questions, Lines 519-532

1. Compare lines 519-520 to *Amores* 1.1.25-26. How are the contexts for these similar lines the same? Different? What connections can be drawn between Ovid in *Amores* 1.1 and Apollo here? What is Cupid's role in both?

2. What role do voice and words play in lines 525-526?

3. How does Apollo's perception of Daphne's beauty change in lines 527-530?

4. How does the *sed* in line 530 signal a shift in Apollo's approach to his pursuit of Daphne?

Certa quidem nostra est, nostra tamen una sagitta
certior, in vacuo quae vulnera pectore fecit.   520
Inventum medicina meum est opiferque per orbem
dicor et herbarum subiecta potentia nobis.
Ei mihi, quod nullis amor est sanabilis herbis,
nec prosunt domino quae prosunt omnibus artes!"
    Plura locuturum timido Peneia cursu   525
fugit, cumque ipso verba imperfecta reliquit;
tum quoque visa decens. Nudabant corpora venti,
obviaque adversas vibrabant flamina vestes,
et levis impulsos retro dabat aura capillos;
aucta fuga forma est. Sed enim non sustinet ultra   530
perdere blanditias iuvenis deus, utque monebat
ipse Amor, admisso sequitur vestigia passu.

"Nostrum quidem spiculum certum est. Attamen unum certius, quod laesit cor liberum. Medicina est reperta a me, et vocor Auxiliaris per mundum. Et vires plantarum sunt nobis addictae. Ei mihi, quod amor nullis herbis est sanabilis. Neque scientia, quae omnes iuvat, iuvat magistrum." Daphne fugit cursu pavido plura dicturum, et destituit verba incompleta cum ipso. Tum etiam visa est pulchra. Aura detegebat corpus, et venti oppositi agitabant amictus reluctantes; et lenia flamina reiciebant in umeros comam incomtam. Et speciosior fuit fuga. Verum iuvenis deus non potest amplius profundere sua blandimenta. Et, pro impulsu ipsius amoris, sequitur vestigia festino gressu.

admitto, admittere, admisi, admissus. to send along, to admit, to hasten

adversus, -a, -um. opposite, facing the opposite direction, in front of

blanditia, -ae. flattery, pleasing speech, compliments; [when plural] sweet nothings, pleasantries

cursus, -us. course, route, path

decens, decentis. fitting, right, appropriate

flamen, flaminis (n.). wind, gust, sharp blast of air

fuga, -ae. flight

herba, -ae. grass, herb, small plant or flower

imperfectus, -a, -um. incomplete, unfinished

impello, impellere, impuli, impulsus. to beat, to strike, to hit against

inventum, -i. discovery, invention

nudo, -are, -avi, -atus. to expose, to reveal, to strip bear or naked

obvius, -a, -um. facing, opposite, opposing

opifer, opifera, opiferum. aid-bringing, help-bringing [literally a bringer (-fer = fero) of aid (op- = ops)]

orbis, orbis (m.). orb, wheel, disc, world, sun [or any other spherical object]

passus, -us. step, gait, stride

Peneius, -a, -um. of or belonging to Peneus; daughter of Peneus

plus, pluris (comp. adj.). more

prosum, prodesse, profui, - (+ dat.). to be useful

quidem (adv.). indeed

retro (adv.). back, backwards

sanabilis, -e. treatable, curable

subicio, subiciere, subieci, subiectus (+ dat.). to control, to put under the control

sustineo, sustinere, sustinui, -. to sustain, to maintain, to do something continuously or consistently

timidus, -a, -um. timid, afraid, hesitant

ultra (adv.). beyond, further

vacuus, -a, -um. empty, hollow; devoid of (+ abl.)

vestigium, -i. vestige, trace, footprint, sign, remnant

vibro, -are, -avi, -atus. to shudder, to shake, to quiver, to make shake

vestis, vestis (f.). clothes, clothing, garment

533-538. *Apollo chasing Daphne is compared to a dog chasing a hare.*

533.   **cum.** To be read with *ut.*
534.   **hic, ille.** Refers to the *canis* and the *lepus* respectively.
535-6. **alter...rostro.** Describes the actions and emotions of the *canis.*
535.   **inhaesuro.** Does not agree with *alter* but rather a substantive future active participle. Understand *cani* or
         uni. What case is it?
         iam iamque. The repetition reflects the pursuit of the *canis.*
         tenere. Not the main verb. With what main verb will this infinitive be read?
536.   **extento.** What is the ablative with which this agrees?
537-8. **alter...relinquit.** Describes the actions and emotions of the *lepus.*
537.   **in ambiguo est = dubitat**
         sit comprensus. The *lepus* remains the subject.
         ipsis. Agrees with the *morsibus* of 538.
538.   **morsibus.** With what is the *lepus eripitur*?
         eripitur. Here with the force of a middle verb: "snatches itself."
         tangentia ora = ora (canis) quae (paene) tangunt (leporem). Describes the closeness with which the *canis*
         is pursuing the *lepus.*

539-542. *Apollo continues to chase Daphne, now devoid of any of the innocent charm with which his earlier
pursuit was characterized.*

539.   **sic.** Connects the end of the simile to the narrative.
         hic...timore = hic (deus) celer spe, illa (virgo celer) timore. Explains the two very different reasons why
         Apollo and Daphne are running quickly.
         spe, timore. To be read with *celer.*
540.   **qui = (is) qui.** The understood *is* is the subject of the *est* of 541.
         pennis. To be read with *adiutus.*
         Amoris. Whose *pennis*?
541.   **fugacis.** Refers to Daphne.

Discussion Questions, Lines 533-542

1. The *Galicus canis* simile that begins in line 533 recalls Apollo's own comparison of him chasing Daphne
    in lines 505-506. What are the similiarities and differences of the two similes? What is the effect of both?
2. Identify specific Latin words or phrases in lines 533-542 that heighten the tension in Ovid's description of
    Apollo's pursuit of Daphne.
3. How do the verbs used in the simile in 533-538 reflect the actions and emotions of the *canis* and the *lepus*?
4. How does *requiem negat* in 541 contrast with Apollo's approach to his pursuit of Daphne in lines 510-511?

Ad Comparanda: Vergil, Aeneid 12.749-757

inclusum veluti si quando flumine nactus
cervum aut puniceae saeptum formidine pennae   750
venator cursu canis et latratibus instat;
ille autem insidiis et ripa territus alta
mille fugit refugitque vias, at vividus Umber
haeret hians, iam iamque tenet, similisque tenenti
increpuit malis, morsuque elusus inani est;   755
tum vero exoritur clamor ripaeque lacusque
responsant circa et caelum tonat omne tumultu.

Ut canis in vacuo leporem cum Gallicus arvo
vidit, et hic praedam pedibus petit, ille salutem,
alter inhaesuro similis iam iamque tenere   535
sperat, et extento stringit vestigia rostro,
alter in ambiguo est an sit comprensus et ipsis
morsibus eripitur tangentiaque ora relinquit.
Sic deus et virgo est, hic spe celer, illa timore.
Qui tamen insequitur, pennis adiutus Amoris   540
ocior est requiemque negat tergoque fugacis
imminet et crinem sparsum cervicibus afflat.

Quemadmodum canis Gallicus, cum vidit leporem in campo aperto, et hic quaerit rapinam pedibus, ille incolumitatem. Alter similis correpturo, iam iamque credit apprehendere, et instat vestigiis porrecto rostro. Alter dubitat, an sit correptus. Et avellitur ipsis morsibus, et destituit rictus pertingentes. Sic deus et puella est, hic spe velox, illa metu. Qui tamen persequitur, sustentatus pennis Amoris, celerior est, neque dat spatium respirandi. Et instat tergo fugaci, et ventilat spiritu capillos diffusos per collum.

afflo, afflare, afflavi, afflatus. to breathe on, to breathe at, to blow on

adiuvo, adiuvare, adiuvi, adiutus. to help

ambiguum, -i. uncertainty, ambiguity; the state of being uncertain or ambiguous

an (conj.). whether, if [*used to introduce "yes/no" indirect questions*]

arvum, -i. field, meadow, open expanse of grass

cervix, cervicis (f.). neck

comprendo, comprendere, comprendi, comprensus. to seize, to catch, to capture, to hold

eripio, eripere, eripui, ereptus. to grab, to take away, to snatch, to steal

extendo, extendere, extendi, extentus. to stretch (out), to reach, to hold (out)

fugax, fugacis. evasive, fleeing [*also used substantively to mean "one fleeing" or "the evasive one"*]

Gallicus, -a, -um. Gallic, of or belonging to Gaul

immineo, imminere, -. - (+ dat.). to hang over, to threaten, to press upon

inhaereo, inhaerere, inhaesi, inhaesurus. to cling to, to stick to, to hold on to, to remain attached

lepus, leporis (m.). rabbit

morsus, -us. jaws, mouth, bite, morsel, nibble

ocior, ocius (comp. adj.; gen. = ocioris). quicker, swifter

requies, requietis (f.; acc. = requiem). rest, respite

rostrum, -i. beak, nose, snout

spargo, spargere, sparsi, sparsus. to splatter, to spray, to stream, to strew

stringo, stringere, strinxi, strictus. to bind, to draw near, to draw (a sword)

vacuus, -a, -um. empty, hollow; devoid of (+ abl.)

vestigium, -i. vestige, trace, footprint, sign, remnant

543-547. The focus shifts from Apollo to Daphne who, no longer able to evade him, now prays to her father to destroy her beauty.

543.   **viribus absumptis.** Describes Daphne's loss of strength. What construction has an ablative noun and an ablative participle?

   illa. Who is the new subject?

   citae. Agrees with the *fugae* of 544.

544a-545. Believed by some to be a post-Ovidian addition to the text. In pre-Ovidian versions of the story, Daphne was saved not by her father but by Mother Earth. Skeptics of these lines read them as a transparent and awkward attempt to recall such earlier versions of the story. Many previous editions of Ovid have omitted these lines (see p. 8 in the Introduction for a comparison chart) but Tarrant's new Oxford Classical Text, the text on which the AP exam is based, includes them. He, however, numbers then differently but keeps them in this order.

544a. **victa labore citae fugae.** Describes Daphne's fatigue from running.

   tellus. Vocative.

   hisce. Not a form of *hic, haec, hoc* but the imperative of a verb.

   istam. Understand the *figuram* of 545 here.

545.   **quae.** Its antecedent is *figuram.*

   facit = "[which] makes it happen [that...]." Introduces the result clause *ut laedar.*

   mutando. How will Daphne's *figuram* be destroyed?

   perde. Not an ablative but a verb parallel in mood to *hisce* and *vela.*

544.   **spectans.** Daphne realizes that she has fled close to her father's river.

546.   **opem.** The object of *fer.*

   flumina habetis. The *flumina* is an appositive to the subject of *habetis,* but here Daphne personifies the river to emphasize the power inherent in her father's divinity.

547.   **qua nimium placui.** Does not mean "which pleases too much." The antecedent of *qua* is *figuram.* Be careful of the case of *qua:* how has Daphne *nimium placui*?

548-552. Daphne's transformation from young woman to laurel tree.

548.   **finita.** Not a nominative.

   artus. Not a nominative. What declension is it?

549.   **tenui.** Not a form of *teneo, tenere* nor a nominative. What declension is it, and so what does it modify?

550.   **in frondem crines.** Understand *crescunt* here.

551.   **modo tam velox.** With *haeret,* emphasizes the suddenness of the change.

552.   **ora.** Not the subject.

   cacumen = cacumen (arboris)

   illa = Daphne

Discussion Questions, Lines 543-552

1. Identify specific Latin words or phrases that indicate Daphne's physical or emotional desperation in lines 543-547.

2. Why is Daphne's *qua nimium placui* in line 547 so pathetic (in its literal sense)?

3. What can *nitor* in line 552 refer to?

Viribus absumptis expalluit illa citaeque	543
victa labore fugae "Tellus," ait, "hisce, vela istam	544a
quae facit ut laedar, mutando perde figuram."	545
Victa labore fugae, spectans Peneidas undas,	544
"Fer, pater," inquit, "opem, si flumina numen habetis;	546
qua nimium placui, mutando perde figuram."	547
Vix prece finita, torpor gravis occupat artus;	
mollia cinguntur tenui praecordia libro;	
in frondem crines, in ramos bracchia crescunt;	550
pes modo tam velox pigris radicibus haeret;	
ora cacumen habet: remanet nitor unus in illa.	

Illa expalluit viribus exhaustis, et superata labore celeris fugae, aspiciens aquas Peneidas, dixit, "Genitor, succurre, si vos fluvii habetis aliquam potestatem. Vel hia, o terra, in qua nimis grata fui, vel dele formam istam, quae causa est ut offendar, convertendo." Vix absoluta oratione, gravis stupor coercet membra. Tenera viscera coarctantur subtili cortice. Capilli augentur in frondes, lacerti in ramos. Pes modo tam celer affixus est segnibus radicibus. Fastigium habet vultus. Solus splendor superest in illa.

absumo, absumere, absumpsi, absumptus. to consume, to waste, to use up, to exhaust, to expend

bracchium, -i. arm, forearm

cacumen, cacuminis (n.). height, peak, top

cingo, cingere, cinxi, cinctus. to bind, to gird, to surround

citus, -a, -um. fast, swift, rapid

cresco, crescere, crevi, cretus. to increase, to develop, to grow

expallesco, expallescere, expallui, -. to grow pale, to grow white

finio, -ire, -ivi, -itus. to finish

frons, frondis (f.). foliage, leafy part of a tree

hisco, hiscere, -, -. to open, to yawn

laedo, laedere, laesi, laesus. to harm, to hurt, to injure, to wound

nimium (adv.). too much, excessively

nitor, nitoris (m.). brightness, light, glory, beauty

ops, opis (f.). power, ability, aid, assistance, wealth

piger, pigra, pigrum. sluggish, slow, inert, still

praecordia, praecordiorum (n. pl.). chest, breast

radix, radicis (f.). root (of a tree or plant)

remaneo, remanere, remansi, -. to remain, to last, to endure

torpor, torporis (m.). sluggishness, numbness, paralysis

velox, velocis. swift, quick

vis, - (f.; defec.; nom. and acc. pl. = vires). strength, power, force

vix (adv.). scarcely, hardly

553-559. Apollo realizes that he has lost Daphne, and addresses her in her new form.

553.   **posita.** Does not agree with *stipite.*
        dextra. Not a nominative.
554.   **sentit…pectus** = sentit pectus adhuc trepidare sub nove cortice
555.   **suis.** Does not agree with *ramos.* With what is he *complexus ramos*?
        ut membra. Describes what part of the body Daphne's *ramos* would be if she were still a young woman.
556.   **refugit tamen oscula lignum.** Daphne, as a tree, still will not love Apollo back.
557.   **cui deus.** These do not agree. Who is speaking and to whom is he speaking?
558.   **mea.** Agrees with *arbor.*
559.   **te, te, te.** The repeated object of *habebunt.*
        coma, citharae, pharetrae. The subjects of *habebunt.*
        laure. Not an ablative. To whom (or what) is Apollo talking?

Discussion Questions, Lines 553-559

1. What movement does the *hanc* of line 553 indicate when read against the *illa* of line 552?
1. How does the *quoque* in line 553 reinforce Cupid's power over Apollo?
2. How does the juxtaposition of *cortice pectus* in line 554 heighten the effect of Daphne's transformation?
3. Is *oscula dat ligno* to be interpreted as a true expression of Apollo's love for Daphne, or an Ovidian farce that completes Apollo's degeneration from his initial heroic pose? Use the surrounding Latin to support your answer.

Hanc quoque Phoebus amat, positaque in stipite dextra
sentit adhuc trepidare novo sub cortice pectus,
complexusque suis ramos, ut membra, lacertis,   555
oscula dat ligno; refugit tamen oscula lignum.
Cui deus, "At quoniam coniunx mea non potes esse,
arbor eris certe," dixit, "mea; semper habebunt
te coma, te citharae, te nostrae, laure, pharetrae.

Apollo amat etiam hanc, et manu admota trunco, sentit pectus micare adhuc sub recenti libro. Et amplexus ramos suis bracchiis, tamquam artus, deosculatur lignum. Lignum tamen oscula refugit. Quam deus sic alloquitur, "At siquidem non potes esse uxor mea, profecto eris arbor mea. Capilli nostri, citharae, pharetrae nostrae semper te ornabuntur, Laure.

adhuc (adv.). still

at (conj.). but, and so, still [*an adversative conjunction that often signals a shift in the story or sense*]

cithara, -ae. lyre

coma, -ae. hair

complector, complecti, complexus. to embrace, to hug

lacertus, -i. arm, upper part of the arm

laurus, -i (f.). laurel tree, laurel branch, sprig of laurel

lignum, -i. wood, bark

membrum, -i. limb, part of the body

pharetra, -ae. quiver [*holder for arrows*]

quoniam (conj.). since, because

refugio, refugere, refugi, -. to flee, to flee from, to shrink back

stipes, stipitis (m.). trunk (of a tree)

trepido, -are, -avi, -atus. to tremble, to quiver, to shiver, to shake

560-563. Ovid connects the transformation of Daphne into a laurel tree to contemporary Augustan Rome.

560.   Daphne's transformation is tied to Ovid's contemporary Rome in two ways: *ducibus Latiis*, recalling the old Italian aristocracy; and *Triumphum* and *longas pompas*, referring to the state-sponsored triumphal parades awarded to victorious generals.

    ducibus Latiis. To be read with *aderis.*

    aderis. From *adsum.*

    laeta. Does not agree with *Triumphum.*

561.   **canet, visent.** Be careful of tense here. These actions have not yet happened.

    Capitolia. The Capitoline hill, and the location of the Roman government.

562.   **postibus Augustis.** To be read with *fidissima.* Augustus had the doorways to his palace adorned with laurel.

    eadem. "same" in the sense of "everlasting."

    custos. Not an accusative, and here feminine because it refers to Daphne.

563.   **tuebere = tueberis.** A second person singular passive.

564-565. Apollo also adopts the laurel for his own ceremonial purposes.

564.   **meum.** What is the neuter noun with which this agrees?

    iuvenale. Not an ablative.

565.   **tu gere.** Latin will often include a subject pronoun with the imperative. English will tend to have difficulty expressing the subject without it sounding like an indicative verb, i.e. "You bear…" vs. "Bear…"

566-567. Apollo finishes addressing Daphne and she, perhaps surprisingly, apparently acquiesces to Apollo in an ending typically Ovidian because of its ambiguity.

566.   **factis ramis.** Describes how Daphne's branches are now fully formed.

    modo. To be read with *factis.*

567.   **ut caput.** To be read with *cacumen*: what did the *cacumen* look like when she shook it?

    visa est. Remember that this verb has a different meaning in the passive.

    agitasse = agitavisse

Overview Discussion Questions

1. What is the role of speech in the Apollo and Daphne story? How does Apollo misuse speech? What is the role of speech for Daphne?

2. Of course, Daphne changes in the story. Does Apollo? Explain your answer in the context of the *Metamorphoses* (refer to the opening lines of the *Metamorphoses* on page 17).

3. Analyze the structure of Apollo's speech to Daphne in lines 504-524. To what extent does it correspond to Roman rhetorical principles? To what extent does it not? Why would Ovid structure the speech in such a way?

4. Analyze how Apollo and Daphne represent the theme of order vs. chaos.

5. Analyze the structure of the Apollo and Daphne story. Identify as part of your answer specific Latin words that signal the transitions between sections.

6. In line 556 Daphne, as a newly formed tree, shrunk from Apollo. In line 567, she seems to have been swayed. Explain this transformation.

7. In lines 560-563 Ovid associates the laurel tree with victory: the triumphal crown, its use in Roman triumphs, and its use by Augustus on his doorposts. How does this association affect or change your interpretation of the story? Identify specific passages whose interpretation is changed when read in the context of victory.

8. How does Ovid use hunting imagery in the Apollo and Daphne story? Is it appropriate? Explain your answer.

Tu ducibus Latiis aderis, cum laeta Triumphum   560
vox canet et visent longas Capitolia pompas;
postibus Augustis eadem fidissima custos
ante fores stabis mediamque tuebere quercum.
Utque meum intonsis caput est iuvenale capillis,
tu quoque perpetuos semper gere frondis honores."   565
Finierat Paean; factis modo laurea ramis
annuit utque caput visa est agitasse cacumen.   567

Tu comitaberis Imperatores Latinos, cum vox alacris provocabit triumphum, et productae pompae ascendent in Capitolium. Eadem affigeris custodia certissima postibus Augustis ante portam, et defendes mediam quercum. Et quemadmodum caput meum est iuvenile coma intacta, tu etiam habe semper gloriam illibatam foliorum." Apollo absolverat. Laurus approbavit ramis modo creatis, et visa est movisse verticem, tamquam caput.

annuo, annuere, annui, annutus. to nod at, to agree, to
     assent
agito, -are, -avi, -atus. to agitate, to stir (up), to shake
Augustus, -a, -um. of or belonging to Augustus, of or
     belonging to the emperor, imperial [*Augustus was the*
     first emperor of Rome, solidifying his power in 27 BCE;
     his name, as Caesar's did, became synonymous with the
     role of emperor and the institution of empire]
cacumen, cacuminis (n.). height, peak, top
Capitolium, -i. the Capitoline Hill
custos, custodis (m./f.). guard
finio, -ire, -ivi, -itus. to finish
foris, foris (f.). door, door post
frons, frondis (f.). foliage, leafy part of a tree
intonsus, -a, -um. uncut, untamed, wild, not trimmed

iuvenalis, -e. youthful, of or belonging to youth
Latius, -a, -um. Latin, of or belonging to the Latins [*the*
     Latins were, according to the Romans at least, the
     people who preceded the Romans at the site of Rome]
laureus, -a, -um. laurel, of or belonging to the laurel tree
Paean, Paeanis (m.). [name; *an epithet for the god Apollo,*
     stemming from his role as god of healers]
pompa, -ae. parade, ceremony, ceremonial procession
postis, postis (m.). doorway, door-frame, door-post
quercus, -us (f.). oak tree, oak leaf
Triumphus, -i. triumph, triumphal procession
tueor, tueri, tuitus. to look at, to gaze at, to protect, to
     defend
viso, visere, visi, -. to look at, to behold, to view

Discussion Questions, Lines 560-567

1. Why does Ovid include Augustus and contemporary Roman history in lines 560-563?

2. How can *adnuit* and *agitasse cacumen* in line 567 be reconciled with Daphne's previous behavior?

3. If you are familiar with the Aeneas and Dido story, how is Daphne's tragedy similar to Dido's? How is it different? (Recall that the *saeva Cupidinis ira* of line 483 at least obliquely connects the stories.)

Ad comparanda: Augustus, *Res Gestae* 34.1-2

In consulatu sexto et septimo, postquam bella civilia exstinxeram, per consensum universorum potitus rerum omnium, rem publicam ex mea potestate in senatus populique Romani arbitrium transtuli. Quo pro merito meo senatus consulto Augustus appellatus sum et laureis postes aedium mearum vestiti publice coronaque civica super ianuam meam fixa est clupeusque aureus in curia Iulia positus, quem mihi senatum populumque Romanum dare virtutis clementiaeque et iustitiae et pietatis causa testatum est per eius clipei inscriptionem.

Chapter Two

Benevolentia Deorum

Amores 1.3
Baucis and Philemon

Introduction

It is rare in the *Metamorphoses* that an interaction with the gods ends positively. Even when the gods interact among themselves, as seen in Apollo and Daphne, it often ends in tragedy. The two selections here, however, illustrate the gods at their best: in *Amores* 1.3, Ovid uses the gods to try to win his *puella*; in the Baucis and Philemon story, Jupiter and Mercury visit the house of a kindly old couple, and ultimately reward them for their kindness by granting them a wish.

Ovid opens *Amores* 1.3 with the very word that Jupiter uses to describe Philemon (line 704): *iustus*. While the English word "just" is derived from *iustus*, perhaps here "fair" or "right" is more appropriate. In the Baucis and Philemon story, Jupiter thanks the kindly old couple for acting fairly toward him and Mercury. He offers them a wish, and with this wish they achieve their own

form of immortality. Indeed Ovid's narrator of the Baucis and Philemon story, a man named Lelex, provides evidence that he himself has seen the trees into which Baucis and Philemon were changed; they have achieved local and lasting fame through the notoriety of their fairness.

Ovid, in *Amores* 1.3, seeks a similar form of notoriety for himself. He prays that his love affair be successful and that his relationship be immortalized in poetry. He cites the gods as allies: Cytherea (Venus) in line 4, Apollo and Dionysius in line 11, and Cupid in line 12, but he also recalls Jupiter's aggressive philandering in lines 21-24, alluding to three of his paramours. No matter, however. While we may not know how successful Ovid's relationship proved, we do know one thing for certain: it was indeed immortalized in the poetry that we are reading right here.

Amores 1.3

Iusta precor: quae me nuper praedata puella est,
    aut amet aut faciat cur ego semper amem.
A, nimium volui: tantum patiatur amari:
    audierit nostras tot Cytherea preces.
Accipe, per longos tibi qui deserviat annos;   5
    accipe, qui pura norit amare fide.
Si me non veterum commendant magna parentum
    nomina, si nostri sanguinis auctor eques,
nec meus innumeris renovatur campus aratris,
    temperat et sumptus parcus uterque parens: 10
at Phoebus comitesque novem vitisque repertor
    hac faciunt, et me qui tibi donat Amor
et nulli cessura fides, sine crimine mores,
    nudaque simplicitas purpureusque pudor.
Non mihi mille placent, non sum desultor amoris: 15
    tu mihi, si qua fides, cura perennis eris;
tecum, quos dederint annos mihi fila sororum,
    vivere contingat teque dolente mori;
te mihi materiem felicem in carmina praebe:
    provenient causa carmina digna sua.   20
Carmine nomen habent exterrita cornibus Io
    et quam fluminea lusit adulter ave
quaeque super pontum simulato vecta iuvenco
    virginea tenuit cornua vara manu.
Nos quoque per totum pariter cantabimur orbem,   25
    iunctaque semper erunt nomina nostra tuis.

Metamorphoses 8.616-724: *Baucis and Philemon*

Obstipuere omnes nec talia dicta probarunt,   616
ante omnesque Lelex animo maturus et aevo,
sic ait: 'Immensa est finemque potentia caeli
non habet, et quidquid superi voluere peractum est.
Quoque minus dubites, tiliae contermina quercus   620
collibus est Phrygiis, medio circumdata muro:
ipse locum vidi; nam me Pelopeia Pittheus
misit in arva suo quondam regnata parenti.
Haud procul hinc stagnum est, tellus habitabilis olim,
nunc celebres mergis fulicisque palustribus undae.   625
Iuppiter huc specie mortali cumque parente
venit Atlantiades positis caducifer alis.
Mille domos adiere, locum requiemque petentes,
mille domos clausere serae. Tamen una recepit,
parva quidem, stipulis et canna tecta palustri,   630
sed pia Baucis anus parilique aetate Philemon
illa sunt annis iuncti iuvenalibus, illa
consenuere casa paupertatemque fatendo
effecere levem nec iniqua mente ferendo.
Nec refert, dominos illic famulosne requiras: 635
tota domus duo sunt, idem parentque iubentque.
      'Ergo ubi caelicolae parvos tetigere Penates
summissoque humiles intrarunt vertice postes,
membra senex posito iussit relevare sedili,
quo superiniecit textum rude sedula Baucis.   640
Inde foco tepidum cinerem dimovit et ignes
suscitat hesternos foliisque et cortice sicco
nutrit et ad flammas anima producit anili,
multifidasque faces ramaliaque arida tecto
detulit et minuit parvoque admovit aeno,   645
quodque suus coniunx riguo collegerat horto
truncat holus foliis; furca levat ille bicorni
sordida terga suis nigro pendentia tigno
servatoque diu resecat de tergore partem
exiguam sectamque domat ferventibus undis.   650
      'Interea medias fallunt sermonibus horas
sentirique moram prohibent. Erat alveus illic

fagineus, dura clavo suspensus ab ansa;
is tepidis impletur aquis, artusque fovendos   654
accipit. In medio torus est de mollibus ulvis   655a
impositus lecto, sponda pedibusque salignis;   656a
concutiuntque torum de molli fluminis ulva   655
impositum lecto sponda pedibusque salignis;   656
vestibus hunc velant, quas non nisi tempore festo
sternere consuerant, sed et haec vilisque vetusque
vestis erat, lecto non indignanda saligno.
Accubuere dei. Mensam succincta tremensque   660
ponit anus, mensae sed erat pes tertius impar;
testa parem fecit, quae postquam subdita clivum
sustulit, aequatam mentae tersere virentes.
Ponitur hic bicolor sincerae baca Minervae
conditaque in liquida corna autumnalia faece   665
intibaque et radix et lactis massa coacti
ovaque non acri leviter versata favilla,
omnia fictilibus. Post haec caelatus eodem
sistitur argento crater fabricataque fago
pocula, qua cava sunt, flaventibus illita ceris.   670
Parva mora est, epulasque foci misere calentes;
nec longae rursus referuntur vina senectae
dantque locum mensis paulum seducta secundis:
hic nux, hic mixta est rugosis carica palmis
prunaque et in patulis redolentia mala canistris   675
et de purpureis collectae vitibus uvae;
candidus in medio favus est. Super omnia vultus
accessere boni nec iners pauperque voluntas.

  'Interea totiens haustum cratera repleri
sponte sua per seque vident succrescere vina: 680
attoniti novitate pavent manibusque supinis
concipiunt Baucisque preces timidusque Philemon
et veniam dapibus nullisque paratibus orant.
Unicus anser erat, minimae custodia villae,
quem dis hospitibus domini mactare parabant;   685
ille celer penna tardos aetate fatigat
eluditque diu tandemque est visus ad ipsos
confugisse deos. Superi vetuere necari
"Di"que "sumus, meritasque luet vicinia poenas

impia," dixerunt; "vobis immunibus huius   690
esse mali dabitur. Modo vestra relinquite tecta
ac nostros comitate gradus et in ardua montis
ite simul." Parent ambo baculisque levati   693
[ite simul." Parent et dis praeeuntibus ambo   693a
membra levant baculis tardique senilibus annis]   693b
nituntur longo vestigia ponere clivo.   694
    'Tantum aberant summo quantum semel ire sagitta   695
missa potest; flexere oculos et mersa palude
cetera prospiciunt, tantum sua tecta manere,
dumque ea mirantur, dum deflent fata suorum,
illa vetus dominis etiam casa parva duobus
vertitur in templum: furcas subiere columnae,   700
stramina flavescunt aurataque tecta videntur
caelataeque fores adopertaque marmore tellus.
Talia tum placido Saturnius edidit ore:
"Dicite, iuste senex et femina coniuge iusto
digna, quid optetis." Cum Baucide pauca locutus   705
iudicium superis aperit commune Philemon:
"Esse sacerdotes delubraque vestra tueri
poscimus, et quoniam concordes egimus annos,
auferat hora duos eadem, nec coniugis umquam
busta meae videam neu sim tumulandus ab illa."   710
Vota fides sequitur: templi tutela fuere,
donec vita data est. Annis aevoque soluti
ante gradus sacros cum starent forte locique
narrarent casus, frondere Philemona Baucis,
Baucida conspexit senior frondere Philemon.   715
Iamque super geminos crescente cacumine vultus
mutua, dum licuit, reddebant dicta "Vale"que
"O coniunx" dixere simul, simul abdita texit
ora frutex. Ostendit adhuc Thyneius illic
incola de gemino vicinos corpore truncos.   720
    'Haec mihi non vani (neque erat cur fallere vellent)
narravere senes; equidem pendentia vidi
serta super ramos ponensque recentia dixi:
"Cura deum di sunt, et qui coluere coluntur."'   724

Amores 1.3 Introduction

Amores 1.1 introduced Ovid's decision to write elegy without providing any specifics about Ovid's lover. *Amores* 1.2 saw Ovid resign himself to writing elegy. In *Amores* 1.3 Ovid will articulate his goals for writing elegy, and introduce himself as an elegiac lover.

Ovid's virtue as a lover, specifically his loyalty or *fides*, and the opportunity for lasting fame through poetry provide the focus of *Amores* 1.3. Ovid alludes to three mythological exemplars to illustrate the effects of poetic fame: Io, Leda, and Europa. This collection of examples immediately follows Ovid's proclamation of undying *fides* to his *puellae*. But the combination of Ovid's *fides* and these exemplars proves problematic: what kind of *fama* have these women achieved? Why are they remembered? They are all victims of Jupiter's sexual aggression and infidelity to Juno. They all represent a conspicuous lack of *fides*, the very *fides* which Ovid has just pledged to his *puella*.

The question then must be asked: what is to be made of Ovid's apparent contradiction? What exactly is Ovid pledging to his *puella* if in one breath he elaborately describes his ironclad *fides* but in the next hopes that his relationship will achieve lasting fame through poetry in the same way that the adulterous relationships of Jupiter have?

Amores 1.3 presents a complex and sophisticated elegiac lover, whose defining charateristic may in fact be his contradictory approach to love, his *puella*, and their relationship. *Amores* 1.1 and *Amores* 1.2 have clearly signalled that Ovid will not write the elegy of his predecessors. *Amores* 1.3 is the first indication that Ovid himself will not be the elegiac lover that his predecssors were. Sure, Ovid is desperate. Sure, Ovid is enslaved to his *puella*. But Ovid forces us to examine to what extent his desperation and enslavement, the defining features of the elegiac lover, are genuine and real for Ovid, and to what extent they are performances for the sake of his audience, masks that can be put on or taken off as the situation dictates. Ovid at least hints that his *puella* will not be the only one misbehaving. Ovid at least hints that he too might have his own illicit life outside of his elegiac relationship, which at least implicitly undermines the validity of the rawness of his elegiac emotions. This questioning of the very personality traits that define the elegiac lover then calls into question the entire poetic persona of the elegiac lover. If the character of the lover can be altered, if the lover can be as deceptive as his *puella*, or if the lover remains ultimately unaffected by his *puella*'s insults and infidelities, doesn't that then imply that the traditional elegiac lover of Ovid's predecessors was an empty and artificial construct? As *Amores* 1.1 was Ovid's introduction to his new brand of elegiac poetry, so *Amores* 1.3 is Ovid's first introduction to this new brand of elegiac lover, characterized by a self-awareness of his role both as lover and as poetic focus, and indicative of Ovid's interest in genre and archetype.

1-6. Ovid's feelings for his still unnamed love create conflict within him: he wants her to love him or he wants to be free of his feelings, and he asks Venus for help.

1.　　**iusta.** Not a nominative. If it's not the subject, what gender (and number) is it likely to be?
　　　quae. Its antecedent is the *puella* that follows it.
　　　puella. The subject of the *amet* and *faciat* of line 2.

2.　　**amet, faciat.** Be careful of the mood here. How can main verb subjunctives be translated?
　　　faciat cur… = "give a reason why…" Don't forget that *faciat* is subjunctive.

3.　　**volui.** What tense is this verb?
　　　patiatur, amari. *Puella* is the subject of both of these verbs, i.e. *(puella) tantum patiatur (se) amari.*

4.　　**audierit.** By form, either a future perfect indicative or a perfect subjunctive, but more likely the future perfect, with the implication: "(By the end of all this,) Venus will have…"

5-6.　**accipe.** The understood antecedent of the *qui* of each line is the object. What is understood as its antecedent is debatable. LaFleur suggests a general antecedent for *qui*: *talem virum*, "such a man who…". Perhaps *me* is better understood because the couplets that precede and follow concern Ovid. Or perhaps a combination of the two: "a man like me who…" or "me, the type of man who…"
　　　deserviat, norit. There are two different interpretations of this subjunctive that have two very different meanings: how would a relative clause of characteristic create a different meaning from a relative clause of purpose?

5.　　**tibi.** To be read with *deserviat.*

6.　　**norit = noverit**

7-10. Ovid offers some background and family history to further commend himself to his **puella.**

7.　　**veterum parentum.** Be careful of case here. What declension are these words? And so what case?

8.　　**si…eques.** Either understand *me non commendant* from the previous line or *est* with *auctor eques.*

10.　　**temperat et** = *et temperat.* What figure of speech is this?
　　　sumptus. Be careful of this form. What declension is it? Why is it not nominative?

Discussion Questions, lines 1-10

1. What is the significance of *puella* in line 1 for the *Amores*?

2. How does the *praedata est* in line 1 continue the imagery of *Amores* 1.1?

3. What is the tone of *A, nimium volui* in line 3? What emotion is Ovid trying to create here, and how does the tense of *volui* contribute to that? How does Ovid continue this tone through the rest of the couplet?

4. What Latin words in line 5-6 are most important for Ovid to convey what he wants? Explain your answer.

5. What are the implications of the tense of *norit* in line 6 for the meaning of the line?

6. What approach towards winning his *puella* does Ovid adopt in lines 7-10?

Iusta precor: quae me nuper praedata puella est,
    aut amet aut faciat cur ego semper amem.
A, nimium volui: tantum patiatur amari:
    audierit nostras tot Cytherea preces.
Accipe, per longos tibi qui deserviat annos;   5
    accipe, qui pura norit amare fide.
Si me non veterum commendant magna parentum
    nomina, si nostri sanguinis auctor eques,
nec meus innumeris renovatur campus aratris,
    temperat et sumptus parcus uterque parens: 10

Aequa oro: aut puella quae nuper me cepit amet, aut praestet quamobrem ego semper amem. Ah! nimium expetivi: tantum sinat se amari. Cytherea exaudiverit tot nostras petitiones. Recipe, qui tibi serviat per multos annos: recipe, qui sciat amare sincera fide. Si nomina magnifica antiquorum avorum non me decorant; nec eques est auctor nostri sanguinis; nec ager meus iteratur innumeris aratris, et parens uterque tenax modum facit impensae;

aratrum, -i. plow
auctor, auctoris (m.). founder, creator
commendo, -are, -avi, -atus. to recommend
Cytherea, -ae. [name] Cytherean one, Venus
deservio, deservire, -, -. to serve, to be a servant
eques, equitis. horseman, cavalryman
fides, -ei. faith, trust, loyalty
iustus, -a, -um. just, lawful, right, appropriate
nimium (adv.). too much, excessively
nosco, noscere, novi, notus. to know
nuper. recently
parcus, -a, -um. thrifty, frugal, parsimonious
parens, parentis (m./f.). parent

patior, pati, passus. to endure, to allow
praedor, praedari, praedatus. to conquer, to plunder, to take as plunder
precor, precari, precatus. to beg, to pray, to ask for
prex, precis (f.). entreaty, prayer
purus, -a, -um. pure, unsullied, uncorrupted
renovo, -are, -avi, -atus. to make new, to revive
sumptus, -us. the act of spending money; expenditure
tempero, -are, -avi, -atus. to control, to temper, to moderate
tot (indecl.). so many
uterque, utraque, utrumque. each (of two), both
vetus, veteris. old

11-14. Ovid identifies forces, both divine and abstract, that are on his side, further reinforcing his bid for the love of his puella.

11-14. See the diagram below for help with the overall structure of this sentence.

11. **novem.** This is an indeclinable adjective; its ending will remain the same whatever it modifies. Who are Apollo's *comites novem*?

   vitis repertor. To what god does this periphrasis refer? Who is the *repertor vitis*?

12. **hac** = hac (**ex parte**) = "on my behalf", "for me" (literally, "from this side").

   me qui tibi donat Amor. Who is giving whom to whom?

13. **nulli.** Remember that this is an irregular adjective. What case is it (it is not genitive)?

   cessura. Be careful of the tense here. What tense of the participal does that *-ur-* signify?

   sine crimine. An adjectival prepositional phrase. What noun does it describe, i.e. what is *sine crimine*?

15. **mille** = mille (**puellae**)

16. **qua.** Remember how this word functions following *si*, i.e. it is not a relative pronoun.

   perennis. What declension is this adjective? And so what case is it?

17. **tecum...mori** = Contingat (mihi) vivere tecum annos, quos fila sororum dederint mihi, (et contingat) **mori, te dolente**

19. **te.** Direct object of *praebe*.

   materiem. How does this expand the meaning of *te*? How are they grammatically connected? What is it called when one noun "modifies "another?

   in carmina. To be read with *praebe*.

20. **causa sua.** To be read with *digna*.

Discussion Questions, lines 11-20

1. What is the effect of the extended polysyndeton in lines 11-14?
2. Explain what the four abstract concepts that Ovid lists in lines 13-14 mean? Why does Ovid group them together? What do they mean when read as a single unit?
3. How does word placement emphasize the point of line 16?
4. Why does Ovid introduce the *fila sororum* in line 17? What does it recall? Why?
5. How does the structure of line 18 emphasize its point?

Lines 11-14 Sentence Diagram

at Phoebus comitesque novem vitisque repertor
hac faciunt, et me qui tibi donat Amor
et nulli cessura fides, sine crimine mores,
nudaque simplicitas purpureusque pudor.

There are eight nominatives for one verb. That verb appears in line 12 in the middle of its subjects. Some subjects are relatively simple, i.e. a lone nominative or a nominative with an adjective, while other subjects are accompanied by modifiers, ranging from a simple genitive to a prepositional phrase to a participial phrase to a relative clause.

at Phoebus comitesque novem vitisque repertor
    hac faciunt, et me qui tibi donat Amor
et nulli cessura fides, sine crimine mores,
    nudaque simplicitas purpureusque pudor.
Non mihi mille placent, non sum desultor amoris: 15
    tu mihi, si qua fides, cura perennis eris;
tecum, quos dederint annos mihi fila sororum,
    vivere contingat teque dolente mori;
te mihi materiem felicem in carmina praebe:
    provenient causa carmina digna sua.   20

at Phoebus, et comites novem, et inventor vitis hoc agant; et amor qui me tuum facit; et fides nulli secunda; mores inculpati; et sincera ingenuitas, et pudor purpureus. Mille non me iuvant; non sum desultor amoris. Tu (si quam mihi fidem habes) eris mihi cura perpetua. Obveniat mihi transigere tecum aetatem quam fila sororum indulserint, et excedere vita te afflicta. Dato te mihi materiam laetam in versus; versus fluent digni sua causa.

at (conj.). but, and so, still [*an adversative conjunction that often signals a shift in the story or sense*]

cedo, cedere, cessi, cessurus (+ dat.). to yield (to), to proceed

contingo, contingere, contigi, contactus. to touch, to contact, to come into contact with; [+ *inf. = impers.*:] it is granted

desultor, desultoris (m.). horse-jumper

dignus, -a, -um (+ abl.) worthy (of)

doleo, dolere, dolui, doliturus. to be sad, to regret

filum, -i. thread

materies, -ei. material, subject matter

morior, mori, mortuus (dep.). to die

mos, moris (m.). custom, character

novem (indecl.). nine

nudus, -a, -um. nude, naked, bare

perennis, -e. eternal

Phoebus, -i. [name; *epithet for Apollo*]

praebeo, praebere, praebui, praebitus. to offer, to furnish, to show, to display

provenio, provenire, proveni, proventurus. to come forth, to come out

pudor, pudoris (m). decency, chastity, shame, embarassment, virtue

repertor, repertoris (m.). discoverer, inventor

simplicitas, simplicitatis (f.). simplicity, unity, sincerity

vitis, vitis (f.). grapevine

1.3.15, *desultor*. The *desultor* ran a horse race which included switching horses in mid-race (note to the left the two horses with only one rider). Ovid does not jump from woman to woman as the *desultor* jumps from horse to horse.

21-24. Ovid here begins a list of three mythological women whose names have been immortalized by poetry.

21. **carmine** = "in song", "because of poetry," "through poetry"
     nomen habent. The literal translation works, but what would be a better way to say this idiom in English?
     cornibus. Ablative of cause. Why is she *exterrita*? What has happened to Io? (See the box at the bottom of the next page for Io's story.)
22. **et quam** = et (ea) **quam.** A different female subject is introduced, the second mythological female, who is identified only by the descriptive relative clause introduced by *quam*.
23. **quaeque** = (et ea) **quae.** A structure similar to that in line 21 is used to introduce the third mythological female.
     simulato. Was the *iuvenco* really a *iuvenco*? Rather, she was a *simulato iuvenco*.
     iuvenco. How was she carried *super pontum*?
24. **virginea, vara.** Use scansion and context to help make clear which nouns each of these adjectives modifies.

25-26. Ovid shifts the focus back to himself, drawing connections between his intentions and aspirations, and the examples of his three mythological heroines.

25. **quoque.** An adverb which connects the list Ovid began in the previous two couplets to this couplet.
26. **tuis** = tuis (nominibus)

Discussion Questions, lines 21-26

1. What is the effect of opening this section of the poem with the *carmine* of line 21?
2. How do the mythological allusions in lines 21-24 subtly contradict Ovid's statement *non sum desultor amoris* of line 15?
3. What figure of speech does Ovid use in lines 21-24 and what is its effect?
4. What is the ambiguity of the *nos* of line 25, especially when compared against the *nostra tuis* of line 26?
5. What is the effect of ending the poem with the *tuis* of line 26? How does this word function with the *nos* of line 25 that began the couplet?

Lines 21-24 Sentence Diagram

Carmine nomen habent exterrita cornibus Io
et quam fluminea lusit adulter ave
quaeque super pontum simulato vecta iuvenco
virginea tenuit cornua vara manu.

Two of the three subjects of **habent** are expressed as the understood antecedent of a relative pronoun (**quam** and **quae**). The gender of the relative indicates how the understood subject should be rendered in English (smooth English cannot leave the subject unstated).

Carmine nomen habent exterrita cornibus Io
 et quam fluminea lusit adulter ave
quaeque super pontum simulato vecta iuvenco
 virginea tenuit cornua vara manu.
Nos quoque per totum pariter cantabimur orbem,   25
 iunctaque semper erunt nomina nostra tuis.

Io tremefacta cornibus, et quam adulter fefellit alite fluviali, nactae sunt famam versibus; et quae, ablata per aequor ficto tauro, corripuit cornua vara manu puellari. Nos etiam pariter celebrabimur per omnes terras, et laus nostra semper erit connexa tuae.

adulter, adulteri. adulterer

avis, avis (f.). bird

exterreo, exterrere, exterrui, exterritus. to scare, to terrify

flumineus, -a, -um. of or belonging to a river; river [*as an adjective*]

Io (acc. = Io; f.). [name: *a lover of Jupiter whom he changed into a cow to hide her identity from his wife Juno*]

iuvencus, -i. young bull

ludo, ludere, lusi, lusus. to play

pariter (adv.). equally; at the same time as [*often used with the preposition* cum]

pontus, -i. sea, water, ocean

simulo, -are, -avi, -atus. to simulate, to pretend, to fabricate, to create

varus, -a, -um. curving, bent

veho, vehere, vexi, vectus. to carry, to convey

virgineus, -a, -um. of or belonging to a maiden; maiden's

The Mythological Females in Lines 21 - 24

Io was a young woman whom Jupiter took as his lover, but his wife Juno suspected what was happening. When she came to check on him, he turned Io into a white cow. Juno, however, understood how Jupiter had disguised Io and asked him for the cow as a gift. Jupiter could not deny her, of course, because then he would be admitting his deception. So he reluctantly gave Io as a cow to Juno who placed Io in the care of Argus, the hundred-eyed monster whose eyes never closed, so that she could not escape. Jupiter still felt bad about what had happened, so he sent Hermes to lull all one hundred eyes of the monster Argus to sleep. He succeeded and Io escaped, but Juno tormented her further, making her wander the earth with a gadfly continually stinging her as punishment.

Leda was a queen of Sparta, whom Zeus loved in the form of a swan. She was also loved on the same night by her mortal husband, and so had four children by two different fathers. Two of these children, Helen (later, Helen of Troy) and Polydeuces (or Pollux), the children of Zeus, were immortal, but the other two, Clytemnestra (the wife of Agamemnon) and Castor, were mortal. Helen is not immortal in Homer, and her later life when immortality would become more relevant is rarely treated by ancient authors.

Europa was a young Phoenician woman with whom Zeus fell in love. When she was playing on the beach with some friends, he changed himself into a bull and approached her. He coaxed her onto his back and started romping around in the shallow water. He gradually moved deeper and deeper into the water until it was too deep for Europa to jump off his back and return to her friends. Zeus took her to the island of Crete.

Baucis and Philemon Introduction

Strangers are at your door asking for shelter. What do you do? Do you take them in? Do you turn them away? Would your economic status affect your decision? What if you had little to offer? This is the decision faced by the ancient couple Baucis and Philemon. They, of course, welcome those strangers and feed them as much as they can, despite their meager resources. Only towards the end of the meal is it revealed that their mysterious guests are more than they appear to be.

The Baucis and Philemon story likely has its origins in an Eastern folktale. Ovid's account in the *Metamorphoses* is the only extant ancient literary version of the story. The transformation of Baucis and Philemon into trees and their house into a temple might also link it to an ancient tree-cult or the worship of a tree deity.

Baucis and Philemon are two of Ovid's most likeable characters. They are realistically human in the best ways. They are kind and generous, while still nervous about the appearance of their hovel and their food before their obviously exalted guests. They are humble and still take pride in their work. Yet they are not perfect. They withhold some food from their guests until they realize that they are gods, and they struggle physically to ascend the mountains with the gods as they escape the impending flood. In *Baucis and Philemon* Ovid shows us humanity as it should be: fundamentally good without being perfect.

The Baucis and Philemon story is introduced and told by Ovid as an illustration of the power of the gods. But it is unclear what aspect of the story illustrates this power: the transformation of Baucis and Philemon and their house is the choice that Ovid makes most obvious, but, according to

Ovid himself and the rest of the *Metamorphoses*, transformation should not count as evidence of the gods' power; they transform people throughout the *Metamorphoses*.

To what else could it refer: the swamping (literally) of an entire region by the gods, transforming village to marshland? Certainly a possibility, but perhaps too predictable for Ovid. And again, such violence, however sweeping its scope might be, doesn't seem entirely out of the realm of possibility for the gods; Jupiter destroyed the entire world in Book 1.

Perhaps Ovid's irony is at work here. Perhaps the true power of the gods, especially in Ovid's hands, lies in their ability to recognize goodness in and show mercy to deserving humans. Consistently throughout the *Metamorphoses*, the gods toy with unsuspecting and often undeserving humans, Daphne being a prime example in the *Metamorphoses* (though not strictly a human, still a pawn in the gods' games) as is Dido from the *Aeneid*. In the Baucis and Philemon story, the couple is indeed tested as so many other humans in the *Metamorphoses* are. But Baucis and Philemon pass the test, the gods recognize their goodness, and reward them for it. For Lelex, the narrator of the story, perhaps the transformation of Baucis and Philemon does indeed illustrate the power of the gods. The reader, however, and even Ovid, knows from the rest of the *Metamorphoses* that transformation alone is all too common to constitute a notable illustration of the power of the gods. Perhaps then the most venerable power of the gods is their capacity for mercy or their anthropomorphic reflection of humans' capacity for good, precisely because of its rarity.

Baucis and Philemon At-A-Glance

Book	8
Lines	616-724
Main Characters (in order of appearance)	Jupiter: king of the gods Mercury: messenger god and, here, companion of Jupiter Baucis: old, kind woman; wife of Philemon Philemon: old, kind man; husband of Baucis
Minor Characters	Lelex: guest at Achelous' feast who tells the Baucis and Philemon story
Context	The Theseus story, beginning in book 7 and stretching into the beginning of book 9
Preceeding Story	Achelous and the Nymphs. Theseus approaches the river Achelous, where he pauses to dine with Achelous and friends. He asks about islands in the distance, and Achelous tells him how they were once nymphs, but were turned into islands.
Transition	One of the banqueters scoffs at Achelous' story and the power of the gods, and another guest, Lelex, tells the story of Baucis and Philemon as further proof of the gods' power.
Subsequent Story	Erysichthon and his Daughter. Theseus wants to hear more about the power of the gods. The Calydonian River introduces Proteus and shape-shifters, and tells the story of Erysichthon's daughter, who was also a shape-shifter. Her father desecrated a sacred tree of Ceres, and so was cursed with insatiable hunger. He sold everything for food, including his daughter. Rather than be sold into slavery, her daughter prayed to Neptune, who allowed her to change her shape to escape.
Primary Topics	the power of the gods the piety (and impiety) of humans *xenia* or the hospitality code the corruption of wealth (or the nobility of poverty)

Baucis and Philemon Vocabulary Frequency

The vocabulary of Baucis and Philemon is the most difficult in the book. Ovid's descriptive focus on the meal that Baucis and Philemon serve necessitates a variety of technical vocabulary. While such technical vocabulary does not appear in the vocabulary frequency list, a study guide for it (to be used prior to reading the sections, during the reading of the sections, or as a review for those sections) is provided on the facing pages.

7 times
deus, -i

6 times
Baucis, -idis
duco, -ere
paro, -are
pono, -ere
sen- [root] old
video, -ere

5 times
parvus, -a, -um
Philemon, -onis
tectum, -i

4 times
annus, -i
coniunx, -iugis
locus, -i
medius, -a, -um

omnis, -e
simul
superus, -a, -um
(superi, -orum)

3 times
do, dare
dominus, -i
domus, -us
dum

duo
lectus, -i
levo, -are
mensa, -ae
mitto, -ere
pes, pedis
salignus, -a, -um
super

Perhaps the most difficult part of *Baucis and Philemon* is the specialized vocabulary concerning food and furniture. Two lists are provided on the next pages to address this difficulty, the first organized alphabetically, the second by line number.

Baucis and Philemon Dinner Vocabulary - Alphabetical List

aenum, -i	bronze kettle	lectus, -i	bench, couch
alveus, -i	tray, basket	malum, -i	apple
ansa, -ae	hook	massa, -ae	mass
baca, -ae	berry		(with *lactis coacti*) cheese
canistrum, -i	basket	mensa, -ae	table
carica, -ae	fig	menta, -ae	mint, mint leaf
cinis, -eris	ashes	nux, -cis	nut
clavus, -i	nail	ova, -ae	egg
clivus, -i	slope	palma, -ae	date (the fruit)
coma, -ae	grass	pes, pedis	foot (of a couch or bed)
cortex, -icis	wood, bark	poculum, -i	cup
crater, -eris	mixing bowl	pruna, -ae	prune, dried fig
faex, -cis	dregs	radix, -icis	radish, (edible) root
fagineus, -a, -um	beech wood	ramalia, -ium	kindling, brushwood
favilla, -ae	bean	salignus, -a, -um	willow wood
favus, -i	bean	sponda, -ae	bed-frame, couch-frame
fax, facis	flame, fire, torch	tergum, -i	back
fictilis, -e	made of earth; clay	tergus, -oris	back
flamma, -ae	flame, heat	testa, -ae	pottery sherd
focus, -i	hearth, fireplace	torus, -i	bench, couch
folium, -i	leaves, kindling	ulva, -ae	grass, sea grass
furca, -ae	fork	uva, -ae	grape
holus, -eris	vegetable	vestis, -is	cloth, cushion
hortus, -i	garden	vinum, -i	wine
ignis, -is	fire	vitis, -is	vine
intiba, -ae	endive (lettuce)		

Baucis and Philemon Dinner Vocabulary - By Line Number

641	focus, -i	hearth, fireplace		660	mensa, -ae	table
	cinis, -eris	ashes		662	testa, -ae	pottery sherd
	ignis, -is	fire			clivus, -i	slope
642	folium, -i	leaves, kindling		663	menta, -ae	mint, mint leaf
	cortex, -icis	wood, bark		664	baca, -ae	berry
643	flamma, -ae	flame, heat		665	coma, -ae	grass
644	fax, facis	flame, fire, torch			faex, -cis	dregs
	ramalia, -ium	kindling, brushwood		666	intiba, -ae	endive (lettuce)
645	aenum, -i	bronze kettle			radix, -icis	radish, (edible) root
646	hortus, -i	garden		666	massa	mass;
647	holus, -eris	vegetable				(with *lactis coacti*)
	furca, -ae	fork				cheese
648	tergum, -i	back		667	ova, -ae	egg
649	tergus, -oris	back			favilla, -ae	bean
652	alveus, -i	tray, basket		668	fictilis, -e	made of earth; clay
	fagineus, -a, -um	beech wood		669	crater, -eris	mixing bowl
653	clavus, -i	nail		670	poculum, -i	cup
	ansa, -ae	hook		672	vinum, -i	wine
655a	torus, -i	bench, couch		674	nux, -cis	nut
	ulva, -ae	grass, sea grass			carica, -ae	fig
656a	lectus, -i	bench, couch			palma, -ae	date (the fruit)
	sponda, -ae	bed-frame, couch-frame		675	pruna, -ae	prune, dried fig
	pes, pedis	foot (of a couch or bed)			malum, -i	apple
					canistrum, -i	basket
	salignus, -a, -um	willow wood		676	vitis, -is	vine
657	vestis, -is	cloth, cushion			uva, -ae	grape
				677	favus, -i	bean

616-618. A group is discussing the power of the gods. Just prior to line 616 one member of the group has scoffed at the power of the gods, an attitude unpopular with the group. Another member of the group, Lelex, will tell the story of Baucis and Philemon to illustrate the power of the gods.

616.   **obstipuere.** Not an infinitive.

       omnes. Refers to the group responding to the comments against the power of the gods.

617.   **-que.** To be read with *ante,* i.e. *anteque*

       animo, aevo. In what ways is Lelex *maturus?*

618-625. Lelex the narrator introduces his story of the power of the gods. He describes the setting of the story in great detail to lend the story verisimilitude, i.e. to convince his audience that he is not making anything up.

618.   **immensa…non habet** = potentia caeli immensa est finemque (potentia) non habet

       caeli = deorum (by metonymy)

619.   **quicquid superi voluere.** The entire clause is the subject of *peractum est.* What is *peractum est?*

       voluere. Not an infinitive.

620.   **quo** = ut. A relative clause of purpose.

       tiliae. Not a nominative; to be read with *contermina.*

       quercus. The subject through line 621.

621.   **collibus Phrygiis** = (in) collibus Phrygiis

       circumdata. Modifies *quercus.*

622.   **ipse.** To emphasize the truthfulness of the story: Lelex is not reporting what other people have seen.

       Pelopeia. Modifies *arva.*

623.   **suo parenti.** To be read with *regnata.* A dative of agent with the perfect passive participle, more common in poetry than in prose.

       quondam. To be read with *regnata.*

624.   **hinc.** Refers to the *arva* and the *quercus* of the previous lines, as the scene shifts to a new location.

       tellus habitabilis olim. Refers to the *stagnum.*

       olim. To be read with *habitabilis.*

625.   **nunc.** Contrasted with the *olim* of 624. What was *olim* is *nunc…* .

       celebres. Does not modify *mergis.*

       mergis…palustribus. To be read with *celebres.*

Discussion Questions, lines 616-625

1. What is the significance of Lelex being described as *animo maturus et aevo* in line 617?

2. Why does Lelex begin his story in line 620 with the image of the *quercus,* rather than Baucis and Philemon themselves?

3. Why is it important that Lelex *ipse* saw the place in line 622?

Obstipuere omnes nec talia dicta probarunt,   616
ante omnesque Lelex animo maturus et aevo,
sic ait: 'Immensa est finemque potentia caeli
non habet, et quidquid superi voluere peractum est.
Quoque minus dubites, tiliae contermina quercus   620
collibus est Phrygiis, medio circumdata muro:
ipse locum vidi; nam me Pelopeia Pittheus
misit in arva suo quondam regnata parenti.
Haud procul hinc stagnum est, tellus habitabilis olim,
nunc celebres mergis fulicisque palustribus undae.   625

Omnes mirati sunt; neque eiusmodi verbis faverunt: et Lelex ante omnes, mente sapiens atque aetate, sic dicit: 'Potestas deorum est infinita, neque terminis ullis comprehenditur: et quodcumque dii cupierunt absolutum est. Et ut minus haesites, quercus est proxima tiliae in vallibus Phrygiis cincta parvo muro. Ego vidi locum: nam Pittheus misit me in agros Pelopeios, qui olim sub potestate fuerant sui patris. Nam longe inde lacus; terra olim hospitalis: nunc aquae frequentatae a mergis et fulicis palustribus.

aevum, -i. age

arvum, -i. field, meadow, open expanse of grass

celeber, celebris, celebre. busy, crowded

circumdo, circumdare, circumdedi, circumdatus. to surround

collis, collis (m.). hill

conterminus, -a, -um (+ dat.). bordering, next to, near

finis, finis (m.). limit, boundary, border, end

fulica, -ae. water bird, water fowl

habitabilis, -e. livable, habitable

haud (adv.). hardly, not, not at all

hinc (adv.). from here, next; [with illinc] on this side

Lelex, Lelegis (m.). [name; a Greek who participated in the Calydonian Boar Hunt, and who is Ovid's narrator for the Baucis and Philemon story]

maturus, -a, -um. mature, developed

mergus, -i. sea gull, sea bird

obstipesco, obstipescere, obstipui, -. to be amazed, to be (dumb)struck, to be (awe)struck, to be stunned

olim. once

paluster, palustris, palustre. swampy, marshy

Pelopeius, -a, -um. of or belonging to Pelops [the father of Pittheus, and the grandfather of Agamemnon and Menelaus, the principle Greek generals in the Trojan War]

perago, peragere, peregi, peractus. to do, to complete

Phrygius, -a, -um. Phrygian, of or belonging to Phrygia [Phrygia is a region along the northeastern border of what is modern-day Turkey; also where the ancient city of Troy was likely located]

Pittheus, -i. [name; son of Pelops]

probo, -are, -avi, -atus. to test, to try, to approve, to prove

procul (adv.). far away, from afar

quercus, -us (f.). oak tree, oak leaf

quisquis, quidquid. whoever, whatever

stagnum, -i. marsh, swamp

superus, -a, -um. high, upper; [as a substantive:] those above, the gods

tilia, -ae. linden tree

626-629. The setting established, the narrative proper begins. Jupiter and his companion Mercury are introduced as they move from house to house, each house ultimately turning them away.

626. **huc.** To be read with *venit*; refers to the setting described in 620-625.
       -que. Connects the two subjects of *venit*. Which two gods *venit*?
627. **Atlantiades.** To be read with *caducifer*.
       postitis alis. Refers to how Mercury sheds the wings on his ankles as part of his human guise. What will *positis* mean then in this context ("put" or "place" alone will not suffice)?
628-629. **mille, mille.** Not nominative here.
       adiere, clausere. Not infinitives.

629-636. The one house that took Jupiter and Mercury in and its inhabitants, Baucis and Philemon, are introduced, with an emphasis on both their poverty and their admirable character.

629. **una = una domus**
       recepit. Whom did the *domus recepit*? The direct object is understood.
630. **parva.** Still the understood *domus* of 629.
       et. Connects the two ablatives that describe the composition of the *tecta*.
631. **sed.** Establishes the contrast between the depressed setting of the *domus* and the elevated character of Baucis and Philemon.
       anus. An appositive to *Baucis*.
       parili aetate. How is Philemon described? How old is he?
632. **illa, illa.** Agree with the *casa* of 633 and are not nominative. What case do they have to be?
       annis iuvenalibus. Since when have Baucis and Philemon been married?
633. **casa.** Not nominative.
633-634. **paupertatem...ferendo:** "They made their poverty insignificant by admitting (that it existed) and by enduring it with a level head."
       fatendo, ferendo. What forms are these?
635. **dominos...requiras.** Understand an *ut* with this clause. It suggests that the social hierarchy of having a master of the house or of having servants does not exist in the house of Baucis and Philemon.
       requiras. Be careful of person here. Who is the subject with that *-s* ending?
636. **tota domus duo sunt.** The singular *tota domus* conflicts grammatically with the plural *duo sunt*, but they do go together. English would likely express *duo* as a singular: "the two/the pair (of them)."
       idem. Indicates that Baucis and Philemon *parent* and *iubent* in equal measure.
       -que, -que = et, et. The use of multiple *-que*'s for "both...and" is more common in poetry than in prose.

Discussion Questions, lines 626-636

1. Why is the *specie mortali* of line 626 an important aspect for Jupiter and Mercury to assume?
2. What figures of speech accentuate the futility of the gods' efforts in lines 628-629? Explain your answer.
3. How does the use of *serae* in line 629, instead of a more prosaic word (*fores, etc.*), emphasize the finality of the doors shutting in the gods' faces?
4. How does the description of the house in lines 629-630 reflect the characterization of Baucis and Philemon?
5. How does the use of *pia* in 631 to describe Baucis emphasize the character of both Baucis and Philemon?
6. Identify specific Latin words or phrases in lines 631-636 that establish Ovid's characterization of Baucis and Philemon.

Iuppiter huc specie mortali cumque parente
venit Atlantiades positis caducifer alis.
Mille domos adiere, locum requiemque petentes,
mille domos clausere serae. Tamen una recepit,
parva quidem, stipulis et canna tecta palustri,   630
sed pia Baucis anus parilique aetate Philemon
illa sunt annis iuncti iuvenalibus, illa
consenuere casa paupertatemque fatendo
effecere levem nec iniqua mente ferendo.
Nec refert, dominos illic famulosne requiras: 635
tota domus duo sunt, idem parentque iubentque.

Jupiter figura humana et caducifer Atlantiades descendit cum patre, omissis alis. Accesserunt ad mille domos, rogantes hospitium et requiem: obices obserarunt mille domos. Tamen una accipit illos, exigua quidem, tecta stipulis et harundine palustri. Verum Baucis pia vetula, atque Philemon in illa convenerunt aetate integra; illo tugurio senectutem contraxerant: et inopiam agnoscendo reddiderunt eam facilem, neque tolerandam averso animo. Neque interest ibi voces heros an servos: universa familia duo sunt; idem et imperant et obtemperant.

adeo, adire, adii / -ivi, aditus. to approach, to come to

aetas, aetatis (f.). age

ala, -ae. wing

anus, -us (f.). old woman

Atlantiades, -ae. [name] Mercury [*here the patronymic as the grandson of Atlas*]

Baucis, Baucidis (f.; acc. sing = Baucida). [name]

caducifer, caduciferi (m.). Mercury, the staff-bearer

canna, -ae. reed

consenesco, consenescere, consenui, -. to become old, to achieve old age

efficio, efficere, effeci, effectus. to make happen, to create, to produce

famulus, -i. slave, servant

fateor, fateri, fassus. to admit, to acknowledge, to confess

huc (adv.). to this place, here

illic (adv.). to that place, there

iniquus, -a, -um. hated, detested; unequal, uneven

iuvenalis, -e. youthful, of or belonging to youth

paluster, palustris, palustre. swampy, marshy

pareo, parere, parui, - (+ dat.). to obey

parens, parentis (m./f.). parent

parilis, -e. equal, similar

paupertas, paupertatis (f.). poverty

Philemon, Philemonis (m.; acc sing. = Philemona). [name]

pius, -a, -um. loyal, faithful, respectful, pious

refero, referre, retuli, relatus. to bring back, to return, to serve again; [*used impersonally:*] it makes a difference, it matters

requies, requietis (f.; acc. = requiem). rest, respite

requiro, requirere, requisivi, requisitus. to seek, to look for, to search for; to ask, to inquire

sera, -ae. lock, bolt, bar (of a door)

species, -ei. appearance, guise, sight

stipula, -ae. stalk of grain, grain

tectum, -i. roof, house

637-640. The gods enter the house of Baucis and Philemon and sit down.

637.   **Penates.** Not a nominative. Here by metonymy referring to the house itself, and recalling the (*domus*) *parva* of line 630.

638.   **submisso vertice.** The *humiles postes* were too short for Jupiter and Mercury to enter standing straight.

639.   **senex** = Philemon
        membra iussit relevare = iussit (deos) relevare (eorum / sua) membra
        posito sedili. Where did the *deos relevare*?

640.   **quo.** An ablative where a dative with the compound *superiniecit* would be expected, and specifically read with *super*, i.e. "over which…" Tarrant's OCT reads *cui* here.
        rude. Not an ablative.

641-647. The preparations of Baucis are described in great detail, from stoking the fire to preparing food.

642.   **foliis et cortice sicco.** How did she build up the fire?

643.   **nutrit.** Understand the *ignis* of line 641 as its object.
        anima. Not a nominative.

644.   **faces.** Here, by synecdoche, meaning "wood" or "firewood" because of the wooden handles of the torches.
        tecto. From where did she *detulit* the *faces ramaliaque*?

645.   **detulit.** Baucis uses, it appears, wood or brush from which the roof is made to stoke the fire.
        minuit. Baucis builds up the heat of the fire but ultimately lets it settle for better cooking, as happens when cooking with wood or, perhaps more recognizable today, charcoal.
        parvo aeno. Dative with the compound *admovit*. She moves the *aeno* to the fire.

Discussion Questions, lines 637-645

1. Identify at least three Latin words or phrases in lines 641-645 that emphasize the poverty of Baucis and Philemon.

2. Why is the synecdoche (or metonymy) *Penates* used for *domos* in 637? What is suggested about Baucis and Philemon by the use of *Penates*?

3. How do the multiple enjambments of lines 641ff. reflect Baucis' mental state and activity level?

'Ergo ubi caelicolae parvos tetigere Penates
summissoque humiles intrarunt vertice postes,
membra senex posito iussit relevare sedili,
quo superiniecit textum rude sedula Baucis.   640
Inde foco tepidum cinerem dimovit et ignes
suscitat hesternos foliisque et cortice sicco
nutrit et ad flammas anima producit anili,
multifidasque faces ramaliaque arida tecto
detulit et minuit parvoque admovit aeno,   645

Postquam igitur dii adierunt exiguam casam, atque subierunt parvam ianuam capite inclinato, senex hortatus est quietem praebere artubus, oblato sedili, quod officiosa Baucis sternit crasso texto. Deinde abstulit calidum cinerem foco, atque excitat ignes hesternos, atque fovet frondibus et cortice arido, et perducit ad flammas spiritu anili; et attulit ligna in multa segmenta divisa, et ramusculos siccos tecto dereptos, et fregit, et admovit exiguo cacabo;

aenum, aeni. bronze vessel, bronze cup, bronze bowl

anilis, -e. of or belonging to an old woman; old woman's

aridus, -a, -um. dry

caelicola, -ae (m./f.). god / goddess; heaven-dweller

cortex, corticis (m.). bark (of a tree), covering

defero, deferre, detuli, delatus. to bring down, to get

dimoveo, dimovere, dimovi, dimotus. to stir, to move around

fax, facis (f.). torch, fire, wedding [*because of the torches that burned at weddings*]; wood

focus, -i. hearth, fireplace

folium, -i. leaf

hesternus, -a, -um. of or belonging to yesterday, yesterday's

minuo, minuere, minui, minutus. to decrease, to lessen, to diminish

multifidus, -a, -um. split, split into pieces, splintered

nutrio, nutrire, nutrivi, nutritus. to nourish, to cultivate, to feed at the breast

Penates, Penatium (m. pl.). [name; *the household gods: gods particular to each household that look over and protect the household; also by synecdoche:*] house

postis, postis (m.). doorway, door-frame, door-post

produco, producere, produxi, productus. to produce, to lead forth, to bring forth, to create, to encourage, to give birth to

ramale, ramalis (n.). branch, twig [*of a tree*]

relevo, -are, -avi, -atus. to lighten, to rest, to ease

rudis, -e. coarse, simple, rudely-fashioned

sedile, sedilis (n.). chair, seat, bench

sedulus, -a, -um. deliberate, painstaking, attentive, focused

siccus, -a, -um. dry

summitto, summittere, summisi, summissus. to send down, to bend low, to lower

superinicio, superinicere, superinieci, superiniectus. to throw over, to cover

suscito, -are, -avi, -atus. to stir up

tango, tangere, tetigi, tactus. to touch, to reach

tepidus, -a, -um. warm, tepid

texo, texere, texui, textus. to weave

vertex, verticis (m). whirlpool, head

646. **quod.** Its antecedent is *holus* in 647.
647. **truncat holus foliis.** Baucis is removing leaves from the vegetables.
      holus. Not the subject. What other case can it be?

647-650. The focus turns to Philemon, who prepares a less-than-gourmet cut of meat for the group.

647. **furca.** Neither a nominative nor an accusative. How did Philemon *levat*?
      ille. Who is now the subject? What gender is this?
648. **sordida.** How would food be *sordida*, i.e. not necessarily "dirty"?
      nigro tigno. Because of build-up from the fire. The house is so small that one main room functions as the main living space: sitting, cooking, and eating, and so smoke from the cooking over the years has colored the wood black.
649. **servato.** Here, "preserved."
      diu. To be read with *servato*, though perhaps also with *resecat* as an indication of the toughness of the cut of meat.
650. **sectam = sectam (partem)**
      domat. Philemon compensated for the poor cut of meat by cooking it in liquid (likely water). Moist cooking of meat can make an otherwise poor cut of meat more tender. Thus he "tamed" (*domat*) the meat, or made it more palatable than it would have been had it been cooked dry over an open flame.

651-652. Conversation occupies Baucis, Philemon, and the gods as a meal is prepared.

651. **medias.** Here, "intervening," referring to the time during which the food was being cooked.
      fallunt. Here, "they wiled away." The idea is that they "deceived" time or that the length of time felt deceiving.
652. **sentiri moram prohibent.** Refers to how the conversation never waned.
      sentiri. Be careful of voice here.

652-655a. The first step of the meal is to wash up. A jug that is filled with water used for washing is introduced.

653. **dura.** Does not agree with *clavo*.
654. **is.** Its antecedent is the *alveus* of 652.
654-655a. **artus fovendos accipit.** The *tepidae aquae* of 654 are used to wash the gods' *artus*.

655a-656. The couch or bench where the gods will sit is described and prepared.

655a. **medio.** Agrees with the *lecto* of 656a.
      est. To be read with the *impositus* of 656a.
      de mollibus ulvis. To be read with, and describing the composition of, the *torus*.
656a. **sponda pedibusque salignis.** A hendiadys that describes the *lecto*. What kind of *sponda* does the *lectus* have? See p. 88 for a diagam of the *lectus* and its parts.
655-656. The validity of these lines, as well as lines 652-654, is debated. Tarrant brackets these lines, indicating his doubt of their validity, as did Anderson, whose explanation of the manuscript difficulties is helpful.
655. **concutiunt torum.** Describes the action of fluffing the cushion to make it more comfortable.
      de molli fluminis ulva. Reiterates the composition of the *torus*.

Discussion Questions, lines 646-656

1. Identify specific Latin words or phrases in lines 647-650 that indicate the economic status of Baucis and Philemon. Are such indicators meant to be read as positives or negatives? Explain your answer.
2. Why does Ovid use such specific vocabulary to describe the house and its furnishings in lines 647-656?

quodque suus coniunx riguo collegerat horto
truncat holus foliis; furca levat ille bicorni
sordida terga suis nigro pendentia tigno
servatoque diu resecat de tergore partem
exiguam sectamque domat ferventibus undis. 650
   'Interea medias fallunt sermonibus horas
sentirique moram prohibent. Erat alveus illic
fagineus, dura clavo suspensus ab ansa;
is tepidis impletur aquis, artusque fovendos 654
accipit. In medio torus est de mollibus ulvis 655a
impositus lecto, sponda pedibusque salignis; 656a
concutiuntque torum de molli fluminis ulva 655
impositum lecto sponda pedibusque salignis; 656

et concidit holera quae suus coniunx collegerat in horto riguo. Ille deripit furca bicorni turpia terga porci pendentia trabe fumida; atque abscindit de tergo diu servato parvam partem; et mollit adscissam aquis bullientibus. Interea taedium tollunt temporis interiecti colloquio, et faciunt ne cunctatio molesta sit. Ibi erat crater fagineus suspensus clavo ab ansa curva: is impletur aquis calidis, atque accipit membra lavanda. In medio erat torus de lentis ulvis impositus lecto, sponda et pedibus salignis.

alveus, -i. bowl

ansa, -ae. handle

bicornis, -e. with two horns, two-horned; with two prongs, two-pronged

clavus, -i. nail, spike

concutio, concutere, concussi, concussus. to shake, to cause to vibrate, to fluff

domo, domare, domui, domitus. to tame, to overcome, to temper

exiguus, -a, -um. slight, paltry, minimal, small, barely noticeable

fagineus, -a, -um. of or belonging to the beech tree; made of beech wood

fallo, fallere, fefelli, falsus. to deceive, to trick

fervens, ferventis. warm, hot, boiling, fervent, steaming

folium, -i. leaf

foveo, fovere, fovi, fotus. to be warm to warm, to keep warm; to cherish

furca, -ae. fork

holus, holeris (n.). vegetable

hortus, -i. garden

illic (adv.). to that place, there

impleo, implere, implevi, impletus. to fill, to fill up

lectus, -i. bed, couch, bench

levo, -are, -avi, -atus. to lift, to raise up, to elevate, to hold up, to support

niger, nigra, nigrum. black

prohibeo, prohibere, prohibui, prohibitus. to prohibit, to forbid

reseco, -are, -avi, -atus. to trim, to slice, to cut off

riguus, -a, -um. well-watered, well-irrigated

salignus, -a, -um. made of willow-wood, willow

seco, secare, secui, sectus. to cut, to slice, to carve

sermo, sermonis (m.). speech, conversation, speaking

sordidus, -a, -um. sordid, dirty, imperfect

sponda, -ae. bed, bed frame

sus, suis (n.). pig, sow

tepidus, -a, -um. warm, tepid

tergum, -i. back

tergus, tergoris (n.). back [*specifically of an animal*]

tignum, -i. piece of wood, plank (of wood), beam

torus, -i. bed, bench, couch, cushion

trunco, -are, -avi, -atus. to split, to break; (+ abl.) to strip (of)

ulva, -ae. water grass

657-660. Ovid now focuses on the covering for the bench or seat, which is rarely used.

657.   **vestibus.** Not "clothes" here. What would Baucis and Philemon *velant* the *lectus* with?

        hunc. The *lecto* of 656a and 656 is its antecedent.

        quas. *Vestibus* is its antecedent.

        non. To be read with the *consuerant* of 658.

        tempore festo. Refers to the only time Baucis and Philemon *consuerant sternere vestes.*

658.   **et = etiam**

658-659. **haec…erat = haec vestis erat vilisque vetusque**

658.   **consuerant.** This form is a contracted form of *consueverant.*

        -que, -que = et, et

659.   **lecto saligno.** Either a dative of agent with *indignanda*, with the *lecto* personified, or a dative of reference.

        indignanda. Agrees with *vestis.*

660-663. Baucis focuses on setting the table in preparation for eating.

660.   **accubuere dei.** Understand *et* before this clause.

        accubuere. Not an infinitive.

        succincta. Refers to Baucis' clothes, similar to how we might roll up our sleeves before getting to work. (Except of course that Baucis doesn't have sleeves. What does she roll up?)

        tremens. Refers to Baucis' age and likely as well her nervousness over wanting to entertain her new guests properly (remember she does not yet know that they are gods).

661.   **ponit.** What will this mean with *mensam*? "Put" or "place" alone will not convey the correct sense.

        mensae. To be read with *pes tertius.*

        impar. Refers to the unevenness and unsteadiness of the table.

662.   **testa.** The ancient equivalent of using today a folded up napkin to level and steady a table.

        parem. Now the *tertius pes* is the same height as the others.

        quae. Its antecedent is the *testa* of 661.

663.   **aequatam = aequatam (mensam).** The table is now level.

        mentae. Neither "table" nor "mind."

Discussion Questions, lines 657-663

1. Why is the *nisi tempore festo* of line 657 ironic?

2. What aspect of Baucis' emotional state does the *impar mensa* of line 661 represent? What specific Latin word that describes Baucis in line 661 does *impar* recall?

3. The *deus* of line 660 is the first use of this word in the story to refer to Jupiter and Mercury. Why does Ovid reserve the first use of this word for here? What contrast is it intended to highlight?

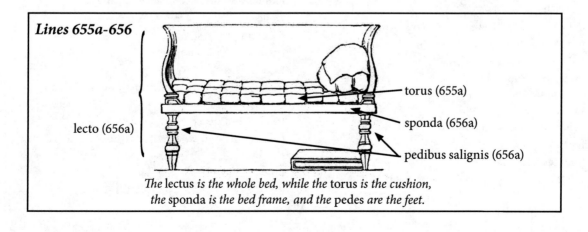

Lines 655a-656

torus (655a)

sponda (656a)

pedibus salignis (656a)

lecto (656a)

The **lectus** *is the whole bed, while the* **torus** *is the cushion,*
the **sponda** *is the bed frame, and the* **pedes** *are the feet.*

vestibus hunc velant, quas non nisi tempore festo
sternere consuerant, sed et haec vilisque vetusque
vestis erat, lecto non indignanda saligno.
Accubuere dei. Mensam succincta tremensque   660
ponit anus, mensae sed erat pes tertius impar;
testa parem fecit, quae postquam subdita clivum
sustulit, aequatam mentae tersere virentes.

Hunc sternunt tapete, quem non nisi tempore festo soliti erant depromere: sed et ille tapes et vilis et vectus erat, non erubescendus lecto saligno. Dii accubuerunt. Anus accincta et tremens admovet mensam; verum pes tertius mensae erat dissidens, later fecit aequalem: qui postquam subiectus dempsit inaequalitatem, mentae virides effinxerunt aequatam.

accumbo, accumbere, accubui, accubiturus. to recline, to sit (down) [*used in the context of sitting down to dinner*]

aequatus, -a, -um. level, flat

anus, -us (f.). old woman

clivus, -i. slope, incline, progression

consuesco, consuescere, consuevi, consuetus. to be accustomed to, to be used to

festus, -a, -um. of or belonging to a party or a festival

indignor, indignari, indignatus. to view as inappropriate, to view as unworthy

mensa, -ae. table, course, food [*i.e. what's on the table*]

menta, -ae. mint, mint-leaf

salignus, -a, -um. made of willow-wood, willow

sterno, sternere, stravi, stratus. to lay low, to lay out, to kill, to slay

subeo, subire, subii / -ivi, subditus. to place under, to support

succingo, succingere, succinxi, succinctus. to gird up, to gather up

suffero, sufferre, sustuli, sublatus. to hold up, to raise up

tergeo, tergere, tersi, tersus. to wipe, to dry

testa, -ae. sherd, terracotta piece, piece of baked clay

tremo, tremere, tremui, -. to tremble, to shake, to vibrate, to shiver, to shudder, to ripple

velo, -are, -avi, -atus. to cover, to hide

vetus, veteris. old

vilis, -e. cheap, inferior, lowly

vireo, virere, virui, -. to grow green, to be fresh, to sprout

mensa tribus pedibus

664-668. A detailed description of the food that is placed on the table.

664.   **ponitur.** Describes what was served for the meal. It is followed by a series of six different nominative nouns that stretch to line 668, all of which are its subjects.
       hic = in mensa. Here the adverb rather than a modfier of *bicolor baca.*
       bicolor sincerae baca Minervae. Refers to the olive by recalling Minerva's / Athena's gift of the olive tree to Athens.
       bicolor. These olives were part green, part black, an indication of lack of ripeness.
665.   **condita.** Agrees with *corna,* and here means "preserved"; storing fruit in a liquid infuses them (and the liquid) with flavor, but more important here also prevents them from spoiling.
       in liquida faece. To be read with *condita.*
       faece. Refers to the sediment that collects at the bottom of red wine. Baucis has used these leftovers to preserve the *autumnalia corna.*
666.   **lactis coacti** = "cheese." Not a nominative.
667.   **non acri** = "warm" (as opposed to *acri* or "hot"). Agrees with *favilla.*
       versata. Does not agree with *favilla.*

668-670. Once the food itself has been described, Ovid now turns his attention to the vessels in which it was served.

668.   **omnia.** Refers to all of the subjects in the previous lines.
       fictilibus. Refers to the vessel(s) in which everything was served.
       haec. Refers to *omnia.*
       caelatus. Does not refer to the gods or the sky. What does this word mean?
       eodem. Agrees with the *argento* of line 669. Baucis and Philemon own nothing that is silver, but here the idea of silver is used to refer to the collection of "finery" in which they are serving everything. Ovid is saying that their non-silver or earthenware serving pieces function in the same way that silver serving pieces function for more wealthy people.
669.   **crater.** What agrees with this? How was this vessel decorated?
       fabricata. Does not agree with *fago.* What is *fabricata*?
670.   **pocula...ceris.** A description that is not exactly clear. The *pocula* are smeared with wax, but it is unclear where and why they are smeared. Perhaps the inside of the cups is smeared with wax because the cups are so old that the wax is used to smooth the interior, or, more probably, the wax is used to fill holes that have worn into (or been eaten into) the cups.
       pocula. Another subject of the *sistitur* of line 669.
       qua. Here adverbial: "where" or "in the place which."

Discussion Questions, lines 664-670

1. What is the significance of Ovid's periphrasis for "olive" (*bicolor...Minervae*) in line 664? Why include in the periphrasis mention of Minerva (Athena)?

2. Why does Ovid include such a detailed list of food in lines 664-667? What is the effect of concluding that list with the *omnia fictilibus* of line 668?

3. Why does Ovid describe the *crater* of line 669 as *caelatus eodem argento*?

Ponitur hic bicolor sincerae baca Minervae
conditaque in liquida corna autumnalia faece   665
intibaque et radix et lactis massa coacti
ovaque non acri leviter versata favilla,
omnia fictilibus. Post haec caelatus eodem
sistitur argento crater fabricataque fago
pocula, qua cava sunt, flaventibus illita ceris.   670

Tum apponitur baca bicolor intemeratae Palladis, et corna autumnalia defruto condita, et cicoreum, et raphanus, et caseus recens, et ova leviter versata in tepido cinere: atque haec omnia in vasibus terreis. Postea sculptus urceus ex eadem terra apponitur, et pocula facta ex fago, obducta ceris flavis, qua parte sunt cava.

argentum, -i. silver

autumnalis, -e. autumnal, of or belonging to autumn

baca, -ae. berry, nut, pearl, jewel

bicolor, bicoloris. having two colors, bi-colored

caelo, -are, -avi, -atus. to etch, to engrave, to incise

cavus, -a, -um. hollow, full of holes, porous

cogo, cogere, coegi, coactus. to force, to compel

cornum, -i. (cornelian) cherry, (cornal) berry

crater, crateris (m.; acc = cratera). [name; *the* crater *was a deep, wide-mouthed Greek vase which was used to mix wine and water*]

fabrico, -are, -avi, -atus. to fashion, to create, to make

faex, faecis (f.). dregs, solids, leftovers

fagus, -i (f.). beech tree

favilla, -ae. ashes (of a fire)

fictile, fictilis (n.). earthenware, (terracotta) vase or pitcher

flavens, flaventis. golden, blonde, yellow

illino, illinere, illevi, illitus. to cover, to smear, to wipe, to coat

intibum, -i. chicory, endive [*a lettuce-like leafy vegetable often used in salads*]

lac, lactis (n.). milk

massa, -ae. lump, mass

ovum, -i. egg

poculum, -i. cup

radix, radicis (f.). root (of a tree or plant)

sincerus, -a, -um. pure, unsullied, unadulterated, unblemished

sisto, sistere, steti, status. to set up, to set down, to establish, to place

verso, -are, -avi, -atus. to turn, to spin

671-673. The main course is served, and quickly removed to make way for dessert.

671.   **epulas.** Not a nominative.

     misere. Not an infinitive. What verb's third principle part is *misi*?

     calentes. Can agree with either *epulas* or *foci*; which makes more sense?

672.   **nec longae senectae.** This genitive of description is to be read with *vina*. The litotes conveys a meaning opposite to *senectae*.

     rursus referuntur. Refers to the serving again of the same wine that was served earlier.

673.   **dant locum paulum.** (*Vina*) *seducta* is the subject. The wine is cleared to make way for the next course.

     mensis. Here, not the "table" itself, but rather what goes on the table.

     paulum. Remember that the table (and entire house) is very small; there is not much room for any kind of feast or multi-course meal.

674-677. The dessert course, consisting of nuts and fruit, is described.

674.   **hic, hic.** Here the adverb and not the nominative of *hic, haec, hoc*.

675.   **pruna, mala.** Understand *collecta sunt* with these nominatives.

676.   **collectae = collectae (sunt)**

677.   **in medio = in medio (mensae)**

677-678. The meal is infused with the good nature and kindness of Baucis and Philemon.

677.   **super omnia.** Refers to how the faces of Baucis and Philemon shine over the whole meal.

678.   **accessere.** Not an infinitive.

     boni. Agrees with the *vultus* of 677.

     nec. Negates both *iners* and *pauper*.

     voluntas. Described by *nec iners pauperque*. What kind of *voluntas* do Baucis and Philemon possess?

Discussion Questions, lines 671-678

1. Identify at least two figures of speech in line 672. Why does Ovid describe the wine in such an elaborate way?

2. What is the significance of the *paulum seducta* of line 673?

3. The list of desserts in lines 674-677 recalls the list of appetizers in lines 664-667. Why are these the foods that Ovid focuses on (and not, say, the main course)? How do these foods reflect or emphasize the characterization of Baucis and Philemon?

4. How is the *super omnia vultus* of line 677 to be read? Is it a poignant perspective on the good-hearted couple? Or is it a cynical exaggeration of their *voluntas*? Explain your answer.

Parva mora est, epulasque foci misere calentes;
nec longae rursus referuntur vina senectae
dantque locum mensis paulum seducta secundis:
hic nux, hic mixta est rugosis carica palmis
prunaque et in patulis redolentia mala canistris   675
et de purpureis collectae vitibus uvae;
candidus in medio favus est. Super omnia vultus
accessere boni nec iners pauperque voluntas.

Breve est tempus, et foci dederunt dapes callidas: neque rursus apponitur vinum vetus; atque haec paulum seposita vicem praestant bellariis. Tum nux, tum ficus aridae iunctae sunt corrugatis dactylis, itemque pruna et mala fragrantia in corbibus, cum racemis collectis ex rubris vitibus. Favus albus est in medio. Laeta facies addita est super omnia, et voluntas neque segnis neque parca.

accedo, accedere, accessi, accessus. to approach, to come (forward)

caleo, calere, calui, -. to be hot, to be warm

candidus, -a, -um. white, yellow

canistrum, -i. basket

carica, -ae. fig

favus, -i. honeycomb

iners, inertis. lazy, slow, lifeless

mensa, -ae. table, course, food [*i.e. what's on the table*]

nux, nucis (f.). nut

palma, -ae. palm, palm tree, fruit of the palm tree, date [*the date is the fruit of the palm tree*]

patulus, -a, -um. broad, gaping, (wide) open

paulus, -a, -um. small, slight, little

pauper, pauperis. poor

prunum, -i. plum

redoleo, redolere, -, -. to be odiferous, to give off a pleasant smell

rugosus, -a, -um. wrinkled, shriveled

rursus (adv.). back, in return, again and again, over and over

secundus, -a, -um. second, favorable

seduco, seducere, seduxi, seductus. to take away, to clear away

senecta, -ae. old age

uva, -ae. grape, bunch of grapes

vinum, -i. wine

vitis, vitis (f.). grapevine

voluntas, voluntatis (f.). wish, desire

679-680. A miracle occurs that is the first indication that the guests of Baucis and Philemon might be a bit more than mortal: the wine never runs out.

679-680. See the sentence diagram at bottom right for structural assistance.

679.   **haustum.** Modifies the Greek accusative singular *cratera.*

  repleri. Not a main verb; to be read with *vident,* with the accusative *cratera* as its subject, likely with a middle sense.

680.   **sponte sua, per se.** These expressions are nearly synonymous. Both emphasize that the wine replenished itself without any outside assistance.

681-683. Baucis and Philemon realize that they are in the presence of gods. They become suddenly scared because they think that they have offended the gods, and they become embarassed by their lack of food and amenities.

681.   **novitate.** To be read with *attoniti.* Refers to the miraculous event described in 679-680.

  pavent. Who is the "they" that is the subject of this verb? Who is *attoniti*?

682.   **concipiunt preces = orant**

683.   **veniam orant.** Refers to how embarassed Baucis and Philemon are by the meagerness of the meal that they served to these honored guests.

  paratibus. Here the noun *paratus, -us.*

684-685. The introduction of the **anser.** *Baucis and Philemon now look to their only living animal to serve as compensation for the paltry fare they have already served.*

684.   **minimae custodia villae.** A tenderly humorous description of the *anser.* A modern equivalent might be when the owners of a small, cute, loud dog introduce it as the guard dog.

685.   **domini.** Not a genitive.

Discussion Questions, lines 679-685

1. How does the repetition of the *sponte sua per seque* of line 680 reflect the reaction of Baucis and Philemon to this wonder?

2. Why is the *succrescere* of line 680 a particularly vivid word in this context?

3. Identify specific Latin words or phrases in lines 681-683 that indicate the emotional state of Baucis and Philemon. How does their emotional state further emphasize their characterization?

3. How does the rhythm of the *unicus anser erat* of line 684 reflect Baucis' and Philemon's actions in response to their embarassment?

4. What is the effect of the *mactare* of line 685? How does the *minimae custodia villae* of line 684 intensify this effect?

'Interea totiens haustum cratera repleri
sponte sua per seque vident succrescere vina: 680
attoniti novitate pavent manibusque supinis
concipiunt Baucisque preces timidusque Philemon
et veniam dapibus nullisque paratibus orant.
Unicus anser erat, minimae custodia villae,
quem dis hospitibus domini mactare parabant;   685

Interea cum advertunt urceum repleri per se quotiens vacuus esset, atque ultro vina augeri, stupentes novitate timent, et Baucis et pavidus Philemon ad preces confugiunt manibus in caelum sublatis, et veniam implorant epulis, atque exiguo apparatui. Unicus anser erat, custos vilissimae villae, quem domini volebant occidere in gratiam deorum hospitum.

anser, anseris (m.). goose

attonitus, -a, -um. astonished, thunderstruck, disbelieving

concipio, concipere, concepi, conceptus. to worship, to speak with respect

crater, crateris (m.; acc = cratera). [name; *the* crater *was a deep, wide-mouthed Greek vase which was used to mix wine and water*]

custodia, -ae. protection, guard, custody

daps, dapis (f.). feast

haurio, haurire, hausi, haustus. to drain, to empty; to drink

macto, -are, -avi, -atus. to sacrifice, to offer as a sacrifice, to slay as part of a sacrifice

novitas, novitatis (f.). novelty, strange or new phenomenon

paratus, -us. preparations, accoutrements, equipment, stuff

paveo, pavere, -, -. to be scared, to be terrified, to be apprehensive

prex, precis (f.). entreaty, prayer

repleo, replere, replevi, repletus. to refill, to replenish, to fill again

sponte (defec.). [*used often with* sua] *sua sponte* = "of one's own volition" or "of one's own choice"

succresco, succrescere, succrevi, -. to rise up

supinus, -a, -um. lying on the back, supine, backwards, upturned

totiens (adv.). whenever, as often as

unicus, -a, -um. lone, sole, single

venia, -ae. grace, thanks, favor, kindness

Sentence Diagram, lines 679-680

Interea totiens haustum cratera repleri
sponte sua per seque vident succrescere vina:

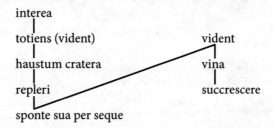

The *totiens* establishes two parallel clauses, each with *vident* as its verb. Follow the line above: the left column is the first clause, with the long diagonal line leading to the second clause. Horizontal alignment indicates parallel grammatical function in each clause.

686-688. The goose runs away, eventually tiring out old Baucis and Philemon. It seeks refuge with the gods, who intervene on its behalf.

686.   **ille** = **anser**

celer penna, tardos aetate. These are parallel expressions, each comprising an adjective modified by an ablative. Note, however, that the two adjectives are not the same case and so do not describe the same nouns. Who is *celer*? And who are *tardos*?

penna. Not nominative. Why is the *anser celer*?

aetate. Why are Baucis and Philemon *tardos*?

687.   **est visus.** *Video, -ere* can have a different meaning in the passive. What is it?

ipsos. What accusative plural noun will this agree with?

688.   **confugisse.** To be read with the *est visus* of 687.

deos. Not the subject of *confugisse*.

vetuere. Not an infinitive.

necari. The subject is an understood *anserem*, which is not killing anything. Be careful of voice here.

689-693. Jupiter and Mercury reveal themselves to Baucis and Philemon, and tell the old couple what they plan to do to their neighbors. They also tell Baucis and Philemon that they will be spared.

690-691. **vobis…dabitur** = **esse immunibus huius mali dabitur vobis.** The *dabitur* will perhaps best be translated impersonally, i.e. "it will be be given…" The *immunibus* is dative because of the *vobis*, even though in English it sounds better as a predicate adjective.

691.   **dabitur.** The infinitive *esse* and everything that goes with it is the subject.

modo = **nunc**

691-692. **relinquite, comitate.** Not ablatives (not even nouns). How are Jupiter and Mercury addressing Baucis and Philemon? What are they telling them to do?

692.   **gradus.** Not nominative. What adjective modifies this?

ardua. A substantive. To what part of the *mons* are they climbing?

693.   **ite.** An uncommon form of an irregular verb. Which verb has its stem as just *i-*?

693-694. Baucis and Philemon begin following Jupiter and Mercury, but have difficulty making the climb.

693.   **parent.** Baucis and Philemon are not preparing anything. This verb is not from *paro, -are.*

694.   **longo clivo** = **(in) longo clivo**

vestigia. Recalls the *gradus* of 692, and its suggestion of the age and infirmity of Baucis and Philemon, but now, as the gods push on ahead of them, their *gradus* leave only *vestigia* behind.

Discussion Questions, lines 686-694

1. How does the *diu* of line 687 reflect the character of Baucis and Philemon?

2. What is the narrative implication of the *visus* of line 687? Why didn't the *anser* simply *confugit ad ipsos deos*?

3. Why is the *ipsos* of line 687 used to describe the *deos* of line 688? Why are they now *deos ipsos* instead of just *deos*?

4. How does the *gradus* of line 692 emphasize the infirmity of Baucis and Philemon and the difficulty of their climb?

5. What is the significance of the *parent ambo* of line 693? What earlier description of Baucis and Philemon does it recall?

ille celer penna tardos aetate fatigat
eluditque diu tandemque est visus ad ipsos
confugisse deos. Superi vetuere necari
"Di"que "sumus, meritasque luet vicinia poenas
impia," dixerunt; "vobis immunibus huius 690
esse mali dabitur. Modo vestra relinquite tecta
ac nostros comitate gradus et in ardua montis
ite simul." Parent ambo baculisque levati 693
nituntur longo vestigia ponere clivo. 694

Ille velox pennis lassat lentos annis, et diu effugit; atque tandem visus est confugisse ad deos ipsos. Illi prohibuerunt occidi, "Diique sumus," inquiunt; "et vicinia impia dabit poenas quas meruit: vobis concederetur esse expertibus huius cladis: deserite tantum vestras sedes, atque sequimini nostra vestigia, et venite una in cacumen montis. Uterque obsequuntur, et sustentati scipionibus conantur ascendere excelsum montem."

ac (conj.). and

aetas, aetatis (f.). age

ambo, ambae, ambo. both [*this is an irregular adjective that only occurs in the plural, and whose masculine and neuter nominative can be misleading because of the -o ending*]

arduus, -a, -um. tall, towering, steep, precipitous; [*as substantive*] height, peak

baculum, -i. stick, staff

clivus, -i. slope, incline, progression

comito, -are, -avi, -atus. to go with, to accompany

eludo, eludere, eludi, elusus. to elude, to escape, to avoid

fatigo, -are, -avi, -atus. to tire, to fatigue, to weary

gradus, -us. slope, grade, step, footstep

immunis, -e. immune, free (from), free (of), exempt (from)

levo, -are, -avi, -atus. to lift, to raise up, to elevate, to hold up, to support

luo, luere, lui, -. to suffer (a punishment), to endure (a punishment)

meritus, -a, -um. deserved, merited, earned

nitor, niti, nixus (+ infin.). to struggle (to do something)

pareo, parere, parui, - (+ dat.). to obey

praeeo, praeire, praeii / -ivi, praeiturus. to move past, to go beyond, to go ahead, to transcend

senilis, -e. of or belonging to an old person; old man's, old woman's

tandem (adv.). finally, at last

tardus, -a, -um. slow, late, sluggish

vestigium, -i. vestige, trace, footprint, sign, remnant

veto, vetare, vetui, vetitus. to forbid, to deny

vicinia, -ae. neighborhood, area nearby, vicinity, proximity

ite simul." Parent et dis praeeuntibus ambo 693a
membra levant baculis tardique senilibus annis 693b

693a-693b. These two lines consist of an alternate reading for line 693 (693a) plus another line that has been otherwise removed from the manuscript tradition (693b).

695-696. Baucis and Philemon are close to the top, where they pause to look back from where they have come.

695-696. **Tantum…potest.** Describes how far they are from the top by comparing that distance to how far an arrow is shot.

695.   **tantum.** Works in conjunction with *quantum*: "as…as…" or "as…so far…"
          summo = summo (montis)
          ire. This infinitive will need to be read with another verb. What verb is it?

696.   **missa.** Is not to be read with *potest*. What does it agree with?

696-697. Baucis and Philemon turn to look back, and see everything except their house under water.

696.   **flexere.** Not an infinitive; in what direction are they looking?
          mersa palude. These words do not agree. What is *mersa*? And by what?

697.   **cetera.** Not the subject of *prospiciunt*.
          tantum. Here the adverb, equivalent to *nunc* or *modo*.
          manere. An infinitive in an indirect statement dependent on *prospiciunt*.

698-700. To the amazement of Baucis and Philemon, their old house becomes a temple.

698.   **fata.** Not the subject of *deflent*. At what are Baucis and Philemon *deflent*?
          suorum. Refers to the family and neighbors that they left behind.

699.   **vetus.** A nominative, but not a masculine, adjective. What does it modify? What is (or was) *vetus*?
          dominis. A dative here, to be read with *parva*. Refers to Baucis and Philemon and their size relative to the size of their *casa*.
          etiam. Does not mean "also" here. What else can it mean?

700.   **vertitur** = vertitur (a deis)

700-702. Ovid details the process of transformation from old house to magnificent temple, focusing on the transformation of specific architectural details of both structures.

          furcas. Not the subject. Here it refers to a vertical architectural member that would support a horizontal member in its "fork" or v-shaped opening.
          subiere. Not an infinitive.

702.   **caelatae fores.** Refers to how the doors are decorated with some pattern or relief sculpture.
          adoperta marmore tellus. What was the *tellus adoperta* with? Refers to the floor of the temple.

Discussion Questions, lines 695-702

1. What detail from Lelex's introduction to his tale does the *mersa palude* of line 696 recall?
2. What is the effect of the asyndeton in line 697?
3. What does the *deflent fata suorum* of line 698 say about the character of Baucis and Philemon?
4. How is line 699 a fitting conclusion to the existence of the *casa* of Baucis and Philemon? And how does the enjambment in line 700 reinforce this?
5. How does the structure of the *dominis etiam casa parva duobus* of line 699 reflect its meaning?
6. Identify specific Latin words or phrases in lines 700 to 702 that contrast the new "house" of Baucis and Philemon to the description of their old house in lines 629ff.
7. What is the significance of the *tellus* of line 702 being the final word of the transformation scene? How does it recall the detailed descriptions of food that Ovid included earlier?

'Tantum aberant summo quantum semel ire sagitta   695
missa potest; flexere oculos et mersa palude
cetera prospiciunt, tantum sua tecta manere,
dumque ea mirantur, dum deflent fata suorum,
illa vetus dominis etiam casa parva duobus
vertitur in templum: furcas subiere columnae,   700
stramina flavescunt aurataque tecta videntur
caelataeque fores adopertaque marmore tellus.

Tantum distabant a cacumine quantum iactus sagittae potest comprehendere: converterunt oculos, et prospiciunt suam domum solam residuam, alia omnia absorpta lacu. Et dum ea stupent; dum lugent sortem suorum, illud antiquum tugurium etiam angustum duobus dominis mutatur in aedem: columnae vices praestiterunt furcarum, tectum flavescit, et terra conspicitur strata marmore, ianua sculpta, et domus auro oblita:

adopertus, -a, -um. covered, veiled

auratus, -a, -um. golden

caelo, -are, -avi, -atus. to etch, to engrave, to incise

defleo, deflere, deflevi, defletus. to weep (for), to mourn

duo, duae, duo (dat. & abl. pl. = duobus). two

flavesco, flavescere, -, -. to become blond, to turn yellow

flecto, flectere, flexi, flexus. to bend, to curve

furca, -ae. fork

marmor, marmoris (n.). marble

mergo, mergere, mersi, mersus. to submerge, to flood, to inundate

palus, paludis (f.). swamp, marsh

prospicio, prospicere, prospexi, prospectus. to see (something) in front, to look at, to gaze at, to stare at

quantus, -a, -um. how much, how many

semel. once, a single time

stramen, straminis (n.). straw, hay, thatch [as in a thatched roof]

subeo, subire, subii / -ivi, subditus. to place under, to support; to replace

vetus, veteris. old

703-705. Jupiter rewards Baucis and Philemon for their piety by asking them to make a wish.

703.   **talia.** To be read with *edidit* and refers to the speech that begins at 704.
        Saturnius. Not here the name "Saturn" but rather the adjective that refers to his son.
704-705. **iuste…digna.** An extended vocative expression.
704.   **coniuge iusto.** To be read with *digna*: what is the *femina digna* of?
705.   **quid optetis.** To be read with *dicite.*

705-708. Baucis and Philemon first ask to return to their home, as priests of the temple that has replaced it.

705.   **cum.** Not the conjunction "when" here.
        pauca. Does not agree with *Baucide*. What did Philemon *locutus*?
706.   **iudicium.** Not so much a "judgment" here. What did Baucis and Philemon make in response to Jupiter's question?
        superis = deis
        commune. Not an ablative. What is the neuter accusative noun that this modifies?
707.   **esse, tueri.** These infinitives need a verb to be read with. What is it?

708-710. Baucis and Philemon also ask, with a bit more uncertainty, that they be allowed to die together. Philemon is speaking: he asks that he not see his wife's grave, and that he not have to be buried by her.

708.   **egimus.** What does this verb mean with expressions of time? (Not "do" or "drive.")
709.   **auferat.** This verb expresses the wish of Baucis and Philemon. What mood is it? How might they address gods when making such a request?
        duos = Baucis and Philemon
        coniugis. To be read with the *busta* of 710 and modified by the *meae* of 710.
710.   **videam, sim.** Note the subject change from the *auferat* of line 709 (but the mood has not changed).
        neu = et ne. A negative conjunction with the subjunctive *sim*. The construction is the same as with *videam* and *auferat.*
        sim tumulandus. It is difficult in English to reconcile the subjunctive in the passive periphrastic. What does Philemon (not) want?

Discussion Questions, lines 703-710

1. How does the *placido* of line 703 set the tone for the scene?
2. How does the *vestra* of the *delubra vestra* of line 707 emphasize the piety of Baucis and Philemon?
3. What aspect of the initial description of Baucis and Philemon in lines 629-636 does the *Cum Baucide… Philemon* of lines 705-706 recall?
4. How does the request of lines 709-710 reflect the already established character of Baucis and Philemon?

Talia tum placido Saturnius edidit ore:
"Dicite, iuste senex et femina coniuge iusto
digna, quid optetis." Cum Baucide pauca locutus   705
iudicium superis aperit commune Philemon:
"Esse sacerdotes delubraque vestra tueri
poscimus, et quoniam concordes egimus annos,
auferat hora duos eadem, nec coniugis umquam
busta meae videam neu sim tumulandus ab illa."   710

cum Jupiter eiusmodi protulit amico ore: "Aperite, iuste senex, et femina digna iusto marito, quid voveatis."
Postquam Philemon pauca locutus esset cum Baucide, diis patefacit commune desiderium: "Petimus esse
sacerdotes, et servare vestra templa; et quoniam aetatem transegimus unanimes, eadem hora utrumque tollat;
neque umquam aspiciam sepulchrum meae uxoris, neve sim sepeliendus ab illa."

aperio, aperire, aperui, apertus. to open, to reveal

aufero, auferre, abstuli, ablatus. to carry away, to bear away, to remove

bustum, -i. funeral marker, funeral pyre, tomb, grave-mound

concors, concordis. in agreement, agreeing, of like mind

delubrum, -i. temple, shrine, small place of worship or devotion

dignus, -a, -um (+ abl.). worthy (of)

edo, edere, edidi, editus. to say, to narrate, to tell, to give forth, to produce

iudicium, -i. decision, judgment

iustus, -a, -um. just, lawful, right, appropriate

loquor, loqui, locutus. to speak

neu. and so that…not [*a negative conjunction often continuing a negative purpose clause or other subjunctive clause*]

opto, -are, -avi, -atus. to choose, to want

placidus, -a, -um. placid, peaceful, calm

posco, poscere, poposci, -. to demand, to ask for

quoniam (conj.). since, because

sacerdos, sacerdotis (m./f.). priest, priestess

Saturnius, -a, -um. of or belonging to Saturn, Saturnian [*In the Roman tradition, Saturn was the father of Jupiter*]

talis, -e. such, of such a sort, of such a type

tueor, tueri, tuitus. to look at, to gaze at, to protect, to defend

tumulo, -are, -avi, -atus. to bury, to cover with a burial mound

umquam (adv.). ever

711-715. Jupiter grants Baucis and Philemon their wish: first they live out their lives taking care of the temple, and then they are joined in death as trees.

711.   **vota.** Not the subject of *sequitur.*
        fides. "Faith" or "trust" will not work here. How does Jupiter respond to Philemon's request?
        templi. Not the subject of *fuere* but to be read with *tutela.*
712.   **donec.** Not "until" here. What else can it mean?
        annis aevoque. A hendiadys to be read with *soluti.*
713-715. See the sentence diagram below for structural assistance with this sentence.
713.   **ante gradus sacros** = ante gradus sacros (templi)
        forte. Not a form of *fortis, -e* but an adverb here.
714.   **casus.** Not a nominative. What declension is this noun?
714-715. **Philemona, Baucida.** Greek accusatives, subjects of *frondere.*
715.   **conspexit.** Governs the infinitives in 714 and 715.

716-719. Baucis and Philemon say their goodbyes as they simultaneously transform into trees.

716.   **super geminos vultus.** To be read with *crescente.* Where was the *cacumine crescente*?
        crescente cacumine. Describes the circumstances under which they were *reddebant.*
717.   **mutua.** Agrees with *dicta.*
        dum licuit. Refers to their mouths remaining uncovered by the tree.
        mutua reddebant dicta = "They were uttering words of the same sentiment to each other."
717-718. **vale, o coniunx.** The two things that Baucis and Philemon *dixere simul.*
718.   **abdita.** Not a nominative.
718-719. **simul...frutex.** Refers to the completion of their transformation, preventing them from speaking anymore even as they speak their final words to one another.

719-720. Lelex's narrative here ends. He concludes with the man who showed him the trees.

719.   **Thyneius.** Not a proper name, but an adjective.
720.   **incola.** What is the gender of this word? And so what agrees with it?
        de gemino corpore. To be read with *truncos,* explaining where the trees came from.

Sentence Diagram, lines 713-715

Cum,
      soluti annis aevoque,

starent forte
      ante gradus sacros

et
(cum)
narrarent
      casus loci

Baucis
(conspexit)
      Philemona frondere
et
senior Philemon
conspexit
      Baucida frondere

ante gradus sacros cum starent forte locique
narrarent casus, frondere Philemona Baucis,
Baucida conspexit senior frondere Philemon.   715

The sentence consists of an initial *cum* clause that establishes the circumstances, and two parallel indirect statements that explain the same phenomenon with reversed subjects and objects.

Vota fides sequitur: templi tutela fuere,
donec vita data est. Annis aevoque soluti
ante gradus sacros cum starent forte locique
narrarent casus, frondere Philemona Baucis,
Baucida conspexit senior frondere Philemon.   715
Iamque super geminos crescente cacumine vultus
mutua, dum licuit, reddebant dicta "Vale"que
"O coniunx" dixere simul, simul abdita texit
ora frutex. Ostendit adhuc Thyneius illic
incola de gemino vicinos corpore truncos.   720

Eventus respondet desideriis: fuerunt aeditui quamdiu vita concessa est. Confecti annis atque senio cum forte essent ante gradus sacros, et referrent fortunam loci, Baucis vidit Philemon frondescere, Philemon senex Baucidem. Iamque fastigio crescente super utriusque faciem, mutuos commutabant sermones, dum licuit; et dixerunt simul, "Vale consors," simul arbor obduxit ora condita. Incola Thyneius ibi adhuc monstrat stipites propinquos factos ex duobus corporibus.

abditus, -a, -um. hidden, concealed

adhuc (adv.). still

aevum, -i. age

cacumen, cacuminis (n.). height, peak, top

casus, -us. misfortune, accident, mishap, tragedy

conspicio, conspicere, conspexi, conspectus. to catch sight of, to see, to view

cresco, crescere, crevi, cretus. to increase, to develop, to grow

donec (conj.). until, as long as

frondeo, frondere, -, -. to become leafy, to sprout leaves

frutex, fruticis (f.). shrub, bush, greenery, hedge

gradus, -us. slope, grade, step, footstep

illic (adv.). to that place, there

licet, licere, licuit, - (impers.). it is permitted (+ dat.); [*when used with a subjunctive verb following:*] although

mutuus, -a, -um. mutual, common

reddo, reddere, redidi, redditus. to return, to reflect, to mirror

solvo, solvere, solvi, solutus. to loosen, to open, to unravel, to unbind, to release

tego, tegere, texi, tectus. to cover

Thyneius, -a, -um. Bithynian, of or belonging to Bithynia [*Bithynia is a region in Asia Minor, modern-day Turkey, that stretches along its northern coast, where it borders the Black Sea*]

truncus, -i. trunk [*either of a tree or a person, i.e. the torso*]

tutela, -ae. defense, protection, guard

vicinus, -a, -um. neighboring, nearby, near, next to

vultus, -us. face, countenance, appearance, expression

Discussion Questions, lines 711-720

1. What will *donec* in line 712 mean? How does *vita data est* answer the question?
2. What is the significance of the actions of Baucis and Philemon (in lines 713-714) as their transformation begins?
3. Identify how Ovid makes his description of the last moments of Baucis and Philemon (in lines 716-719) cinematic.
4. Why is it important that he *Thyneius incola ostendit* the *vicinos truncos* in lines 719-720? How can *gemino vicinos corpore truncos* be read as an iconic structure or word picture?

721-722. Lelex the narrator reports from where he heard the story of Baucis and Philemon and asserts the validity of his source.

721. **haec.** Not a nominative. Refers to the narrative Lelex just recited.
       non vani = "truthful," "believable." A litotes that literally means "not unreliable."
       neque…vellent. Defending the description of the *senes* as *non vani*.
       neque erat cur = "and there is no reason why"

722-724. Lelex the narrator reports that he himself has seen the trees and has left an offering. He includes a moral to the story to close his narration.

722. **equidem.** Not an accusative but an adverb.
       pendentia. Agrees with the *serta* of 723.
       vidi. Note the change in subject.
723. **serta.** Refers to garlands or offerings left by those who are familiar with the Baucis and Philemon story.
       super ramos. To be read with the *pendentia* of 722.
       recentia. Refers to how Lelex himself left an offering, which also lends validity to his tale.
724. **cura…coluntur** = (illi qui sunt) cura deum sunt di, et (illi) qui coluere (deos) coluntur

Discussion Questions, lines 721-724

1. Identify specific Latin words or phrases that lend credence to Lelex's tale, and explain how they do so.
2. Why is it important that Lelex left something at the two trees (beyond lending validity to his tale)?
3. Identify specific ways in which Ovid uses rhetoric to signal the importance of line 724.
4. Explain the meaning of the *cura…coluntur* of line 724.

Overview Discussion Questions

1. What is the role of nature and natural materials in the Baucis and Philemon story?
2. Identify myths or stories (not necessarily ancient) parallel to the Baucis and Philemon story. Explain the connections between them.
3. Few artistic depictions of Baucis and Philemon focus on their transformation into trees, while a majority of artistic depictions of Daphne focus on her transformation into a tree. Why might this discrepancy exist? What aspect of each story might produce such a focus, or lack of focus?

'Haec mihi non vani (neque erat cur fallere vellent)
narravere senes; equidem pendentia vidi
serta super ramos ponensque recentia dixi:
"Cura deum di sunt, et qui coluere coluntur."'   724

Senes nequaquam mendaces mihi ista retulerunt: neque erat cur vellent mentiri. Equidem vidi corollas pendentes ex ramis; atque affigens novas dixi, "Pii sunt curae Diis, et qui eos honoraverunt honorantur."'

colo, colere, colui, cultus. to cultivate, to worship; to till, to farm

equidem (adv.). indeed

fallo, fallere, fefelli, falsus. to deceive, to trick

neque (conj.). and...not [*equivalent to* et...non; *used with another* nec:] neither...nor

pendeo, pendere, pependi, -. to hang

ramus, -i. branch

recens, recentis. new, recent, recently plucked or picked

senex, senis (adj.). old; [*often used substantively*] old man, old woman

serta, -orum (n. pl.). garland (of flowers), wreath (of flowers)

vanus, -a, -um. empty, foolish, silly, unreliable

Chapter Three

Amoris Difficilia

Amores 1.9	*Amores 1.12*
Amores 1.11	*Pyramus and Thisbe*

Introduction

The classic love story: the smiling couple rides off into the sunset together to live happily ever after. But how often does this happen in real life? Certainly less than the movies would have us believe. And for the elegiac lover, that less-than-idealized reality was a fact of life (even if only poetic life). Trial and pain, often in sharp contrast to expectation and hope, are more common for the elegiac lover; if they weren't, he would have nothing to write about.

Ovid focused on the pain of love in his earlier work, the *Heroides*, in which notable females wrote letters to their male counterparts to vent their frustrations over how they were treated in their relationships. Ovid's *Heroides* are the all-stars of ancient tragic love: Dido, Ariadne, Deianira, Medea, Phaedra. While some of these women's lives end relatively peacefully (Penelope of the *Odyssey*, and perhaps Briseis and Helen of the *Iliad*), most end tragically. Ovid does not imbue the *Amores* with such tragedy; his elegies are not the ponderous love poems of his elegiac predecessors Propertius and Tibullus. *Amores* 1.9, 1.11, and 1.12 will approach the pain of love in less traditional, and less tragic, ways. But in the *Metamorphoses*, where the realm of mythology by definition encompasses fewer intrusions of reality, Ovid explores the pain of love in all of its permutations. Although only the Pyramus and Thisbe story is included in this chapter as an illustration of this theme from the *Metamorphoses*, the Apollo and Daphne story, the Daedalus and Icarus story, and even the Pygmalion story could just as easily have been included.

Ovid surveys the pain of love in three very different ways here. First, in *Amores* 1.9, through an extended metaphor between lover and soldier: each fights his own battle, each faces his own enemies, each struggles similarly. Second, in *Amores* 1.11 and 1.12, Ovid writes to his *puella* and excitedly awaits her reply, only to find that she has rejected his offer. He channels his frustration against the writing tablet that betrayed him with its bad news. Finally, in Ovid's classic tragic love story *Pyramus and Thisbe*, which ultimately will become the inspiration for Shakespeare's *Romeo and Juliet*, the two young lovers, through a tragic misunderstanding, meet a fateful end.

To quote a bad '80s band: "Love Stinks." Indeed it does if one person loves another without reciprocation, or if there are impediments to that love. More broadly speaking, the profound emotional effect that love has makes it inherently problematic. Our lives are predicated on predictability and routine. We take comfort in some basic expectations of what each day will bring. Love inherently interrupts such predictability. And when such predictability is interrupted, only trouble can ensue.

Amores 1.9

Militat omnis amans, et habet sua castra Cupido:
    Attice, crede mihi, militat omnis amans.
Quae bello est habilis, Veneri quoque convenit aetas:
    turpe senex miles, turpe senilis amor.
Quos petiere duces annos in milite forti,   5
    hos petit in socio bella puella viro;
pervigilant ambo; terra requiescit uterque:
    ille fores dominae servat, at ille ducis.
Militis officium longa est via: mitte puellam,
    strenuus exempto fine sequetur amans;   10
ibit in adversos montes duplicataque nimbo
    flumina, congestas exteret ille nives,
nec freta pressurus tumidos causabitur Euros
    aptave verrendis sidera quaeret aquis.
Quis nisi vel miles vel amans et frigora noctis   15
    et denso mixtas perferet imbre nives?
Mittitur infestos alter speculator in hostes,
    in rivale oculos alter, ut hoste, tenet.
Ille graves urbes, hic durae limen amicae
    obsidet; hic portas frangit, at ille fores.   20
Saepe soporatos invadere profuit hostes
    caedere et armata vulgus inerme manu.
Sic fera Threicii ceciderunt agmina Rhesi,
    et dominum capti deseruistis equi.
Nempe maritorum somnis utuntur amantes,   25
    et sua sopitis hostibus arma movent.
Custodum transire manus vigilumque catervas
    militis et miseri semper amantis opus.
Mars dubius, nec certa Venus: victique resurgent,
    quosque neges umquam posse iacere, cadunt.   30
Ergo desidiam quicumque vocabat amorem,
    desinat: ingenii est experientis Amor.
Ardet in abducta Briseide maestus Achilles:
    dum licet, Argeas frangite, Troes, opes;

Hector ab Andromaches conplexibus ibat ad arma,   35
    et galeam capiti quae daret, uxor erat.
Summa ducum, Atrides, visa Priameide, fertur
    Maenadis effusis obstipuisse comis.
Mars quoque deprensus fabrilia vincula sensit:
    notior in caelo fabula nulla fuit.   40
Ipse ego segnis eram discinctaque in otia natus:
    mollierant animos lectus et umbra meos;
impulit ignavum formosae cura puellae,
    iussit et in castris aera merere suis.
Inde vides agilem nocturnaque bella gerentem: 45
    qui nolet fieri desidiosus, amet.

Amores 1.11

Colligere incertos et in ordine ponere crines
    docta neque ancillas inter habenda Nape
inque ministeriis furtivae cognita noctis
    utilis et dandis ingeniosa notis,
saepe venire ad me dubitantem hortata Corinnam,   5
    saepe laboranti fida reperta mihi,
accipe et ad dominam peraratas mane tabellas
    perfer et obstantes sedula pelle moras.
Nec silicum venae nec durum in pectore ferrum
    nec tibi simplicitas ordine maior adest;   10
credibile est et te sensisse Cupidinis arcus:
    in me militiae signa tuere tuae.
Si quaeret quid agam, spe noctis vivere dices;
    cetera fert blanda cera notata manu.
Dum loquor, hora fugit: vacuae bene redde tabellas;   15
    verum continuo fac tamen illa legat.
Aspicias oculos mando frontemque legentis:
    et tacito vultu scire futura licet.
Nec mora, perlectis rescribat multa iubeto:
    odi, cum late splendida cera vacat.   20
Comprimat ordinibus versus, oculosque moretur
    margine in extremo littera rasa meos.
Quid digitos opus est graphio lassare tenendo?
    Hoc habeat scriptum tota tabella "VENI."
Non ego victrices lauro redimire tabellas   25
    nec Veneris media ponere in aede morer.
Subscribam VENERI FIDAS SIBI NASO MINISTRAS
    DEDICAT. AT NUPER VILE FUISTIS ACER.

Amores 1.12

Flete meos casus: tristes rediere tabellae!
    infelix hodie littera posse negat.
Omina sunt aliquid: modo cum discedere vellet,
    ad limen digitos restitit icta Nape.
Missa foras iterum, limen transire memento   5
    cautius atque alte sobria ferre pedem.
Ite hinc, difficiles, funebria ligna, tabellae,
    tuque, negaturis cera referta notis,
quam, puto, de longae collectam flore cicutae
    melle sub infami Corsica misit apis.   10
At, tamquam minio penitus medicata, rubebas:
    ille color vere sanguinulentus erat.
Proiectae triviis iaceatis, inutile lignum,
    vosque rotae frangat praetereuntis onus.
Illum etiam, qui vos ex arbore vertit in usum,   15
    convincam puras non habuisse manus.
Praebuit illa arbor misero suspendia collo,
    carnifici diras praebuit illa cruces;
illa dedit turpes raucis bubonibus umbras,
    vulturis in ramis et strigis ova tulit.   20
His ego commisi nostros insanus amores
    molliaque ad dominam verba ferenda dedi?
Aptius hae capiant vadimonia garrula cerae,
    quas aliquis duro cognitor ore legat;
inter ephemeridas melius tabulasque iacerent,   25
    in quibus absumptas fleret avarus opes.
Ergo ego vos rebus duplices pro nomine sensi:
    auspicii numerus non erat ipse boni.
    Quid precer iratus, nisi vos cariosa senectus
    rodat, et immundo cera sit alba situ?   30

Metamorphoses 4.55 - 166

Pyramus et Thisbe, iuvenum pulcherrimus alter,   55
altera, quas Oriens habuit, praelata puellis,
contiguas tenuere domos, ubi dicitur altam
coctilibus muris cinxisse Semiramis urbem.
Notitiam primosque gradus vicinia fecit;
tempore crevit amor. Taedae quoque iure coissent,   60
sed vetuere patres; quod non potuere vetare,
ex aequo captis ardebant mentibus ambo.
Conscius omnis abest; nutu signisque loquuntur,
quoque magis tegitur, tectus magis aestuat ignis.
Fissus erat tenui rima, quam duxerat olim,   65
cum fieret, paries domui communis utrique.
Id vitium nulli per saecula longa notatum
(quid non sentit amor?) primi vidistis amantes
et vocis fecistis iter, tutaeque per illud
murmure blanditiae minimo transire solebant.   70
Saepe, ubi constiterant hinc Thisbe, Pyramus illinc,
inque vices fuerat captatus anhelitus oris,
"Invide" dicebant "paries, quid amantibus obstas?
Quantum erat, ut sineres toto nos corpore iungi?
Aut, hoc si nimium est, vel ad oscula danda pateres?   75
Nec sumus ingrati: tibi nos debere fatemur
quod datus est verbis ad amicas transitus aures."
Talia diversa nequiquam sede locuti
sub noctem dixere "Vale" partique dedere
oscula quisque suae non pervenientia contra.   80
Postera nocturnos Aurora removerat ignes,
solque pruinosas radiis siccaverat herbas:
ad solitum coiere locum. Tum, murmure parvo
multa prius questi, statuunt ut nocte silenti
fallere custodes foribusque excedere temptent,   85
cumque domo exierint, urbis quoque tecta relinquant.
Neve sit errandum lato spatiantibus arvo,
conveniant ad busta Nini, lateantque sub umbra
arboris: arbor ibi niveis uberrima pomis,
ardua morus, erat, gelido contermina fonti.   90

Pacta placent; et lux, tarde discedere visa,
praecipitatur aquis, et aquis nox exit ab isdem.
    Callida per tenebras, versato cardine, Thisbe
egreditur fallitque suos adopertaque vultum
pervenit ad tumulum, dictaque sub arbore sedit;   95
audacem faciebat amor. Venit ecce recenti
caede leaena boum spumantes oblita rictus,
depositura sitim vicini fontis in unda;
quam procul ad lunae radios Babylonia Thisbe
vidit et obscurum timido pede fugit in antrum,   100
dumque fugit, tergo velamina lapsa reliquit.
Ut lea saeva sitim multa compescuit unda,
dum redit in silvas, inventos forte sine ipsa
ore cruentato tenues laniavit amictus.
    Serius egressus, vestigia vidit in alto   105
pulvere certa ferae, totoque expalluit ore
Pyramus; ut vero vestem quoque sanguine tinctam
repperit, "Una duos" inquit "nox perdet amantes,
e quibus illa fuit longa dignissima vita;
nostra nocens anima est. Ego te, miseranda, peremi,   110
in loca plena metus qui iussi nocte venires
nec prior huc veni. Nostrum divellite corpus
et scelerata fero consumite viscera morsu,
o quicumque sub hac habitatis rupe leones!
Sed timidi est optare necem." Velamina Thisbes   115
tollit, et ad pactae secum fert arboris umbram,
utque dedit notae lacrimas, dedit oscula vesti,
"Accipe nunc" inquit "nostri quoque sanguinis haustus."
Quoque erat accinctus, demisit in ilia ferrum:
nec mora, ferventi moriens e vulnere traxit.   120
Ut iacuit resupinus humo, cruor emicat alte,
non aliter quam cum vitiato fistula plumbo
scinditur, et tenues stridente foramine longe
eiaculatur aquas, atque ictibus aera rumpit.
Arborei fetus aspergine caedis in atram   125
vertuntur faciem, madefactaque sanguine radix
purpureo tingit pendentia mora colore.
    Ecce, metu nondum posito, ne fallat amantem,
illa redit, iuvenemque oculis animoque requirit,

quantaque vitarit narrare pericula gestit.   130
Utque locum et visa cognoscit in arbore formam,
sic facit incertam pomi color: haeret an haec sit.
Dum dubitat, tremebunda videt pulsare cruentum
membra solum retroque pedem tulit oraque buxo
pallidiora gerens exhorruit aequoris instar,   135
quod tremit, exigua cum summum stringitur aura.
Sed postquam remorata suos cognovit amores,
percutit indignos claro plangore lacertos
et, laniata comas amplexaque corpus amatum,
vulnera supplevit lacrimis, fletumque cruori   140
miscuit, et gelidis in vultibus oscula figens
"Pyrame," clamavit, "quis te mihi casus ademit?
Pyrame, responde! Tua te, carissime, Thisbe
nominat; exaudi vultusque attolle iacentes."
Ad nomen Thisbes oculos iam morte gravatos   145
Pyramus erexit visaque recondidit illa.
Quae, postquam vestemque suam cognovit et ense
vidit ebur vacuum, "Tua te manus" inquit "amorque
perdidit, infelix. Est et mihi fortis in unum
hoc manus, est et amor: dabit hic in vulnera vires.   150
Persequar exstinctum, letique miserrima dicar
causa comesque tui, quique a me morte revelli
heu sola poteras, poteris nec morte revelli.
Hoc tamen amborum verbis estote rogati,
o multum miseri meus illiusque parentes,   155
ut quos certus amor, quos hora novissima iunxit,
componi tumulo non invideatis eodem.
At tu, quae ramis arbor miserabile corpus
nunc tegis unius, mox es tectura duorum,
signa tene caedis pullosque et luctibus aptos   160
semper habe fetus, gemini monimenta cruoris."
    Dixit et, aptato pectus mucrone sub imum,
incubuit ferro, quod adhuc a caede tepebat.
Vota tamen tetigere deos, tetigere parentes;
nam color in pomo est, ubi permaturuit, ater,   165
quodque rogis superest, una requiescit in urna.

Amores 1.9 Introduction

In the Apollo and Daphne story, Apollo chides Cupid for playing with the bow and arrow, weapons, according to Apollo, more fitting for a warrior than a young boy. Cupid of course provides Apollo with ample evidence of the power of his arrows, and at the same time Ovid introduces the martial aspect of Cupid and his power. Cupid's arrows can wreak emotional havoc just as Apollo's arrows can kill the mighty Python. In *Amores* 1.9 Ovid further develops the connections between the lover and the soldier, or between love and violence, in an explicit and extended comparison of the two roles.

All's fair in love and war. The universality of the cliche reflects the long tradition of connecting the lover to the solider. Hellenistic Greek literature seems to provide its first real development into a cogent analogy, and Ovid's predecessors utilized it widely. Ovid, however, is the first to develop the analogy between lover and solider into a full poetic treatment. Ovid is the first to carry the analogy through a series of comparisons and situations that comprise the bulk of the poem. There is no narrative proper to *Amores* 1.9, but rather a series of short vignettes that illustrate both the struggles of the lover and the soldier, and the connections between them.

Amores 1.9 then becomes a literary exercise for Ovid: In how many permutations can he illustrate the parallel lives of the soldier and lover? How nuanced can he make distinctions between the two? How many situations can he invent in which they would act or react similarly? Where Ovid's predecessors were satisfied to use the lover-as-soldier comparison for momentary illustrative purposes only, Ovid here develops it into the subject of his entire poem.

It is worth considering here the role of the soldier and the lover in Augustan politics. While the love poetry of Propertius and Tibullus was accepted, if not officially praised, the epic poetry of Vergil that grounded Rome's imperial nature in mythology was certainly preferred by Augustus for its propagandistic potential. The rising prominence of the literary lover, however, could not have pleased Augustus: Aeneas of course conspicuously eschewed his role as lover (to Dido) and Ovid himself would ultimately be exiled for missteps regarding love. Augustus, at least officially, was promoting a Rome in which the (literary) lover would not thrive.

Yet the poem is characteristically ambiguous at its close. Apparently Ovid has written the poem to answer a charge of laziness (lines 41-44; perhaps levelled by the poem's otherwise unknown addressee Atticus), responding that the goads of love are enough to set anyone into action. But Ovid closes the poem with potentially confounding questions: Is he in love only as a way to cure his laziness? Is there any true emotional underpinning to his love, or does it exist for purely practical purposes? It is characteristically Ovidian, especially in the *Amores*, to question the validity of such depths of emotion.

1-2. The dedication and introduction of the poem, where Ovid establishes the subject and parameters of the poem: soliders and lovers have a lot in common.

1.   **militat.** There is no direct object for this verb. What does *omnis amans* do?
        Cupido. Not an ablative.

3-8. The connections between the soldier and the lover are drawn.

3.   **Quae.** Its antecedent is *Veneri* later in the line.
        Veneri. Not the subject.
        aetas. Not an accusative plural.

4.   **turpe…miles, turpe…amor** = turpe (est) senex miles, turpe (est) senilis amor
        turpe, turpe. A neuter substantive of the adjective, describing in a derogatory way what the *senex miles* and the *senilis amor* are.

5-6.   **Quos…viro** = Animos, quos duces petiere in milite forti, hos (animos) bella puella petit in socio viro. Ovid here continues the parallelism between the lover and the soldier by equating the sort of spirit a leader wants in his soldier and the kind of spirit a girl wants in her lover.

5.   **animos.** This is the noun shared by the two clauses. It is the direct object of the *petit* of line 6, and the antecedent of the *quos* in line 5.

6.   **hos.** Emphasizes the parallelism between the two clauses. Here almost equivalent to *tales animos*: "this kind of spirit…"
        bella. Not a form of *bellum, -i.*

7.   **ambo, uterque.** The *miles* and *vir* of the previous lines are now discussed as one.
        terra. Not a nominative. Where will *uterque requiescit?*

8.   **ille, ille.** Separates the *miles* and *vir* again into separate clauses.

Discussion Questions, lines 1-8

1. How do both the first word and the first couplet set the tone for the poem?
2. Scan the first couplet. How does the meter and the repetition of *militat omnis amans* reflect the meaning of the couplet and the theme of the poem?
3. What is the effect of the apostrophe in line 2?
4. How does the *quoque* of line 3 establish the parallelism of the line?
5. What is the effect of the repetition of *turpe* in line 4?
6. What qualities are described in lines 7-8?

Militat omnis amans, et habet sua castra Cupido:
    Attice, crede mihi, militat omnis amans.
Quae bello est habilis, Veneri quoque convenit aetas:
    turpe senex miles, turpe senilis amor.
Quos petiere duces annos in milite forti,   5
    hos petit in socio bella puella viro;
pervigilant ambo; terra requiescit uterque:
    ille fores dominae servat, at ille ducis.

Omnis amator bellum gerit, et Cupido habet sua castra: fidem mihi habe, Attice, omnis amator arma tractat. Anni qui ad bellum sunt apti, apti sunt quoque ad Venerem. Miles senex est res indecora, amor senilis est indecorus. Quam aetatem imperatores voluerunt in strenuo milite, hanc pulchra puella expetit in lecto iugali. Uterque noctes insomnes ducunt: ambo cubant humi. Ille custodit portam dominae, at iste imperatoris.

Atticus, -i (m.). [name: *an otherwise unspecified man to whom Ovid addresses some of his poems*]

bellum, -i. war

bellus, -a, -um. beautiful, charming

convenio, convenire, conveni, conventurus. to be convenient, to be useful

habilis, -e. useful

milito, -are, -avi, -aturus. to be a soldier, to serve as a soldier

pervigilo, -are, -avi, -atus. to keep guard all night, to keep watch all night

requiesco, requiescere, requievi, requietus. to rest, to lie at rest

senex, senis (adj.). old; [*often used substantively*] old man, old woman

senilis, -e. of or belonging to an old person; old man's, old woman's

turpis, -e. foul, disgusting, offensive

uterque, utraque, utrumque. each (of two), both

9-16. The journey that the soldier and lover must undergo is another element that they share. The journey is introduced in lines 9 and 10, and described in terms of its difficulty and challenges in lines 11-16.

9.   **Militis...via** = Officium militis est longa via
      via. Here, likely with its military meaning, "march," but could also be used more figuratively as "road."
      mitte puellam = si puella mittitur
      mitte. With the idea of "introduce" or "reveal."
10.   **exempto fine** = sine fine
      amans. What agrees with this noun? What kind of *amans* will *sequetur exempto fine*?
11.   **ibit.** The subject is still the *amans* of line 10.
      adversos. Refers to the location of the *montes* as the *amans* approaches them.
      duplicata. Agrees with the *flumina* of line 12.
12.   **exteret.** Not an imperfect subjunctive. It is the same tense as the *sequetur* of line 10.
13.   **freta.** The object of *pressurus.*
      pressurus. Agrees with the *amans* of line 10, which is still the subject.
14.   **verrendis aquis.** To be read with *apta.*
      quaeret. Be careful of tense here. It is the same as the *exteret* of line 12.
15.   **et.** Not "and" here but to be read with the *et* of line 16. What does *et...et* mean? What two things would the *miles vel amans perferet*?
16.   **denso imbre.** To be read with *mixtas.*

17-20. The soldier and the lover face their enemies, both people (lines 17-18) and places (lines 19-20).

17.   **mittitur.** With the sense of "sent (out on a mission)."
      alter speculator. Refers to the *miles*, i.e. the military half of the equation.
18.   **rivale.** An accusative parallel to the *infestos hostes* of line 17.
      alter. Refers to the *amans*, i.e. the love half of Ovid's equation.
      ut hoste. To be read with *rivale*, rather than with *alter.*
      tenet. "Hold" will not quite work here. What will this mean with *oculos in rivale*?
19.   **graves urbes.** The object of the *obsidet* of line 20.
      durae. Refers to the refusal of the *amica* to acknowledge the *amans.*
20.   **portas, fores.** The doors (or gates) of a defensive wall versus the doors of a house.

Discussion Questions, lines 9-20

1. How does word placement in line 10 illustrate Ovid's combining of the soldier and the lover?
2. Identify specific words and phrases in lines 11-16 that Ovid uses to make more vivid his description. Why is such vividness especially appropriate for his subject matter here?

Militis officium longa est via: mitte puellam,
    strenuus exempto fine sequetur amans;   10
ibit in adversos montes duplicataque nimbo
    flumina, congestas exteret ille nives,
nec freta pressurus tumidos causabitur Euros
    aptave verrendis sidera quaeret aquis.
Quis nisi vel miles vel amans et frigora noctis   15
    et denso mixtas perferet imbre nives?
Mittitur infestos alter speculator in hostes,
    in rivale oculos alter, ut hoste, tenet.
Ille graves urbes, hic durae limen amicae
    obsidet; hic portas frangit, at ille fores.   20

Munus militis est prolixum iter: ablega puellam; fortis amator sine fine consequetur. Curret in colles oppositos, et torrentia aucta imbribus: ille calcabit nives cumulatas. Nec navigaturus culpabit Euros turgidos; nec requiret astra idonea aquis tranandis. Quis, nisi vel miles vel amator, usque toleret et frigora noctis et nives confusas cum spissis nimbis? Alter dimittitur explorator in hostes infensos: alter defigit oculos in aemulo, tamquam in hoste. Ille oppugnat urbes molestas, hic limen crudelis amicae: hic proterit portas, at ille fores.

adversus, -a, -um. opposite, facing the opposite direction, in front of

aptus, -a, -um. appropriate, easy, apt

causor, causari, causatus. to complain about, to make an excuse of

congestus, -a, -um. accumulated, piled up

duplicatus, -a, -um. doubled, double in size, increased, swollen

Eurus, -i. east wind

eximo, eximere, exemi, exemptus. to remove, to take away

extero, exterere, extivi, exterritus. to crush, to wear down, to compress

finis, finis (m.). limit, boundary, border, end

frango, frangere, fregi, fractus. to break, to shatter

fretum, -i. water, sea, strait, channel

frigor, frigoris (n.). cold, chill, frost

imber, imbris (m.). rain

infestus, -a, -um. savage, violent

limen, liminis (n.). door, threshold

nimbus, -i. cloud

nix, nivis (f.). snow

obsideo, obsidere, obsedi, obsessus. to besiege

perfero, perferre, pertuli, perlatus. to carry through, to deliver

premo, premere, pressi, pressus. to press down, to compress, to touch

quaero, quaerere, quaesivi, quaesitus. to seek, to look for, to ask for

speculator, speculatoris (m.). spy, scout

strenuus, -a, -um. energetic, enthusiastic

tumidus, -a, -um. swollen, grown, expanded

vereor, vereri, veritus. to fear, to be afraid

21-26. The solider lover goes into battle, first invading the enemies' camp and then slaying them. The **Iliad** *is alluded to with the story of Rhesus, whom Odysseus and Diomedes killed, and whose horses deserted him during a nighttime raid when the enemy soldiers were asleep.*

21.   **profuit.** An impersonal verb.

22.   **caedere et = et caedere.** To be read with *profuit*, as *invadere* is.

      armata. Not a nominative singular. With what noun does this agree?

      vulgus. Not a nominative singular. What gender is this noun?

      inerme. Not an ablative singular.

23.   **sic.** Indicates that this clause will be a specific example of what was described in the previous clause.

      Threicii Rhesi. Not a nominative plural. What other case can these be? Whose *fera agmina ceciderunt*?

24.   **dominum.** Not a nominative singular.

      capti equi. A vocative with *deseruistis*.

25.   **maritorum.** To be read with *somnis*.

      utuntur. In what case does this verb takes its object?

26.   **movent.** The subject is still the *amantes* of line 25; it has its military meaning here: "brandish."

27-28. The risk of being caught is introduced.

27-28. **Custodum…opus = Opus (est) militis et miseri semper amantis transire manus custodum vigilumque catervas**

27.   Other than the infinitive *transire*, this line is comprised of a pair of direct objects, each of which has with it a genitive.

      transire. Here with the sense of "to cross in front of" or "to be visible to."

      manus. Here with its military meaning: "band (of men)," "platoon."

28.   **semper.** To be read with *opus (est)*.

      opus. When used with a form of *sum, esse* (usually *est*; here understood), it means "it is necessary for [genitive] to [infinitive]."

29-30. The difficulty of final victory and the need for the soldier-lover to persevere is described.

29.   **Mars…Venus.** Understand an *est* with both of these clauses.

      nec. To be read with *certa* rather than the understood *est*.

      resurgent. Not a present tense verb.

30.   **quos.** Has an understood antecedent (*illi* or *ei*) which is the subject of *cadunt*.

      neges umquam = dicas numquam

      iacere = vinci. *Iaceo* has the connotation of lying down after having been defeated.

Discussion Questions, lines 21-30

1. What is the significance of the allusion to both Rhesus and the *Iliad*?
2. What is the connection of the apostrophe to Rhesus' horses in line 24 to Ovid's subject matter?
3. What is the effect of the alliteration in lines 25-26?
4. How does the placement of *opus* in line 28 at the end of its couplet impact the effect of that couplet?
5. Identify two figures of speech from *Mars…Venus* (there are at least three) in line 29. Why might Ovid call so much rhetorical attention to that clause?

Saepe soporatos invadere profuit hostes
    caedere et armata vulgus inerme manu.
Sic fera Threicii ceciderunt agmina Rhesi,
    et dominum capti deseruistis equi.
Nempe maritorum somnis utuntur amantes,   25
    et sua sopitis hostibus arma movent.
Custodum transire manus vigilumque catervas
    militis et miseri semper amantis opus.
Mars dubius, nec certa Venus: victique resurgent,
    quosque neges umquam posse iacere, cadunt.   30

Saepe utile fuit adoriri hostes sopitos, et mactare vulgus nudum manu armis instructa. Sic acres copiae Rhesi Threicii deletae sunt, et, equi correpti, destituistis dominum. Amantes utuntur saepe sopore maritorum; et concutiunt sua arma hostibus somno oppressis. Effugere globos custodum, et manus excubitorum, est munus militis, et amantis semper miseri. Mars incertus, nec Venus fida; et subacti eriguntur: et quos credas numquam posse interimi, opprimuntur.

caedo, caedere, cecidi, caesus. to attack, to strike, to kill, to slaughter

caterva, -ae. crowd

custos, custodis (m./f.). guard

desero, deserere, deserui, desertus. to desert, to leave

iaceo, iacere, iacui, iaciturus. to lie down, to lie still, to lie motionless

inermis, -e. unharmed

invado, invadere, invasi, invasus. to invade, to attack

maritus, -i. husband

nempe. of course, certainly

opus, operis (n.). work, deed; [*often when used with a form of* sum, esse:] to be necessary

prosum, prodesse, profui, -- (+ dat.). to be useful

resurgo, resurgere, resurrexi, resurrecturus. to rise again

Rhesus, -i (m.). [name: *a Thracian who was an ally of Priam, the king of the Trojans, in the Trojan War; he was killed by Odysseus and Diomedes during their night raid on the Trojan camp*]

sopitus, -a, -um. sleeping, asleep

soporatus, -a, -um. asleep, put to sleep

Threcius, -a, -um. Thracian, of or belonging to Thrace [*a region in the northeastern corner of Greece, on the northern coast of the Aegean Sea*]

umquam (adv.). ever

utor, uti, usus (+ abl.). to use, to take advantage of [*one of the so-called VPUFF verbs: deponents who take their object in the ablative; the term VPUFF comes from the first letters of the verbs: vescor, potior, utor, fungor and fruor (including their compounds)*]

vigil, vigilis (m.). guard, watchman

vulgus, vulgi (n.). crowd, multititude, throng

31-32. Ovid warns against underestimating the power of love.

31.   **desidiam, amorem.** Double accusatives with *vocabat*, i.e. calling one thing another thing.

32.   **desinat.** The clause in line 31 introduced by *quicumque* is the subject of this verb. Be careful of the mood of this verb. It is not indicative.
       ingenii experientis. Genitive of description with *Amor*: "Love is of…" or "Love has…"

33-40. Mythological examples of the mixing of love and war are introduced. See the box below for summaries of their stories.

33.   **in abducta Briseide.** To be read with *maestus*.

34.   **frangite.** Be careful of the mood here.
       Troes. Vocative.
       opes. Here with its military sense: "defenses."

35.   **ab Andromaches complexibus.** Hector was not going "from Andromache" but *ab complexibus Andromaches*.
       ad arma = ad bella

36.   **galeam…erat = (ea) erat uxor quae daret galeam capiti**
       galeam capiti. Grammatically, an accusative direct and dative indirect object with *daret*. But English wouldn't say "give a helmet to his head." What would it say?
       daret. Could be a relative clause of characteristic, i.e. "she was the sort of wife who…", but more likely a relative clause of purpose, i.e. "she was his wife to…"

37.   **summa ducum = summus dux.** To be read in apposition to *Atrides*.
       visa. Not a nominative singular.
       fertur. What does *fero* mean in the passive, especially wih the infinitive *obstipuisse* in 38?

38.   **Maenadis.** Here genitive, but almost with the force of a simile.
       obstipuisse. To be read with the *fertur* of line 37.

The Mythological Allusions of lines 33-40.
All four allusions refer to Homer's *Iliad*, and three of the four come directly from the *Iliad*.

Achilles and Briseis. During the Trojan War, the Greek warrior Achilles captured the girl Briseis in battle. The Greek general Agamemnon also captured a girl in battle, whose father, a priest of Apollo, asked for her return. When Agamemnon refused, Apollo sent a plague upon the Greek army until Agamemnon relented. Because he lost his girl, he took Briseis, the girl of Achilles. Achilles almost killed Agamemnon in anger, but he was restrained by the goddess Athena. Instead, Achilles removed himself from the Trojan War, so that the Greeks would realize how indispensible he was to their success.

Hector and Andromache. Hector, the premier fighter of the Trojans in the Trojan War, was married to Andromache. In Book VI of the *Iliad*, Homer describes Hector's return to war. His son Astyanax is scared by the helmet on Hector's head, and Andromache begs him not to go. It is one of the most poingant scenes in the *Iliad*.

Agamemnon and Cassandra. Agamemnon, the general of the Greek army in the Trojan War, here sees Cassandra, the daughter of Priam, who was cursed with the paradoxical gift of prophecy that no one would heed. He brings Cassandra home with him as a spoil of war and, as described by the Greek tragedian Aeschylus in his play the *Agamemnon*, both are killed by his wife Clytemnestra. Cassandra foresaw the deaths but of course was not heeded.

Mars, Venus, and Vulcan. Venus, the goddess of love, was married to Vulcan, the lame god of the forge, but was having an affair with the war god Mars. Vulcan set a trap to catch them. He wove a net of gold filament so thin that it was invisible, laid it in his bed, and invited the rest of the gods as witnesses. He indeed did trap Venus and Mars, but was ridiculed by Mercury, who quipped that he only wished he could be caught in such a way.

Ergo desidiam quicumque vocabat amorem,
    desinat: ingenii est experientis Amor.
Ardet in abducta Briseide maestus Achilles:
    dum licet, Argeas frangite, Troes, opes;
Hector ab Andromaches complexibus ibat ad arma,   35
    et galeam capiti quae daret, uxor erat.
Summa ducum, Atrides, visa Priameide, fertur
    Maenadis effusis obstipuisse comis.
Mars quoque deprensus fabrilia vincula sensit:
    notior in caelo fabula nulla fuit.   40

Ergo quicumque nominabit amorem segnitiem, id omittat: amor est ingenii multa molientis. Tristis Achilles flagrat in Briseide abrepta. Troiani, proterite vires Argolicas, dum datur. Hector ruebat in arma ab amplexibus Andromaches: et coniunx erat quae aptaret cassidem capiti. Atrides dux ducum dicitur spectata Priameide haesisse in sparsis capillis Maenadis. Mars quoque correptus sensit laqueos fabriles. Nulla fabula fuit magis vulgata caelo.

Achilles, Achillis (m.). [name: *most famous Greek warrior and main character of Homer's* Iliad]

Andromache, Andromaches (f.). [name: *the wife of Hector, who is the most famous Trojan warrior*]

Argeus, -a, -um. Argive; of or belonging to Argus; Greek [*refers to a city in the northeast of the Peloponnese which dominated early Greece and whose name became synonymous with Greece*]

Atrides, Atridae (m.). son of Atreus; *either* Menelaus *or* Agamemnon

Briseis, Briseidos (abl. sing. = Briseide) (f.). [name: *woman whom Achilles claimed as a prize of war, but whom Agamemnon took from Achilles when Agamemnon lost his own war prize; Agamemnon's taking of her resulted in Achilles' withdrawal from the Trojan War*]

coma, -ae. hair

complexus, -us. embrace, hug

deprendo, deprendere, deprendi, deprensus. to seize, to catch

desidia, -ae. laziness, sloth, leisure, idleness

desino, desinere, desivi, desitus. to stop, to cease

effusus, -a, -um. flowing, undone, spread out

experiens, experientis. active

fabrilis, -e. of or beloning to a crafstman; craftsman's, blacksmith's

fero, ferre, tuli, latus. to bring, to bear, to carry, to endure; fertur: "it is said" [*used with an infinitive*]

galea, -ae. helmet

Hector, Hectoris (m.). [name: *the most famous Trojan warrior, who is eventually killed by Achilles*]

Maenas, Maenadis (f.). Maenad [*female follower, characterized by her crazed devotion to the god of wine, Bacchus or Dionysius*]

maestus, -a, -um. sad, weary

obstipesco, obstipescere, obstipui, -. to be amazed, to be (dumb)struck, to be (awe)struck, to be stunned

ops, opis (f.). power, ability, aid, assistance, wealth

Priameis, Priameidos (f. patron.; abl. = Priameide). daughter of Priam

quicumque, quaecumque, quodcumque. whoever, whatever

Tros, Trois (m.; nom. & voc. pl. = Troes). Trojan

Discussion Questions, lines 31-40

1. What is the effect of the apostrophe in line 34? Why address the Trojans directly?

2. Why use *fertur* in line 37? What about this allusion might require the sort of narrative distance that this word creates?

3. Why might Ovid make the statement that he makes in line 40 (consider also that it is entirely Ovid's invention; he certainly does not know which *fabulae* are *notiores in caelo*)?

4. How do the allusions in lines 33-40 fit the theme of the poem?

5. Why might Ovid connect the allusions in lines 33-40 so closely to the *Iliad*?

41-45. Ovid claims that he is naturally lazy, and that the only thing that pushes him to action is the battle he wages over love.

41. **segnis.** Not a dative or ablative plural.

43. **ignavum** = ignavum (me)

 formosae. Not nominative and does not modify *cura*.

44. **iussit et** = et iussit

 iussit. The subject is still the *cura* of line 43.

 aera. Here a synecdoche for "military pay" or "wages." Does it make more sense as the object of *iussit* or of *merere*?

45. **agilem, gerentem** = (me) agilem, (me) gerentem

 gerentem. What will this mean with the object *bella*?

46. The moral of the story, where Ovid generalizes the message of the previous five lines to his readers.

46. **qui.** Has an understood, generalized antecedent who will be the subject of *amet*.

 amet. Be careful about the mood of this verb. It is not indicative.

Discussion Questions, lines 41-46

1. How does the *ipse* of line 41 serve as a transition into this final part of the poem?

2. How do lines 41-44 lack romance? What reason does Ovid give for his pursuit of his girl? What are the implications of line 44 for the previous question?

3. Explain the moral of the poem as articulated in line 46.

Ipse ego segnis eram discinctaque in otia natus:
    mollierant animos lectus et umbra meos;
impulit ignavum formosae cura puellae,
    iussit et in castris aera merere suis.
Inde vides agilem nocturnaque bella gerentem: 45
    qui nolet fieri desidiosus, amet.

Ipse ego deses eram, et genitus in otia dissoluta: lectus et umbra enervaverant mea pectora. Amor pulchrae puellae excitavit desidiosum; et imperavit stipendia facere in castris suis. Inde cernis me alacrem et moventem arma nocturna. Qui nolet fieri segnis, amet.

aes, aeris (n.). copper, bronze, metal; currency, money

agilis, -e. swift, quick, agile, nimble

cura, -ae. care, concern

desidiosus, -a, -um. idle, lazy

discinctus, -a, -um. relaxed, easy-going, unbound, loosely-fitting

formosus, -a, -um. handsome, beautiful

ignavus, -a, -um. cowardly, lazy

impello, impellere, impuli, impulsus. to strike against, to beat, to compel

inde (adv.). from there, next

lectus, -i. bed, couch

mereo, merere, merui, meritus. to deserve, to earn

mollio, mollire, mollivi, mollitus. to make soft, to grow soft, to soften, to make pliable

nascor, nasci, natus. to be born

nolo, nolle, nolui, -. to not want

otium, -i. leisure

segnis, -e. lazy, sluggish

Amores 1.11 and 1.12 Introduction

Blame. Where does it lie when things go wrong? Especially when things that are out of our control go wrong? Someone who trips might jokingly blame the doorstep over which he tripped. An athlete might blame the ball or her equipment for a missed shot. Writers might vent their frustration on their pen or computer when the words stop coming. Ovid, in these two poems, does exactly that. Rather than see the real forces at work that impeded his relationship, he blames that insignificant object that was the bearer of bad news.

The two poems form what is called a diptych: a two-panelled hinged unit for writing or illustration that can be open or closed. In its literary context, it refers to pairs of poems that form a single narrative unit, i.e. the second poem continues or responds to the first one. Ovid has bid the maid of his *puella* to bring her a note that asks her to meet him. The first poem of the diptych closes with the text of Ovid's note. The second poem finds Ovid distraught over having received a negative response to his request; his *puella* has turned him down. The second poem then becomes an extended invective against the writing tablet itself. It is the object that bore Ovid's note and his *puella*'s response that receives Ovid's wrath.

Amores 1.11 is divided in half. In the first section, up to line 14, Ovid entreats Corinna's servant, a woman named Nape, to do for him what he wishes. Ovid flatters her, Ovid sympathizes with her, Ovid encourages her. Ovid will do anything to ensure that his note is delivered. The second half of the poem anticipates *Amores* 1.12 by speculating on both Corinna's reaction to receiving the note and her potential responses to it. Ovid even swears to dedicate the tablet to Venus should he receive a positive outcome. Ovid

very deliberately establishes his naïve enthusiasm to intensify the antithetical tone of the companion poem.

Amores 1.12 opens unequivocally. Ovid makes clear from the first three words the result of his request, and it is not good. In the first couplet, Ovid explains what has happened. In the next two couplets, he briefly blames Nape for tripping over the doorstep on her way to deliver the note. The rest of the poem, twenty-four lines, is dedicated to Ovid's outpouring of negative energy toward the tablet itself.

Ovid's poetic diptych is iconic, i.e. its physical layout mimics its meaning: as Ovid the character writes to and then awaits a reply from Corinna, so does Ovid the author write a poem about the act of writing and a companion poem about Corinna's reply. But in the reply appears Ovid's characteristic ambiguity. Where we would expect Ovid to blame Corinna for her negative response, he instead blames the tablets themselves. Where we would expect Ovid to lament the state of his relationship, instead he remains silent about it. Corinna's absence from *Amores* 1.12 begs the question: does Ovid not blame Corinna to reinforce his role as the atypical elegiac lover, able to accept such a rejection without appearing desperate? Or does Ovid not blame Corinna for just the opposite reason, out of a naïve avoidance of the truth about his relationship? Or, does Ovid use his extended focus on the tablet as an extended metaphor for Corinna herself? The answer to any of these questions lies in large part in how we read Ovid as an elegiac poet and lover. But the very fact that Ovid requires so much of us in interpreting these two poems is both his most frustrating and his most impressive quality as a poet.

*1-6. Ovid introduces the addressee of the poem, a certain Nape, a slave of his **puella** Corinna. Nape, in an elaborate vocative expression, is described in admirable and flattering terms, as she is the way for Ovid to access his **puella**.*

1.   **colligere, ponere.** To be read with the *docta* of line 2.
      incertos. "Uncertain" won't really work here. How are Nape's *crines* arranged?
2.   **docta.** Here, "adept at" or "skilled at" with the infinitives *colligere* and *ponere*.
      ancillas inter = inter ancillas
      habenda. With the sense that she is useful or worth keeping.
3.   **in ministeriis.** To be read with *cognita*; we might say "for" for *in*.
      furtivae noctis. To be read with *ministeriis*.
4.   **utilis.** To be read with *cognita* with an understood *esse* connecting them.
5.   **saepe.** To be read with *hortata*.
6.   **saepe.** To be read with *reperta*.
      fida. To be read with *reperta* with an understood *esse* connecting them.
      laboranti. Refers to Ovid's attempt to win Corinna.

7-8. Ovid finally tells Nape what he wants her to do: take a letter, deliver it to Corinna, and wait for her reply.

7.   **accipe.** Finally, the main verb.
      mane. Not an imperative but the adverb, and to be read with *peraratas*.
8.   **sedula.** Agrees with the subject of the imperative *pelle*. English often prefers adjectives that modify a nominative pronoun (or here unstated subject) to be adverbs.
      pelle obstantes moras. Refers to Ovid's desire for Nape not to delay and for a quick response to his missive.

Sentence Diagram, lines 1-8

Nape
    docta
                colligere
                            incertos crines in ordine
                ponere
    habenda
                inter ancillas
    cognita
                in ministeriis
                            furtivae noctis
    utilis
    ingeniosa
                dandis notis
    hortata
                dubitantem Corinnam
                            venire
                                ad me
    fida
    reperta
                laboranti mihi
accipe..
perfer…
pelle…

Colligere incertos et in ordine ponere crines
        docta neque ancillas inter habenda Nape
inque ministeriis furtivae cognita noctis
        utilis et dandis ingeniosa notis,
saepe venire ad me dubitantem hortata Corinnam,   5
        saepe laboranti fida reperta mihi,
accipe et ad dominam peraratas mane tabellas
        perfer et obstantes sedula pelle moras.

The sentence is comprised simply of a subject (*Nape*) and three main verbs (*accipe, perfer,* and *pelle*). Everything before *accipe* either modifies *Nape* or is to be read with something that modifies *Nape*. The bold words modify *Nape*; the words or phrases indented below the bold words are to be read with the bold words.

Amores 1.11

Colligere incertos et in ordine ponere crines
　　docta neque ancillas inter habenda Nape
inque ministeriis furtivae cognita noctis
　　utilis et dandis ingeniosa notis,
saepe venire ad me dubitantem hortata Corinnam,　　　　　　　5
　　saepe laboranti fida reperta mihi,
accipe et ad dominam peraratas mane tabellas
　　perfer et obstantes sedula pelle moras.

Nape, perita cogere et componere capillos turbatos, neque reponenda in famularum numero; et inventa indonea in servitiis noctis clandestinae; et callida in edendis signis; saepe hortata Corinnam haesitantem ad me proficisci; saepe inventa fidelis mihi dolenti; corripito et deferto ad dominam tabellas mane perscriptas; et tolle diligens moras importunas.

ancilla, -ae. slave woman

cognosco, cognoscere, cognovi, cognotus. to recognize, to learn; [*in the perfect tense*] to know

colligo, colligere, collegi, collectus. to assemble, to gather, to collect

Corinna, -ae. [name: *the name of Ovid's love and the subject of his love poetry*]

furtivus, -a, -um. furtive, secret

hortor, hortari, hortatus. to encourage

ingeniosus, -a, -um. clever, gifted

laboro, -are, -avi, -atus. to work

mane (adv.). in the morning, early

ministerium, -i. activity, duty

mora, -ae. delay, wait, pause; [*sometimes used with a negative to mean:*] without delay

Nape, Napes (f.). [name: *the servant of Ovid's girlfriend Corinna*]

obsto, obstare, obstiti, obstaturus (+ dat.). to obstruct, to be in the way of, to stand in the way of, to hinder, to prevent

pello, pellere, pepuli, pulsus. to strike, to beat, to beat away, to banish

peraro, -are, -avi, -atus. to plow through, to inscribe, to write on

perfero, perferre, pertuli, perlatus. to carry through, to deliver

reperio, reperire, repperi, repertus. to find, to discover, to come upon

sedulus, -a, -um. deliberate, painstaking, attentive, focused

tabella, -ae. tablet, writing tablet

Discussion Questions, lines 1-8

1. What image is created by opening the poem with the *colligere* of line 1? How does this image represent the difference between the reality of Nape's existence and the way Ovid imagines her carrying out his task?

2. What is the significance of the *ancillas inter* of line 2?

3. What is the ambiguity implicit in line 3?

4. What is the effect of the juxtaposition of the *dubitantem hortata Corinnam* in line 3?

5. What is the effect of postponing for so long the imperative *accipe* in line 7?

6. To what extent in lines 1-7 is Ovid flattering Nape, and to what extent are these perhaps backhanded compliments? Explain your answer.

9-10. Ovid characterizes Nape first by suggesting that she is not cold and unfeeling, and second by mentioning her overarching simplicity.

9. **silicum.** Not an accusative singular. What declension is this noun?
   venae. Nominative plural subject of *adest.* The verb is singular because the closest of its three subjects is singular.

10. **tibi.** Dative of possession with *adest*: "…are present in you."
    simplicitas ordine maior. A very subtle phrase, but one whose subtlety is not entirely clear. Is this a veiled insult, as Ovid says that Nape's simplicity is greater than those in her class? Or is it a subtle compliment, as Ovid says conversely that her discretion is greater? The exact implication of *simplicitas* is unclear.

11-12. Ovid equates his position to Nape's: they are both soliders, but soldiers of love.

11. **arcus.** Not a nominative singular. What has Nape *sensisse*?
12. **tuere.** The passive imperative (of a deponent), here meaning "defend" or "accept."

13-14. The focus now shifts to Corinna. Ovid encourages Nape to flatter Corinna for him: he can't wait to see her; he's sent a flattering note to her.

13. **quaeret.** Corinna becomes the subject.
    quid agam. Here the idiom "how I'm doing."
    spe noctis. Why does Ovid *vivere*? What are the implications of *spe noctis*? What does Ovid hope for?
    vivere = (me) vivere
    dices. Be careful of tense here. This is not present.

14. **cetera.** A neuter substantive object of *fert.*
    cera notata. Refers to the tablet which Ovid has written and wants delivered.
    blanda. Agrees with *manu.*

15-19. Ovid begins to get antsy. He wants the letter delivered quickly so Corinna can read it, and wants Nape to note how Corinna reacts to reading it.

15. **vacuae = vacuae (dominae).** Here dative rather than genitive, referring to Corinna being alone so that she can properly read Ovid's letter.
16. **fac illa legat.** "Make it that she read (it)" or "Make her read (it)." The subjunctive following *facere* indicates cause.
17. **Aspicias…legentis = Mando (ut) aspicias oculos (Corinnae) frontemque (Corinnae) legentis.** Ovid wants Nape to register how Corinna reacts (via her eyes and forehead) as she reads his message.
18. **et = etiam**
    futura. The neuter substantive object of *scire.*

Discussion Questions, lines 9-18

1. What three Latin words in line 9 create imagery? Explain the imagery.
2. What approach does Ovid take towards convincing Nape in lines 11-12?
3. What is the significance of the *si* in line 13? What is Ovid's implied concern?
4. How does Ovid characterize himself in lines 13-18? Identify specific Latin words or phrases to support your answer.
5. What is Ovid assuming in lines 17-18? Is he justified in such an assumption? Explain your answer.

Nec silicum venae nec durum in pectore ferrum
    nec tibi simplicitas ordine maior adest;   10
credibile est et te sensisse Cupidinis arcus:
    in me militiae signa tuere tuae.
Si quaeret quid agam, spe noctis vivere dices;
    cetera fert blanda cera notata manu.
Dum loquor, hora fugit: vacuae bene redde tabellas;   15
    verum continuo fac tamen illa legat.
Aspicias oculos mando frontemque legentis:
    et tacito vultu scire futura licet.

Nec venae saxorum nec durum ferrum in pectore, nec simplicitas tibi inest maior tua sorte. Verisimile est te etiam expertam esse tela amoris. Defende in me signa tuae militiae. Si petat quid faciam; respondebis vitam ducere spe noctis. Tabellae miti manu scriptae indicant reliqua. Dum loquor, tempus effluit. Apte tradito litteras otiosae: verum fac tamen illa legat protinus. Iubeo intuearis oculos et vultum legentis.

ago, agere, egi, actus. to do, to drive, to discuss

arcus, -us. bow

blandus, -a, -um. flattering, encouraging, enticing, inviting

continuo (adv.). immediately

credibilis, -e. believable, credible

frons, frontis (f.). forehead

mando, -are, -avi, -atus. to entrust, to hand over; [*with* ut:] to request, to demand

militia, -ae. military service

noto, -are, -avi, -atus. to note, to mark, to scribe, to mar; to recognize, to know

perlego, perlegere, perlegi, perlectus. to read completely, to read through

silex, silicis (m.). hard rock, stone

simplicitas, simplicitatis (f.). simplicity, unity, sincerity

tacitus, -a, -um. quiet

tueor, tueri, tuitus. to look at, to gaze at, to protect, to defend

vacuus, -a, -um. empty, hollow; alone, without company; devoid of (+ abl.)

vena, -ae. vein, blood-vessel, blood

verum (conj.). but

vultus, -us. face, countenance, appearance, expression

19-20. Ovid wants Corinna to write back quickly; he hates an empty tablet.

19.　　nec mora = sine mora
　　　　perlectis = (tabellis) perlectis
　　　　rescribat multa iubeto = iubeto (ut illa) rescribat multa.
　　　　multa. The neuter plural substantive accusative object of *rescribat*.
20.　　late splendida cera vacat. In direct juxtaposition to the *multa* of 19: as Ovid wants her to *rescribat multa*,
　　　　so too would he detest an empty tablet in response.
　　　　late. An adverb here referring to the expanse (width) of the tablet.

*21-24. Ovid first envisions Corinna's reply as filled with words, even in the margins, but ultimately decides that
he would prefer a single word for a reply: an invitation for him to join her.*

21.　　comprimat. Corinna is still the subject. What mood is this verb?
　　　　ordinibus. Refers to how the *versus* are arranged on the *tabella*.
　　　　versus. Here refers to lines written on the *tabella* in response, instead of the perhaps more common lines
　　　　of poetry.
　　　　moretur. The subject is the *littera* of 22. What mood is this verb? With *oculos* as the object, "remain" or
　　　　"delay" won't quite work.
22.　　margine in extremo. Refers to little notes that Corinna might have written.
　　　　rasa. Likely here "written" or "inscribed" rather than "erased," as Ovid envisions Corinna's reply.
23.　　quid = cur
　　　　digitos = (meos) digitos
　　　　opus est. What is the idiom here?
　　　　graphio tenendo. Why would Ovid's *digitos lassare*?
24.　　hoc scriptum. Refers to the single word response he hopes for: *veni*; the *hoc* especially anticipates the
　　　　identification of the specific message.

*25-28. Ovid now glorifies the tablets for their anticipated success and good service. First he equates them to a
victorious general returning and rewarded with laurel, and finally he dedicates them to Venus.*

25.　　victrices. Describes *tabellas*.
　　　　redimire. To be read (along with the *ponere* of 26) with the *morer* of 26.
26.　　Veneris. To be read with *aede*.
　　　　media. Agrees with *aede*.
　　　　ponere = ponere (tabellas)
　　　　morer. Potential subjunctive.
27.　　sibi. Dative of possession with *ministras*.
　　　　Naso. Not a dative / ablative.
　　　　ministras. Refers to the *tabellas*. Ovid here personifies them by making them his servants.
28.　　vile. Not an ablative singular. What gender is *acer*?

Discussion Questions, lines 19-28

1. What is the implication of the *iubeto* of line 19? Why might Nape have to *iubeto* Corinna?
2. Ovid likely has in mind in line 20, with *odi* as the opening word, Catullus' short poem 85:
   > *Odi et amo. Quare id faciam, fortasse requiris.*
   > *Nescio, sed fieri sentio et excrucior.*

   Why might Ovid be recalling Catullus' poem here? What are the connections between the two?
3. What reasons in lines 21-24 does Ovid give for first wanting Corinna to write a lot, and then for her to
   write only one word?
4. What is the effect of the personification of the *tabellas* in lines 25-26? Why do they become a holy object?
5. What is the irony of the inscription that closes the poem? What might we expect the inscription to be?

Nec mora, perlectis rescribat multa iubeto:
    odi, cum late splendida cera vacat.   20
Comprimat ordinibus versus, oculosque moretur
    margine in extremo littera rasa meos.
Quid digitos opus est graphio lassare tenendo?
    Hoc habeat scriptum tota tabella "VENI."
Non ego victrices lauro redimire tabellas   25
    nec Veneris media ponere in aede morer.
Subscribam VENERI FIDAS SIBI NASO MINISTRAS
    DEDICAT. AT NUPER VILE FUISTIS ACER.

Licet prospicere futura ex ore silente. Et statim, admoneto plurima rescribat perlectis. Doleo cum cera nitida late est vacua. Denset versus ordinibus, et litera exarata in ultima ora detineat meos oculos. Quid opus est fatigare digitos stylo eum tractando? Integra tabella contineat hoc exaratum, "Adesto." Ego non cunctabor coronare tabellas victrices lauro, nec collocare in medio templo Veneris. Subscribam, "Naso sacras facit famulas fideles Veneris: at non ita pridem fuistis acer minimi pretii."

acer, acris (n.). maple tree, maple wood

aedes, aedis (f.). temple, shrine

at (conj.). but, and so, still [*an adversative conjunction that often signals a shift in the story or sense*]

comprimo, comprimere, compressi, compressus. to compress, to condense

extremus, -a, -um. outer edge, side

graphium, -i. stylus, writing implement, "pencil"

lasso, -are, -avi, -atus. to fatigue, to wear out, to tire

late (adv.). far and wide

laurus, -i (f.). laurel tree, laurel branch, sprig of laurel

margo, marginis (m.). edge, border, margin

ministra, -ae. maid, female servant

moror, morari, moratus. to delay, to wait, to remain

Naso, Nasonis (m.). [name: *Ovid's cognomen*]

nuper. recently

odi, odisse (defec.). to hate

perlego, perlegere, perlegi, perlectus. to read completely, to read through

rado, radere, rasi, rasus. to scrape, to wipe; to pass closely, to sneak around

redimio, redimire, redimii, redimitus. to wreathe, to encircle

subscribo, subscribere, subscripsi, subscriptus. to write underneath, to append

vaco, -are, -avi, -atus. to be empty, to be free, to be vacant

Venus, Veneris (f.). [name; *the Roman goddess of love, also used by metonymy for love itself*]

victrix, victricis (f.). female victor

vilis, -e. cheap, inferior, lowly

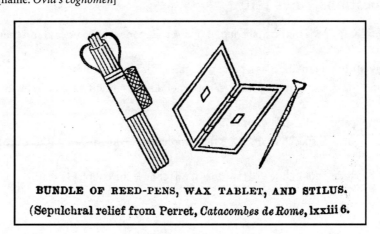

BUNDLE OF REED-PENS, WAX TABLET, AND STILUS.
(Sepulchral relief from Perret, *Catacombes de Rome*, lxxiii 6.

1-2. Ovid introduces the connection between this poem and the previous poem: the request he sent to Corinna via her servant Nape has been rejected.

1.   **casus.** Not a nominative singular. What declension is this word? And so what case is it?
2.   **posse.** Its subject is the request from the letter of 1.11, that Ovid wants Corinna to tell him "*Veni;*" he has now found out that she (via the *tabella*) *negat posse*.

3-6. Ovid blames the rejection on a bad omen that occurred as Nape was leaving for Corinna's house: she tripped over the doorstep.

3.   **omina.** Not *omnia*.
      sunt. Here with the sense of "mean."
      discedere. Refers to Nape leaving Ovid (or Ovid's house) to deliver the *tabella* of 1.11
      vellet. With the sense of being ready (moreso than wanting).
4.   **ad limen.** To be read with *digitos icta*, or the object of a passive verb used in a middle sense, but likely also to be read with *restitit*.
      digitos. An accusative of respect with *icta*, and here "toes" instead of "fingers."
      icta. What did Nape do *ad limen* to her *digitos*? What is the English expression?
5.   **Missa foras iterum.** Refers to how Nape tries again after the mishap of the first attempt.
      limen transire. Refers to clearing the threshold cleanly instead of tripping over it as she did before.
      memento. The future imperative, equivalent in meaning to a present imperative, but with a softened tone, here perhaps used sarcastically.
6.   **cautius.** To be read with *transire*.
      alte. How should Nape *ferre pedem* to avoid tripping?
      sobria. Agrees with Nape, the subject of *memento*.

7-10. Ovid addresses directly both the tablets and the wax that contained the message, including with his address to the wax a description of its origin.

7.   **ite.** Not *ita* ("thus," "in this way") but the imeperative of *eo, ire*.
      difficiles tabellae. A vocative with the imperative *ite*.
      funebria ligna. In apposition to *difficiles tabellae*.
8.   **cera.** Refers to the *tu*. Ovid personifies both the *tabellae* in the previous line, and here the wax in which the message was written.
9-10. **quam...apis =** quam, collectam de flore longae cicutae sub infami melle, puto, Corsica apis misit.
10.   **melle sub infami.** The honeycomb (*melle*) has sunk to the bottom of whatever collection vessel is being used.
      Corsica apis. Corsican honey in the ancient world was known for its bitterness.

Discussion Questions, lines 1-10

1. Identify specific Latin words in the first couplet that set the tone for the poem (and that respond to the previous poem).
2. Why does Ovid cite *omina* in line 3 as a potential reason for his bad news?
3. How does *cautius* in line 6 create suspense? What other adverbs might have been expected given Ovid's mood?
4. What are the implications of *sobria* in line 6?
5. Identify specific figures of speech in lines 7-8 that emphasize Ovid's attitude (there are at least three). Explain how they do so.
6. Why does Ovid include *puto* in line 9? How does it affect how the couplet is read?

Amores 1.12

Flete meos casus: tristes rediere tabellae!
  infelix hodie littera posse negat.
Omina sunt aliquid: modo cum discedere vellet,
  ad limen digitos restitit icta Nape.
Missa foras iterum, limen transire memento   5
  cautius atque alte sobria ferre pedem.
Ite hinc, difficiles, funebria ligna, tabellae,
  tuque, negaturis cera referta notis,
quam, puto, de longae collectam flore cicutae
  melle sub infami Corsica misit apis.   10

Lugete meam calamitatem: lugubres tabellae reverterunt. Flebilis epistula negat posse hodie. Praesagia sunt aliquid: cum modo Nape vellet proficisci, haesit illisa pedes ad limen. Recorderis missa denuo foras transgredi limen prudentius; et sobria pedem tollere. Discedite, morosae tabellae, lignum triste: et tu, cera, plena lineis abnuentibus: quam arbitror coactam de flore procerae cicutae apis Corsica digessit sub melle famoso.

altus, -a, -um. high, deep
apis, apis (f.). bee
casus, -us. misfortune, accident, mishap, tragedy
cautus, -a, -um. cautious, careful
cicuta, -ae. hemlock, hemlock plant
Corsicus, -a, -um. of or belonging to Corsica, Corsican [the northernmost of two large islands off of Italy's west coast, Corsica belonging to France, and Sardinia, to its south, belonging to Italy]
digitus, -i. finger, toe
discedo, discedere, discessi, discessurus. to depart, to leave
fleo, flere, flevi, fletus. to weep
flos, floris (m.). flower
foras (adv.). outside
funebris, -e. of or belonging to a funeral, funeral

hinc (adv.). from here, next; [with illinc] on this side
icio, icere, ici, ictus. to strike, to beat
infamis, -e. infamous, notorious, of ill repute
iterum (adv.). again and again, over and over, repeatedly
lignum, -i. wood, bark
limen, liminis (n.). door, threshold
mel, mellis (n.). honey
memini, meminisse (defec.). to remember
Nape, Napes (f.). [name: the servant of Ovid's girlfriend Corinna]
refertus, -a, -um. packed (with), stuffed (with)
resisto, resistere, restiti, -. to stop, to pause, to halt, to cause to stop
sobrius, -a, -um. sober

11-12. As Ovid described the origin of the wax in the previous couplet, he now creates a negative explanation for its red color.

11.   **minio.** Refers to the red color with which the wax was dyed.

        medicata. Agrees with the "you" of *rubebas*, still the *cera* from line 8.

12.   **ille color** = ille color (cerae)

        sanguinulentus. In contrast to the *minio* of line 11: while cinnabar was the customary means to dye something red, Ovid suggests that, because of the negative message from Corinna that the *tabellae* deliver, its wax gets its color from blood.

*13-14. Ovid imagines a fittingly nasty end for his now detested **tabellae**: he imagines them run over and shattered by the wheel of a wagon.*

13.   **proiectae.** Agrees with the understood *tabellae*, which are also the subject of *iaceatis*.

        triviis. Here with a negative connotation. The image is similar to us tossing something out of a car window in frustration.

        iaceatis. Be careful of mood here. What does that *-ea-* signify?

        inutile lignum. In apposition to the understood *tabellae*.

14.   **vos.** Still the *tabellae*, but here no longer nominative.

        rotae praetereuntis onus. The image here is of a cart wheel crushing the *tabellae*, the *onus* referring to the weight of the cart transferred to its *rotae*.

        frangat. The mood here, as with the *iaceatis* of 13, distinguishes between a cart wheel that will crush the *tabellae* versus a cart wheel that Ovid hopes will (but may not) crush the *tabellae*.

        onus. Not an accusative here. What other case can it be?

*15-16. Ovid now turns his attention to the origin of the **tabellae**: the tree from which they were made. He begins with the man who cut the tree down: he could not have been pure to have created such impure **tabellae**.*

15-16. **illum…manus** = Convincam illum, qui vertit vos ex arbore in usum, non habuisse puras manus

15.   **illum.** The subject accusative of the indirect statement introduced by *convincam* (and not the main subject of the sentence).

        ex arbore in usum. Describes the process of making the *tabellae*: they began as an *arbor* and were turned *in usum* as *tabellae*.

16.   **convincam.** Unlike the *iaceatis* and *frangat* of 13 and 14, likely here a future indicative instead of a subjunctive.

*17-20. Ovid imagines the awful uses of the wood which was used to make the **tabellae**: as the tree was used for such negative purposes, so it makes sense that the wood that comes from it would have treated Ovid so poorly.*

17.   **misero collo.** Dative with *praebuit*.

        suspendia. Refers to the tree branch from which criminals are hanged.

18.   **illa** = illa (arbor), the same as in line 17.

        carnifici. Dative with *praebuit*.

20.   **volturis.** To be read with *ova*.

        tulit = illa (arbor) tulit

Discussion Questions, lines 11-20

1. Why does *sanguinulentus* stand out in line 2? Why might Ovid have made it so prominent?

2. How does *sanguinulentus* in line 2 maintain Ovid's tone from the previous couplet?

3. How does Ovid's attitude towards the tablets intensify in lines 13-14?

4. How do lines 15-20 connect to the *omina* of line 3?

5. Could the *illum* of line 15 refer obliquely to Ovid himself (and the *collo* of line 17 to Ovid's neck)? Explain your answer.

At, tamquam minio penitus medicata, rubebas:
    ille color vere sanguinulentus erat.
Proiectae triviis iaceatis, inutile lignum,
    vosque rotae frangat praetereuntis onus.
Illum etiam, qui vos ex arbore vertit in usum,   15
    convincam puras non habuisse manus.
Praebuit illa arbor misero suspendia collo,
    carnifici diras praebuit illa cruces;
illa dedit turpes raucis bubonibus umbras,
    vulturis in ramis et strigis ova tulit.   20

At prorsus rubebas tamquam illita minio. Ille color erat vere cruentus. Abiectae tabellae iaceatis lignum futile in triviis, et pondus rotae transeuntis vos proterat. Probare etiam possim illum qui vos accommodavit ad usum ex trunco, non habuisse manus insontes. Illud lignum pro patibulo fuit collo infelici: illud suppeditavit saevas cruces tortori. Illa arbor praebuit obscenas umbras raucis bubonibus: habuit ora vulturis et strigis in ramis.

bubo, bubonis (m.). owl, horned owl

carnifex, carnificis (m.). killer, executioner

collum, -i. neck

convinco, convincere, convici, convictus. to overcome; [*when used with an infinitive*] to prove

crux, crucis (f.). cross

dirus, -a, -um. grim, awful, dire, horrible

iaceo, iacere, iacui, iaciturus. to lie down, to lie still, to lie motionless

inutilis, -e. useless

lignum, -i. wood, bark

medicatus, -a, -um. medicated, treated; dyed [*as in a color*]

minium, -i. cinnabar [*a vibrant reddish-orange mineral that was used as both a dye and a medicine*]

ovum, -i. egg

penitus (adv.). completely, thoroughly

praebeo, praebere, praebui, praebitus. to offer, to furnish, to show, to display

praetereo, praeterire, praeterii / -ivi, praeteritus. to move past, to go beyond, to transcend

proicio, proicere, proieci, proiectus. to eject, to throw out, to expel

ramus, -i. branch

raucus, -a, -um. loud, raucous, noisy, noticeable

rota, -ae. wheel, revolution, circle

rubeo, rubere, -, -. to become red, to redden, to turn red

sanguinulentus, -a, -um. bloody, red

strix, strigis (f.). screech owl [*a bird often associated with bad omens*]

suspendium, -i. the act of hanging [*referring specifically to suicide*]

tamquam. as if

trivium, -i. crossroad

turpis, -e. foul, disgusting, offensive

vere (adv.). truly

verto, vertere, verti, versus. to turn, to spin

vultur, vulturis (m.). vulture

21-22. Ovid becomes incredulous that he even sent the letter in the first place.

21.   **his.** Refers to the *tabellae*. How did *ego commisi*?
22.   **ad dominam.** To be read with *ferenda* rather than with *dedi*.
       dedi. Understand the *his* of line 21 with this verb also.

23-26. Ovid realizes that his wax would better serve not for a love letter but rather for a more pedestrian use, either a summons to court or an account book.

23.   **aptius.** Here an adverb. Is it positive, comparative, or superlative?
       hae. Still the *tabellae*.
       capiant = "would hold." A potential subjunctive.
24.   **duro ore.** Refers to the look with which the *cognitor legat*.
       legat. Subjunctive here in a relative clause of purpose.
25.   **-que.** Connects *ephemeridas* and *tabulas*, the objects of *inter*.
       iacerent. Potential subjunctive. Its subject is the *cerae* of line 23.
26.   **in.** "In" will not work with the verb *fleret*. How in English do we *fleret in* something?
       quibus. Refers to the *ephemeridas* and *tabulas* of line 25.
       avarus. Here a substantive, referring to a generalized, unnamed character.
       opes. Not a nominative. What participle modifies it?

27-30. Ovid turns his attention back to Corinna, finishing the poem by insulting her.

27.   **rebus.** Ablative of respect, referring to everything that has happened in 1.11 and 1.12.
       pro nomine. To be read with *duplices*.
28.   **auspicii…boni.** Explains how Ovid should have known that his message for Corinna was ill-fated from the outset because of the very nature of the tablets on which they were sent: their literal duplicity reflects her duplicity.
       auspicii boni. Genitive of description with *erat*.
       numerus. Refers to the double meaning of *duplices* in 27: as she is *duplex* because of her deception, so too are the two tablets *duplices*, because of their two, hinged, single tablets.
29.   **quid = cur**
       vos. Not a nominative.
       senectus. Not a masculine noun. What adjective agrees with it?
30.   **immundo situ.** To be read with *alba*.

Discussion Questions, lines 21-30

1. How does Ovid characterize himself in lines 21-22?
2. Why does Ovid choose the *cognitor* and the *avarus* of lines 24 and 26 as alternate users of the *tabellae*? Use Ovid's description of them to support your answer.
3. What is the effect of the juxtaposition in line 27?
4. How does Ovid's tone change in the last couplet? Why might he end the poem on such a note?

His ego commisi nostros insanus amores
    molliaque ad dominam verba ferenda dedi?
Aptius hae capiant vadimonia garrula cerae,
    quas aliquis duro cognitor ore legat;
inter ephemeridas melius tabulasque iacerent,   25
    in quibus absumptas fleret avarus opes.
Ergo ego vos rebus duplices pro nomine sensi:
    auspicii numerus non erat ipse boni.
Quid precer iratus, nisi vos cariosa senectus
    rodat, et immundo cera sit alba situ?   30

Ego demens his credidi nostros amores, et tradidi blandas voces deferendas ad dominam? Hae tabellae convenientius contineant vadimonia loquacia, quas aliquis iudex legat vultu aspero. Convenientius iacerent inter tabulas diarias, in quibus avarus lugeret divitias expensas. Ergo ego expertus sum vos duplices esse effectis pro ratione nominis? Ipse numerus non erat laeti augurii. Quid orem infensus, nisi vetustas cariem inducens vos exedat, et cera sit cana turpi squalore?

absumo, absumere, absumpsi, absumptus. to consume, to waste, to use up, to exhaust, to expend

albus, -a, -um. white

aptus, -a, -um. appropriate, easy, apt

auspicium, -i. omen, sign; the act of reading omens, augury

avarus, -a, -um. greedy

cariosus, -a, -um. decayed, rotten

cognitor, cognitoris (m.). lawyer, representative

committo, committere, commisi, commissus. to entrust

duplex, duplicis (adj.). double, deceiving, two-faced, folded over

ephemeris, ephemeridis (f.; acc. pl. = ephemeridas). date book, account book

ergo. therefore

garrulus, -a, -um. talkative, garrulous, chatty

immundus, -a, -um. unclean, sordid, dirty

ops, opis (f.). power, ability, aid, assistance, wealth

precor, precari, precatus. to beg, to pray, to ask for

rodo, rodere, rosi, rosus. to erode, to waste away, to nibble (at)

senectus, senectutis (f.). old age

situs, -us. site, location

tabula, -ae. account book, financial record

vadimonium, -i. bond, summons [*in the sense of a legal obligation to appear in court*]

Pyramus and Thisbe Introduction

Two households, both alike in dignity,
In fair Verona, where we lay our scene,
From ancient grudge break to new mutiny,
Where civil blood makes civil hands unclean.
From forth the fatal loins of these two foes
A pair of star-cross'd lovers take their life;
- Shakespeare, *Romeo and Juliet*, Prologue.1-6

Verona. Mercutio. Tybalt. Capulets. Montagues. Even Leonardo di Caprio.

Romeo and Juliet. Perhaps the most famous lovers of all time. Pyramus and Thisbe? Who are they? A different time. A different place. Different details. A different author. But in the hands of Ovid, this otherwise unknown story becomes a tragi-comic inspiration that yielded not only Shakespeare's *Romeo and Juliet* but also the concluding scene to his *A Midsummer Night's Dream*.

Ovid's story has no clear literary antecedent. Folk vestiges remain in Asia Minor and perhaps Cyprus: there is a river Pyramus who apparently fell in love with a nymph Thisbe and was unable to realize that love; mosaics attest to this story. But Ovid's narrative appears to be largely his own invention: he has maintained the names and the theme of failed love, but moved the setting to the East, removed any divinity from Pyramus and Thisbe, introduced the lovers' parents as the obstacle to their love, and of course incorporated both the story's metamorphosis and the story's tragic ending. *Romeo and Juliet*, while changing many of the details of the setting, maintains many of Ovid's narrative details.

But Shakespeare also incorporated the Pyramus and Thisbe narrative into his comic play *A Midsummer Night's Dream*. Written about the same time as *Romeo and Juliet* (in fact, it is unknown which was written first), the play focuses on the marriage of Theseus, the Athenian hero best known for killing the Minotaur, and Hippolyta, his Amazon bride. As part of their wedding celebration, they have issued an open invitation to the townspeople to provide entertainment. This entertainment is ultimately provided by a group of craftsmen and artisans from town called the Mechanicals. Their entertainment for the wedding:

our play is, The most lamentable comedy, and most cruel death of Pyramus and Thisby

-Shakespeare, *A Midsummer Night's Dream*, 1.2.11-13

But the Mechanicals don't have any concept of what their "most lamentable comedy" involves. Not only is it tragic, but it is also a tragic love story to be performed at a wedding celebration. Their play is full of miscues: an uncooperative moon to light the way for Pyramus and Thisbe to Ninus' tomb, the wall played by a reluctant actor, and a death scene from Pyramus that was indeed anything but tragic. At the end, the naive charm of the Mechanicals wins the favor of Theseus and Hippolyta, despite the subject matter of the play.

So where did Shakespeare get the Mechanicals' comic version of Pyramus and Thisbe? Did he do what Ovid did? Did he take Ovid's existing narrative and rewrite it humorously? Probably not. Ovid's narrative is of course tragic. But Ovid rarely writes pure tragedy without imbuing it with at least some sense of the tragically humorous (or the humorously tragic). Thus, in Ovid's hands, Pyramus' wound spouts blood in the same way that the Black Knight spouts blood in *Monty Python and the Holy Grail*, or the fictional Julia Child spouts blood when parodied by Dan Aykroyd on *Saturday Night Live*. Ovid juxtaposes the extremes of humor and tragedy in Pyramus and Thisbe as a reminder of their close emotional affinity: they both cause physical reactions (laughter and weeping) to extreme emotions. Ovid intentionally imbues

Pyramus and Thisbe with an ambiguity that may or may not heighten its tragedy: does the subtle humor of the story of Pyramus and Thisbe convey a sense of realism which then makes the tragedy more accessible? Or does the humor, by its very appearance in the story, distract the reader from and undercut the tragic nature of the story? Characteristically, Ovid will only raise the question. But the pursuit of its answer is what has made this story not only endure, but also exist in its iconic form thanks to Shakespeare's incorporation of it in *Romeo and Juliet*.

Pyramus and Thisbe At-A-Glance

Book	4
Lines	55-166
Main Characters (in order of appearance)	Pyramus: young man who lives in Babylon Thisbe: young woman who lives in Babylon
Minor Characters	the parents of Pyramus and Thisbe lioness
Context	The Theban king Pentheus is punished for his denial of the divinity of Dionysius (Bacchus) by having his mother, possessed by a Dionysiac frenzy, kill him. In response to the punishment of Pentheus, a holiday is declared in Thebes to allow all women to worship Dionysius.
Preceeding Story	The Daughters of Minyas (or Minyades) still refuse to worship Dionysius. Instead, they decide to tell stories.
Transition	Pyramus and Thisbe is the first story the Minyades tell.
Subsequent Story	The exposure of the affair of Mars and Venus.
Primary Topics	the rashness of youth separation vs. togetherness gender expectations and roles

Pyramus and Thisbe Vocabulary Frequency

8 times
video, -ere

7 times
amor, -oris
Thisbe, -es
ut

6 times
arbor, -oris
dico, -ere
Pyramus, -i

5 times
amans, -ntis
do, dare
nox, -ctis

4 times
caedes, -is
corpus, -oris
facio, -ere
os, oris
osculum, -i
tego, -ere
unus, -a, -um

3 times
aqua, -ae
cognosco, -ere
color, -oris
cruor, -oris
domus, -us
fallo, -ere

inquit
locus, -i
longus, -i
mors, -rtis
multus, -a, -um
pomum, -i
sanguis, -inis
tenuis, -e
ubi
venio, -ire
vestis, -is
vulnus, -eris
vultus, -us

55-58. The characters and setting of the story are introduced. Pyramus and Thisbe live next door to one another in the Eastern city of Bablyon, ruled by the mythical queen Semiramis.

55.   **alter.** How is *alter* translated when it is used with another *alter* (here, *altera*)?
56.   **quas.** Its antecedent is *puellis*.
        praelata puellis. If Pyramus is *pulcherrimus iuvenum*, how is Thisbe described similarly?
57.   **contiguas.** What does this word modify? What is the gender of *domos*?
        tenuere. Not an infinitive. Be careful of principle parts.
57-58. **ubi...fecit = ubi Semiramis dicitur cinxisse altam urbem coctilibus muris**

59-64. Their neigboring houses are the source of their love, even though their fathers forbid their relationship.

59.   **Notitiam...fecit.** How did the lovers meet?
        gradus. Declension is important for understanding the case of this word. What modifies it?
60.   **taedae coissent.** What would have happened if their fathers didn't forbid it?
61.   **vetuere, potuere.** Not infinitives. Be careful of principle parts.
62.   **ex aequo.** An idiom. How does each love the other?
64.   **magis, magis.** These words create parallel clauses: what made their love increase?
        tegitur = (ignis) tegitur
        tectus. Brings the action of the first clause into the parallel second clause.

Discussion Questions, lines 55-64

1. What is the effect of describing Pyramus and Thisbe as *pulcherrimus iuvenum* (line 55) and *praelata puellis* (line 56)?
2. Why is the location of the story (the *Oriens* of line 56) important?
3. What is the parallel drawn between the *muris* of Semiramis in line 58 and the *contiguas domos* in line 57?
4. How is the love of Pyramus and Thisbe characterized in lines 60-64? Identify specific Latin words and phrases that describe the kind of love that they were experiencing.

Ad comparanda

The underlined words in the Latin below correspond to similar or the same words in line 63. The noun *digitus*, finger, used in both selections below, is used to indicate the same type of communication that Ovid identifies in *Pyramus and Thisbe* with *signis*.

> neu te decipiat <u>nutu</u>, <u>digito</u>que liquorem
>   ne trahat et mensae ducat in orbe notas.
>   - Tibullus 1.6.19-20

> Nil opus est *digitis*, per quos arcana loquaris,
>   Nec tibi per <u>*nutus*</u> accipienda nota est:
>   - Ovid, *Ars Amatoria*, 1.137-138

Pyramus et Thisbe, iuvenum pulcherrimus alter,   55
altera, quas Oriens habuit, praelata puellis,
contiguas tenuere domos, ubi dicitur altam
coctilibus muris cinxisse Semiramis urbem.
Notitiam primosque gradus vicinia fecit;
tempore crevit amor. Taedae quoque iure coissent,   60
sed vetuere patres; quod non potuere vetare,
ex aequo captis ardebant mentibus ambo.
Conscius omnis abest; nutu signisque loquuntur,
quoque magis tegitur, tectus magis aestuat ignis.

Pyramus et Thisbe, alter elegantissimus iuvenum, altera formosissima virginum quas Oriens habuit, incoluerunt domos conterminas, ubi Semiramis dicitur clausisse excelsum urbem lateribus excoctis. Vicinia stravit primam viam et conciliavit consuetudinem. Amor auctus est mora; faces etiam iure convenissent, sed patres prohibuerunt quod non potuerunt prohibere. Uterque pariter incensi erant animis correptis. Omnis arbiter abest; verba faciunt nutu et notis: et quo magis ignis obducitur, magis obductus incalescit.

aequus, -a, -um. level, even; **ex aequo** [*expr.*]: equally, with the same intensity

aestuo, -are, -avi, -atus. to flare, to blaze, to burn fiercely

cingo, cingere, cinxi, cinctus. to bind, to gird, to surround

coctilis, -e (adj.). brick, baked, made of fired bricks

coeo, coire, coii / coivi, coitus. to come together; [*both in a literal sense and in a figurative sense, i.e. in a union, in marriage, etc.*], to assemble

conscius, -i. accomplice, witness

contiguus, -a, -um. connected

cresco, crescere, crevi, cretus. to increase, to develop

gradus, -us. slope, grade, step, footstep

ius, iuris (n.). law, rule, precept, guide, legal sanction, legal authority, control [*sometimes used in the ablative to mean "by law," "under the law," or "with legal authority"*]

notitia, -ae. acquaintance, notice, familiarity

nutus, -us. nod [*especially one that indicates familiarity or assent*]

orior, oriri, ortus. to rise [*often used with reference to the sun and where the sun rises, the east*]

praelatus, -a, -um. distinguished, preferred

Pyramus, -i. [name]

Semiramis, Semiramidis (f.). [name: *legendary queen of Assyria, wife of Ninus, founder of Babylon*]

taeda, -ae. wedding torch, wedding, marriage

tego, tegere, texi, tectus. to cover, to hide

Thisbe, Thisbes. [name; *declined as a Greek noun: gen = -es, acc. sing. = -en*]

veto, vetare, vetui, vetitus. to forbid, to deny

vicinia, -ae. neighborhood, area nearby, vicinity, proximity

65-70. The means by which Pyramus and Thisbe communicate is introduced and explained.

65.　**fissus erat.** Be careful about the subject of this verb (it's not *rima*). What was split?
66.　**paries...utrique.** How does the synchesis here help you with agreement and case?
67.　**id vitium.** Can this be a nominative with its verb *vidistis*?
　　nulli. Be careful about case here. This is an irregular adjective, and not a genitive singular or nominative plural.
68.　**quid...amor?** This is an aside, a self contained grammatical unit, that interrupts the sentence around it.
　　amantes. In apposition to the subject of *vidistis*.
69.　**vocis iter.** What is the *rima* allowing Pyramus' and Thisbe's voices to do?
　　-que. Note how the subject changes in this new clause.
　　illud. What is the gender of this word? And how does that help you determine its antecedent?

Discussion Questions, lines 65-70

1. Why is the *rima* described as *tenui* in line 65?
2. What is the thematic significance of beginning the sentence that introduces the *paries* of line 66 with the *fissus erat* of line 65?
3. Discuss the imagery of the synchesis in line 66.
4. The *quid non sentit amor* is an aside from Ovid. Why does he, the author, interject himself into the story? What is the effect? What is he trying to say and why is such an abrupt aside the most effective or appropriate way to say it?
5. What are the immediate and extended implications of the *tutae* in line 69?

Fissus erat tenui rima, quam duxerat olim,   65
cum fieret, paries domui communis utrique.
Id vitium nulli per saecula longa notatum
(quid non sentit amor?) primi vidistis amantes
et vocis fecistis iter, tutaeque per illud
murmure blanditiae minimo transire solebant.   70

Murus medius inter utramque domum hiabat exigua fissura, quam quondam traxerat, cum strueretur. Ille defectus a nemine observatus per diutina tempora (quid non cognoscit amor?) a vobis amantibus primo fuit cognitus; et fecistis viam voci; et securae blanditiae solebant transire per eam, tenuissimo strepitu.

blanditia, -ae. flattery, pleasing speech, compliments; [*when plural*] sweet nothings, pleasantries

communis, -e. common, shared

findo, findere, fidi, fissus. to split apart, to open

fio, fieri, factus. to become, to happen, to be made, to be done

murmur, murmuris (n.). murmur, whisper

noto, -are, -avi, -atus. to note, to mark, to scribe, to mar; to recognize, to know

nullus, -a, -um. none, no [*an irregular adjective whose genitive singular ends in -ius and whose dative singular ends in -i*]

olim. once

paries, parietis (m.). wall [*an interior wall that divides houses or rooms, as opposed to a* murus *that is an exterior fortification wall*]

rima, -ae. crack, opening

saeculum, -i. age, generation; **per saecula** [*expr.*]: through the generations, through the ages

soleo, solere, solitus. to be accustomed, to be used (to do something) [*often followed by an infinitive*]

tenuis, -e. thin, slight

uterque, utraque, utrumque. each (of two), both [*an irregular adjective whose genitive singular ends in -ius and whose dative singular ends in -i*]

vitium, -i. fault, crack, imperfection, blame

71-77. Ovid describes the routine of Pyramus and Thisbe when they talk, and their frustration over the obstacle that separates them.

71.   constiterant...illinc. Describes the positioning of Pyramus and Thisbe when they talk through the wall.
72.   fuerat captatus = captatus erat. Be careful of your subject here.
       anhelitus oris. These words are different cases. What action of the lovers do they refer to?
73.   Invide. What is being addressed here? And so what does this modify?
       quid = cur
74-75. Quantum...pateres = Quantum esset ut sineres nos iungi toto corpore aut, si hoc est nimium, (quantum esset) vel pateres ad oscula danda
75.   ad oscula danda. The form of *danda* is essential to understanding this construction: why would the *paries pateres*? What do Pyramus and Thisbe want to do?
77.   quod...aures. Why do *fatemur debere*? What does the wall do for Pyramus and Thisbe?
       amicas. Not the noun here. What does this adjective modify?

78-80. Still frustrated, Pyramus and Thisbe leave one another.

78.   talia. Not a nominative. For what verb will this be the object?
       diversa. Does not modify *talia*. What case is it? And so what does it modify?
79.   sub noctem. When do Pyramus and Thisbe depart one another (not of course "under the night")?
80.   quisque. The subject of *dedere*, despite that it is singular. A singular collective noun can sometimes take a plural verb, even though it is grammatically singular, because it refers to a plural. British English will tend to do this: "The team are…" vs. American English "The team is…"
       suae. There is only one word this can agree with (and it is not nominative plural). What is it?
       oscula non pervienientia contra. What are Pyramus' and Thisbe's kisses not doing?

Discussion Questions, lines 71-80

1. Discuss the visual effect of the imagery of the chiasmus in line 71.
2. What is the effect of the periphrasis *anhelitus oris* in line 72? What detail does it focus on that a more prosaic description might not?
3. Why is the wall addressed as *invide* in line 73?
4. Discuss the personification of the wall in lines 73ff. How does the personification intensify the sympathy Ovid creates for Pyramus and Thisbe? What theme does the personification introduce?
4. How should lines 71-80 be read? Is it a tender depiction of two desperate lovers trying to communicate? Or is it a cyncial depiction of the foolish lengths to which love can drive people? Explain your answer.

Saepe, ubi constiterant hinc Thisbe, Pyramus illinc,
inque vices fuerat captatus anhelitus oris,
"Invide" dicebant "paries, quid amantibus obstas?
Quantum erat, ut sineres toto nos corpore iungi?
Aut, hoc si nimium est, vel ad oscula danda pateres?   75
Nec sumus ingrati: tibi nos debere fatemur,
quod datus est verbis ad amicas transitus aures."
Talia diversa nequiquam sede locuti
sub noctem dixere "Vale" partique dedere
oscula quisque suae non pervenientia contra.   80

Saepe postquam convenissent, hinc Thisbe, Pyramus illinc, et spiritus oris esset utrobique captatus, "Livide mure," dicebant, "quamobrem prohibes amantes? Quam parum esset, ut patereris nos convenire toto corpore! Aut si hoc nimium, saltem apertus esses ad iungenda suavia! Neque sumus ingrati. Nos agnoscimus tibi debere, quod via facta est vocibus ad aures amicas." Postquam eiusmodi frustra e diverso loco dixissent, adventante nocte dixerunt "Vale"; et quisque obtulerunt basia suae parti, non praetereuntia in alteram.

amicus, -a, -um. friendly, eager; belonging to a friend or lover

anhelitus, -us. a breathing, a gasping

auris, auris (f.). ear

capto, -are, -avi, -atus. to keep taking, to keep grabbing, to try to touch

consisto, consistere, constiti, constitus. to stand still, to stop, to establish oneself

contra (adv.). in return, in response, opposite, facing

diversus, -a, -um. different, opposite

fateor, fateri, fassus. to admit, to acknowledge, to confess

hinc (adv.). from here, next; [*with* illinc] on this side

illinc (adv.). from that side; [*with* hinc] on that side

ingratus, -a, -um. ungrateful

invidus, -a, -um. hateful, spiteful, malevolent

iungo, iungere, iunxi, iunctus. to join

nequiquam (adv.). uselessly

obsto, obstare, obstiti, obstaturus (+ dat.). to obstruct, to be in the way of, to stand in the way of, to hinder, to prevent

os, oris (n.). mouth, face

pateo, patere, patui, -. to lie open, to be open, to open

pervenio, pervenire, perveni, perventurus (+ ad + acc.). to arrive at, to reach

sedes, sedis (f.). seat, location, spot

sino, sinere, sivi, situs. to allow

transitus, -us. passage, path, way

(in) vices. each in turn, alternately, back and forth

Ad comparanda: Tibullus 1.2.5-10.

The Roman poet Tibullus devotes a poem to the door (*ianua*) that separates him from his girlfriend. Some of the early lines of that poem are included below.

Nam posita est nostrae custodia saeva puellae,   5
    clauditur et dura ianua firma sera.
Ianua difficilis domini, te verberet imber,
    te Iovis imperio fulmina missa petant.
Ianua, iam pateas uni mihi, victa querellis,
    neu furtim verso cardine aperta sones.   10

81-92. Pyramus and Thisbe's frustration leads them to formulate a plan for escape.

81.   **Postera.** Be careful of the part of speech of this word: what does it modify?
83.   **coiere.** Be careful of all those vowels in a row: what form is this (not an infinitive…)?
83-89. **Tum…arboris.** See the chart below for a structural diagram of this sentence.
84.   **multa.** Not a feminine. What other gender can it be?
       prius. What happens first that spurs Pyramus and Thisbe to *statuunt* next?
       silenti. Not a noun. What does this agree with?
87.   **neve sit errandum spatiantibus** = "Or so that they, wandering, might not get lost…" This is an impersonal passive periphrastic with the *spatiantibus* a dative of agent. Ultimately, the agent will function better in English as the subject.
89-90. **arbor…fonti.** The parenthetical introduces why the *arbor,* under whose shade Pyramus and Thisbe will meet, will be important for the story: the *niveis pomis* of the *arbor* will undergo the metamorphosis in the story.
90.   **morus.** This has an unexpected gender. What agrees with it?
91-92. **lux…isdem.** A periphrasis for sunset and night-rise.
91.   **tarde discedere visa.** A universal statement about the speed with which time passes when we are anticipating something exciting.
92.   **aquis.** Refers to the horizon.

Discussion Questions, lines 81-92

1. How does the rhythm of Ovid's language change within lines 81-92? What effect does that change have?
2. How does the *prius questi* of line 84 explain the decisions introduced by the *statuunt* in line 84?
3. How does the *nocte* of line 84 signify a change in the relationship of Pyramus and Thisbe?
4. Why does Ovid include so many details of Pyramus' and Thisbe's plan in lines 84-90?
5. Is *exierint* in line 86 an indicative or a subjunctive? Explain your answer.

Sentence Diagram, lines 83-90

                              Tum, murmure parvo
        multa prius questi, statuunt ut nocte silenti
        fallere custodes foribusque excedere temptent,
        cumque domo exierint, urbis quoque tecta relinquant.
        Neve sit errabunda lato spatiantibus arvo,
        conveniant ad busta Nini, lateantque sub umbra
        arboris

There are six subjunctive verbs, four of which are dependent on *statuunt*, whose subject has a participial phrase agreeing with it. The other two subjunctive verbs are used in dependent clauses within the clauses dependent on *statuunt*.

Tum,
 murmure parvo multa prius <u>questi</u>,
statuunt
        <u>ut</u> nocte silenti fallere custodes foribusque excedere *temptent,*
                cum<u>que</u> domo exierint

        urbis quoque tecta *relinquant,*

                <u>neve</u> sit erranda lato spatiantibus arvo
conveniant ad busta Nini,

        lateant<u>que</u> sub umbra arboris

Postera nocturnos Aurora removerat ignes,
solque pruinosas radiis siccaverat herbas:
ad solitum coiere locum. Tum, murmure parvo
multa prius questi, statuunt ut nocte silenti
fallere custodes foribusque excedere temptent, 85
cumque domo exierint, urbis quoque tecta relinquant,
neve sit errandum lato spatiantibus arvo,
conveniant ad busta Nini, lateantque sub umbra
arboris: arbor ibi niveis uberrima pomis,
ardua morus, erat, gelido contermina fonti. 90

Sequens Aurora fugaverat sidera nocturna, atque Sol exsiccaverat gramina pruina conspersa radiis; convenerunt in eundem locum. Tum prius conquesti plurima voce summissa, decernunt, ut nocte intempesta conentur fallere ianitores, et valvis egredi; et postquam domo prodierint, egrediantur insuper urbe; et ne opus sit vagari per vastos agros, coeant ad tumulum Nini, et latitent sub umbra arboris. Ibi erat morus arbor procera fecundissima pomis candidis, proxima fonti frigidissimo. Conditiones probantur, et dies sero credita transire praecipitatur in aquas, et nox excitatur ab iisdem aquis.

arduus, -a, -um. tall, towering, steep, precipitous; [*as substantive*] height, peak

arvum, -i. field, meadow, open expanse of grass

Aurora, -ae. dawn, the Goddess of the Dawn

bustum, -i. funeral marker, funeral pyre, tomb, grave-mound

coeo, coire, coii / coivi, coitus. to come together; [*both in a literal sense and in a figurative sense, i.e. in a union, in marriage, etc.*], to assemble

conterminus, -a, -um (+ dat.). bordering, next to, near

discedo, discedere, discessi, discessurus. to depart, to leave

erro, -are, -avi, -atus. to wander aimlessly, to go astray

excedo, excedere, excessi, excessurus. to go out, to leave

fallo, fallere, fefelli, falsus. to deceive, to trick

fons, fontis (m.). fountain, spring

foris, foris (f.). door, door post

gelidus, -a, -um. cool, chilled

herba, -ae. grass, herb, small plant or flower

lateo, latere, latui, -. to take shelter, to hide, to lie in hiding, to be hiding

morus, -i (f.). the mulberry tree

murmur, murmuris (n.). murmur, whisper

Ninus, -i. [*name: king of Assyria, founder of Nineveh, husband of Semiramis*]

niveus, -a, -um. snowy white, white

nocturnus, -a, -um. nocturnal, of or belonging to night

pactum, -i. pact, agreement, plan [*Latin will sometimes use a plural where English will use a singular*]

pomum, -i. fruit

posterus, -a, -um. next, following

praecipito, -are, -avi, -atus. to plunge, to sink, to hurl downward

prior, prius. first (of two), previous

pruinosus, -a, -um. frosty, dewy

queror, queri, questus. to complain, to protest

radius, -i. ray (of light / from the sun)

relinquo, relinquere, reliqui, relictus. to leave behind

sicco, -are, -avi, -atus. to dry

silens, silentis. silent, quiet, calm

solitus, -a, -um. usual, accustomed

spatior, spatiari, spatiatus. to walk about, to wander

statuo, statuere, statui, statutus. to decide; [*often accompanied by* ut + *a subjunctive verb:*] to decide (that)

tempto, -are, -avi, -atus. to try, to attempt

uber, uberis (adj.). copious, abundant, rich (in + abl.)

93-96. Thisbe is the first to leave home. Ovid focuses on her departure and her arrival at the appointed spot, with little attention paid to the journey there.

93.   **callida.** Does not agree with *tenebras.*
        versato cardine. This expression describes one of the first, albeit simple, things that happens for the door to open.

94.   **suos.** Does not agree with any noun. Who are Thisbe's *suos?*
        vultum. An accusative of respect dependent on *adoperta.*

95.   **dicta.** In this context, "said" will not be sufficient. What is the *dicta arbore?*

96.   **audacem.** Who is *audacem?* Why?

96-101. A lioness surprises Thisbe, who runs away and in the process drops her shawl.

96-98. **Venit...unda** = Ecce, leaena, oblita spumantes rictus recenti caede boum, venit, despositura sitim in unda vicini fontis

98.   **despositura.** Be careful of tense here: it is not a very commonly used form.

99.   **Quam.** Does not refer to Thisbe. What does *Thisbe vidit?*

101.   **tergo...reliquit** = (Thisbe) reqliquit velamina lapsa tergo

102-104. The lioness finds Thisbe's shawl and mauls it with its bloody mouth.

102-3. **Ut...silvas.** Establishes the setting for the following line and a half with two different temporal clauses.

103.   **inventos.** The word that this modifies does not look like an accusative.
        sine ipsa. Refers to the *velamen's* lack of its owner.

104.   **amictus.** Be careful of the declension of this word. What case is it?

Discussion Questions, lines 93-104

1. How does Ovid's use of *leaena* and *lea* (in lines 97 and 102) confuse gender roles? Explain your answer in terms of both the lioness' role in the story and the specific ways in which Ovid describes her.

2. What atmosphere does the *tenebras* of line 93 establish? Explain your answer.

3. Why does Ovid include the detail of the *versato cardine* of line 93?

4. What are the implications of the *dicta* in line 95? What does it say about Thisbe? What does it say about Pyramus?

5. What is the relevance of the *audacem* of line 96?

6. What is the effect of opening the sentence at line 96 with *venit*? Whom do we expect to be coming?

7. Why is the *despositura sitim* of line 98 an important detail? What does it say about the role of chance in the story?

8. What is the tone of lines 99-101? Identify specific Latin words that contribute to this tone and explain how they do so.

Pacta placent; et lux, tarde discedere visa,
praecipitatur aquis, et aquis nox exit ab isdem.
   Callida per tenebras, versato cardine, Thisbe
egreditur fallitque suos adopertaque vultum
pervenit ad tumulum, dictaque sub arbore sedit;   95
audacem faciebat amor. Venit ecce recenti
caede leaena boum spumantes oblita rictus,
depositura sitim vicini fontis in unda;
quam procul ad lunae radios Babylonia Thisbe
vidit et obscurum timido pede fugit in antrum,   100
dumque fugit, tergo velamina lapsa reliquit.
Ut lea saeva sitim multa compescuit unda,
dum redit in silvas, inventos forte sine ipsa
ore cruentato tenues laniavit amictus.

Solers Thisbe erumpit per opaca noctis, cardine dimoto, et suos decipit, et velatum os habens pervenit ad sepulchrum, et substitit sub praestituta arbore. Amor praestabat audentem. Ecce leaena adest infectum habens os aestuans recenti caede boum, sedatura sitim aqua fontis proximi. Quam Thisbe Bablylonia intuita est e longinquo ad lucem Lunae, et pede tremente dilabitur in tenebrosam speluncam: et fugiendo omittit a tergo lapsa velamina. Postquam credelis leaena sedavit sitim multa aqua, dum revertitur in nemus, forte discerpit rictu sanguinolento subtilia vela reperta sine Thisbe.

adopertus, -a, -um. covered, veiled	**luna, -ae.** moon
amictus, -us (m.). cloak	**oblino, oblinere, oblevi, oblitus.** to smear, to cover
antrum, -i. cave	**obscurus, -a, -um.** dark, gloomy
audax, audacis. bold, arrogant, cocky	**radius, -i.** ray (of light / from the sun)
Babylonius, -a, -um. Babylonian	**recens, recentis.** new, recent, recently plucked or picked
bos, bovis (m./f.; gen pl. = boum). cow, ox	**redeo, redire, redii / -ivi, reditus.** to return, to go back
caedes, caedis (f.). slaughter, gore	**rictus, -us.** jaws, open mouth
callidus, -a, -um. clever, crafty	**sitis, sitis (f.; acc. = sitim).** thirst
cardo, cardinis (m.). pivot, door-hinge, door	**spumo, -are, -avi, -atus.** to foam, to be covered with foam
compesco, compescere, compescui, -. to quench, to satisfy	**tenebrae, -arum.** darkness, shadows
cruento, -are, -avi, -atus. to stain with blood, to pollute	**tergum, -i.** back
depono, deponere, deposui, depositus. to satisfy, to quench	**tumulus, -i.** grave, grave mound, tomb
labor, labi, lapsus. to slip, to fall (off or from)	**velamen, velaminis (n.).** cloak, shawl
lanio, -are, -avi, -atus. to tear, to shred, to mutilate	**verso, -are, -avi, -atus.** to turn, to spin
lea, -ae. lioness	**vicinus, -a, -um.** neighboring, nearby, near, next to
leaena, -ae. lioness	**vultus, -us.** face, countenance, appearance, expression

105-112. Pyramus, having left Babylon after Thisbe, now arrives at the appointed place, and finds signs of Thisbe's presence that he will tragically misinterpret.

105.   **egressus.** Change of gender indicates change of focus. Who is now being discussed?
       vestigia. What did Thisbe leave *in alto pulvere* (as she fled the lioness)?
106.   **certa.** Modifies neither *pulvere* or *ferae.*
       ferae. To be read with *certa.*
108.   **repperit.** This action is the next step (after *vidit* and *expalluit*) in Pyramus' erroneous assumption about what happened.
       una duos. Neither the intentional juxtaposition nor the isolation that the quotes create mean that these words go together. What noun does each modify?
       perdet. Be careful of the tense of this verb.
109.   **e quibus illa** = *illa (una) e quibus. Illa* functions as the "part" of the partitive expression *e quibus,* i.e. it specifies to which of the *amantes* this clause refers.
       longa vita. Not nominative and to be read with *dignissima.*
111.   What word will connect this line to the previous?
       in loca plena. To be read with *venires.*
       metus. To be read with *plena.*
       iussi nocte venires = *iussi (ut tu) nocte venires*

112-114. Pyramus now addresses directly the beast whom he blames for Thisbe's death.

114.   **o quicumque…leones** = *o quicumque leones habitatis sub hac rupe*
       habitatis. *Leones* is its subject; the verb is second person because of the vocative.

Discussion Questions, lines 105-114

1. What aspects of Pyramus' personality are revealed in lines 105-114? (Identify at least 3.)
2. Identify two juxtapositions in Pyramus' speech in lines 108-114. What are their effects?
3. What is the significance of the tense of *perdet* in line 108?
4. What assumptions is Pyramus making in lines 111-112? Are they valid? Explain your answer.
5. What is the effect of the apostrophe in lines 112-114?
6. How does Pyramus (or Ovid) rhetorically embellish the apostrophe in lines 112-114?

    Serius egressus, vestigia vidit in alto   105
pulvere certa ferae, totoque expalluit ore
Pyramus; ut vero vestem quoque sanguine tinctam
repperit, "Una duos" inquit "nox perdet amantes,
e quibus illa fuit longa dignissima vita;
nostra nocens anima est. Ego te, miseranda, peremi,   110
in loca plena metus qui iussi nocte venires
nec prior huc veni. Nostrum divellite corpus
et scelerata fero consumite viscera morsu,
o quicumque sub hac habitatis rupe leones!

Pyramus, qui tardius exierat, aspexit in ultimo pulvere indubitata vestigia ferae, et toto vultu expalluit. Postquam autem invenit amictum infectum etiam cruore: "Una nox," inquit, "conficiet duos amantes, e quibus illa fuit dignissima producta vita. Anima nostra est in culpa. Ego te perdidi, deflenda, qui monui ut venires noctu in loca pavore obsita, neque primus huc affui. O leones, quicumque incolitis haec saxa, convellite impia praecordia saevo morsu.

consumo, consumere, consumpsi, consumptus. to devour, to consume

dignus, -a, -um (+ abl.). worthy (of)

divello, divellere, divelli, divulsus. to tear apart, to tear to pieces

egredior, egredi, egressus. to depart, to leave

expallesco, expallescere, expallui, -. to grow pale, to grow white

ferus, -a, -um. wild; [*often used substantively as:*] wild beast, wild animal

huc (adv.). to this place, here

miserandus, -a, -um. to be pitied; miserable, wretched

morsus, -us. jaws, mouth, bite, morsel, nibble

nocens, nocentis (adj.). guilty

perdo, perdere, perdidi, perditus. to destroy, to ruin

perimo, perimere, peremi, peremptus. to ruin, to destroy, to kill

plenus, -a, -um. full, complete

pulvis, pulveris (m.). dust

quicumque, quaecumque, quodcumque. whoever, whatever

reperio, reperire, repperi, repertus. to find, to discover, to come upon

rupes, rupis (f.). rocky cliff, crag

sceleratus, -a, -um. sinful, wretched

serus, -a, -um. late

tingo, tingere, tinxi, tinctus. to stain, to soak, to color, to dye, to paint

vero (adv.). truly, indeed, for certain

vestigium, -i. vestige, trace, footprint, sign, remnant

vestis, vestis (f.). clothes, clothing, garment

viscus, visceris (n.). entrails, innards, guts [*often used in the plural, as in English, i.e. you can't have one gut or one innard*]

115-117. Pyramus' lament concludes, and his dramatic reaction to the evidence around him continues.

115.   **Sed timidi est optare necem** = Vir (qui est) timidus necare optat. A general statement about a certain type of man, i.e. the type that *optat necare.*
       timidi. A genitive of description, literally "It is of a fearful man…"
       Thisbes. Neither a nominative nor an accusative plural. Whose *velamina* is it?
116.   **ad.** What is the object of this preposition? Where did Pyramus carry the veil?
       pactae arboris. Not the object of *ad.* With what will these be translated?
       fert. Understand the object of the previous clause with this verb.
117.   **notae vesti.** To be read with both of the *dedit*-clauses in this line.

118-121. Pyramus utters one final lament, before he kills himself.

118.   **haustus.** Make certain to know the declension of this word to determine its case (it can't be the subject of *accipe*).
119.   **Quoque** = et quo. The antecedent of *quo* is *ferrum.*
       ilia. This is not a form of *ille, illa, illud.*
120.   **nec mora** = et statim
       traxit. The object is still the *ferrum* of line 119.
121.   **humo.** Not the word *homo.* Where did Pyramus *iacuit*?
       alte. In what direction is the *cruor emicat*?

121-124. The gore of Pyramus' wound is described by one of Ovid's best known similes. His blood spurts through the hole like a stream of water forced through a tiny hole in a pipe.

122.   **non aliter quam cum** = sicut cum. A litotes that introduces the simile.
       vitiato plumbo. Explains why the *fistula scinditur.*
123.   **longe.** Adverbial, and not grammatically connected to *stridente foramine.* Explains where the *fistula eiaculatur tenues aquas.*
124.   **ictibus.** How does the *fistula rumpit aera*?
125-126. **arborei…faciem** = arborei fetus vertuntur in atram faciem aspergine caedis
126.   **faciem.** Does not here mean "face."
       madefacta. Does not modify *sanguine.*

Discussion Questions, lines 115-127

1.   What does Pyramus mean by *timidi est optare necem* in line 115? How does it change our reading of his suicide?
2.   In the description of Pyramus' suicide Ovid includes a number of potentially gratuitous details. Why might Ovid have included them?
3.   What is the significance of Pyramus stabbing himself *in ilia*? How does this action correspond to the ways in which Ovid has characterized Pyramus up to this point?
4.   What aspect of the *paries* of line 66 does the *vitiato* of line 122 specifically recall? Why does Ovid connect the broken pipe to the wall?

Sed timidi est optare necem." Velamina Thisbes   115
tollit, et ad pactae secum fert arboris umbram,
utque dedit notae lacrimas, dedit oscula vesti,
"Accipe nunc" inquit "nostri quoque sanguinis haustus."
Quoque erat accinctus, demisit in ilia ferrum,
nec mora, ferventi moriens e vulnere traxit.   120
Ut iacuit resupinus humo, cruor emicat alte,
non aliter quam cum vitiato fistula plumbo
scinditur, et tenues stridente foramine longe
eiaculatur aquas, atque ictibus aera rumpit.
Arborei fetus aspergine caedis in atram   125
vertuntur faciem, madefactaque sanguine radix
purpureo tingit pendentia mora colore.

Sed proiecti est animi mortem cupere." Colligit velum Thisbes, et portat secum ad umbram arboris constitutae. Et sicuti dedit lacrimas, dedit quoque suavia amictui: "Deinde," inquit, "habeas nunc etiam undas nostri sanguinis;" et infigit gladium, quo erat instructus, in latus; et sine cunctatione, moriens educit e vulnere exaestuante. Cum stratus fuit humi resupinus, sanguis exsilit in altum, non aliter quam cum tubus aperitur laeso plumbo, et longe exspuit subtiles aquas, foramine strepente, atque impetu aerem verberat. Fructus arboris mutantur rubore sanguinis in nigrum colorem, et radix cruore imbuta inficit mora pendentia colore rubro.

accingo, accingere, accinxi, accinctus. to equip, to gird

aes, aeris (n.). copper, bronze, metal; currency, money

aliter (adv.). different(ly), otherwise

arbor, arboris (f.). tree

arboreus, -a, -um. of a tree, belonging to a tree, tree's

aspergo, asperginis (f.). a sprinkling, a spattering

ater, atra, atrum. black, dark

caedes, caedis (f.). slaughter, gore

cruor, -oris (m.). blood, gore

demitto, demittere, demisi, demissus. to thrust, to send into, to lower; [with animum:] to put one's mind to

eiaculor, eiaculari, eiaculatus. to shoot out, to discharge

emico, -are, -ui, -atus. to spurt out, to spurt upward

facies, -ei. face, appearance

fervens, ferventis. warm, hot, boiling, fervent, steaming

fetus, -us. fruit, offspring

fistula, -ae. pipe, tube; syrinx, pan-pipe

foramen, foraminis (n.). hole, crack, break, aperture

haustus, -us. a drink, a helping

humus, -i (f.). earth, dirt, soil

ictus, -us. a blow, a strike, a pounding

ilium, -i. groin [often used in the plural]

late (adv.). far and wide, all over

madefacio, madefacere, madefeci, madefactus. to drench, to soak

mora, -ae. delay, wait, pause; [sometimes used with a negative to mean:] without delay

morior, mori, mortuus. to die

morum, -i. mulberry, the fruit of the mulberry tree

nex, necis (f.). death

pactus, -a, -um. agreed upon, predetermined, specified

plumbum, -i. lead

purpureus, -a, -um. purple, dark blue

radix, radicis (f.). root (of a tree or plant)

resupinus, -a, -um. flat on one's back, lying flat on one's back

rumpo, rumpere, rupi, ruptus. to break, to burst (under pressure)

scindo, scindere, scidi, scissus. to cut, to construct, to make

strido, stridere, stridi, -. to hiss

tingo, tingere, tinxi, tinctus. to stain, to soak, to color, to dye, to paint

tollo, tollere, sustuli, sublatus. to lift up, to raise

velamen, velaminis (n.). cloak, shawl

verto, vertere, verti, versus. to turn, to spin

vitio, -are, -avi, -atus. to make faulty, to corrupt, to weaken

128-130 The scene shifts back to Thisbe, who now returns to meet Pyramus, hoping that the lioness that scared her away has left.

128.   **metu nondum posito.** A concessive ablative absolute, i.e. "Although *metu nondum posito, illa redit…*"
         ne fallat amantem. What does Thisbe not want to do?

130.   **quantaque…gestit** = et (illa) gestit narrare (Pyramo) quanta pericula vita(ve)rit.

131-136. Thisbe returns but does not recognize the place because of the change in color of the fruit, until she sees Pyramus' body before her.

131.   **et.** Cannot connect *locum* and *visa*. What is the other accusative to be connected with *locum*?
         formam. Refers to the shape of the fruit.

132.   **facit.** *Illa* (she) is no longer the subject.
         incertam. A substantive. Whom does it describe (note its gender)?
         haeret an haec sit = (illa) est (incerta) an haec sit (arbor dicta).

133-136. See sentence diagram below.

133.   **dubitat.** Still referring to Thisbe's uncertainty of 132.
         tremebunda. Does not modify the subject. What other case and gender could it be?
         pulsare. What is Pyramus doing? And what part of him is doing it (a gruesome detail)?

134.   **ora.** The object of *gerens*, modified by *pallidiora*: Thisbe is literally "wearing" an *ora pallidiora*.
         buxo. To be read with *pallidiora*.

136.   **quod.** What is the neuter antecedent of this pronoun? What is *tremit*?
         exigua. Not nominative.
         summum. Here a noun, i.e. *summum (aequoris)*.

Sentence Structure Diagram, lines 133-136

> Dum dubitat, tremebunda videt pulsare cruentum
> membra solum, retroque pedem tulit, oraque buxo
> pallidiora gerens exhorruit aequoris instar,
> quod tremit, exigua cum summum stringitur aura.

Dum <u>dubitat,</u>

   tremebunda
<u>videt</u>
   pulsare *cruentum* **membra** *solum,*

retroQUE pedem <u>tulit,</u>

   *ora*QUE buxo *pallidiora* <u>gerens</u>
<u>exhorruit</u> **aequoris** instar,
    QUOD tremit
      exigua CUM summum stringitur *aura.*

- there are three main verbs and one subordinate verb with Thisbe as their subject
- there are two other subordinate verbs
- underlined words refer to Thisbe, the subject
- italicized and bolded words agree with each other within their line (except for *aequoris* and *quod*)
- conjunctions are in all capitals

Ecce, metu nondum posito, ne fallat amantem,
illa redit, iuvenemque oculis animoque requirit,
quantaque vitarit narrare pericula gestit.   130
Utque locum et visa cognoscit in arbore formam,
sic facit incertam pomi color: haeret an haec sit.
Dum dubitat, tremebunda videt pulsare cruentum
membra solum retroque pedem tulit oraque buxo
pallidiora gerens exhorruit aequoris instar,   135
quod tremit, exigua cum summum stringitur aura.

Ecce illa, ne decipiat amantem, revertitur, pavore nondum sedato; et vestigat iuvenum oculis et mente, et laetatur referre quantum discrimen effugerit. Et postquam cognovit locum, et formam mutatum in arbore, dubitat an haec sit, ita color fructus facit incertam. Dum haeret, aspicit artus trementes quatere terram sanguinolentam; et gressum repressit, et vultus habens pallidiores buxo, exhorruit sicut mare quod strepit, cum superficies impellitur levi vento.

an (conj.). whether, if [*used to introduce "yes/no" indirect questions*]

buxus, -i (f.). the box-wood tree [*a tree known for the pale color of its bark*]

cruentus, -a, -um. bloody

dubito, -are, -avi, -atus. to doubt, to be uncertain

exhorresco, exhorrescere, exhorrui, -. to shudder (with fear)

exiguus, -a, -um. slight, paltry, minimal, small, barely noticeable

forma, -ae. shape, form, external appearance, body

gero, gerere, gessi, gestus. to bear, to carry, to wear, to reveal, to show, to indicate

gestio, gestire, gestivi, -. to really want, to desire

haereo, haerere, haesi, haesus. to stick, to be stuck, to cling, to be uncertain

instar (indecl.). the equivalent (of) [*sometimes used with a genitive noun to draw comparisons, i.e. something is the equivalent [*instar*] of [gen.] something else*]

membrum, -i. limb, part of the body

metus, -us. fear

nondum (adv.). not yet

pallidus, -a, -um. pale, colorless

pomum, -i. fruit

pulso, -are, -avi, -atus. to beat, to strike

requiro, requirere, requisivi, requisitus. to seek, to look for, to search for; to ask, to inquire

retro (adv.). back, backwards

solum, -i. ground, earth

stringo, stringere, strinxi, strictus. to bind, to draw near, to draw (a sword)

tremebundus, -a, -um. trembling, quivering

tremo, tremere, tremui, -. to tremble, to shake, to vibrate, to shiver, to shudder, to ripple

vito, -are, -avi, -atus. to avoid

Discussion Questions, lines 128-136

1. How does the *metu nondum posito* of line 128 connect to the *audacem faciebat amor* of line 96?
2. What is the effect of the description of Thisbe's actions in lines 128-130? How do they heighten our sympathy for her?
3. What is the narrative function of the *pomi color* of line 132?
4. How does the *tremebunda* of line 133 foreshadow Thisbe's reaction to Pyramus' death?
5. What is the effect of the enjambments in lines 133-135?
6. How does alliteration in line 133 reflect the meaning of the line?

137-144. *Thisbe tragically figures out what has happened and her reaction is described, until she finally cries out to Pyramus directly.*

137.   **suos amores = suum amorem**

139.   **comas.** An accusative of respect with *laniata*.

        amatum. Cannot be "lover." What form is this? And what neuter noun does it modify?

140.   **vulnera = vulnera (Pyrami)**

142.   **quis = qui.** Used here as an adjective that modifies *casus*.

        mihi = a me. A dative of separation with a verb of taking away, or a dative of disadvantage.

143.   **carissime = carissime (Pyrame)**

144.   **exaudi = exaudi (me).** Parallel in form to the *responde* of line 143 and the *attolle* of line 144.

145-146. *In a painful moment of recognition, Pyramus hears and reacts to Thisbe's words.*

145.   **Thisbes.** Whose *nomen* is it?

        iam, morte. To be read with *gravatos*, as indicated by framing.

146.   **visaque recondidit illa = et (Pyramus) recondidit, illa visa.** Neither *illa* nor *visa* are nominative.

Discussion Questions, lines 137-146

1. What is the effect of the *amatum* of line 139? Why does Ovid use *amatum* instead of *amoris* or *amantis* (both of which would fit the meter)?

2. What does the imagery of mixing and mingling in lines 140-141 represent?

3. Lines 142-144 represent the first time Pyramus and Thisbe are doing something. What is it? (For a hint, see line 63.)

4. How does the enjambment of *nominat* in line 144 reflect Thisbe's mindset?

5. How does the juxtaposition of *tua te* in line 143 emphasize Thisbe's devotion to Pyramus?

"Pyrame," clamavit, "quis te mihi casus ademit?
Pyrame, responde! Tua te, carissime, Thisbe
nominat; exaudi vultusque attolle iacentes!"

Sed postquam remorata suos cognovit amores,
percutit indignos claro plangore lacertos
et, laniata comas amplexaque corpus amatum,
vulnera supplevit lacrimis, fletumque cruori   140
miscuit, et gelidis in vultibus oscula figens
"Pyrame," clamavit, "quis te mihi casus ademit?
Pyrame, responde! Tua te, carissime, Thisbe
nominat; exaudi vultusque attolle iacentes."
Ad nomen Thisbes oculos iam morte gravatos   145
Pyramus erexit visaque recondidit illa.

Sed postquam per temporis spatium suum amatorem agnovisset, plangit immerita bracchia magnis ictibus: et discerpens capillos, et complexa corpus dilectum opplevit plagas lacrimis, et miscuit fletum sanguini; et deosculans os frigidum, "Pyrame," clamavit, "quod infortunium te mihi sustulit? Pyrame, responde: tua Thisbe te vocat, suavissime: exaudi, et erige vultus languentes." Pyramus aperuit oculos iam morte pressos ad nomen Thisbes, et ea conspecta clausit.

adimo, adimere, ademi, ademptus. to take away, to remove

amplector, amplecti, amplexus. to embrace

attollo, attollere, -, -. to lift (up), to raise (up)

casus, -us. misfortune, accident, mishap, tragedy

clarus, -a, -um. clear, loud, sharp

cognosco, cognoscere, cognovi, cognotus. to recognize, to learn; [*in the perfect tense*] to know

coma, -ae. hair

cruor, -oris (m.). blood, gore

erigo, erigere, erexi, erectus. to raise, to lift up

exaudio, exaudire, exaudivi, exauditus. to hear, to listen to

figo, figere, fixi, fixus. to drive in, to insert, to fix, to affix, to attach

fletus, -us. lamentation, sorrow, weeping

gelidus, -a, -um. cool, chilled

gravo, -are, -avi, -atus. to be heavy, to be weighed down, to oppress

lacertus, -i. arm, upper part of the arm

lanio, -are, -avi, -atus. to tear, to shred, to mutilate

misceo, miscere, miscui, mixtus. to mix, to blend, to mingle

nomino, -are, -avi, -atus. to call, to address, to name

percutio, percutere, percussi, percussus. to shake violently, to scratch, to tear at, to strike, to beat, to hit

plangor, plangoris (m.). lamentation, wailing, beating of the breast [*as a sign of distress or mourning*]

recondo, recondere, recondidi, reconditus. to put away, to close

remoror, remorari, remoratus. to delay, to pause

suppleo, supplere, supplevi, suppletus. to fill (with a liquid)

147-153. Thisbe addresses the dead Pyramus, and reveals her tragic intentions.

147.   **Quae = Thisbe.** A connective relative.
       -que. Here with the *et* of *cognovit et*: "both…and."
       ense. To be read with *vacuum.*
148.   **ebur.** Not the subject of *vidit*. What gender is this noun? And so what case?
       tua. Be careful about what this word modifies. Of *manus* and *amor*, which is feminine?
149.   **infelix.** Nominative, agreeing with *amor.*
       et = etiam
149-150. **in unum hoc = in unum hoc (factum),** referring to Thisbe's final act.
150.   **amor.** Parallel to *manus* of the previous clause.
       hic = hic (amor)
       in vulnera. To be read with *vires.*
       vires. Not a form of *vir, viri.*
151.   **Persequar, dicar.** Be careful of tense here.
       exstinctum = (te) exstinctum
151-152. **letique…tui = (et) dicar (esse) miserrima causa leti (tui) comesque (tua)**
151.   **dicar.** Be careful about voice here. This does not mean "I will say."
152-153. **quique…revelli = (et tu) qui heu poteras revelli a me morte sola, (tu non) poteris revelli morte**
152.   **a me.** This is not an ablative of agent (despite the passive *revelli*).

Discussion Questions, Lines 147-153

1. What is the effect of the enjambments in almost every line in lines 147-153?
2. Is the *amor* in line 148 *tuus amor, meus amor,* or *noster amor*? How does each reading change the emotional register of Thisbe's question?
3. Editors have read *infelix* in line 149 either with or without a comma preceding. What is the effect, both grammatical and interpretive, of the presence or absence of the comma? Which reading do you prefer? Explain your answer.
4. What is the significance of the *fortis* of line 149?
5. What is the effect of the postponement of the *amor* in line 150?
6. What is the effect of Ovid's parallel structure in lines 152-153?

Quae, postquam vestemque suam cognovit et ense
vidit ebur vacuum, "Tua te manus" inquit "amorque
perdidit, infelix. Est et mihi fortis in unum
hoc manus, est et amor: dabit hic in vulnera vires.   150
Persequar exstinctum, letique miserrima dicar
causa comesque tui, quique a me morte revelli
heu sola poteras, poteris nec morte revelli.

Quae postquam et agnovit velum suum, et vidit eburneam vaginam inanem gladio: "Manus tua," inquit, "et amor te mactavit, miser. Manus est etiam mihi strenua ad hoc unum; est etiam amor: hic sufficiet vires ad plagas. Prosequar mortuum, et infelicissima dicar causa et socia tuae mortis; et, heu!, qui poteras seiungi a me sola morte, neque poteris seiungi morte.

comes, comitis (m./f.). companion

ebur, eboris (n.). ivory, something made of ivory

ensis, ensis (m.). sword

exstinguo, exstinguere, exstinxi, exstinctus. to extinguish [*in both a literal and a figurative sense, i.e. a fire or a life*]

letum, -i. death

perdo, perdere, perdidi, perditus. to destroy, to ruin

persequor, persequi, persecutus. to follow completely, to pursue

revello, revellere, revelli, revulsus. to tear away, to remove with force

solus, -a, -um. alone, lone [*an irregular adjective whose genitive singular ends in* -ius *and whose dative singular ends in* -i]

vacuus, -a, -um. empty, hollow; devoid of (+ abl.)

vis, - (f.; defec.; nom. and acc. pl. = vires). strength, power, force

154-157. Thisbe now addresses both her parents and Pyramus' parents, asking them for a final favor.

154. **Hoc.** A neuter pronoun that refers to what will be *rogati*.
      estote rogati = rogabimini, but with a less harsh sense, i.e. "you shall" or "may you" instead of "you will."
155. **o…parentes.** This is one large vocative expression.
      multum miseri = miserrimi
      meus illiusque parentes = mei parentes et Pyrami parentes. Both *meus* and *illius* show possession, the former as a possessive adjective, the latter as a genitive of *ille.*
156. **ut.** Introduces a noun clause that functions as the object of *estote rogati* or an appositive to the *hoc* of 154.
      quos certus amor. What is the verb for this clause? How does parallel structure help?
      quos, quos. Have as their antecedent an understood *nos.*
      novissima. Will not mean "new" in this context.
157. **componi.** Be careful of voice here.
      invideatis. Has as its object the understood *nos* of 156 and the two clauses that go with it.

158-161. Thisbe now turns her attention to the tree itself.

158-159. **At tu…duorum = At tu, arbor, quae nunc tegis ramis miserabile corpus unius, (arbor quae) mox tectura es (corpora miserabilia) duorum…**
158. **miserabile.** Not an ablative.
159. **nunc tegis, mox es tectura.** The *tegis* refers to the current situation (*nunc*); the *tectura* refers to the future situation (*mox*).
160. **signa.** Refers to the visible change that will occur as a result of the death of Pyramus and Thisbe.
      caedis. To be read with *signa.*
161. **gemini.** Does not agree with *monimenta.*

Discussion Questions, Lines 154-161

1. How does Ovid rhetorically embellish Thisbe's request in lines 154-157?
2. What is the significance of the *amborum* of line 154?
3. What is the effect of the extended vocative of line 155?
4. How does the *at* of line 158 signal a change in focus for Thisbe's speech?
5. What is the significance of addressing in the second person both the parents in lines 154-157, and the tree in lines 158-161?
6. How does the mood of the verbs impact the tone of Thisbe's address to her parents and the tree?

Hoc tamen amborum verbis estote rogati,
o multum miseri meus illiusque parentes,   155
ut quos certus amor, quos hora novissima iunxit,
componi tumulo non invideatis eodem.
At tu, quae ramis arbor miserabile corpus
nunc tegis unius, mox es tectura duorum,
signa tene caedis pullosque et luctibus aptos   160
semper habe fetus, gemini monimenta cruoris."

Attamen, o parentes meus et illius valde infelices, estote rogati amborum nomine, ut non prohibeatis condi eodem sepulchro quos amor verus, quos hora ultima in unum coegit. At tu, arbor, quae nunc operis ramis corpus luctuosum unius, mox es opertura duorum, habe indicia necis, et serva fructus nigros et idoneos luctibus, documenta duplicis sanguinis."

ambo, ambae, ambo. both [*this is an irregular adjective that only occurs in the plural, and whose masculine and neuter nominative can be misleading because of the* -o *ending*]

aptus, -a, -um. appropriate, easy, apt

compono, componere, composui, compositus. to assemble, to put together

fetus, -us. fruit, offspring

geminus, -i. twin, double

invideo, invidere, invidi, invisus. to refuse, to begrudge, to be resentful that

luctus, -us. grief, lamentation

miser, misera, miserum. miserable, wretched, sad, pitiable, awful

miserabilis, -e. miserable, distraught

monimentum, -i. monument, memorial

pullus, -a, -um. dark, dreary-colored

tego, tegere, texi, tectus. to cover, to hide

teneo, tenere, tenui, tentus. to have, to hold, to keep

tumulus, -i. grave, grave mound, tomb

unus, -a, -um. one, lone, alone [*an irregular adjective whose genitive singular ends in* -ius *and whose dative singular ends in* -i]

162-164. The resolution of the story. Thisbe completes the tragedy, and her prayers are heard and answered by both the gods and her and Pyramus' parents.

162.   **dixit.** This marks the end of Thisbe's speech.
         aptato pectus mucrone sub imum. What did Thisbe put where? What construction is this?
         pectus sub imum. To be read with *aptato*.
163.   **a caede = a caede (Pyrami)**

165-166. The final two lines of Ovid's tale are devoted to the commemoration of the tragic lives of Pyramus and Thisbe.

165.   **in pomo.** To be read with *color*.
166.   **quod rogis superest = (illud) quod rogis superest.** Refers to the cremation of Pyramus and Thisbe; the entire clause (or the understood antecedent) is the subject of *requiescit*.
         rogis. Not the subject of *superest*.

Discussion Questions, Lines 162-166

1. What is the significance of the *adhuc a caede tepebat* of line 163?
2. Why does Ovid include the *vota tetigere deos* in line 164? Does this contribute to or detract from the tragedy of the story? Explain your answer.

Overview Discussion Questions

1. Count how many apostrophes occur in the Pyramus and Thisbe story. Count how many dialogues occur. What is the thematic significance of this ratio?
2. Analyze the mechanics of separation in the story. How does Ovid use the concept of separation and togetherness as a means of unifying the story?
3. The story of Semiramis, the legendary queen of Babylon, focuses on her anomalous role as a female ruler, with some versions even suggesting that she killed her husband (Ninus) to assume power over Babylon. How should the inclusion of Semiramis at the outset of Ovid's story affect our reading of Thisbe and her role in the story?
4. The Pyramus and Thisbe story appears in the *Metamorphoses* as one of many stories told by the Minyades, or the daughters of Minyas. These women lived in the Greek city of Thebes, where the god Dionysius (Roman Bacchus) had just punished those who refused to worship him. In response to this punishment, a feast day for Dionysius was declared, and all women were ordered to stop working and to worship the god of wine. The Minyades, however, refused to participate and instead chose to tell stories instead. The story of Pyramus and Thisbe is the first story they told. How does this context change your reading of the story?

Dixit et, aptato pectus mucrone sub imum,
incubuit ferro, quod adhuc a caede tepebat.
Vota tamen tetigere deos, tetigere parentes;
nam color in pomo est, ubi permaturuit, ater,
quodque rogis superest, una requiescit in urna.

165

Dixit, et cuspide accommodato ad infimum pectus immisit se gladio, qui adhuc calidus erat a sanguine Pyrami. Ceterum preces moverunt deos, moverunt parentes. Nam color est niger in fructu mori, ubi ad maturitatem pervenit; et quod reliquum est ex pyris compositum est in una urna.

adhuc (adv.). still

apto, -are, -avi, -atus. to put, to place, to fit

ater, atra, atrum. black, dark

imus, -a, -um. the lowest (part of)

incumbo, incumbere, incubui, - (+ dat.). to fall (on), to lie down (on), to thrust oneself (on)

mucro, mucronis (m.). the sharp end of a sword, the point, the tip

permaturesco, permaturescere, permaturui, -. to become fully ripe, to ripen

requiesco, requiescere, requievi, requieturus. to rest, to lie at rest

rogus, -i. funeral pyre

supersum, superesse, superfui, -. to remain, to be left over

tango, tangere, tetigi, tactus. to touch, to reach

tepeo, tepere, -, -. to be warm, to have warmth, to grow warm, to heat up

urna, -ae. vase, (funerary) urn [*for holding the remains of a cremation*]

votum, -i. prayer

Chapter Four

Ars Latet Arte Sua

Amores 3.15
Daedalus and Icarus
Pygmalion

Introduction

> *If people knew how hard I worked to get my*
> *mastery, it wouldn't seem so wonderful at all.*
> *- Michelangelo*

> *I said, "A line will take us hours maybe;*
> *Yet if it does not seem a moment's thought,*
> *Our stitching and unstitching has been naught."*
> *- W. B. Yeats, "Adam's Curse"*

Painters. Sculptors. Writers. Actors. Engineers. Designers. Even athletes. The creative impulse is in all of us, yet some are clearly better at channeling it into something beautiful or inspirational or controversial or insightful than others. Ovid, as one of these creators, is especially interested in this creative process; it is in fact the theme perhaps most seminal to his work, next to love and its psychology. And in this final chapter, Ovid examines this process in three very different ways.

Amores 3.15 is the final poem of the *Amores,* and he uses it as an opportunity to reflect on the collection and its place in literary history: what has he created as an artist with his *Amores,* and how will history receive it? Artistic themes also

appear repeatedly in the *Metamorphoses*. In the story of Arachne, the young woman who bragged that she was a better weaver than Athena and who was turned into a spider after losing (perhaps) a weaving contest to the goddess, Ovid spends much of the story with an elaborate ekphrasis of the tapestries that each woman wove. The story of Procne and Philomela, one of Ovid's darkest and most disconcerting stories in the *Metamorphoses,* details how a new husband raped his bride's sister and then cut her tongue out to prevent her from telling anyone. She responds by weaving her story into a tapestry and sending it to her sister. Both stories illustrate the use of art as a means of communication and as an extension of the voice of the artist. Whether that artist is Ovid himself or Ovid's character is a question that Ovid leaves unanswered.

The creative impulse is for Ovid the artistic expression of the same emotional processes that produce love: as the lover loves, so the artist creates. Thus Ovid will explore art and the creative process in a variety of situations, from the tragic to the ideal, parallelling the variety of incarnations of love in the *Metamorphoses*. The two stories from the *Metamorphoses* that are included here cover the potential of art for both tragedy and beauty: Daedalus, the master Athenian craftsman, watches his art lead to the death of his son, while Pygmalion, the Cypriot sculptor who retreats to his art after rejecting society, is rewarded by Venus for his creation of the ultimate beauty.

Art and love in many ways share similar characteristics. Both produce in us emotions which can affect us profoundly and inexplicably. Both are constantly explored because of our inability to explain them adequately. And both are sublime in their mystery; vestiges of the divine exist in both. And in the amalgam of myth, emotion, and psychology that underlies both artistic production and love, perhaps we find the best representation of Ovid's artistic output, certainly in the *Metamorphoses* and its explicit focus on myth, but also in the *Amores* and the rest of Ovid's *oeuvre*.

Amores 3.15

Quaere novum vatem, tenerorum mater Amorum:
    raditur haec elegis ultima meta meis;
quos ego composui, Paeligni ruris alumnus,
    (nec me deliciae dedecuere meae)
si quid id est, usque a proavis vetus ordinis heres,   5
    non modo militiae turbine factus eques.
Mantua Vergilio gaudet, Verona Catullo;
    Paelignae dicar gloria gentis ego,
quam sua libertas ad honesta coegerat arma,
    cum timuit socias anxia Roma manus.   10
Atque aliquis spectans hospes Sulmonis aquosi
    moenia, quae campi iugera pauca tenent,
"Quae tantum," dicet, "potuistis ferre poetam,
    quantulacumque estis, vos ego magna voco."
Culte puer puerique parens Amathusia culti,   15
    aurea de campo vellite signa meo:
corniger increpuit thyrso graviore Lyaeus;
    pulsanda est magnis area maior equis.
Imbelles elegi, genialis Musa, valete,
    post mea mansurum fata superstes opus.   20

Metamorphoses 8.183-235: **Daedalus and Icarus**

Daedalus interea Creten longumque perosus   183
exilium tactusque soli natalis amore
clausus erat pelago. "Terras licet" inquit "et undas   185
obstruat, at caelum certe patet; ibimus illac!
Omnia possideat, non possidet aera Minos."
Dixit et ignotas animum dimittit in artes
naturamque novat. Nam ponit in ordine pennas,
a minima coeptas, longam breviore sequente,   190
ut clivo crevisse putes: sic rustica quondam
fistula disparibus paulatim surgit avenis.
Tum lino medias et ceris alligat imas
atque ita compositas parvo curvamine flectit
ut veras imitetur aves. Puer Icarus una   195
stabat et, ignarus sua se tractare pericla,
ore renidenti modo, quas vaga moverat aura,
captabat plumas, flavam modo pollice ceram
mollibat lusuque suo mirabile patris
impediebat opus. Postquam manus ultima coepto   200
imposita est, geminas opifex libravit in alas
ipse suum corpus motaque pependit in aura.
Instruit et natum "Medio"que "ut limite curras,
Icare," ait, "moneo, ne, si demissior ibis,
unda gravet pennas, si celsior, ignis adurat: 205
inter utrumque vola, nec te spectare Booten
aut Helicen iubeo strictumque Orionis ensem;
me duce carpe viam." Pariter praecepta volandi
tradit et ignotas umeris accommodat alas.
Inter opus monitusque genae maduere seniles   210
et patriae tremuere manus. Dedit oscula nato
non iterum repetenda suo pennisque levatus
ante volat comitique timet, velut ales ab alto
quae teneram prolem produxit in aera nido,
hortaturque sequi damnosasque erudit artes.   215
Et movet ipse suas et nati respicit alas.
Hos aliquis tremula dum captat harundine pisces,
aut pastor baculo, stivave innixus arator
vidit et obstipuit, quique aethera carpere possent

credidit esse deos. Et iam Iunonia laeva   220
parte Samos (fuerant Delosque Parosque relictae),
dextra Lebinthos erat fecundaque melle Calymne,
cum puer audaci coepit gaudere volatu
deseruitque ducem caelique cupidine tractus
altius egit iter. Rapidi vicinia solis   225
mollit odoratas, pennarum vincula, ceras.
Tabuerant cerae; nudos quatit ille lacertos
remigioque carens non ullas percipit auras,
oraque caerulea patrium clamantia nomen
excipiuntur aqua, quae nomen traxit ab illo.   230
At pater infelix nec iam pater "Icare" dixit,
"Icare," dixit, "ubi es? Qua te regione requiram?"
"Icare" dicebat: pennas aspexit in undis
devovitque suas artes corpusque sepulcro
condidit; est tellus a nomine dicta sepulti.   235

Metamorphoses: 10.238-297: Pygmalion

    Sunt tamen obscenae Venerem Propoetides ausae   238
esse negare deam; pro quo sua numinis ira
corpora cum forma primae vulgasse feruntur,   240
utque pudor cessit sanguisque induruit oris,
in rigidum parvo silicem discrimine versae.
    Quas quia Pygmalion aevum per crimen agentes
viderat, offensus vitiis quae plurima menti
femineae natura dedit, sine coniuge caelebs   245
vivebat thalamique diu consorte carebat.
Interea niveum mira feliciter arte
sculpsit ebur formamque dedit, qua femina nasci
nulla potest, operisque sui concipit amorem.
Virginis est verae facies, quam vivere credas   250
et, si non obstet reverentia, velle moveri:
ars adeo latet arte sua. Miratur et haurit
pectore Pygmalion simulati corporis ignes.
Saepe manus operi temptantes admovet, an sit
corpus an illud ebur, nec adhuc ebur esse fatetur,   255
oscula dat reddique putat loquiturque tenetque
sed credit tactis digitos insidere membris
et metuit, pressos veniat ne livor in artus,
et modo blanditias adhibet, modo grata puellis
munera fert illi, conchas teretesque lapillos   260
et parvas volucres et flores mille colorum
liliaque pictasque pilas et ab arbore lapsas
Heliadum lacrimas. Ornat quoque vestibus artus;
dat digitis gemmas, dat longa monilia collo,
aure leves bacae, redimicula pectore pendent: 265
cuncta decent; nec nuda minus formosa videtur.
Collocat hanc stratis concha Sidonide tinctis
appellatque tori sociam acclinataque colla
mollibus in plumis tamquam sensura reponit.
    Festa dies Veneris tota celeberrima Cypro   270
venerat, et pandis inductae cornibus aurum
conciderant ictae nivea cervice iuvencae,
turaque fumabant, cum munere functus ad aras

constitit et timide, "Si, di, dare cuncta potestis,
sit coniunx, opto," (non ausus "eburnea virgo"   275
dicere) Pygmalion "similis mea" dixit "eburnae."
Sensit, ut ipsa suis aderat Venus aurea festis,
vota quid illa velint et, amici numinis omen,
flamma ter accensa est apicemque per aera duxit.
Ut rediit, simulacra suae petit ille puellae   280
incumbensque toro dedit oscula visa tepere est:
Admovet os iterum, manibus quoque pectora temptat;
temptatum mollescit ebur positoque rigore
subsedit digitis ceditque, ut Hymettia sole
cera remollescit tractataque pollice multas   285
flectitur in facies ipsoque fit utilis usu.
Dum stupet et dubie gaudet fallique veretur,
rursus amans rursusque manu sua vota retractat.
Corpus erat! saliunt temptatae pollice venae.
Tum vero Paphius plenissima concipit heros   290
verba quibus Veneri grates agit, oraque tandem
ore suo non falsa premit, dataque oscula virgo
sensit et erubuit, timidumque ad lumina lumen
attollens pariter cum caelo vidit amantem.
Coniugio, quod fecit, adest dea, iamque coactis   295
cornibus in plenum noviens lunaribus orbem
illa Paphon genuit, de quo tenet insula nomen.   297

Amores 3.15 Introduction

How far has Ovid come since *Amores* 1.1? The last poem of his collection of love poems, *Amores* 3.15 should indicate some sense of progress on Ovid's part throughout the *Amores*; if nothing else, it forces us to reconsider the opening poem of the *Amores*. If you remember, *Amores* 1.1 opened with Ovid hoping and trying to write epic. Cupid stepped in, stole a foot, and forced Ovid to write love elegy. Now, three books later, is Ovid any more accustomed to his adopted genre? Has he eventually assimilated to the poetry that Cupid has forced him to write? It would seem not.

The premise of *Amores* 3.15 is a standard one for the closing poem of a collection. Called the *sphragis* poem (from the Greek word for "seal" because it seals the collection), it not only concludes the poetic collection but also declares the poet's desire for lasting fame through his poetry. Ovid's *sphragis* poem is no different. He establishes himself and his literary worth, and closes with the hope that his poetry will live on beyond him.

But Ovid, as we should expect, cannot close his collection in a purely conventional way. He returns to the martial imagery that characterized *Amores* 1.1 by alluding to his hometown's role in the Social Wars of 90 BC. He refers to his elegies as *imbelles*, "unwarlike," recalling the epic that he wanted to write but could not. And he both opens and closes the poem with the related, competitive imagery of the chariot race, with its obvious suggestions of battle. The question remains, however: why? Why does Ovid persist in such imagery?

The tone of *Amores* 3.15 seems to be dismissive: Ovid has done what Cupid has forced him to do, but now can return to the epic poetry he originally set out to write. Ovid both opens and closes the poem with imperatives, both of which ask their addressee to in effect go away. Ovid uses such imperatives to say goodbye to his poetic collection, but he forces us to ask whether he is at the same time saying goodbye (and good riddance) to love elegy.

If Ovid is indeed bidding elegy farewell, he also returns to and perhaps answers the question of genre that he has been exploring throughout the *Amores*. If Ovid wrote *Amores* 1.1 and other poems in the *Amores* to purposefully flaunt the conventions of elegiac poetry and so to force us to question to what extent his elegies are true elegies, and if *Amores* 3.15 closes the collection on a similarly flaunting note, it suggests that Ovid was never writing true elegy. It suggests that Ovid was only writing elegy to satisfy the aggressive elegiac Cupid of *Amores* 1.1. Now that Ovid has fulfilled his requirements, now that he has done what he was supposed to do, he will happily, if dispassionately, wrap up the collection of poetry that he was reluctant to write to begin with.

It is characteristic of Ovid to leave more questions asked than answered. But perhaps at the close of the *Amores* Ovid does in fact answer one of his own questions. Perhaps indeed he confirms that he has been writing deliberately self-conscious love poetry whose fundamental goal is to call into question the conventions of elegy by presenting an elegiac lover defined not by his passion but rather by his lack of passion.

Artists are rarely paid millions. They don't have highlight shows. They live in relative obscurity. So how then is the fame of an artist measured? Artists achieve immortality through the fame of their work. Classical poets in particular frequently included a bid for such fame in the last poem of their collection. *Amores* 3.15 is Ovid's bid for such fame.

1-2. Ovid orders Venus to find a new poet; he is finished with his love poetry.

1.   **mater.** A vocative with the imperative *quaere.*
2.   **raditur ultima meta.** The image is of rounding the turning post in a chariot race. See the accompanying illustration at bottom right.

3-6. Ovid offers a description of his background: where he is from, his ancestors, and their social status.

3.   **quos.** Its antecedent is *elegis,* and here is a connective relative.
         ruris. Not a dative or ablative plural. What declension is this word?
         alumnus. In apposition to *ego.*
5.   **si quid id est** = "If it is anything" or "If it means anything."
         quid. Remember what *quid* means after *si* (and *nisi, num,* and *ne*).
         usque. To be read with *a.*
         proavis. Does not agree with *ordinis.*
         vetus. Agrees with *heres* but describes *ordinis.* What figure of speech is this?
5-6.   **heres, eques.** In apposition to the *ego* of line 3 (as is *alumnus*).
6.   Ovid's family is equestrian by their own virtue rather than being promoted just because of the necessities of war. Many Roman families rose in social status because of a relaxing of the requirements for military service. As such requirements were relaxed, families who would not have otherwise been able to serve in the military could suddenly serve. With such service came an increase in social status. Ovid says here that his familiy was not of these families.
         non modo. To be read with *turbine.*

Discussion Questions, lines 1-6

1. How does line 1 recall the opening of *Amores* 1.1? Does Ovid intend it to be read ironically or not? Explain your answer.
2. Explain the imagery in line 2. Why does Ovid use such imagery?
3. What is the effect of Ovid referring to himself as a *Paeligni ruris alumnus* in line 3?

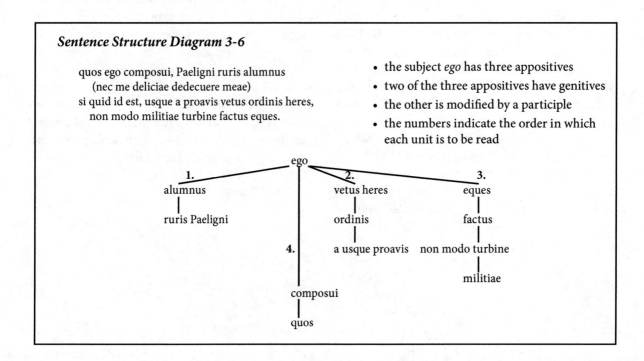

Sentence Structure Diagram 3-6

    quos ego composui, Paeligni ruris alumnus
        (nec me deliciae dedecuere meae)
    si quid id est, usque a proavis vetus ordinis heres,
        non modo militiae turbine factus eques.

- the subject *ego* has three appositives
- two of the three appositives have genitives
- the other is modified by a participle
- the numbers indicate the order in which each unit is to be read

Quaere novum vatem, tenerorum mater Amorum:
    raditur haec elegis ultima meta meis;
quos ego composui, Paeligni ruris alumnus,
    (nec me deliciae dedecuere meae)
si quid id est, usque a proavis vetus ordinis heres,   5
    non modo militiae turbine factus eques.

Mater mollium amorum, quaere alium poetam: ultima meta hic teritur meis elegis; quos ego alumnus agri Paeligni conscripsi: nec mei lusus mihi dedecori fuerunt; mihi inquam, si id est aliquid, qui sum antiquus heres ordinis equestris usque a proavis, non nuper creatus eques motibus belli.

alumnus, -i. native, child

dedecet, dedecere, dedecuit, - (impers.). it is not fitting, it is inappropriate

delicia, -ae. pleasure, enjoyment, delight

elegi, -orum (m. pl.). elegiac verses, elegiac poetry

eques, equitis. horseman, cavalryman

heres, heredis (m.). heir

meta, -ae. turning-point; turning post [*the post around which chariots turned in Roman chariot races; often used metaphorically to refer to a turning point or shift in events*]

militia, -ae. military service

Paelignus, -a, -um. Paelignian; of or belonging to the Paelignians [*an ancient tribe of central Italy*]

proavus, -i. ancestor, forefather

rado, radere, rasi, rasus. to scrape, to wipe; to pass closely, to sneak around

turbo, turbinis (m.). something spinning; whirlpool, whirlwind

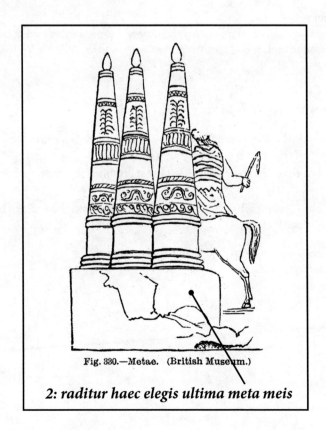

Fig. 330.—Metae. (British Museum.)

2: raditur haec elegis ultima meta meis

7-10. Ovid associates himself and his fame with his hometown of Sulmo (modern Sulmona), and cites the hometowns of Vergil and Catullus, and their admiration for their poets, as parallels.

7. The Roman poet Vergil was from Mantua in Northern Italy and the Roman poet Catullus was from Verona, also in Northern Italy. But neither *Vergilio* nor *Catullo* are nominatives.

8. **dicar** = dicar (esse). Be careful of voice here. Also, is this verb future indicative or present subjunctive?

9. **sua.** Refers to the *Paelignae gentis* of 8. The *sua libertas* is the *libertas* the Paelignians wanted when they joined the uprising against Rome of the Italian cities whose citizens did not possess Roman citizenship to gain greater political influence. This uprising of 90 BC was also known as the Social War, and was resolved quickly when Rome agreed to confer citizenship on the inhabitants of all cities south of the Po, a river in Northern Italy.

    libertas. Not an accusative plural.

    honesta. An adjective. What does it agree with? Its meaning justifies the role of the Paelignians in the Social War.

10. **timuit.** The subject here is postponed. What is the nominative in this line?

    socias. Not a noun. What does it modify?

    anxia. Reflects the effect of the Social War on Rome itself, and foreshadows its success.

    manus. Not a nominative. What declension is this?

11-14. Ovid introduces an anonymous visitor to his hometown of Sulmo as a way both to mention the strength of its walls, and to include an objective commentator to reinforce the impressiveness of Ovid's achievement.

11. **hospes.** Not a plural noun. What modifies it?

    spectans. This verb will take an object. What is it? (Be careful of the enjambment.)

12. **moenia.** Be careful of the gender of this word.

    quae. There is no feminine to be the antecedent of this pronoun. What other gender can it be?

    campi. Not the subect of *tenent*. What other case can it be?

13. **quae...voco** = ...dicet, "Ego voco vos (moenia) **magna, quantulacumque estis, quae potuistis ferre tantum poetam.**"

    quae. The antecedent is the *vos* of 14.

    dicet. Be careful of tense here. Remember that the *hospes* has not yet arrived at the *moenia*.

14. **vos.** Refers to the *moenia*, and so will retain the gender of *moenia*. What adjective modifies this?

Discussion Questions, lines 7-14

1. Why does Ovid include the historical note in lines 9-10? How does that reinforce what he is saying about himself?

2. Identify specific Latin words or phrases in lines 9-14 that establish the contrast between the Paelignians and the Romans.

3. What two words in lines 13-14 establish a contrast between Ovid and the walls of his hometown? What is the intention of this contrast?

Mantua Vergilio gaudet, Verona Catullo;
   Paelignae dicar gloria gentis ego,
quam sua libertas ad honesta coegerat arma,
   cum timuit socias anxia Roma manus.   10
Atque aliquis spectans hospes Sulmonis aquosi
   moenia, quae campi iugera pauca tenent,
"Quae tantum," dicet, "potuistis ferre poetam,
   quantulacumque estis, vos ego magna voco."

Mantua sibi plaudit Virgilio, Verona Catullo: ego perhibebor laus nationis Paelignae: quam sua libertas impulerat ad arma decora, cum Roma solicita metuit manus sociales. Atque aliquis peregrinus intuens muros Sulmonis aquatici, qui complectuntur pauca iugera agri, "Qui," inquiet, "potuistis sustinere tantum poetam, quantulicumque estis, ego vos nomino magnos."

anxius, -a, -um. anxious, worried, concerned

aquosus, -a, -um. watery, well-watered

cogo, cogere, coegi, coactus. to force, to compel

iugerum, -i. measure of land, acre, acreage

libertas, libertatis (f.). freedom, liberty

Mantua, -ae. [name: *a town in northern Italy where the Roman poet Vergil was born*]

Paelignus, -a, -um. Paelignian; of or belonging to the Paelignians [*an ancient tribe of central Italy*]

quantuluscumque, quantulacumque, quantulumcumque. however small

socius, -a, -um. of or belonging to a companion

Sulmo, Sulmonis (m.). [name: *modern Sulmona, a town just east of Rome over the mountains where Ovid was born*]

Vergilius, -i. [name: *Vergil, the Roman poet of the* Aeneid *and a poetic influence on Ovid*]

Verona, -ae. [name: *a city in northern Italy where the poet Catullus was born*]

15-18. Ovid uses the same juxtaposition between martial imagery and references to love poetry with which he began the **Amores** *(1.1), invoking both Cupid and Venus, as well as Bacchus.*

15.   **culte…culti.** An extensive vocative expression that addresses two people.
      culte. Not an ablative. Remember what this line is doing and in what case it will then be.
      puer. Not nominative. What modifies it?

16.   **vellite.** What kind of verb will often (but not always) accompany a vocative? This verb will have a special meaning with *signa*. What is it?

17.   **graviore.** "Heavier" will not really work here. What else can the comparative mean?

18.   **pulsanda est.** When used with *equis*, what will this verb mean?
      area. Roughly equivalent in meaning to the *campo* of line 16.

19-20. A final prediction on the longevity of Ovid's work.

19.   **elegi, Musa.** Both vocatives here.

20.   **post…opus = superstes opus, mansurum post mea fata**
      mansurum. "About to remain" does not quite capture the meaning here. A relative clause will work better.
      superstes. A very tricky form: neither plural nor masculine / feminine. What does this modify? What will be *superstes*?

Discussion Questions, lines 15-20

1.   How is the imagery of lines 15 and 17 juxtaposed against the imagery of lines 16 and 18? Identify specific Latin words or phrases that support your answer.

2.   Identify figures of speech in lines 15-18 that intensify Ovid's conclusion.

3.   How does the final couplet change the tone of Ovid's conclusion? Why does he address both the *elegi* and the *Musa* directly?

4.   What is the significance of *opus* as the last word of the last poem of Ovid's *Amores*?

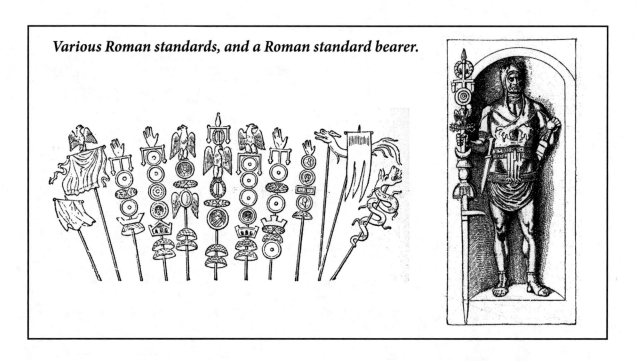

Various Roman standards, and a Roman standard bearer.

Culte puer puerique parens Amathusia culti,   15
    aurea de campo vellite signa meo:
corniger increpuit thyrso graviore Lyaeus;
    pulsanda est magnis area maior equis.
Imbelles elegi, genialis Musa, valete,
    post mea mansurum fata superstes opus.   20

Splendide puer, et mater Amathusia pueri splendidi, tollite signa splendida de meo agro. Corniger Lyaeus me perculit thyrso maiore: vastior campus est premendus magnis equis. Elegi molles, genialis Musa, opus duraturum superstes post meum obitum, valete.

Amathusius, -a, -um. Amathusian; of or belonging to Amathusia [*a city in Cyrprus where Venus is said to have been born*]

area, -ae. area, (open) space

aureus, -a, -um. golden, of gold

corniger, cornigera, cornigerum. horned, horn-bearing

cultus, -a, -um. cultivated, elegant, refined

elegi, -orum (m. pl.). elegiac verses, elegiac poetry

genialis, -e. genial, friendly, appealing, jovial

imbellis, -e. not warlike, unsuited to war

increpo, increpare, increpui, increpitus. to beat loudly, to strike loudly; to make noise, to make a loud noise

Lyaeus, -i. [name: *an alternate name for Bacchus, the god of wine*]

pulso, -are, -avi, -atus. to beat, to strike

superstes, superstitis. surviving, living, alive

thyrsus, -i. thyrsus [*the staff carried by Bacchus and his retinue; it was topped with some sort of vegetation, often a pine cone*]

vello, vellere, vulsi, vulsus. to pull out, to remove, to pull up; [*with signa*]: to remove an army's standards [*to indicate the departure of the army from that place*]

Ad Comparanda.

The sphragis of Ovid's *Metamorphoses*, and the sphragis poem of the poet Horace's collection.

Iamque opus exegi, quod nec Iovis ira nec ignis
nec poterit ferrum nec edax abolere vetustas.
Cum volet, illa dies, quae nil nisi corporis huius
ius habet, incerti spatium mihi finiat aevi:
parte tamen meliore mei super alta perennis
astra ferar, nomenque erit indelibile nostrum,
quaque patet domitis Romana potentia terris,
ore legar populi, perque omnia saecula fama,
siquid habent veri vatum praesagia, vivam.
        (*Metamorphoses* 15.871-879)

Exegi monumentum aere perennius
regalique situ pyramidum altius,
quod non imber edax, non Aquilo impotens
possit diruere aut innumerabilis
annorum series et fuga temporum.
        (Horace, *Odes* 3.30.1-5)

Introduction to *Daedalus and Icarus*

iPods. Cell phones. Wireless networks. Bluetooth. Blackberries. The Greek word *techne*, from which the English word "technology" is derived, means "art" or "skill" and is essentially synonymous with the Latin *ars*. Any new application of skill (or art; to the Greeks and Romans, much less of a distinction between the two would be made than we do today) then is a form of technology.

Daedalus, the architect of the Labyrinth, was by this definition an early Bill Gates. He was an engineer, in the sense that his job was to design things to solve problems. Originally an Athenian, he left Athens because of a murder charge; whom he murdered is disputed, but in some versions it was the murder of his pupil Perdix, who Daedalus feared was a better craftsman than he (and whose story follows Daedalus' in the *Metamorphoses*). Daedalus fled to the island of Crete, where he was welcomed by the Cretan king Minos. Minos, however, would soon regret Daedalus' arrival.

Minos' wife Pasiphae, because of an insult to the gods (whether Minos insulted Poseidon or Pasiphae insulted Venus is disputed), was made to fall in love with a bull. She went to Daedalus with her problem, and he designed for her a hollow cow so that she might realize her love for the bull. From their union was born the half-man, half-bull Minotaur. Minos, enraged at Daedalus for his role in Pasiphae's affair, had him build the labyrinth, an elaborate maze at the center of which the Minotaur lived, and then imprisoned him as well. Daedalus' imprisonment and resentment of Minos is where Ovid begins his story.

Daedalus' story, in Ovid's hands, becomes in turns poignant and heartwarming, fantastic and awe-inspiring, tragic and painful. He is the careful and conscientious craftsman. He is the old designer hunched over his table and his tools. He is the tender and loving father. His son Icarus could not be more different. Icarus hops around his father's workshop. You imagine him touching everything, moving carefully placed tools out of place, humming and tapping, being a nuisance.

He understands none of the precision that goes into his father's work, and worse, is pathetically unaware of the fate that awaits him. But, despite his obvious shortcomings, he remains his father's son. Ovid leaves no doubt that Daedalus loves his son. In the end, however, all Daedalus can do is warn him of the danger of his endeavor, and hope that he listens. We know of course that Icarus does not listen; Ovid describes the beginning of Icarus' fall the way we might imagine a teenager getting carried away behind the wheel of a car. All parents must ultimately let their children (in this case literally) spread their wings; every child strives for independence from his parents. Icarus' story, however, captures the pain when that bid for independence goes horribly wrong.

Ultimately, we learn what Daedalus learns: that technology is a double-edged sword. While on the one hand, Daedalus' skill as an engineer has always brought him renown and fame, on the other hand, it now has brought him pain and tragedy. The success of technology is entirely dependent on its user or its application. While Daedalus' wings brought him freedom, they brought tragedy to him and his ill-fated son Icarus. Deadalus' lesson then becomes our lesson; its universality is one of the reasons his story has remained so popular: with great power comes great responsibility.

Daedalus and Icarus At-A-Glance

Book	8
Lines	183-235
Main Characters (in order of appearance)	Daedalus: Athenian master craftsman who lives on Crete Icarus: Daedalus' son
Minor Characters	Minos: King of Crete fisherman, shepherd, ploughman: observers of Daedalus and Icarus flying in the sky
Context	The Theseus story, beginning in book 7 and stretching into the beginning of book 9
Preceeding Story	Minos and Scylla. Scylla killed her father, Minos' enemy, because of her love for Minos. Minos, however, horrified by her deed, refused her love but punished her people. She tried to follow Minos to Crete but was attacked by her father who had been changed into a bird. She too was turned into a bird.
Transition	The Minotaur. Daedalus builds the labyrinth to house the Mintoaur but hates being away from home and working for his enemy Minos.
Subsequent Story	Perdix. Perdix, the partridge, observes Daedalus' grief after Icarus' death and rejoices. Perdix was Daedalus' nephew, whom his sister gave to Daedalus to mentor. (The story happens before Daedalus' exile to Crete and so before the Daedalus and Icarus story, even though Ovid tells Perdix's story afterward.) Perdix's skills were prodigious, perhaps even surpassing Daedalus'. Daedalus, out of jealousy, whether because his own son was not as skilled as Perdix or because Perdix was more skilled than Daedalus himself, pushed Perdix from the roof of the temple of Athena, but she saved him by turning him into a bird (the partridge).
Primary Topics	hubris the golden mean the rashness of youth the advantages and disadvantages of technology

Daedalus and Icarus Vocabulary Frequency

5 times
    dico, -ere
    Icarus, -i
    penna, -ae

4 times
    cera, -ae

3 times
    ala, -ae
    ars, artis
    aura, -ae
    coepi, -isse
    moveo, -ere
    natus, -i
    nomen, -inis
    unda, -ae
    volo, -are

Journey of Daedalus, lines 220-221

220-221: *Et iam Iunonia laeva parte Samos*

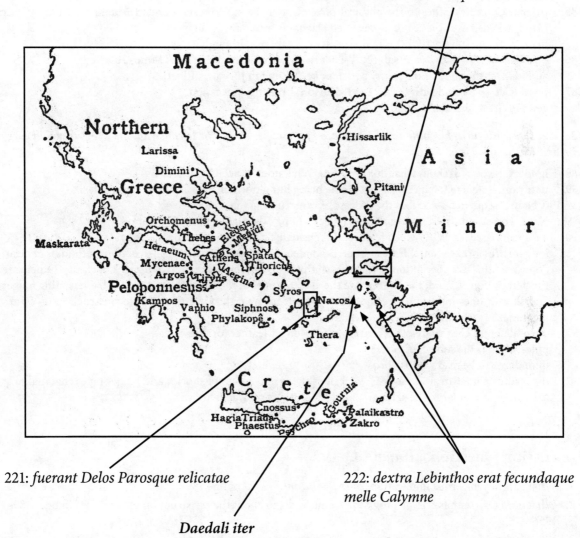

221: *fuerant Delos Parosque relicatae*

222: *dextra Lebinthos erat fecundaque melle Calymne*

Daedali iter

183-187. Daedalus desperately wants to leave Crete, and identifies only one means of escape since both land and sea are closed to him.

183.   **Creten.** A Greek accusative singular. To be read with *perosus*.
         longum. Does not agree with *Creten*. What is the other accusative in this clause?
         perosus. What does this agree with? Who is *perosus* and what is he *perosus*?
184.   **tactus.** Not a main verb.
         loci natalis. Daedalus is an Athenian and not a Cretan.
         amore. By what is Daedalus affected? What does he miss?
185.   **pelago.** Can refer either to the physical proximity of the sea that surrounds Daedalus or to the power Minos wielded over the sea that prevented Daedalus from any escape.
         licet. With the subjunctive, this will express concession: "although."
186.   **obstruat.** Has "Minos" as its subject. What are its two objects? What does Minos rule?
         at. Balances the concession of *licet obstruat*, i.e. "although [*licet*]...still [*et*]..."
187.   **possideat.** To be read with the *licet* of 185, also expressing concession.
         aera. A Greek singular accusative.

188-192. Daedalus turns his mind to a new solution for escape. He begins to construct the wings that will carry him and Icarus away from Crete.

188.   **ignotas.** Be careful about what this modifies. What noun is accusative plural?
189.   **naturam.** Refers to the qualities that define being human which Daedalus will try to alter.
189-190. **Nam...sequente.** Describes the process of constructing the wings.
189.   **Nam.** Transitions from *novat naturam* by describing how Daedalus *novat naturam*.
190.   **a minima coeptas.** With which feathers did Daedalus begin constructing the wings?
         longam breviore sequente. The exact correspondence of this to Daedalus' construction methods is unclear. Some read this as a corruption in the manuscript tradition that has resulted in a lack of clarity. Others see the description as valid: the *minima* are the shortest ones at the tip of the feather, with alternating longer and shorter ones following. See the illustration at below right for a potential reconstruction of Ovid's meaning. Tarrant, in his OCT, brackets the lines.
191.   **clivo.** Refers to the progression from shorter to longer feather (or vice versa).
         putes. Who is the subject of *putes*?
         quondam. To be read with *rustica*.
192.   **disparibus paulatim surgit avenis.** Describes the arrangement of shorter and longer pipes that make up the pan pipe, similar to the arrangment of the feathers on Daedalus' wing.

Discussion Questions, Lines 183-192

1. What are the dangerous implications of the *naturam...novat* of line 189?
2. What does Ovid emphasize by providing so much detail about the construction of the wings in lines 189-195?
3. What is the significance of the comparison of the wings to the *rustica fistula* in lines 191-192?

Daedalus interea Creten longumque perosus							183
exilium tactusque soli natalis amore
clausus erat pelago. "Terras licet" inquit "et undas							185
obstruat, at caelum certe patet; ibimus illac!
Omnia possideat, non possidet aera Minos."
Dixit et ignotas animum dimittit in artes
naturamque novat. Nam ponit in ordine pennas,
a minima coeptas, longam breviore sequente,							190
ut clivo crevisse putes: sic rustica quondam
fistula disparibus paulatim surgit avenis.

Interea Daedalus exosus Creten et longum exilium, et ductus amore terrae patriae, retentus erat mari. "Quamquam," ait, "claudat terras et aquas, at profecto aer est apertus: discedemus illac. Minos imperet cunctis, non imperium obtinebit in aerem." Dixit; et convertit ingenium ad artes inauditas, et novat naturam: nam concinnat pennas coeptas a minima, breviore sequente longam; ut credas in collem auctas esse. Pari modo fistula agrestis sensim fuit olim composita inaequalibus harundinibus.

aer, aeris (m.). air [*a two syllable nominative singular and a three syllable genitive singular*]

avena, -ae. oat, hollow stalk

claudo, claudere, clausi, clausus. to close, to shut

clivus, -i. slope, incline, progression

coepi, coepisse, coeptus (defec.). to begin

cresco, crescere, crevi, cretus. to increase, to develop

Crete, Cretes (f.). [name; *large island in the Mediterranean that lies due south of mainland Greece; its capital city was Knossos, home to King Minos, the Minotaur, and the Labyrinth*]

dimitto, dimittere, dimisi, dimissus. to apply, to send to

dispar, disparis. unequal, disparate, uneven

fistula, -ae. pipe, tube; syrinx, pan-pipe [*an ancient flute-type instrument that was made of reed pipes of differing lengths*]

Minos, Minois (m.). [name; *legendary king of Crete*]

natalis, -e. of or related to birth, birth

obstruo, obstruere, obstruxi, obstructus. to be a barrier, to be in the way, to block

pateo, patere, patui, -. to lie open, to be open, to open

paulatim (adv.). little by little, in stages, gradually

pelagus, -i. sea, water, ocean

perosus, -a, -um. hating, detesting, hateful of

rusticus, -a, -um. rustic, old, ancient, archaic

solum, -i. earth, ground, land

surgo, surgere, surrexi, surrecturus. to rise (up), to get up

tango, tangere, tetigi, tactus. to touch, to reach

Nam ponit in ordine pennas

Nam ponit in ordine pennas
a minima coeptas longam breviore sequente
ut clivo crevisse putes; sic rustica quondam
fistula disparibus paulatim surgit avenis.

a minima coeptas								breviore sequente

longam

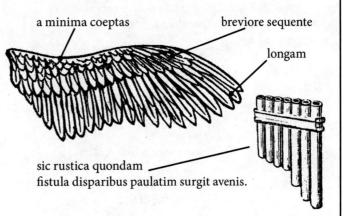

sic rustica quondam
fistula disparibus paulatim surgit avenis.

193-195. After the feathers have been laid out, they are bound together and shaped in the way that birds' wings are shaped.

193.   **medias, imas.** Still agree with the *pennas* of 189.
         alligat. The subject is still Daedalus.
194.   **ita.** To be read with *compositas*, i.e. explaining how they are *compositas* by referring to the description of the previous lines.
195.   **imitetur.** The subject is *curvamen* from the *curvamine* of 194.

195-200. Daedalus' son Icarus is introduced. Ovid's focus is on Icarus' youth and immaturity.

195-200. **Puer...opus.** See the sentence diagram below for structural assistance.
195.   **una** = una (cum Daedalo); here adverbial
196.   **ignarus...pericla** = (Icarus) ignarus se (Icarum) tractare sua pericla
         tractare. To be read with *ignarus.*
197.   **quas.** To be read with the *plumas* of 198.
198.   **flavam.** The first word of the next clause; the comma separates the two clauses where a conjunction might be expected.
199.   **mirabile.** Not an ablative. What case is it and what noun does it modify?
         patris. To be read with the *opus* of 200.

200-202. Daedalus has finished his creation. He fits it to himself and tries it out.

200.   **manus.** Remember the (unexpected) gender of this word. What adjective modifies it?
201.   **opifex.** Refers to Daedalus.
202.   **corpus.** What gender is this word? And so what case is it?
         mota aura. Refers to the effect on the air of the flapping of the wings.

Sentence Diagram, lines 195-200

Puer Icarus una
stabat et, ignarus sua se tractare pericla,
ore renidenti modo quas vaga moverat aura
captabat plumas, flavam modo pollice ceram
mollibat lusuque suo mirabile patris
impediebat opus

Puer Icarus una STABAT
et
    ignarus sua se tractare pericla
ore renidenti
modo
                        quas vaga moverat aura
CAPTABAT **plumas**
flavam *modo* pollice ceram *MOLLIBAT*
lus*que* suo mirabile patris IMPEDIEBAT opus

1. While the *et* and *-que* do the real connecting of clauses, the two instances of *modo* indicate parallelism between these clauses and indicate that they should be read together.

2. The four capitalized verbs are the main actions of the sentence; the italicized ones are parallel because of the *modo... modo.*

3. the relative clause *quas...aura* has as its antecedent *plumas*, which follows, instead of precedes, the clause, as indicated by bold type.

Tum lino medias et ceris alligat imas
atque ita compositas parvo curvamine flectit
ut veras imitetur aves. Puer Icarus una   195
stabat et, ignarus sua se tractare pericla,
ore renidenti modo, quas vaga moverat aura,
captabat plumas, flavam modo pollice ceram
mollibat lusuque suo mirabile patris
impediebat opus. Postquam manus ultima coepto   200
imposita est, geminas opifex libravit in alas
ipse suum corpus motaque pependit in aura.

> Tum connectit medias lino, et infimas ceris: atque ita constructas curvat exiguo flexu, ut imitentur veras aves. Puer Icarus una aderat; et nescius se tenere sua discrimina, nunc laeto vultu corripiebat pennas, quas ventus mobilis abstulerat; nunc subigebat flavam ceram pollice, atque morabatur opus admirandum parentis suo ludo. Postquam novissima manus addita inceptis, ipse artifex commisit suum corpus in alas, et sustentatus est aere agitato.

ala, -ae. wing

alligo, -are, -avi, -atus. to bind, to attach, to join

capto, -are, -avi, -atus. to keep touching, to keep grabbing, to try to touch

cera, -ae. wax

coeptum, -i. undertaking

curvamen, curvaminis (n.). curve, arc, bent shape

imitor, imitari, imitatus. to appear as, to imitate, to resemble

libro, -are, -avi, -atus. to balance, to position

linum, -i. thread, string

lusus, -us. game, play, fooling around

mollio, mollire, mollivi, mollitus. to make soft, to grow soft, to soften, to make pliable

opifex, opificis (m.). craftsman, artisan [*literally a maker* (-fix = facio) *of stuff* (op- = opus)]

pendeo, pendere, pependi, -. to hang

pollex, pollicis (m.). thumb

renideo, renidere, -, -. to glow, to shine, to smile

tracto, -are, -avi, -atus. to tug, to keep pulling, to keep dragging, to keep rubbing, to handle repeatedly, to work over and over

vagus, -a, -um. wandering, shifting

Discussion Questions, Lines 193-202

1. Identify specific Latin words or phrases in lines 195-200 that emphasize the immaturity of Icarus. Explain your answer.
2. What are the implications of the *ignarus sua se tractare pericla* of line 196?
3. What is the effect of the transferred epithet of *ultima* in line 200?

203-209. Daedalus now addresses his son, warning him about flying too high or too low, and the potential consequences.

203.   **et = etiam.** As Daedalus already experimented with the wings himself in the previous sentence, so now he instructs Icarus.

       medio ut limite curras. To be read with the *moneo* of 204.

204-205.   **ne…adurat.** To be read with *curras* of 203 and not *moneo*: why fly the middle course? (The negative *ne* necessitates this reading.)

       si…ibis, si celsior. These conditionals describe the directions in which Icarus should not fly to avoid the consequences described in the purpose clause.

205.   **adurat.** Understand *pennas*.

206.   **utrumque.** Refers to the two choices described in 204-205.

206-7.   **Booten, Helicen, Orionis.** These are all constellations that Daedalus uses as points of reference for Icarus' flight, i.e. he should not see these (or he has flown off course).

207.   **Orionis.** Does not maintain the parallelism of *Booten* and *Helicen*. What is the direct object on which this genitive depends?

208.   **me duce.** Daedalus encourages Icarus to follow him and not to wander off on his own.

       volandi. What kind of *praecepta* did Daedalus *tradit*?

209.   **ignotas.** Foreshadows Icarus' folly.

Discussion Questions, Lines 203-209

1.   What does the confused structure of Daedalus' words in lines 203-205 convey about his emotional state?

2.   The Golden Mean says "everything in moderation." How are Daedalus' instructions to Icarus reflective of the Golden Mean? What other myths reflect such moderation?

3.   How does the use of constellations in lines 206-207 broaden the scope of Icarus' tragedy?

4.   Daedalus' final words to Icarus, *carpe viam*, recall Horace's famous admonition from his poem 1.11, *carpe diem*. Why is Daedalus' recollection of *carpe diem* ironic?

Instruit et natum "Medio"que "ut limite curras,
Icare," ait, "moneo, ne, si demissior ibis,
unda gravet pennas, si celsior, ignis adurat: 205
inter utrumque vola, nec te spectare Booten
aut Helicen iubeo strictumque Orionis ensem;
me duce carpe viam." Pariter praecepta volandi
tradit et ignotas umeris accommodat alas.

Accommodat etiam alas filio; atque inquit, "Hortor te, Icare, ut voles medio spatio: ne si inferior eas, aqua impediat pennas, si altior, ignis inflammet: vola inter utrumque. Neque impero te intueri Booten aut Ursam, et gladium evaginatum Orionis: tene iter me duce." Docet similiter leges volandi; et aptat humeris alas ignotus.

accomodo, -are, -avi, -atus. to fit, to attach

aduro, adurere, adussi, adustus. to scorch, to burn

Bootes, Bootae. (m.). [name: *a constellation*]

celsus, -a, -um. high, lofty, in the air

demitto, demittere, demisi, demissus. to thrust, to send into, to lower; [with *animum*:] to put one's mind to

ensis, ensis (m.). sword

gravo, -are, -avi, -atus. to be heavy, to be weighed down, to oppress

Helice, Helices (acc. = Helicen). [name; *the constellation Ursa Major*]

instruo, instruere, instruxi, instructus. to build, to construct; (+ abl.) to equip, to furnish

limes, limitis (m.). route, limit, path, boundary, course

Orion, Orionis (m.). [name; *a constellation named after the great mythological hunter*]

pariter (adv.). equally; at the same time as [*often used with the preposition* cum]

praeceptum, -i. advice, wisdom, rule, suggestion

stringo, stringere, strinxi, strictus. to bind, to draw near, to draw (a sword)

uterque, utraque, utrumque. each (of two), both

volo, -are, -avi, -atus. to fly

Icarus. Gutzon Borglum, 1919, The University of Virginia, Charlottesville, VA; photograph by the author.

210-215. The departure. Daedalus becomes emotional as he realizes the gravity of their journey, and says goodbye to his son.

210.   **opus.** Refers to the construction of the wings.
211.   **patriae.** The adjective here.
212.   **non interim repetenda.** Agrees with *oscula.* The emotion of these lines culminates here: Ovid reminds us that this is the last time that Daedalus will kiss his son.
        suo = suo (filio)
213.   **ante.** Here adverbial, indicating space instead of time.
        comiti. Be careful of case here. How does this case fit with *timet* (he is not afraid *of* his companion)?
        velut. Here begins a simile describing the poignancy of this moment for Daedalus.
        ales. The simile compares Daedalus to an *ales* with the *quae* of 214 and then describes what the *ales* does.
        ab alto = ab alto (nido)
214.   **aera.** A greek accusative singular. Of what preposition is it the object?
215.   **hortatur sequi = hortatur (natum / Icarum) sequi**

216. Daedalus takes off and looks back at Icarus for one final time.

216.   **suas alas.** To be read with both *movet* and *respicit.* The separation of a noun and its modifier into two coordinate clauses often indicates that the word group is used with both clauses; Latin prefers not to repeat both words in both clauses. Ovid used a similar structure at line 468 of the Apollo and Daphne story: *qui dare certa ferae, dare vulnera possumus hosti.*

Discussion Questions, Lines 210-216

1. What aspects of the *inter...manus* of lines 210-211 emphasize Daedalus' emotional state? Explain your answer.
2. How does Ovid's earlier description of Icarus render the *inter...manus* of lines 210-211 all the more poignant?
3. How does the sound of the *dedit...suo* in lines 211-212 reflect the action that it describes?
4. Based on Ovid's earlier description of Icarus, why would Daedalus *comiti timet* (beyond the implications of the simile that follows)?
5. How does the inclusion of *alto* with *nido* and the separation of *ab alto* from *nido* in lines 213-214 foreshadow Icarus' fall?
6. What are the implications of the *nati respicit alas* of line 216?

An *arator* from line 218 on page 195.

Inter opus monitusque genae maduere seniles   210
et patriae tremuere manus. Dedit oscula nato
non iterum repetenda suo pennisque levatus
ante volat comitique timet, velut ales ab alto
quae teneram prolem produxit in aera nido,
hortaturque sequi damnosasque erudit artes.   215
Et movet ipse suas et nati respicit alas.

> Genae seniles humidae sunt factae inter opus et praecepta; atque manus patriae trepidarunt. Obtulit suavia filio suo, non iterum renovanda: atque pennis sustentatus ante volat, et metuit comiti; sicut avis quae protulit mollem progeniem in aerem ab excelso nido. Admonet sequi; et docet artes noxias; et ipse agitat suas, et respicit alas filii.

ales, alitis (m./f.). (large) bird

erudio, erudire, erudivi, eruditus. to teach, to pass on

gena, -ae. cheek

hortor, hortari, hortatus. to encourage

levo, -are, -avi, -atus. to lift, to raise up, to elevate, to hold up, to support

madesco, madescere, madui, -. to grow wet, to grow moist

nidus, -i. nest

produco, producere, produxi, productus. to produce, to lead forth, to bring forth, to create, to encourage, to give birth to

proles, prolis (f.). offspring, child

repeto, repetere, repetivi, repetitus. to seek (repeatedly), to ask for

senilis, -e. of or belonging to an old person; old man's, old woman's

tener, tenera, tenerum. tender, soft, kind, loving

tremo, tremere, tremui, -. to tremble, to shake, to vibrate, to shiver, to shudder, to ripple

velut (conj.). just as [*introducing a simile*]

volo, -are, -avi, -atus. to fly

Ad Comparanda: Horace Odes 1.11

Tu ne quaesieris (scire nefas) quem mihi, quem tibi
finem di dederint, Leuconoe, nec Babylonios
temptaris numeros. Ut melius quicquid erit pati,
seu pluris hiemes seu tribuit Iuppiter ultimam,
quae nunc oppositis debilitat pumicibus mare   5
Tyrrhenum. Sapias, vina liques et spatio brevi
spem longam reseces. Dum loquimur, fugerit invida
aetas: carpe diem, quam minimum credula postero.

217-220. The perspective of the story changes. Ovid describes the flight of Daedalus and Icarus through the eyes of random onlookers who happen to see them in the air: someone fishing, a shepherd, and a plowman.

217-220. **Hos…deos** = Aliquis, tremula dum captat harundine pisces, aut pastor (innixus) baculo stivave innixus arator vidit et obstipuit hos (et) credidit (hos), qui aethera carpere possent, esse deos

217.   **Hos.** Who are the two masculines to whom this will refer?

         tremula. Not a nominative. What other case can it be and so what will it modify?

218.   **innixus.** To be read with both *pastor* and *arator*.

219.   **qui.** Its antecedent is the *hos* of 217.

         -que. This is the conjunction, and not part of a compound word with *qui*.

         possent. Relative clauses in indirect statements will have their verbs in the subjunctive.

220.   **credidit esse deos.** What did Daedalus and Icarus look like to the three unsuspecting viewers on the ground?

220-226. The route Daedalus and Icarus are flying is described in terms of the islands past which they fly, at which point Icarus' arrogance takes over and he begins to fly off course. His wings begin to malfunction.

220-222. See the map in the introduction (page 185) for a visual guide to the places mentioned here.

220.   **Iunonia laeva.** These words do not go together. What nouns can each modify?

221.   **parte.** On what side was Samos?

221-222. **Samos, Delos, Paros, Lebinthos, Calymne.** What are the genders of these words? And so what adjectives modify them?

222.   **dextra** = dextra (parte)

         melle. To be read with *fecunda* (but they don't agree).

223.   **audaci.** Who is *audaci*? This adjective does not agree with what it describes. Its placement next to *puer* but its agreement with another noun emphasize its descriptive double duty.

224.   **caeli.** To be read with *cupidine*.

225.   **Rapidi.** Does not agree with *vicinia*.

226.   **pennarum vincula.** Figuratively describes the *ceras*: a poignant reminder of what the *ceras* should do, and what it no longer does.

Discussion Questions, Lines 217-226

1. What is the contrast intended between the three observers described in lines 217-220 and Daedalus and Icarus themselves? How does *obstipuit…deos* in lines 219-220 reinforce this contrast?

2. How is the *deos* of line 220 to be read? Is it simply a way of describing the way two flying humans must have appeared to those on the ground? Or is it a reflection of the hubris of Daedalus? Explain your answer.

3. Why is Ovid so specific in his geography of Daedalus' route? What is the connection between such description and the shift of the narrative focus to Icarus' fall?

Hos aliquis tremula dum captat harundine pisces,
aut pastor baculo, stivave innixus arator
vidit et obstipuit, quique aethera carpere possent
credidit esse deos. Et iam Iunonia laeva   220
parte Samos (fuerant Delosque Parosque relictae),
dextra Lebinthos erat fecundaque melle Calymne,
cum puer audaci coepit gaudere volatu
deseruitque ducem caelique cupidine tractus
altius egit iter. Rapidi vicinia solis   225
mollit odoratas, pennarum vincula, ceras.

Dum aliquis piscatur virga tremula, aut pastor fultus scipione, vel arator stiva, intuitus est istos, et miratus est; atque arbitratus est esse deos, qui possent tenere aerem. Et iam Samos Junonia, et Delos, et Paros fuerant praeteritae a parte sinistra: Lebynthos et Calymne melle affluens erant a dextra: cum adulescens coepit exultare volatu temerario, et reliquit ducem, atque impulsus desiderio caeli, carpsit viam sublimiorem. Propinquitas solis fervidi liquefacit ceras odoratas quae erant vincula pennarum.

aether, aetheris (m.). air, heaven

arator, aratoris (m.). plowman

baculum, -i. stick, staff

Calymne, Calymnes (f.). [name: *one of the Sporades islands, located off the southwest coast of Asia Minor (modern-day Turkey)*]

capto, -are, -avi, -atus. to keep touching, to keep grabbing, to try to touch

Delos, Deli (f.). [name: *an island; one of the larger of the Cyclades, a group of islands off the east coast of mainland Greece*]

desero, deserere, deserui, desertus. to desert, to leave

fecundus, -a, -um. fertile, rich (in)

harundo, harundinis (f.). reed, something made of reed, shaft; long, slender pole [*as in a fishing rod*]

innixus, -a, -um (+ abl.). leaning on

Iunonius, -a, -um. of or belonging to Juno, Juno's

laevus, -a, -um. left

Lebinthos, Lebinthi (f.). [name: *one of the Sporades islands, located off the southwest coast of Asia Minor (modern-day Turkey)*]

mel, mellis (n.). honey

mollio, mollire, mollivi, mollitus. to make soft, to grow soft, to soften, to make pliable

obstipesco, obstipescere, obstipui, -. to be amazed, to be (dumb)struck, to be (awe)struck, to be stunned

odoratus, -a, -um. fragrant

Paros, Pari (f.). [name: *an island; one of the Cyclades, a group of islands off the east coast of mainland Greece*]

pastor, pastoris (m.). shepherd

relinquo, relinquere, reliqui, relictus. to leave behind.

Samos, -i (f.). [name: *a large island just off the southwest coast of Asia Minor, modern-day Turkey*]

stiva, -ae. plow-handle

traho, trahere, traxi, tractus. to drag, to pull

tremulus, -a, -um. trembling, shaking, shivering

-ve (encl. conj.). or; and

vicinia, -ae. neighborhood, area nearby, vicinity, proximity

vinculum, -i. chain, fetter

volatus, -us. flying, the act of flying, flight

227-230. Icarus' demise is complete, and he realizes what has happened. He calls to his father, as he falls into the water which will bear his name.

227.   **ille.** To whom does this refer? Who is *quatit nudos lacertos*?

228.   **carens.** What case does this verb's object go into? And so what is its object?
        non ullas percipit auras. Refers to Icarus' inability to fly.

229.   **caerulea.** Does not agree with *ora* but recalls the color of the sky and foreshadows Icarus' consumption by the water.
        patrium. Not the noun "father" but the adjective. What does it agree with?

230.   **quae nomen traxit ab illo.** Refers to the origin of the name of the body of water into which Icarus fell.
        illo = Icaro

231-235. Daedalus realizes something is wrong. He calls out to Icarus but gets no response, until he sees feathers in the water. He curses his mind and the disaster it has brought him, and buries Icarus.

231.   **nec iam pater.** Refers to Daedalus' former role as father now that Icarus is dead.

232.   **Qua.** To be read with *regione*.
        requiram. This form can be either future indicative or present subjunctive. How does each reading change the meaning of Daedalus' questions? Which is the stronger reading? Why?

234.   **artes.** Refers to Daedalus' design and construction of the wings.
        corpus. Not a nominative.

235.   **sepulti = (Icari) sepulti (ibi).** A substantive participle.

Discussion Questions, Lines 227-235

1. How does Ovid's description of Icarus' failure (lines 227-230, *nudos...aqua*) emphasize the pathos of his situation?

2. How does Icarus' reaction to his situation in lines 227-230 reflect Ovid's initial characterization of him (focus especially on his behavior while Daedalus was working)?

3. How does the *pater infelix nec iam pater* of line 231 reflect both Daedalus' character and Ovid's narrative?

4. How does the repetition of *Icare* reflect Daedalus' emotional state?

5. What is the force of the imperfect *dicebat* in line 233 (especially when considered against the *dixit* of 231 and 232)?

6. Why is the *pennas* of line 233 emphatic (beyond its primary position)?

7. Why does Ovid conclude the story so quickly? What does it say about his particular focus in this story? What is his purpose in concluding so quickly?

Overview Discussion Questions

1. Icarus' name occurs five times in the story. Daedalus' occurs only once, in the first line of the story. How do you explain this disparity?

2. If this story occurs in the *Metamorphoses*, what is the metamorphosis of the story? Explain your answer.

3. Is Ovid the old, deliberate craftsman Daedalus, or is Ovid the rash, impulsive youth Icarus? Explain your answer.

4. What is the lesson that Daedalus learns? Identify a modern example that parallels this lesson.

Tabuerant cerae; nudos quatit ille lacertos
remigioque carens non ullas percipit auras,
oraque caerulea patrium clamantia nomen
excipiuntur aqua, quae nomen traxit ab illo.   230
At pater infelix nec iam pater "Icare" dixit,
"Icare," dixit, "ubi es? Qua te regione requiram?"
"Icare" dicebat: pennas aspexit in undis
devovitque suas artes corpusque sepulcro
condidit; est tellus a nomine dicta sepulti.   235

Cerae tabuerant: ille movet bracchia nuda, et destitutus remigio, nullo sustentatur aere: et ora citantia nomen patrium excipiuntur aqua caerulea, quae habuit nomen ab illo. At miser parens, neque iam parens, "Icare," inquit, "Icare," inquit, "ubi es? Qua ora te vestigem, Icare?" dicebat: vidit pennas inter fluctus, et maledixit suis artibus; et sepulturae mandavit corpus; atque terra appellata est a nomine conditi.

aspicio, aspicere, aspexi, aspectus. to look at, to gaze

caeruleus, -a, -um. blue

careo, carere, carui, cariturus (+ abl.). to need, to lack
    [takes its object in the ablative]

devoveo, devovere, devovi, devotus. to curse, to damn

excipio, excipere, excepi, exceptus. to consume, to devour,
    to capture

lacertus, -i. arm, upper part of the arm

patrius, -a, -um. of or belonging to a father; father's

percipio, percipere, percepi, perceptus. to grab, to seize, to
    grab hold of

quatio, quatere, -, quassus. to shake, to flap

remigium, -i. means of propulsion

requiro, requirere, requisivi, requisitus. to seek, to look
    for, to search for; to ask, to inquire

sepelio, sepelire, sepelivi, sepultum. to bury, to entomb

sepulchrum, -i. tomb

tabesco, tabescere, tabui, -. to melt, to dwindle, to
    diminish, to disappear

ullus, -a, -um. any

Introduction to *Pygmalion*

What is the relationship between an artist and his art? This is the fundamental question behind Ovid's Pygmalion story. In its simplest form, it is the story of a sculptor who becomes fed up with society, and so loses himself in his art. But he loses himself so completely that the line between art and life becomes blurred: Pygmalion falls in love with the statue he has created, and begins to treat it / her as if she were his girlfriend. Ultimately, he prays to Venus to grant him his wish that she come to life: Venus hears him, and grants his wish.

Ovid takes the myth from what is likely a local Cypriot legend, that a deviant king of Cyprus lusted after a statue of the goddess Venus. This legend only survives in an obscure literary source, and Ovid's version of the myth, which differs significantly from its predecessor, has become the accepted version. Pygmalion turns to his sculpture because of his disgust at the profligate behavior of the Propoetides (in some versions, all of Cyprus' women). He then seeks to create their antithesis in his art; he strives for the perfection of the female form that the Propoetides lacked. In Ovid's hands, however, the statue remains largely inert and lifeless. There is no exploration of her as anything but a statue, or a form; she remains lifeless and without personality. She eventually acquires a name, Galatea, but later readers confer this upon her; she remains nameless in Ovid.

The statue's lack of obsequiousness also raises questions about the role of Pygmalion: Is he truly her master? Or is it merely a function of Ovid's narrative that he does not describe the mechanics of their relationship? What does Pygmalion expect of his now-alive statue? That she develop a full personality that would, of course, include flaws? Or does he expect her to remain to him in life the way she was in stone: obedient, inert, silent? Characteristically, Ovid leaves such questions unanswered; his complex narrative must continue with the eponymous purpose of the story. Pygmalion and the now-living statue have a child, Paphos, who ultimately lends his name to that city of Cyprus.

The Pygmalion story's legacy is its allegory, i.e. the fact that Pygmalion's loving treatment of his statue, and her transformation from cold stone to warm flesh, can be read as an allegory for his mentoring of a young woman until she can enter society steeled against its vices and evils. We will never know whether Ovid indeed intended this allegorical reading, but it has certainly influenced later readers of the story. The most notable of such readers is the Irish playwright George Bernard Shaw. While his 1916 play *Pygmalion* might not have embedded itself in pop culture, certainly its Broadway adaptation, *My Fair Lady*, has. The story of the snobbish Professor Higgins and his bet-induced social training of the eager but untrained Eliza Doolittle owes its existence to the potential allegory of Ovid's myth.

But Shaw and Broadway are only the beginning. The themes of the Pygmalion myth resonate with both artists and consumers alike. From the silliness of both the 1985 movie *Weird Science*, in which two hapless nerds strive to create their perfect woman using a computer (and then have to face the consequences of their creation), and the 1987 movie *Mannequin*, in which a department-store window designer falls in love with a mannequin who has already come to life, to the more serious treatments of the 1990 movie *Pretty Woman* and the unsettling promo for season three of the FX series *Nip / Tuck*, the themes of the Pygmalion story still resonate today in the mass media and in our own constant striving for perfection.

Pygmalion At-A-Glance

Book	10
Lines	238-297
Main Characters (in order of appearance)	Pygmalion: sculptor from Cyprus statue
Minor Characters	Propoetides: women who insulted Venus and were changed to stone Venus: goddess of love
Context	The heroic poet Orpheus loses his wife Eurydice suddenly to a snake bite shortly after they are married. Overcome with grief, he travels to the Underworld to bring her back. Moved by the poetry of Orpheus, Hades and Persephone agree to release Eurydice to Orpheus on one condition: that he not turn around to look at her until they are out of the underworld. Just as Orpheus approaches the exit, he cannot help himself. He turns to look at Eurydice and immediately Hermes appears to bring her back to the Underworld forever. Orpheus mourns by singing the stories of famous lovers.
Preceeding Story	The Propoetides are women who deny the divinity of the goddess Venus. She punishes them by forcing them into prostitution and eventually they are turned to stone.
Transition	Pygmalion is so disgusted by the behavior of the Propoetides that he swears off women and retreats to his studio to sculpt.
Subsequent Story	Myrrha and Cinyras. Cinyras was Pygmalion's grandson, the son of Paphos whose birth ends the Pygmalion story. Cinyras' daughter Myrrha fell in love with him and eventually realized her love for him. Distraught and shamed by her actions, she is turned into a tree.
Primary Topics	art and the artist fantasy or perfection vs. reality

Pygmalion Vocabulary Frequency

8 times
do, dare

4 times
corpus, -oris
ebur, -oris
os, oris
tempto, -are
Venus, -eris
video, -ere

3 times
ars, -tis
credo, -ere
digitus, -i
manus, -us
osculum, -i
pectus, -oris
Pygmalion, -onis
sentio, -ire
virgo, -inis

Perhaps the most difficult part of *Pygmalion* is the specialized vocabulary concerning jewelry, gifts, and finery that Pygmalion lavishes on his statue. Two lists are provided below to address this difficulty, the first organized alphabetically, the second by line number.

Pygmalion Finery Vocabulary - Alphabetical List

acclino, -are	to recline, to let down	lilia, -ae	lily
artus, -us	limb (of a body)	mollis, -e	soft
auris, -is	ear	monile, -is	necklace
baca, -ae	pearl, jewel	pila, -ae	ball
collum, -i	neck	pluma, -ae	feather
concha, -ae	shell, conch shell, purple dye	redimiculum, -i	garland, wreath
		stratum, -i	sheets (of a bed)
digitus, -i	digit, finger	teres, teretis	smooth, polished
flos, floris	flower	tingo, -ere	to dye
formosus, -a, -um	pretty, attractive	vestis, -is	clothes
gemma, -ae	gem	volucer, -cris	bird
lapillus, -i	stone, gem		

Pygmalion Finery Vocabulary - By Line Number

260	concha, -ae	shell, conch shell	265	auris, -is	ear
	teres, teretis	smooth, polished		baca, -ae	pearl, jewel
	lapillus, -i	stone, gem		redimiculum, -i	garland, wreath
261	volucer, -cris	bird	266	formosus, -a, -um	pretty, attractive
	flos, floris	flower	267	stratum, -i	sheets (of a bed)
262	lilia, -ae	lily		concha, -ae	conch shell, purple dye
	pila, -ae	ball			
263	vestis, -is	clothes		tingo, -ere	to dye
	artus, -us	limb (of a body)	268	acclino, -are	to recline, to let down
264	digitus, -i	digit, finger			
	gemma, -ae	gem		collum, -i	neck
	monilie, -is	necklace	269	mollis, -e	soft
	collum, -i	neck		pluma, -ae	feather

238-242. The Propoetides insult Venus and are punished for that insult by being turned to stone.

238-239. **sunt…deam** = tamen obscenae Propoetides ausae sunt negare Venerem esse deam
238.   **sunt.** To be read with *ausae.*
       obscenae. Does not agree with *Venerem.*
239.   **esse.** The infinitive of an indirect statement introduced by *negare.*
       negare. To be read with the *ausae sunt* of 238.
       pro quo. Refers to the denial of the divinity of Venus by the Propoetides described in lines 238-239.
       sua. Agrees with the *corpora* of 240.
       numinis ira = ira numinis (Veneris). Why did the Propoetides corrupt their bodies?
240.   **forma.** Not nominative. What else did they corrupt besides their *corpora*?
       primae. Agrees with the *Propoetides* who are the subject of *feruntur.* An awkward combination for English to accommodate: *(Propoetides) feruntur (esse primae) vulgasse…*
       vulgasse = vulgavisse
       feruntur. Does not mean "to bear" or "to carry." What is the meaning of this verb when used in the passive with an infinitive dependent on it?
241.   **ut.** Does not mean "so that." What does *ut* mean with indicative verbs?
       sanguis, oris. One of these is the subject of *induruit* and one is a genitive.
242.   **parvo discrimine.** Wryly referring to the lack of distinction in the Propoetides from their previous human, but emotionally stony, state to their now physically stony state.
       versae = versae sunt. A passive form that could be read as a middle.

Discussion Questions, Lines 238-242

1. Identify specific Latin words or phrases in lines 238-240 that portray the Propoetides negatively.
2. The *pudor cessit* of line 241, because of the range of meanings of *pudor*, can be ambiguous. What are two different ways to read this and how do the different readings affect the way the Propoetides are viewed?
3. How does the transformation of the Propoetides reflect their psychological state? Why is it appropriate for who they are that they turned to stone?

Sunt tamen obscenae Venerem Propoetides ausae 238
esse negare deam; pro quo sua numinis ira
corpora cum forma primae vulgasse feruntur, 240
utque pudor cessit sanguisque induruit oris,
in rigidum parvo silicem discrimine versae.

Tamen turpes Propoetides non sunt veritae inficiari Venerem esse deam: quamobrem eius ira dicuntur primae in propatulo habuisse corpora cum pulchritudine. Postquam autem pudor eiectus est, et sanguis oris diriguit, mutatae sunt in durum saxum levi discrimine.

---

cesso, -are, -avi, -atus. to delay, to remain unchanged, to be idle

discrimen, discriminis (n.). difference, distinction

induresco, indurescere, indurui, -. to harden, to grow hard, to stiffen

obscenus, -a, -um. awful, obscene, disgusting, inappropriate

Propoetides, Propoetidum (f. pl.). [name: *the daughters of Propoetus of Cyprus; they were considered the first prostitutes*]

pudor, pudoris (m). decency, chastity, shame, embarassment, virtue

silex, silicis (m.). hard rock, stone

verto, vertere, versi, versus. to turn, to spin

vulgo, -are, -avi, -atus. to prostitute, to corrupt

243-246. Pygmalion, horrified at the example of the Propoetides, removes himself from society and swears off women.

243.   **quas.** Its antecedent is the *Propoetides.*
        aevum. To be read with *agentes.* What is the idiom here?
        crimen. Refers to their life of prostitution.
244.   **quae.** Its antecedent is *vitiis* and it is the neuter object of the *dedit* of 245.
        plurima. Agrees with *quae:* "most of which."
245.   **femineae.** Not the noun meaning "woman" but an adjective meaning something similar. And it does not agree with *natura.*
246.   **carebat.** This verb does not take its object in the accusative. What was Pygmalion *carebat*?

247-249. Pygmalion, having withdrawn from society, turns to his art for solace. He sculpts a woman more beautiful than any mortal, and ultimately falls in love with it.

247.   **niveum.** What did Pygmalion *sculpsit* that is *niveum*?
248.   **sculpsit.** Subject is Pygmalion.
        formam dedit = formam (eburi) dedit
        qua. Not a nominative. Its antecedent is *formam.* With what could *nulla femina nasci*?
        nasci. To be read with the *potest* of 249.
249.   **operis sui.** Refers to the *ebur* or statue.

250-252. Ovid here steps away from the narrative to convey the subtle and nuanced skill with which Pygmalion sculpts. This section, punctuated by the **sententia** *of 252, is perhaps Ovid's most cogent articulation of art and his own poetry.*

250.   **virginis.** Not the subject.
        verae. Does not modify *facies.*
        credas. A perhaps unexpected subject change.
251.   **si non obstet reverentia.** Refers to our (*credas* of 250 involving the reader) hesitatation to admit to the feelings to which Pygmalion has already admitted, and which will become even more surprising as the narrative continues.
        velle moveri. This expression is dependent on the *credas* of 250 (as *vivere* is), but one infinitive will have to govern the other.

252-253. The description of Pygmalion's love for his statue continues.

253.   **simulati corporis.** For what has Pygmalion *haurit ignes*?

Discussion Questions, Lines 243-253

1. What is the role of *natura* in line 245? Does the role of *natura* affect the interpretation of the Propoetides positively or negatively? What is its connection to this transformation?
2. How does the narrative compression of lines 247-249 reflect the artistic process? What are the connections between the creative process and the artist's psychology?
3. Is the *operis sui concipit amorem* of line 249 to be viewed seriously? Or is Ovid poking Ovidian fun at Pygmalion and the creative process?
4. What are the different implications of *virginis* in line 250? What is the role of *verae* in interpreting *virginis*? And how does this contrast to the Propoetides?
5. Why does Ovid shift into the second person with *credas* in line 250? What does the reader's role become in the story with this shift?
6. What is the role of *reverentia* in line 251?
7. What does *ars adeo latet sua* in line 252 mean?

Quas quia Pygmalion aevum per crimen agentes
viderat, offensus vitiis quae plurima menti
femineae natura dedit, sine coniuge caelebs 245
vivebat thalamique diu consorte carebat.
Interea niveum mira feliciter arte
sculpsit ebur formamque dedit, qua femina nasci
nulla potest, operisque sui concipit amorem.
Virginis est verae facies, quam vivere credas 250
et, si non obstet reverentia, velle moveri:
ars adeo latet arte sua. Miratur et haurit
pectore Pygmalion simulati corporis ignes.

Quas quia Pygmalion viderat aetatem transigentes per crimen, deterritus vitiis, quae natura indidit plurima ingenio muliebri, vivebat caelebs sine uxore, atque diu carebat socia thalami. Interea sculpsit feliciter ebur candidum mira arte, atque addidit speciem, qua nulla puella potest nasci; et tactus est amore sui operis. Vultus est verae puellae, quam arbitreris vivere, et nisi prohibeat modestia, velle moveri: usque adeo ars celatur arte sua. Pygmalion miratur, et pectore concipit ardores corporis ficti.

adeo (adv.). to such an extent, so

aevum, -i. age

caelebs, caelibis. unmarried

careo, carere, carui, cariturus (+ abl.). to need, to lack [takes its object in the ablative]

consors, consortis (m./f.). consort, spouse

ebur, eboris (n.). ivory, something made of ivory

facies, -ei. face, appearance

femineus, -a, -um. womanly, of or belonging to a woman

haurio, haurire, hausi, haustus. to drain, to suck (up) to, draw (off)

lateo, latere, latui, -. to take shelter, to hide, to lie in hiding, to be hiding

mirus, -a, -um. wondrous, amazing, wonderful

nascor, nasci, natus. to be born

niveus, -a, -um. snowy white, white

obsto, obstare, obstiti, obstaturus (+ dat.). to obstruct, to be in the way of, to stand in the way of, to hinder, to prevent

simulo, -are, -avi, -atus. to simulate, to pretend, to fabricate, to create

thalamus, -i. bed

vitium, -i. fault, crack, imperfection, blame

254-256. Pygmalion attempts to ascertain whether or not his statue is indeed still a statue or whether it is alive.

254.   **manus.** Not the subject. What does Pygmalion *admovet*?
       operi. To be read with *admovet*. A dative of direction whose more familiar equivalent would be *ad opus*.
       temptantes. Refers to Pygmalion's uncertainty about both his feelings for the statue and his actions here. Does not modify the subject of *admovet*. What is *temptantes*?
       an. Introduces an indirect question following *temptantes*.
       sit. Its subject is the *illud* of 255.
254-255. **an...ebur.** Pygmalion is deceived by his own sculpture. It is so lifelike that he is uncertain whether it is flesh or statue.
       esse. Its subject is also the *illud* of earlier.
256.   Tarrant's OCT brackets this line.
       reddi putat = putat (oscula) reddi. The voice of *reddi* is essential here.
       loquitur, tenet. What is the object of these verbs? To what is Pygmalion *loquitur* and what is he *tenet*?

257-258. Pygmalion is so convinced that his statue is alive that he thinks that the stone is flesh and that his handling of it will injure the flesh.

257.   **tactis membris.** Dative with *insidere*. The *tactis* indicates the action immediately prior to the *insidere*.
       digitos. The subject of *insidere*.
258.   **metuit.** What kind of clause is this verb going to introduce when followed by *ne*?
       pressos. Agrees with *artus*. Indicates the action that occurred before *metuit*.
       ne. Would in prose be read after *metuit*.
       artus. Be careful of declension here. What case is this?

259-265. Pygmalion now begins to treat the statue like his girlfriend. He gives her gifts of jewels and flowers, dresses her, and accessorizes her with jewelry.

259.   **et = etiam**
       modo, modo. These used in tandem indicate simultaneous action.
       puellis. To be read with *grata*.
260.   **illi.** Refers to the statue. This is not a nominative plural.
260-263. All of these nouns are in apposition to the *munera* of 260, explaining specifically what kinds of *munera* Pygmalion *fert illi*.
261.   **mille.** Pygmalion did not *fert illi* one thousand flowers.
       colorum. Not an accusative. What kind of *flores* did Pygmalion *fert illi*?
262-263. **ab arbore...lacrimas = lacrimas Heliadum, lapsas ab arbore.** The Heliades were the sisters of Phaeton who recklessly drove the chariot of the sun until Jupiter killed him. Upon his death, the Heliades mourned so much that they were turned into poplar trees, and their tears became amber. Here, the reference likely refers to amber-colored jewels that Pygmalion gave to the statue.
265.   **aure leves bacae.** Understand *pendent* with this clause as well.

266. A final statement on the appropriateness of Pygmalion's adornment of the statue.

266.   **nuda, formosa.** Both agree with the subject of *videtur*, "she" or "the statue," but both belong to the predicate, rather than the subject, i.e. both follow rather than precede the verb.
       minus. To be read with *formosa*.
       videtur. What does *video* mean in the passive? (Not here "to be seen.")

Discussion Questions, lines 254-266

1. What is the nuance of the *adhuc* in line 255?
2. What figures of speech emphasize Pygmalion's interaction with the statue in lines 259-265?
3. Is the dressing of the statue in lines 263-265 meant to be read as touching and poignant or deviant and strange? Explain your answer.
4. Is the *cuncta decent* of 266 Ovid speaking simply as narrator or rather as sarcastic commentator? Explain your answer.

Saepe manus operi temptantes admovet, an sit
corpus an illud ebur, nec adhuc ebur esse fatetur,   255
oscula dat reddique putat loquiturque tenetque
sed credit tactis digitos insidere membris
et metuit, pressos veniat ne livor in artus,
et modo blanditias adhibet, modo grata puellis
munera fert illi, conchas teretesque lapillos   260
et parvas volucres et flores mille colorum
liliaque pictasque pilas et ab arbore lapsas
Heliadum lacrimas. Ornat quoque vestibus artus;
dat digitis gemmas, dat longa monilia collo,
aure leves bacae, redimicula pectore pendent: 265
cuncta decent; nec nuda minus formosa videtur.

Saepe admovet operi manus explorantes an illud sit corpus an ebur: neque tamen agnoscit esse ebur. Offert suavia, et credit reponi: et affatur, et tangit; et putat digitos infigi artubus tactis, et timet ne livor succedat in membra pressa. Et nunc blanditiis utitur, nunc illi porrigit conchas, et lapillos expolitos, dona accepta puellis, itemque aviculas, et flores mille colorum, et lilia, et pilas pictas, et lacrimas lapsas ab arbore Heliadum. Decorat quoque membra vestibus; inserit gemmas articulis, aptat amplos torques collo. Expolitae margaritae pendent ex auribus, redimicula ex pectore. Omnia sunt decori, neque minus pulchra videtur nuda.

adhibeo, adhibere, adhibui, adhibitus. to use, to employ

adhuc (adv.). still

an (conj.). whether, if [*used to introduce "yes/no" indirect questions*]

baca, -ae. berry, nut, pearl, jewel

blanditia, -ae. flattery, pleasing speech, compliments; [*when plural*] sweet nothings, pleasantries

color, coloris (m.). color

concha, -ae. conch, shellfish, pearl [*i.e. that which is found in a shell*]

decet, decere, decuit, - (impers.). it is fitting, it is right, it is appropriate

fateor, fateri, fassus. to admit, to acknowledge, to confess

flos, floris (m.). flower

formosus, -a, -um. handsome, beautiful

gemma, -ae. gem, jewel

gratus, -a, -um. pleasing

Heliades, Heliadum (f. pl.). [name: *daughters of the sun god and sisters to Phaeton; when their brother died after unsuccessfully driving the chariot of the sun, they were changed into poplar trees, from which amber is "wept"*]

insido, insidere, insedi, insessus. to sink into, to press into

lapillus, -i. small stone, gem

labor, labi, lapsus. to slip, to fall (off or from)

lilium, -i. lily [*a flower*]

livor, livoris (m.). bruise

membrum, -i. limb, part of the body

metuo, metuere, metui, metutus. to fear, to be afraid

monile, monilis (n.). necklace

munus, muneris (n.). gift

orno, -are, -avi, -atus. to decorate, to adorn, to embellish

pendeo, pendere, pependi, -. to hang

pictus, -a, -um. painted, colored

pila, -ae. ball, bauble

premo, premere, pressi, pressus. to press down, to compress, to touch

reddo, reddere, redidi, redditus. to return, to reflect, to mirror

redimiculum, -i. garland, wreath

tango, tangere, tetigi, tactus. to touch, to reach

tempto, -are, -avi, -atus. to try, to attempt

teres, teretis. smooth, polished, rounded

vestis, vestis (f.). clothes, clothing, garment

volucris, volucris (f.). bird

267-269. Having adorned the statue, Pygmalion now puts it to bed for the night, being very careful as he handles it.

267.   **hanc.** Refers to the statue.

   conlocat. Pygmalion is the subject.

   stratis concha Sidonide tinctis. The chiasmus here helps with agreement.

   concha Sidonide. To be read with *tinctis*.

268.   **appellat tori sociam = appellat (hanc) tori sociam.** The *sociam* is the second of a double accusative with *appellat*, the first being an understood *hanc*.

   acclinata colla. Part of the new clause, but not its subject.

269.   **tamquam sensura.** Refers to the statue's ability to feel the softness upon which Pygmalion has laid her.

270-274. The scene changes. Pygmalion attends a festival of Venus where he intends to ask her for his new wife.

270.   **tota Cypro.** Could be read with either *venerat* or *celeberrima*, but the stronger reading is likely with *celeberrima*.

271-272.   **pandis…iuvencae = iuvencae, inductae aurum pandis cornibus, ictae nivea cervice, conciderant.** Describes both a young bull and its sacrifice.

271.   **aurum.** A retained accusative or an accusative of respect with *inductae*: "with gold applied…"

   pandis cornibus. Dative with the compound *inductae*: where was "gold applied?"

273.   **cum.** Not a preposition here.

   munere. What case does *functus* take its object in?

   ad. "To" does not quite capture the sense of *ad aras* with *constitit* (in 274).

274-276. Pygmalion now prays to the gods for a wife (but he cannot admit to the gods what / who he really wants for his wife).

274.   **timide.** To be read with the *dixit* of 276.

275.   **opto.** Here, the aside: "I wish" or "please."

276.   **mea.** Agrees with the *coniunx* of 275, but also describes *eburnae*.

   eburnae. To be read with *similis*.

Discussion Questions, Lines 267-276

1. Identify specific Latin words or phrases in lines 267-269 that reveal Pygmalion's feelings for the statue.

2. Why are the rituals of the *festa dies Veneris* described in such detail in lines 270-273?

3. Identify specific Latin words or phrases in lines 273-276 that reveal Pygmalion's reverence for Venus.

271-2: A Roman sacrifice

Collocat hanc stratis concha Sidonide tinctis
appellatque tori sociam acclinataque colla
mollibus in plumis tamquam sensura reponit.
    Festa dies Veneris tota celeberrima Cypro   270
venerat, et pandis inductae cornibus aurum
conciderant ictae nivea cervice iuvencae,
turaque fumabant, cum munere functus ad aras
constitit et timide, "Si, di, dare cuncta potestis,
sit coniunx, opto," (non ausus "eburnea virgo"   275
dicere) Pygmalion "similis mea" dixit "eburnae."

Hanc componit in stratis infectis concha Sidonia; et vocat consortem lecti, atque collocat collum demissum, tamquam sensurum, in mollibus plumis. Dies Veneri sacra, celeberrima tota Cypro, aderat: et vaccae candido collo, habentes cornua varia circumdata auro, percussae procubuerant; et thura fumabant: cum donis exhibitis constitit Pygmalion ad altaria, atque pavide, "Si dii potestis omnia praebere, cupio sit uxor mea," (non ausus est dicere puella aburnea) dixit, "similis eburneae."

acclino, -are, -avi, -atus. to lay down, to put down, to lie on; to rest, to lean

celeber, celebris, celebre. busy, crowded

cervix, cervicis (f.). neck

colloco, -are, -avi, -atus. to establish, to set up, to place

concido, concidere, concidi, concisus. to fall down, to strike, to impact

consisto, consistere, constiti, constitus. to stand still, to stop, to establish oneself

cornu, -us (n.). horn, ivory, something made of ivory, tip

Cyprus, -i (f.). [name: *a large island in the northeastern corner of the Mediterranean, south of Turkey*]

eburneus, -a, -um. ivory, made of ivory

eburnus, -a, -um. ivory, made of ivory

festus, -a, -um. of or belonging to a party or a festival

fumo, -are, -avi, -. to smoke, to give off smoke

fungor, fungi, functus. to experience, to utilize, to incorporate

icio, icere, ici, ictus. to strike, to beat

induco, inducere, induxi, inductus. to lead up, to lead in, to lead into; to cover

iuvenca, -ae. female cow

munus, muneris (n.). gift

niveus, -a, -um. snowy white, white

pandus, -a, -um. curving, curved, bent

pluma, -ae. feather

repono, reponere, reposui, repositus. to put back, to lay back, to put down; to do again; to put back in a former position

sentio, sentire, sensi, sensus. to sense, to feel, to understand

Sidonis, Sidonidis. Sidonian; of or belonging to Sidon [*a city on the Phoenician coast famous for its production of purple dye taken from the* murex, *the conch shell*]

stratum, -i. cover, quilt; [*in pl.*] bed

tamquam. as if

tingo, tingere, tinxi, tinctus. to stain, to soak, to color, to dye, to paint

torus, -i. bed, bench, couch, cushion

tus, turis (n.). frankincense

277-279. Venus hears Pygmalion's prayer, and responds with a sign.

277. **sensit.** Its subject is Venus.
       suis festis. To be read with *aderat*. Where was Venus *aderat*?
278. **vota quid = quid vota.** This whole clause (to *velint*) is to be read with *sensit*.
       illa vota. Refers to lines 274-276.
       amici. Not the noun here, but the adjective.
       omen. An appositive to the *flamma* of 279.
279. **apicem = apicem (flammae)**

280-286. Pygmalion returns from the festival, and begins to wonder if his prayer has been answered: is the statue coming to life?

280. **Ut rediit = Ut (Pygmalion) rediit (domum)**
       simulacra. Refers to the statue.
282. **os.** Not the subject of *admovet*. What did Pygmalion *admovet*?
       temptat = tangit. Refers to Pygmalion carefully touching the statue to determine whether or not it is alive.
283. **temptatum.** What was *temptatum*? What does this agree with?
       mollescit. The subject is not Pygmalion. What *mollescit*?
       posito. As often with *pono*, here "put aside."
       rigore. Refers to the rigidity of the stone of the statue.
284. **credit = credit (ebur vivere)**
284-286. **ut...usu.** A simile introducing the image of wax (clay might be a better modern equivalent) softening as it is manipulated to represent the process of the statue slowly softening into flesh.
       Hymettia. Does not modify *sole*. Mt. Hymettius is a mountain near Athens famous for its honey, and so its wax.
285. **tractata.** Not a nominative. What does it modify?
       multas. Not a direct object.
286. **ipso usu =** "by its very use" or "just by its use"

287-289. Pygmalion has begun to think that indeed the statue is coming to life, but can't convince himself that it is true. He thinks it's some kind of trick.

287. **falli.** Be careful of voice here. Pygmalion is not deceiving.
288. **sua vota.** Refers here not to the prayers themselves, but rather the statue, which is the object of his prayers.
289. **pollice.** As if he were taking her pulse.

Discussion Questions, Lines 277-289

1. What are the different meanings that the *sensit* of line 277 can convey?
2. To what does *vota quid illa velint* refer? What specifically does Venus *sensit*?
3. What is the symbolism of *flamma accensa est* in line 279?
4. How does the placement of *simulacra* in line 280 reflect Pygmalion's emotional state?
5. How does the use of *temptat* in line 282 reflect Pygmalion's doubt? And how does the recurrence of *temptatum* in line 283 emphasize the diminishing of that doubt?
6. What previous part of the story does the *subsedit digitis* of line 284 recall? How?
7. What are the different comparisons between the softening wax simile of lines 284-286 and the statue? Is this a positive or negative comparison? Explain your answer.
8. How does the placement of *saliunt* in line 289 emphasize the action? What / who else might be *salit* besides the *venae*?

Sensit, ut ipsa suis aderat Venus aurea festis,
vota quid illa velint et, amici numinis omen,
flamma ter accensa est apicemque per aera duxit.
Ut rediit, simulacra suae petit ille puellae   280
incumbensque toro dedit oscula: visa tepere est.
Admovet os iterum, manibus quoque pectora temptat;
temptatum mollescit ebur positoque rigore
subsedit digitis ceditque, ut Hymettia sole
cera remollescit tractataque pollice multas   285
flectitur in facies ipsoque fit utilis usu.
Dum stupet et dubie gaudet fallique veretur,
rursus amans rursusque manu sua vota retractat.
Corpus erat! saliunt temptatae pollice venae.

Cum Venus splendida adesset suis sacris, cognovit quid illa vota significent; atque in praesagium benevoli numinis flamma ter emicuit, et impulit apicem per aerem. Postquam ille rediit, adit effigiem suae virginis: atque devolutus in lectum obtulit suavia. Visa est tepere. Denuo os admovet; explorat etiam pectus manibus; ebur exploratum mollescit, atque omissa duritiae flectitur et cedit digitis; sicut cera Hymettia remollescit sole, atque ficta pollice ducitur in multas figuras, et fit ductilis ipso usu. Dum haeret et cunctanter laetatur, et timet decipi, rursus amans, rursus retentat manu sua desideria. Erat corpus; venae exploratae pollice micant.

accendo, accendere, accendi, accensus. to burn, to smolder, to kindle, to enflame

aer, aeris (m.). air [*a two syllable nominative singular and a three syllable genitive singular*]

apex, apicis (m.). top, tip, point

aureus, -a, -um. golden, of gold

cera, -ae. wax

dubius, -a, -um. doubtful

facies, -ei. face, appearance

fallo, fallere, fefelli, falsus. to deceive, to trick

festus, -a, -um. of or belonging to a party or a festival

flecto, flectere, flexi, flectus. to bend, to curve

Hymettius, -a, -um. Hymettian; of or belonging to Mt. Hymettius [*a mountain near Athens noted for its honey*]

incumbo, incumbere, incubui, - (+ dat.). to fall (on), to lie down (on), to thrust oneself (on)

iterum (adv.). again and again, over and over, repeatedly

mollesco, mollescere, -, -. to grow soft, to soften

pollex, pollicis (m.). thumb

remollesco, remollescere, -, -. to resoften, to become soft again

retracto, -are, -avi, -atus. to handle repeatedly, to feel over and over, to touch again and again

rigor, rigoris (m.). rigor, stiffness

rursus (adv.). back, in return, again and again, over and over

salio, salire, salui, saltus. to jump, to pulse, to beat

simulacrum, -i. statue, likeness, representation

stupeo, stupere, stupui, -. to be amazed, to gape

subsido, subsidere, subsedi, - (+ dat.). to yield (to), to give way (to)

tepeo, tepere, -, -. to be warm, to have warmth, to grow warm, to heat up

tracto, -are, -avi, -atus. to tug, to keep pulling, to keep dragging, to keep rubbing, to handle repeatedly, to work over and over

usus, -us. use, something useful

vena, -ae. vein, blood-vessel, blood

vereor, vereri, veritus. to fear, to be afraid

290-292. Pygmalion thanks Venus for listening to his prayer, and can finally embrace his new wife-to-be.

290.   **Paphius.** An adjective identifying Pygmalion's geographic origin.
        plenissima. Agrees with the *verba* of 291.
        heros. Not an accusative.
291.   **quibus.** How did Pymalion *grates agit*?
        ora = ora (eburis / puellae)
        tandem. To be read with the *non falsa* of 292. The statue's *ora* is *tandem non falsa*, after all of Pygmalion's waiting.

292-294. The focus shifts to the newly alive statue, as she feels Pygmalion kissing her and as she looks out for the first time at the world around her.

292.   **data oscula.** Not the subject.
293.   **timidum.** Not an adverb. With what neuter noun does it agree?
        lumina, lumen = lumina (Pygmalionis), lumen (suum). Not "light" here.
294.   **pariter...amantem.** The newly alive statue sees both Pygmalion and the sky behind him at the same time.

295-297. Pygmalion and his new wife marry and conceive a child, Paphos, who will give his name to the island of Cyprus.

295.   **Coniugio.** Not the subject. To be read with *adest*.
        quod fecit. Refers to the role of Venus in making the marriage happen.
295-296. **coactis...orbem.** A periphrasis for pregnancy: "after the lunar horns were forced into their full orb nine times…" The imagery refers to the crescent moon filling itself into the full moon, with each filling comprising a month. Nine of these cycles equals the full term of a pregnancy.
297.   **Paphon de quo.** Some manuscripts, and Tarrant's OCT, read *de qua* here, taking *Paphon* as a feminine noun. Although most traditions identify Paphos as a son, the gender of the word is uncertain.
        tenet. Here with *nomen*: "takes."

Discussion Questions 290-297

1. How does the use of *heros* in 290 signal a shift in the way the reader should perceive Pygmalion? What has caused this shift? Is Ovid's use of this word ironic? Explain your answer.
2. What are *plenissima verba* (lines 290-291)?
3. What is the effect of the litotes in line 292 and the polyptoton in lines 292-293?
4. What is the effect of the series of enjambments in lines 290-294?
5. What are the implications of *erubuit* in line 293? Is this action a positive or negative? Explain your answer.
6. What are the implications of the statue seeing *amantem cum caelo* in line 294? How are *amans* and *caelum* connected?
7. What is the effect of the periphrasis in lines 295-296 for the statue's pregnancy? Why would Ovid use such complex language here?

Overview Discussion Questions

1. The verb *tempto, -are* is used four times in reference to Pygmalion and the statue. Why? What does it reveal about Pygmalion? What is Ovid's perspective on Pygmalion?
2. Ovid often associates metamorphosis with the ability to use voice, i.e. his descriptions of metamorphosis will often focus on the loss of voice as part of the transformation. What then is the significance of the statue's transformation into a human (instead of from a human) but her lack of any words or speaking?

Tum vero Paphius plenissima concipit heros   290
verba quibus Veneri grates agit, oraque tandem
ore suo non falsa premit, dataque oscula virgo
sensit et erubuit, timidumque ad lumina lumen
attollens pariter cum caelo vidit amantem.
Coniugio, quod fecit, adest dea, iamque coactis   295
cornibus in plenum noviens lunaribus orbem
illa Paphon genuit, de quo tenet insula nomen.   297

> Tum vero heros Paphius comprehendit voces perfectissimas, quibus gratias agat Veneri; et denique urget ora non ficta ore suo: atque puella sensit suavia oblata, et erubuit; et erigens oculos timidos versus ostium spectavit simul amantem cum caelo. Dea adest conubio, quod paravit; atque illa, cornibus lunaribus iam novies coactis in plenum orbem, peperit Paphon, de quo insula habet nomen.

attollo, attollere, -, -. to lift (up), to raise (up)

cogo, cogere, coegi, coactus. to force, to compel

concipio, concipere, concepi, conceptus. to worship, to speak with respect

erubesco, erubescere, erubui, -. to blush, to turn red, to feel shame

gigno, gignere, genui, genitus. to give birth to, to create

grates (defec. f. pl.). thanks

heros, heroidis (m.). hero

noviens (adv.). nine times

Paphius, -a, -um. Paphian; of or belonging to Paphos [*a city on the island of Cyprus, in the northeastern corner of the Mediterranean Sea*]

Paphos, -i (m; acc sing. = Paphon). [name: *the child of Pygmalion and his statue-turned-woman*]

pariter (adv.). equally; at the same time as [*often used with the preposition* cum]

tandem (adv.). finally, at last

vero (adv.). truly, indeed, for certain

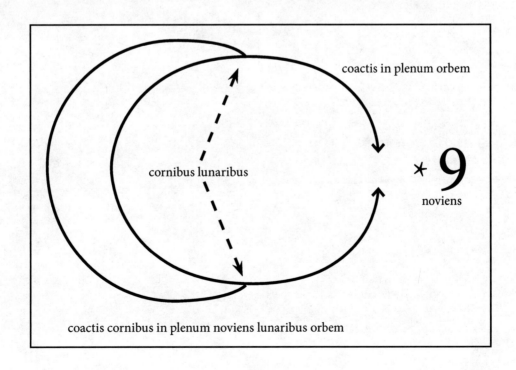

coactis in plenum orbem

cornibus lunaribus

✳ **9**
noviens

coactis cornibus in plenum noviens lunaribus orbem

Appendix One

Vocabulary Frequency

The Vocabulary Frequency List includes all words that appear in the text except common prepositions (*in, ad, a/ab, e/ex, per*), the relative and interrogative pronoun, *sum* and *non*; these words were deemed too common, both in terms of students' knowledge and appearance in the text, to be included. Proper vs. non-proper nouns were not considered separate words, e.g. the twenty-six times that *amor* occurs includes both *amor* the abstract emotion and *Amor* the deity. While the Vocabulary Frequency List should be used for vocabulary assistance, it should also be used to target forms review, e.g. the forms of *is, ea, id* appear only four times in the text, while the forms of *ille, illa, illud* appear forty-four times. The list can be used similarly for some grammatical constructions: *ut*, as might be expected, occurs frequently (twenty-two times, though not necessarily all with the subjunctive); *an*, a word that might require review, appears five times (enough that it would seem to merit review).

44 times
ille, illa, illud

40 times
ego, mei, mihi, me, me

33 times
hic, haec, hoc

31 times
dico, -ere
do, dare
suus, -a, -um

30 times
tu, tui, tibi, te, te

29 times
video, -ere

27 times
nec

26 times
amor, -oris

23 times
ut

22 times
cum

18 times
meus, -a, -um

16 times
deus, -i
facio, -ere
os, oris

15 times
manus, -us

14 times
amans, -ntis
si

13 times
habeo, -ere
ipse, ipsa, ipsum
longus, -a, -um
noster, -tra, -trum
pono, -ere

12 times
corpus, -oris
possum, posse
tuus, -a, -um

215

11 times
cera, -ae
fero, ferre
opus, -eris
osculum, -i

10 times
at
dum
modo
nomen, -inis
omnis, -e
pes, -dis
sic
teneo, -ere
Venus, -eris

9 times
arbor, -oris
certus, -a, -um
fugio, -ere
iam
locus, -i
medius, -a, -um
parvus, -a, -um
pater, -tris
pectus, -oris
penna, -ae
puer, -i
sentio, -ire
sub
tamen
unus, -a, -um
venio, -ire

8 times
alter, -era, -erum
amo, -are
eo, ire
nox, -ctis
puella, -ae
unda, -ae

7 times
annus, -i
ars, -tis
aut
coniunx, -iugis

fallo, -ere
levis, -e
mitto, -ere
oculus, -i
parens, -ntis
peto, -ere
Phoebus, -i
relinquo, -ere
saepe
Thisbe, -es
totus, -a, -um
vestis, -is

6 times
accipio, -ere
aqua, -ae
arma, -orum
aura, -ae
Baucis, -idis
color, -oris
digitus, -i
domus, -us / -i
duo, duae, duo
dux, ducis
hostis, -is
idem, eadem, idem
ignis, -is
iubeo, -ere
loquor, -qui
miser, -era, -erum
moveo, -ere
multus, -a, -um
nos, nostri / -um, nobis,
   nos, nobis
nullus, -a, -um
pendeo, -ere
Pyramus, -i
ramus, -i
semper
sequor, -qui
tabella, -ae
timidus, -a, -um
ubi
verbum, -i
vos, vestri / -um, vobis,
   vos, vobis
volo, velle
vultus, -us

5 times
ago, -ere
ait
altus, -a, -um
ambo, -ae, -a
an
ante
aptus, -a, -um
atque
caelum, -i
carmen, -inis
collum, -i
colo, -ere
cornu, -us
credo, -ere
cupido, -inis
dominus, -i
ebur, -oris
foris, -is
forma, -ae
iaceo, -ere
Icarus, -i
inquit
lacertus, -i
maneo, -ere
membrum, -i
miles, -itis
mollis, -e
mora, -ae
ne
nego, -are
ordo, -inis
perdo, -ere
Philemon, -onis
primus, -a, -um
sanguis, -inis
tectum, -i
tego, -ere
tellus, -eris
tempto, -are
tum
vacuus, -a, -um
votum, -i
vulnus, -eris

4 times

adsum, adesse
adhuc
admoveo, -ere
aer, aeris
ala, -ae
aliquis, -quid
animus, -i
artus, -us
arvum, -i
bellum, -i
caedis, -is
capillus, -i
causa, -ae
cognosco, -ere
colligo, -ere
coma, -ae
cresco, -ere
crinis, -is
durus, -a, -um
fax, facis
ferus, -a, -um
fides, -ei
fleo, -ere
fuga, -ae
gaudeo, -ere
geminus, -a, -um
gravis, -e
hora, -ae
inter
interea
is, ea, id
iungo, -ere
lectus, -i
lego, -ere
levo, -are
licet, licere
lignum, -i
magnus, -a, -um
mille
natus, -i
nimium
notus, -a, -um

novus, -a, -um
nudus, -a, -um
numerus, -i
opto, -are
paro, -are
pars, -rtis
placeo, -ere
postquam
premo, -ere
puto, -are
redeo, -ire
sagitta, -ae
-, sui, sibi, se, se
senex, -is
signum, -i
simul
sine
specto, -are
super
tango, -ere
torus, -i
umbra, -ae
uterque, -traque,
   -trumque
velo, -are
volo, velle
verto, -ere
vestigium, -i
veto, -are
vinco, -ere
virgo, -inis
vivo, -ere

3 times

acer, -cris, -cre
acutus, -a, -um
aetas, -atis
arcus, -us
ardeo, -ere
baculum, -i
blanditia, -ae
cacumen, -inis
campus, -i

caput, -itis
capto, -are
capio, -ere
casus, -us
cado, -ere
cedo, -ere
cervix, -icis
cingo, -ere
clivus, -i
concipio, -ere
compono, -ere
consisto, -ere
crimen, -inis
cruor, -oris
cunctus, -a, -um
cur
cura, -ae
custos, -odis
debeo, -ere
decet, decere
dignus, -a, -um
diu
domina, -ae
dubito, -are
ergo
etiam
facies, -ei
fateor, -eri
ferrum, -i
festus, -a, -um
fio, -eri
flamma, -ae
flavus, -a, -um
flecto, -ere
flumen, -inis
forte
fortis, -e
frango, -ere
gero, -ere
gradus, -us
haereo, -ere
herba, -ae
hinc

huc
illic
impono, -ere
infelix, -icis
insequor, -qui
iste, ista, istud
iustus, -a, -um
iuvenis, -is
lacrima, -ae
laedo, -ere
lateo, -ere
limen, -inis
Mars, -rtis
mensa, -ae
mens, -ntis
Minerva, -ae
minimus, -a, -um
mollio, -ire
moneo, -ere
mons, -ntis
mors, -rtis
nam
narro, -are
neque
nervus, -i
nisi
niveum, -i
numen, -inis
nunc

nuper
nympha, -ae
o
obsto, -are
obstipesco, -ere
ops, opis
orbis, -is
pariter
pateo, -ere
pharetra, -ae
plenus, -a, -um
pollex, -icis
pomum, -i
potentia, -ae
praebeo, -ere
precor, -ari
prex, -cis
purpureus, -a, -um
Pygmalion, -onis
quaero, -ere
quidem
radix, -icis
radius, -i
reddo, -ere
regno, -are
requiro, -ere
rursus
saevus, -a, -um
salignus, -a, -um

senilis, -e
silva, -ae
similis, -e
sol, solis
spero, -are
sto, -are
stringo, -ere
summus, -a, -um
superus, -a, -um
tango, -ere
talis, -e
tardus, -a, -um
tempus, -oris
tergum, -i
tingo, -ere
transeo, -ire
tueor, -eri
turpis, -e
urbs, -bis
vates, -is
vel
verus, -a, -um
versus, -us
vester, -tra, -trum
vetus, -eris
vicinia, -ae
volo, -are

Appendix Two

Rhetorical Figures

The glossary includes all figures included on the AP syllabus. They are defined, and examples in both Latin (from the texts in this volume whenever possible, and from other AP syllabi otherwise) and modern English are included. Where further explanation is deemed helpful, a discussion section is included.

allegory. A form of comparative representation that uses an extended narrative to stand for an abstract idea, a series of relationships, or another narrative, often without specifying explicitly the connection between the two.

> *Latin example.* It was common in the Middle Ages for Christian writers to allegorize (i.e. make an allegory of) stories from Ovid's *Metamorphoses*: the Apollo and Daphne story has been allegorized as Satan chasing the pure soul which is saved by divine intervention. The Pygmalion story, in which a sculptor sculpts the perfect woman after being disgusted with the women around him, has been allegorized as a mentor teaching a young woman the skills necessary to survive in society.

> *English example.* George Orwell's *Animal Farm*, in which the Soviet totalitarianism and the ensuing political wrangling is allegorized via an animal fable in which the animals overthrow their human overseer and then struggle among themselves to establish power.

> *Discussion.* The traditional definition of allegory as an "extended metaphor" is potentially misleading. The difficult conceptual aspect to allegory is the relationship between the allegory itself or the allegorical narrative, and that which the allegory represents. In a metaphor (or a simile for that matter) elements of the comparison are made clear, e.g. "Apollo is a monster" or "Apollo is like a monster." The allegory, however, does not provide the "Apollo" element. It is left to the reader to understand that the "monster" refers to Apollo. In many allegories, these connections do not require explanation (Orwell's *Animal Farm* above is one such example, as is Dante's *Divine Comedy*), but the idea of allegory does enable readers to "see" allegories where none were intended (e.g. the TV sitcom *Gilligan's Island* has been, not with much credibility, interpreted as an allegory for the seven deadly sins).

alliteration. The repetition of the same letter or sounds.

> *Latin example.*   deseruitque ducem caelique cupidine tractus (*Met.* 8.224, Daedalus and Icarus)

> *English example.* "A bridal bower becomes a burial bier of bitter bereavement." (*A Funny Thing Happened on the Way to the Forum*)

anaphora. The unnecessary repetition of words for emphasis.

    Latin examples. nec <u>quid</u> Hymen, <u>quid</u> amor, <u>quid</u> sint conubia curat. (*Met.* 1.480, Apollo and Daphne); semper habebunt / <u>te</u> coma, <u>te</u> citharae, <u>te</u> nostrae, laure, pharetrae. (*Met.* 1.558-559, Apollo and Daphne)

    English example. "To raise a happy, healthy, and hopeful child, it <u>takes</u> a family; it <u>takes</u> teachers; it <u>takes</u> clergy; it <u>takes</u> business people; it <u>takes</u> community leaders; it <u>takes</u> those who protect our health and safety. It <u>takes</u> all of us." (Hillary Clinton, 1996 Democratic National Convention); "<u>If</u> my opponent <u>had been</u> at the moon launch, <u>it would have been</u> a risky rocket scheme. <u>If he had been</u> there when Edison was testing the lightbulb, <u>it would have been</u> a risky anti-candle scheme. And <u>if he'd have been there</u> when the internet was invented..." (George W. Bush, 2000 Republican National Convention)

aposiopesis. The abrupt breaking off in mid-sentence for rhetorical effect.

    Latin example. Iam caelum terramque meo sine numine, venti,
        miscere, et tantas audetis tollere moles?
        <u>Quos ego</u> — (Vergil, *Aeneid* 1.135)

    English example. "If my opponent had been at the moon launch, it would have been a risky rocket scheme. If he had been there when Edison was testing the lightbulb, it would have been a risky anti-candle scheme. <u>And if he'd have been there when the internet was invented...</u>" (George W. Bush, 2000 Republican National Convention)

apostrophe. The direct address of someone or something not present.

    Latin example. sic fera Threicii ceciderunt agmina Rhesi,
        et dominum capti deseruistis equi. (*Amores* 1.9.23-24)

    English example. "O, pardon me, thou bleeding piece of earth, / That I am meek and gentle with these butchers! / Thou art the ruins of the noblest man / That ever lived in the tide of times." (Shakespeare, *Julius Caesar*, Act 3, Scene 1).

    "O Captain, my Captain" (Walt Whitman)

asyndeton. The conspicuous lack of a conjunction.

    Latin example. Vota tamen tetigere deos, tetigere parentes; (*Met.* 4.164, Pyramus and Thisbe)

    English example. "But, in a larger sense, we cannot dedicate, we cannot consecrate, we cannot hallow this ground." (President Abraham Lincoln, Gettysburg Address)

chiasmus. The arranging of words, phrases, or clauses in an A B B A format.

                  A   B   B   A
    Latin example. innumeris tumidum Pythona sagittis. (*Met.* 1.460, Apollo and Daphne)

                                     A   B
    English example. "And so, my fellow Americans, ask not what your country can do for you; ask

              A   B
    what you can do for your country." (John F. Kennedy, Inaugural Address, January 20, 1961)

ecphrasis. The verbal or literary description of an image or visual, usually nature or a work of art.

Latin example. cumque domo exierint, urbis quoque tecta relinquant,
neve sit errandum lato spatiantibus arvo,
conveniant ad busta Nini, lateantque sub umbra
arboris: arbor ibi niveis uberrima pomis,
ardua morus, erat, gelido contermina fonti.
(*Met.* 4.86-90, Pyramus and Thisbe)

Ornat quoque vestibus artus:
dat digitis gemmas, dat longa monilia collo,
aure leves bacae, redimicula pectore pendent:
cuncta decent; nec nuda minus formosa videtur.
(*Met.* 10.263-266, Pygmalion)

Discussion. Ecphrasis is an important figure for Ovid and figures prominently in his work because of his interest in the creative process and the role of the artist. Ovid will regularly (see the Pyramus and Thisbe example above) describe an idyllic natural scene only to destroy it with an act of extreme violence. The Pygmalion example above is intentionally ambiguous, and perhaps worth discussion. Is Ovid describing the statue as a work of art? Or is he describing it as the woman that Pygmalion envisions it as?

ellipsis. The omission of an easily understood syntactical element. (The bracketed words in the examples are not part of the text itself; their omission is the ellipsis.)

Latin example. hic portas frangit, at ille [*frangit*] fores. (*Amores* 1.9.20)

English example. And he to England shall [go] along with you. (Shakespeare, *Hamlet* 3.3.4)

enjambment. When a sentence or clause no longer aligns with the poetic structure. Or, when a sentence or clause begins at the end of a poetic line or ends at the beginning of a poetic line. (End-stopping or end-stopped lines are the opposite of enjambment, i.e. when a clause aligns with the poetic structure.)

Latin example. Arma gravi numero violentaque bella parabam
edere, materia conveniente modis. (*Amores* 1.1.1-2)

English example. I think that I shall never see
A poem as lovely as a tree. (Joyce Kilmer, "Trees")

Discussion. Enjambment, unlike many of the figures here, is unique to poetry because it depends on the poetic structure for its existence. Enjambment renders poetry more conversational (we don't pause at regular intervals when we speak) and is the reason why, when we read poetry, we don't pause at the end of lines, but rather at the end of syntactical units. In the English example above, the meaning becomes very different if the reader pauses at the end of the first line. In the Latin example, it is unclear what the narrator is preparing until the first word of the second line, thereby creating suspense.

hendiadys. Two nouns joined by a conjunction that would otherwise be a noun - adjective pair or a noun - genitive pair.

Latin example. annis aevoque soluti (*Met.* 8.712, Baucis and Philemon); lux et veritas (motto of Yale University)

English example. Law and Order (= the order of law; TV show); Love and Transformation (= the transformation of love / that love brings, or a love of transformation; book title)

Discussion. A hendiadys lends equal emphasis to two concepts rather than, in the non-hendiadys version, one concept having a more prominent syntactical place. The effect can be simply one of emphasis or can introduce an element of ambiguity. The second English example above more likely means "the transformation that love brings," but because the book is an Ovid book, the opposite reading becomes a more plausible reading than it might have otherwise been because of Ovid's interest in metamorphosis, i.e. "the love of transformation."

hyperbaton. A deliberate confusion of normal word order.

Latin example.   oraque caerulea patrium clamantia nomen
                    excipiuntur aqua (*Met.* 8.229-230, Daedalus and Icarus)

English example. "A prophecy that misread, could have been." (Yoda from the movie *Star Wars, Episode III: Revenge of the Sith*; even for Yoda, a particularly confused sentence)

hyperbole. A deliberate and extreme exaggeration for emphasis or rhetorical effect.

Latin example.   stravimus <u>innumeris</u> tumidum Pythona sagittis. (*Met.* 1.460, Apollo and Daphne)

English example. "My guest tonight: an actor who has starred in over <u>500 million</u> films. His latest is *Snakes on a Plane*" (Jon Stewart, introducing an interview with Samuel Jackson on *The Daily Show*)

hysteron proteron. The reversal of the natural order of events.

Latin example.   Quos petiere duces <u>annos</u> in milite <u>forti</u> (*Amores* 1.9.5)

                    <u>Moriamur</u>, et in media arma <u>ruamus</u> (*Aeneid* 2.353)

English example. to put on one's shoes and socks; lock and load

irony. Implying the opposite of what one says to mock or deride.

Latin example.   Me miserum, ne prona cadas indignave laedi
                    crura notent sentes, et sim tibi causa doloris!
                    Aspera, qua properas, loca sunt. Moderatius, oro,
                    curre fugamque inhibe; <u>moderatius insequar ipse.</u>
                    (*Met.* 1.508-511, Apollo and Daphne)

English example. Brutus is an honorable man. (Shakespeare, *Julius Caesar* 3.2.10)

litotes. An understatement achieved by emphasizing something's opposite.

Latin example.   oraque tandem
                    ore suo <u>non falsa</u> premit, (*Met.* 10.291-292, Pygmalion)

                    <u>non aliter</u> quam cum… (*Met.* 4.122, Pyramus and Thisbe)

English example. "A <u>not unblack</u> dog was chasing a <u>not unsmall</u> rabbit across a <u>not ungreen</u> field" (George Orwell, "Politics and the English Language")

metaphor. A direct comparison between a narrative element and an element independent of the narrative for emphasis or clarification.

Latin example.   non sum desultor amoris (*Amores* 1.3.15)

English example. "Why, this country is a shining city on a hill" (Mario Cuomo, 1984 Democratic National Convention)

metonymy. Identifying something by way of association or suggestion

Latin example. submissoque humiles intrarunt <u>vertice</u> postes (*Met.* 8.638, Baucis and Philemon)

suos cognovit <u>amores</u> (*Met.* 4.137, Pyramus and Thisbe)

English example. "City Hall" for the government; the Italian "calcio," meaning "kick" for soccer

Discussion. Some overlap exists between metonymy and synecdoche, e.g. referring to someone as a "suit" could be construed as a synecdoche because the suit is a part of its wearer, or as a metonymy because the "suit" suggests the profession of its wearer. Some have suggested not distinguishing between the two.

onomatopoeia. When the sound of a word represents the meaning of the word.

Latin example. tutaeque per illud
<u>murmure</u> blanditiae minimo transire solebant. (*Met.* 4.69-70, Pyramus and Thisbe)

Venit ecce recenti
caede leaena boum <u>spumantes</u> oblita rictus, (*Met.* 4.96-97, Pyramus and Thisbe)

English example. The <u>moan</u> of doves in <u>immemorial</u> elms
And <u>murmuring</u> of <u>innumerable</u> bees (Alfred Lord Tennyson, "The Princess")

Also, common words like "bang," "crash," "moo," etc.

oxymoron. An expression that apparently contradicts itself.

Latin example. et in <u>vacuo pectore regnat</u> Amor. (*Amores* 1.1.26)

English example. Why, then, O brawling love! O loving hate!
O any thing, of nothing first create!
O heavy lightness! serious vanity!
Mis-shapen chaos of well-seeming forms!
Feather of lead, bright smoke, cold fire, sick health!
Still-waking sleep, that is not what it is! (Shakespeare, *Romeo and Juliet*, 1.1)

Also, common phrases like "friendly fire," "virtual reality," "freezer burn," "jumbo shrimp"

personification. Imbuing an inanimate object with human qualities.

Latin example. <u>ferrea</u> cum vestris <u>bella valete</u> modis. (*Amores* 1.1.28)

English example. "Once again, the heart of America is heavy. The spirit of America weeps for a tragedy that denies the very meaning of our land." (Lyndon Baines Johnson on the death of Martin Luther King, Jr., April 5, 1968)

pleonasm. The use of excessive or syntactically unnecessary words; repetition of the same idea with different words.

Latin example. in <u>rigidum</u> parvo <u>silicem</u> discrimine versae (*Met.* 10.242, Pygmalion)

English example. "<u>No one anywhere in the world</u> can doubt the enduring resolve and boundless capacity of the American people." (President Bill Clinton, State of the Union Address, January 19, 1999)

polyptoton. The use of two or more forms of the same word or root.

> *Latin example.*   Omnia <u>possideat</u>, non <u>possidet</u> aera Minos. (*Met.* 8.187, Daedalus and Icarus)
>
> <u>ars</u> adeo latet <u>arte</u> sua (*Met.* 10.252, Pygmalion)
>
> *English example.* "Do? Do? Hey I'm doing what I do. And I've always done what I do. I'm doing what I do. The way I've always done it. The way I'll always do it." (Kramer from *Seinfeld* "The Trip 2." August 18, 1992)

polysyndeton. The use of more conjunctions than necessary.

> *Latin example.*   oscula dat reddi<u>que</u> putat loquitur<u>que</u> tenet<u>que</u>. (*Met.* 10.256, Pygmalion)
>
> *English example.* "It's more than a game. And regardless of what level it is played upon, it still demands those attributes of courage <u>and</u> stamina <u>and</u> coordinated efficiency <u>and</u> goes even beyond that…" (Vince Lombardi)
>
> *Discussion.* Polysyndeton often conveys a sense of enthusiasm or energy, sometimes with an element of youthfulness or naïvete. The extra conjunctions give the impression that the speaker is thinking too quickly to be able to foresee when the series will end.

praeteritio. Saying something by saying that it will not be said.

> *Latin example.*   Quid Thesea magnum
> quid memorem Alciden? (*Aeneid* 6.122-123)
>
> *English example.* "I'm not going to tell you what they spent on that wedding, but $40,000 is a lot of money." (from the TV show *Friends*)

prolepsis. The introduction of a syntactical unit before it is appropriate, i.e. a word, phrase, or clause that cannot mean anything until some additional element is read after it.

> *Latin example.*   <u>Quos petiere duces animos in milite forti,</u>
> <u>hos</u> petit in socio bella puella viro: (*Amores* I.9.5-6)
>
> *English example.* "<u>Whatever I give her</u>, she's going to be bringing in experts from all over the country to interpret the meaning behind <u>it</u>." (from the TV show *Seinfeld*, "The Deal", May 2, 1991)

prosopopoeia. When the words or actions of someone absent are introduced by the narrator.

> *Latin example.*   Hector ab Andromaches complexibus ibat ad arma,
> et galeam capiti quae daret, uxor erat. (*Amores* 1.9.35-36)
>
> *English example.* "My momma always said, 'Life was like a box of chocolates. You never know what you're gonna get.'" (Forrest Gump from the movie *Forrest Gump*)
>
> *Discussion.* It is worth noting that the Latin example is both an allusion and prosopopoeia, while the English example, because it does not involve anyone famous, is only a prosopopoeia.

simile. An indirect comparison between a narrative element and an element independent of the narrative for emphasis or clarification. Latin similes will be often introduced by *ut, velut, veluti,* or *qualis,* while English similes will be introduced by "like" or "as."

> *Latin example.*   Illa <u>velut crimen</u> taedas exosa (*Met.* 1.483, Apollo and Daphne)
>
> ut Hymettia sole
> cera remollescit tractataque pollice multas
> flectitur in facies ipsoque fit utilis usu. (*Met.* 10.284-286, Pygmalion)

English example. "She came up to me in the gym tonight; she looked at me <u>like I was a leper</u>" (from the movie *Sixteen Candles*)

synchesis. The arrangement of words, phrases, or clauses in an A B A B pattern.

A   B   A   B

Latin example.   in rigidum parvo silicem discrimine versae. (*Met.* 10.242, Pygmalion)

synecdoche. The use of a whole to represent the part or a part to represent the whole.

Latin example.   modo vestra relinquite <u>tecta</u> (*Met.* 8.691, Baucis and Philemon)

demisit in ilia <u>ferrum</u> (*Met.* 4.119, Pyramus and Thisbe)

English example. "Nice wheels"; "Nice threads"; "Hand me the phone" (the whole phone standing for the receiver, which is really what will be handed); "To watch the tube" (i.e. the cathode ray tube that generates the picture of a TV); etc.

"He may be struggling with the <u>leather</u>, but he didn't [*sic*] with the <u>lumber</u>" (*SportsCenter*, 7/22/06, on Yankees' third-baseman Alex Rodriguez's struggles in the field)

Discussion. [see the discussion on "metonymy" above]

tmesis. The cutting or splitting of a word for the insertion of another word.

Latin example.   succepitque ignem foliis, atque arida <u>circum</u>
nutrimenta <u>dedit</u>, (*Aeneid* 1.175-176)

English example. "Kanga-bloody-roo." (Russel Crowe from an interview on *The Daily Show*); "Abso-bloomin'-lutely" (from *My Fair Lady*)

transferred epithet. An adjective that agrees with a noun that it does not describe, or an adjective that describes a noun with which it does not agree.

Latin example.   inque patris <u>blandis</u> haerens cervice lacertis (*Met.* 1.485, Apollo and Daphne)

English example. FoodTV's Jamie Oliver is known as the Naked Chef, also the title of his first and most prominent TV show. He, however, is hardly naked; rather his food is naked, or unadorned.

tricolon crescens. A group of three or more elements (usually nouns or clauses), the last of which is more complex than the previous.

Latin example.   laudat digitosque manusque
bracchiaque et nudos media plus parte lacertos;
(*Met.* 1.500-501, Apollo and Daphne)

English example. "But if we keep our religion at home, keep our religion in the closet, keep our religion between ourselves and our God…" (Malcolm X, The Ballot or the Bullet Speech); "Single moms struggling to feed the kids and pay the rent. Immigrants starting a hard life in a new world. Children without fathers in neighborhoods where gangs seem like friendship, where drugs promise peace, and where sex sadly seems the closest thing to belonging." (George W. Bush, 2000 Republican National Convention; one tricolon crescens within another)

zeugma. The use of a word (usually a verb) in a both a literal and figurative sense. Or the use of a word (usually a verb) in two senses, only one of which reflects common usage.

Latin example.   iuvenemque oculis animoque requirit, (*Met.* 4.129, Pyramus and Thisbe)

English example. "I'm gonna go inside and grab my bag…and my date, I guess" (Jim, played by Jason Biggs, from the movie *American Pie*, when leaving the prom)

Appendix Three

Metrics and Scansion

The folowing summary is intended to provide a quick reference source for the information necessary to scan successfully the two meters included in this volume: the dactylic hexameter of Ovid's *Metamorphoses* and the elegiac couplet of the *Amores*. Words that are italicized in a definition are also defined in the list.

Terminology

dactyl. A poetic *foot* comprised of a long *syllable* followed by two short *syllables*.

dactylic hexameter. The *meter* of epic poetry, comprised of six feet of *dactyls* or *spondees* (see also *substitution*).

diphthong. Two or more vowels that are pronounced as one sound.

elision. When two words, the first ending in a vowel, the second beginning with a vowel, are blended together in pronunciation. (The specific rules for elision are explained in greater detail below.)

foot. The building block of a *meter*; a metric line will comprise a fixed number of feet.

hiatus. When an *elision* should occur, but does not occur. Hiatus often occurs with single letter vowel words (o!) or at a clause break, but there is no rule or set pattern for identifying hiatus.

macron. The mark used to label long *syllables*: a straight line over the vowel (ā).

meter. A specific rhythmic pattern for poetic lines.

quantity. The length of a *syllable*, either long or short.

spondee. A poetic *foot* comprised of two long *syllables*.

substitution. The phenomenon by which the second long *syllable* of a *spondee* can replace the two short *syllables* of a *dactyl*. Thus, the first four *feet* in a line of *dactylic hexameter* can be either four *dactyls* or, by substitution, four *spondees*.

syllable. A group of letters that form a sound; each syllable must have a vowel.

Elision

Elision is essential to scansion because it will affect the total number of syllables in a line and so the metrical pattern of the line.

When one word ends with a vowel and the following word begins with a vowel, the last syllable of the first word will drop out.

> *Colligere incertos et = Colliger(e) incertos et = Colligerincertos et* (*Amores* 1.11.1)

When the second word in an elision is *es* or *est* (forms of *sum, esse*), the "e" of *es* or *est* drops out instead of the terminal vowel of the first word.

> *ingenii est experientis = ingenii (e)st experientis = ingeniist experientis* (*Amores* 1.9.32)

When a word ends with an "m" and is followed by a word that begins with a vowel, these words will elide.

> *nec durum in pectore = nec dur(um) in pectore = nec durin pectore* (*Amores* 1.11.9)

When a word ends with a vowel and the following word begins with an "h," these words will elide.

> *Ite hinc, difficiles, funebria = It(e) (h)inc, difficiles, funebria = Itinc, difficiles, funebria*
> (*Amores* 1.12.7)

Although rare, when a word ends in "m" and begins with "h," elision will occur.

> *dubitantem hortata Corinnam = dubitant(em) (h)ortata Corinnam = dubitantortata Corinnam* (*Amores* 1.11.5)

To sum up, the four scenarios in which an elision occurs are the following:

1st word	2nd word
-[vowel]	[vowel]-
-m	[vowel]-
-[vowel]	h-
-m	h-

On occasion an elision will not occur when it should occur. This is called *hiatus*.

Long by Position

A vowel followed by two or more consonants is long by position.

These two or more consonants can stretch across word breaks, i.e. the final syllable of a word that ends in a single consonant and is followed by a word that begins with a single (or double consonant) will be long. A word that ends in a vowel followed by a word that begins with two or more consonants can be long but will not always be long (see Ambiguity: Stop - Liquid Combination below).

> *super pontum*: the "e" in *super*, normally short, is made long because of the "p" in *pontum* (*Amores* 1.3.23)

The letter "i" can function as a vowel or consonant. This determination should be made largely by context, but often consonantal "i" is followed by the vowel "u," e.g. *iungo, iubeo*, etc., and less often by the vowel "a," e.g. *iaceo*, or "o," e.g. *iocum*.

Certain consonants function contrary to expectation.

- "h" is not considered a consonant for the purpose of long by position. A syllable that ends a word with a single consonant followed by a word that begins with "h" is not long by position. ("h" will also affect elisions; see above.)

  Carmine nomen habent: the "e" in *nomen* is short because it is naturally short and the second consonant that follows it is the "h" of *habent* which does not count toward making a vowel long by position. (*Amores* 1.3.21)

- "x" and "z" are considered double consonants and will render vowels preceding them long.

  radix et lactis massa: the "i" in *radix* is long, even though it is followed by a single consonant, because that single consonant is "x" (*Baucis and Philemon* 666)

- "k" is considered a double consonant and will render vowels preceding it long. (No "k" appears in this volume, so no example is included.)

- "ph" and "th" are considered single consonants and will not render vowels preceding them long.

  duo tela pharetra: the "a" in *tela* is short, even though it is followed by a double consonant, because that double consonant is "ph" (*Apollo and Daphne* 467)

  versato cardine Thisbe: the "e" in *cardine* is short, even though it is followed by a double consonant, because that double consonant is "th" (*Pyramus and Thisbe* 93)

Long by Nature: Diphthongs

ae, au, ei, eu, oe, ui
Diphthongs do not exist when straddling the stem and ending of a form.

  e.g. *fuisti* is a three syllable word, despite the "ui" because the "u" is part of the stem and the "i" is part of the ending

The "u" in "qu" and "gu" does not form a diphthong when followed by another vowel. It is taken with the preceding "q" or "g" instead (much the same way that in English the "q" cannot function without a corresponding "u").

si qua fides: the "a" in *qua* is short; the "u" that precedes it is part of the "qu" of *qua* and does not form a diphthong. (*Amores* 1.3.16)

Long by Nature: Common Naturally Long Syllables

1st, 2nd, and 5th declensions, dative and ablative plural	-īs, -ēbus
1st, 2nd, and 5th declensions, genitive plural	-ārum, -ōrum, -ērum
All declensions (excepting the 3rd declension: -ĕ) ablative singular	-ā, -ō, -ī, -ū, -ē
All declensions nominative plural (excepting neuter forms: -ă)	-ī, -ēs, -ūs
All declensions accusative plural (excepting neuter forms: -ă)	-ās, -ōs, -ēs, -ūs
All conjugations, 1st person singular present active	-ō
All conjugations, 1st person singular perfect active	-ī
1st, 2nd, 4th conjugations, present active infinitive characteristic vowel	-ā, -ē, -ī

Ambiguity: Stop-Liquid Combination

When a vowel is followed by a the combination of a stop and a liquid consonant, that vowel can be either long or short, depending on the poet's needs. Most double consonants that begin words will be stop-liquid combinations.

The stop-consonants: b, c, d, g, k, p, t

The liquid-consonants: l, r

iusta precor: the "a" in *iusta* can be either long or short because of the "pr" of *precor*; in this instance it will be short. (*Amores* 1.3.1)

anima producit: the second "a" in *anima* can be either long or short because of the "pr" of *producit*; in this instance it will be long. (*Baucis and Philemon* 643)

Ambiguity: Syllaba Anceps

The last syllable of a line is considered long, whether it is naturally long or short, because of the natural lengthening that will occur on that last syllable.

The proper symbol for a *syllaba anceps* is a short symbol over a macron. The AP exam allows the *syllaba anceps* to be scanned long in all instances.

Glossary

The glossary defines every word within the text. Words are listed alphabetically with the guide word, and all of its dictionary forms bolded. The identification of part of speech is included in parentheses only when not otherwise obvious. Definitions appear in plain type. Any additional comments are included in italics. Proper names of either people or places will be identifed simply by "name" in brackets [name]. If there is an English equivalent other than the nominative form, it will then be given. If the English equivalent is the same as the nominative, nothing will be given. In either case, a brief explanatory note will be given in italics; this should not be considered part of the definition, but rather information to help understand the context of the name. Brief grammatical explanations will also be included in italics with words of particular difficulty or ambiguity (e.g. *ut, ne, ipse, sui,* etc.). Vowels that can be read as either long or short (e.g. the "i" in *mihi, tibi,* or *ibi* [2nd "i"]) will be left short in the glossary.

Often, more than one definition will be included with a word. This multiplicity is not to be considered an invitation for arbitrary choice on the student's part. Rather, definitions are intended to provide the student with a sense of a given word's range of meaning. That range should be applied to the individual context within which the word appears. No dictionary, however big, can include specific definitions to fit every context of a word. It is (and should be) up to the student to make an informed choice to render a word into an English equivalent that will both capture the sense of the Latin and maintain a conventional and understandable English idiom.

The following abbreviations will be used throughout the glossary. Students should familiarize themselves with them, their terms, and their definitions.

prep.	preposition
conj.	conjunction
pron.	pronoun
impers.	impersonal (verbs that have "it" as the subject that replaces a clause, instead of a personal subject, e.g. *licet* = "it is permitted to…")
dep.	deponent (verbs that are passive in form and active in meaning)
semi-dep.	semi-deponent (verbs that function as non-deponent verbs in the present system and deponent verbs in the perfect system)
defec.	defective (a verb that is missing certain forms and/or principle parts)
disyll.	disllyabic (a word with two syllables)
expr.	expression (referring to a colloquialism or idiom that would not translate directly)
patron.	patronymic (identifying someone by the name of their father or ancestor)
m., f., n.	[gender]
sing., pl.	[number]
nom., gen., dat., acc., abl.	[case names]
encl.	enclitic (a word that is attached to another word as an additional syllable, e.g. *-que, -ne*)

ā (interj.). oh, ah

ā, ab (prep. + abl.). from, away from; by [*only with a passive verb*]

abditus, -a, -um. hidden, concealed

abdūcō, abdūcere, abduxī, abductus. to lead away, to take away, to carry off

abeō, abīre, abiī / -īvī, abitus. to go away, to leave; to pass, to transform

absum, abesse, āfuī, -. to be away, to be absent, to not notice

absūmō, absūmere, absumpsī, absumptus. to consume, to waste, to use up, to exhaust, to expend

ac (conj.). [*see at*]

accēdō, accēdere, accessī, accessus. to approach, to come (forward)

accendō, accendere, accendī, accensus. to burn, to smolder, to kindle, to enflame

accingō, accingere, accinxī, accinctus. to equip, to gird

accipiō, accipere, accēpī, acceptus. to accept, to receive

acclīnō, -āre, -āvī, -ātus. to lay down, to put down, to lie on; to rest, to lean

accommodō, -āre, -āvī, -ātus. to fit, to attach

accumbō, accumbere, accubuī, accubiturus. to recline, to sit (down) [*used in the context of sitting down to dinner*]

acer, aceris (n.). maple tree, maple wood

ācer, ācris, ācre. sharp, piercing, hot

Achillēs, Achillis (m.). [name: *most famous Greek warrior and main character of Homer's* Iliad]

acūtus, -a, -um. sharp

ad (prep. + acc.). to, towards, at

addūcō, addūcere, adduxī, adductus. to lead to, to lead back, to pull back, to pull tight

adeō (adv.). to such an extent, so

adeō, adīre, adiī / -īvī, aditus. to approach, to come to

adhibeō, adhibēre, adhibuī, adhibitus. to use, to employ

adhūc (adv.). still

adimō, adimere, adēmī, ademptus. to take away, to remove

adiuvō, adiuvāre, adiūvī, adiūtus. to help

admittō, admittere, admīsī, admissus. to send along, to admit, to hasten

admoveō, admovēre, admōvī, admōtus. to move (close) to, to approach

adoleō, adolēre, adoluī, adultus. to burn, to scorch, to set on fire

adopertus, -a, -um. covered, veiled

adsum, adesse, adfuī, adfuturus. to be present, to be there

adulter, adulterī. adulterer

adūrō, adūrere, adussī, adustus. to scorch, to burn

adversus, -a, -um. opposite, facing the opposite direction, in front of

aedēs, aedis (f.). temple, shrine

aemula, -ae. (female) rival

ăēnum, ăēnī. [*a three syllable nominative and genitive*] bronze vessel, bronze cup, bronze bowl

aequātus, -a, -um. level, flat

aequor, aequoris (n.). the sea, a level surface (*such as the sea*)

aequus, -a, -um. level, even; **ex aequo** [*expr.*] equally, with the same intensity

āēr, āeris (m.). air [*a two syllable nominative singular and a three syllable genitive singular*]

aes, aeris (n.). copper, bronze, metal; currency, money

aestuō, -āre, -āvī, -ātus. to flare, to blaze, to burn fiercely

aetās, aetātis (f.). age

aethēr, aetheris (m.). air, heaven

aevum, -ī. age

affectō, -āre, -āvī, -ātus. to attempt, to try, to strive (for)

afflō, afflāre, afflāvī, afflātus. to breathe on, to breathe at, to blow on

agilis, -e. swift, quick, agile, nimble

agitō, -āre, -āvī, -ātus. to agitate, to stir (up), to shake

agmen, agminis (n.). battle line, battle formation

agna, -ae. a young lamb [*specifically a ewe lamb, which is a female sheep under one year of age and/or a female sheep which has not yet given birth*]

agō, agere, ēgī, actus. to do, to drive, to discuss

āiō (defec.). to say, to assent [*often used as the verb for direct quotes*]

āla, -ae. wing

albus, -a, -um. white

āles, ālitis (m./f.). (large) bird

aliquis, aliquid (pron.). some, any; someone, something; anyone, anything [*the indefinite pronoun that is declined like the interrogative* quis, quid *with the prefix* ali- *attached*]

aliter (adv.). different(ly), otherwise

alligō, -āre, -āvī, -ātus. to bind, to attach, to join

alter, altera, alterum. [*often appears in pairs:*] one...the other [*an irregular adjective whose genitive singular ends in* -ius *and whose dative singular ends in* -ī]

altus, -a, -um. high, deep

alumnus, -ī. native, child

alveus, -ī. bowl

amans, amantis (m./f.). lover

Amathūsius, -a, -um. Amathusian; of or belonging to Amathusia [*a city in Cyprus where Venus is said to have been born*]

ambiguum, -ī. uncertainty, ambiguity; the state of being uncertain or ambiguous

ambitiōsus, -a, -um. eager, ambitious, adventurous

ambō, ambae, ambō. both [*an irregular adjective that only occurs in the plural, and whose masculine and* *neuter nominative can be misleading because of the -ō ending*]

amīca, -ae. (female) friend

amictus, -ūs (m.). cloak

amīcus, -a, -um. friendly, eager; belonging to a friend or lover

amō, -āre, -āvī, -ātus. to love

amor, amōris (m.). love; [*when capitalized*] Cupid [*the son of Venus and also the god of love*]

amplector, amplectī, amplexus. to embrace

an (conj.). whether, if [*used to introduce "yes/no" indirect questions*]

ancilla, -ae. slave woman

Andromachē, Andromachēs (f.). [name: *the wife of Troy's most famous warrior Hector*]

anhēlitus, -ūs. a breathing, a gasping

anīlis, -e. of or belonging to an old woman; old woman's

anima, -ae. breath, spirit, soul, heart

animal, animālis (n.). animal, creature

animus, -ī. spirit, soul, maturity, heart

annuō, annuere, annuī, annūtus. to nod at, to agree, to assent

annus, -ī. year

ansa, -ae. handle

anser, anseris (m.). goose

ante (adv., prep. + acc.). before, in the past; in front of

antrum, -ī. cave

anus, -ūs (f.). old woman

anxius, -a, -um. anxious, worried, concerned

Āonius, -a, -um. of or belonging to Aonia or Boeotia [*the region in Greece where Mt. Helicon is located, a peak sacred to Apollo and the Muses*]

aperiō, aperīre, aperuī, apertus. to open, to reveal

apex, apicis (m.). top, tip, point

apis, apis (f.). bee

Apollineus, -a, -um. of or belonging to Apollo; Apollonean

appellō, -āre, -āvī, -ātus. to call, to name

aptō, -āre, -āvī, -ātus. to put, to place, to fit

aptus, -a, -um. appropriate, easy, apt

aqua, -ae. water

aquila, -ae. eagle, bird of prey

aquōsus, -a, -um. watery, well-watered

āra, -ae. altar

arātor, arātōris (m.). plowman

arātrum, -ī. plow

arbor, arboris (f.). tree

arboreus, -a, -um. of a tree, belonging to a tree, tree's

arcus, -ūs. bow

ardeō, ardēre, arsī, arsurus. to burn, to be on fire

arduus, -a, -um. tall, towering, steep, precipitous; [*as substantive*] height, peak

ārea, -ae. area, (open) space

argentum, -ī. silver

Argēus, -a, -um. Argive; of or belonging to Argos; Greek [*refers to a city in the northeast of the Peloponnese (the southern half of Greece), which dominated early Greece and whose name became synonymous with Greece itself*]

āridus, -a, -um. dry

arista, -ae. grain [*specifically the awn or beard of a stalk of grain, which is the upper part of a stalk of grain that crumbles in the hand*]

arma, -ōrum (n. pl.). arms, weapons

armātus, -a, -um. armed

armentum, -ī. herd (of cattle)

ars, artis (f.). art, skill

artus, -ūs. limb [*of the body*]

arvum, -ī. field, meadow, open expanse of grass

arx, arcis (f.). citadel, summit, stronghold, lofty perch

asper, aspera, asperum. rough, harsh, forbidding, dangerous

aspergō, asperginis (f.). a sprinkling, a spattering

aspiciō, aspicere, aspexī, aspectus. to look at, to gaze

asserō, asserere, asserruī, assertus. to claim, to lay claim to, to identify as one's own, to possess

at (conj.). but, and so, still [*an adversative conjunction that often signals a shift in the story or sense*]

āter, ātra, ātrum. black, dark

Atlantiadēs, -ae (m.). [name] Mercury [*here the patronymic as the grandson of Atlas*]

atque. [*see* at]

Atrīdēs, Atridae (m.). son of Atreus; *either* Menelaus *or* Agamemnon

attenuō, -āre, -āvī, -ātus. to make thin, to weaken

Atticus, -ī (m.). [name: *an otherwise unspecified man to whom Ovid addresses some of his poems*]

attollō, attollere, -, -. to lift (up), to raise (up)

attonitus, -a, -um. astonished, thunderstruck, disbelieving

auctor, auctōris (m./f.). founder, creator

audax, audācis (adj.). bold, arrogant, cocky

audeō, audēre, ausus (semi-dep.). to dare

audiō, audīre, audīvī, audītus. to hear

auferō, auferre, abstulī, ablātus. to carry away, to bear away, to remove

augeō, augēre, auxī, auctus (semi-dep.). to increase, to augment

Augustus, -a, -um. of or belonging to Augustus; of or belonging to the emperor; imperial [*Augustus was the first emperor of Rome, solidifying his power in 27 BC; his name here is used synonymously with the role of emperor and the institution of empire*]

aura, -ae. breeze, wind, air

aurātus, -a, -um. golden

aureus, -a, -um. golden, of gold

auris, auris (f.). ear

Aurōra, -ae. dawn; [name: *the goddess of the dawn*]

aurum, -ī. gold

auspicium, -ī. omen, sign; the act of reading omens, augury

aut (conj.). or; [*when used with multiple* aut*'s*] either...or

autumnālis, -e. autumnal, of or belonging to autumn

avārus, -a, -um. greedy

avēna, -ae. oat, hollow stalk

āversor, āversārī, āversātus. to reject, to spurn

avis, avis (f.). bird

āvius, -a, -um. remote, wild, without paths or roads

Babylōnius, -a, -um. Babylonian

bāca, -ae. berry, nut, pearl, jewel

baculum, -ī. stick, staff

Baucis, Baucidis (f.; acc. sing = Baucida). [name]

bellum, -ī. war

bellus, -a, -um. beautiful, charming

bene (adv.). well

bicolor, bicolōris (adj.). having two colors, bi-colored

bicornis, -e. with two horns, two-horned; with two prongs, two-pronged

blanditia, -ae. flattery, pleasing speech, compliment; [*when plural*] sweet nothings, pleasantries

blandus, -a, -um. flattering, encouraging, enticing, inviting

bonus, -a, -um. good

Boōtēs, Boōtae. (m.). [name: *a constellation*]

bōs, bovis (m./f.; gen. pl. = boum). cow, ox

brācchium, -i. arm, forearm

brevis, -e. short, brief

Brīsēis, Brīsēidos (f.; abl. sing. = Brīsēide). [name: *woman whom Achilles claimed as a prize of war, but whom Agamemnon took from Achilles when Agamemnon lost his own war prize; Agamemnon's taking of her resulted in Achilles' withdrawal from the Trojan War*]

būbō, būbonis (m.). owl, horned owl

bustum, -ī. funeral marker, funeral pyre, tomb, grave-mound

buxus, -ī (f.). the box-wood tree [*a tree known for the pale color of its bark*]

cacūmen, cacuminis (n.). height, peak, top

cadō, cadere, cecidī, cāsus. to fall, to fall down, to sink down, to trip

cādūcifer, cādūciferī (m.). Mercury, the staff-bearer

caedēs, caedis (f.). slaughter, gore

caedō, caedere, cecīdī, caesus. to attack, to strike, to kill, to slaughter

caelebs, caelibis (adj.). unmarried

caelicola, -ae (m./f.). god / goddess; heaven-dweller

caelō, -āre, -āvī, -ātus. to etch, to engrave, to incise

caelum, -ī. sky, heaven

caeruleus, -a, -um. blue

caleō, calēre, caluī, -. to be hot, to be warm

callidus, -a, -um. clever, crafty

Calymnē, Calymnēs (f.). [name: *one of the Sporades islands, located off the southwest coast of Asia Minor (modern-day Turkey)*]

campus, -ī. field, open space, plain

candidus, -a, -um. white, yellow

canis, canis (m./f.). dog

canistrum, -ī. basket

canna, -ae. reed

canō, canere, cecinī, cantus. to sing

cantō, -āre, -āvī, -ātus. to sing

capillus, -ī. hair

capiō, capere, cēpī, captus. to take, to capture

Capitōlium, -ī. the Capitoline Hill [*the hill in Rome where the government met*]

captīvus, -a, -um. captive, captured, taken

captō, -āre, -āvī, -ātus. to keep taking, to keep grabbing, to try to touch

caput, capitis (n.). head

cardō, cardinis (m.). pivot, door-hinge, door

careō, carēre, caruī, cariturus (+ abl.). to need, to lack [*takes its object in the ablative*]

cārica, -ae. fig

cariōsus, -a, -um. decayed, rotten

carmen, carminis (n.). song, poem

carnifex, carnificis (m.). killer, executioner

carpō, carpere, carpsī, carptus. to seize, to grab at, to travel, to devour, to consume, to harvest

cārus, -a, -um. dear

casa, -ae. little house, hut, hovel

castra, -ōrum (n. pl.). camp

cāsus, -ūs. misfortune, accident, mishap, tragedy

caterva, -ae. crowd

Catullus, -ī. [name: *a Roman poet born in 86 BC in Verona and a poetic predecessor of Ovid*]

causa, -ae. cause, reason

causor, causārī, causātus. to complain about, to make an excuse of

cautus, -a, -um. cautious, careful

cavus, -a, -um. hollow, full of holes, porous

cecid-. [*see* cado *or* caedo]

cēdō, cēdere, cessī, cessūrus (+ dat.). to yield (to), to proceed

celeber, celebris, celebre. busy, crowded

celer, celeris, celere. swift, quick

celsus, -a, -um. high, lofty, in the air

cēra, -ae. wax

Cerēs, Cereris (f.). [name: *the Roman goddess of the harvest*]

certē (adv.). certainly, of course

certus, -a, -um. certain, definite, true

cerva, -ae. female deer, doe

cervix, cervīcis (f.). neck

cessō, -āre, -āvī, -ātus. to delay, to remain unchanged, to be idle

cēterus, -a, -um. the rest, other

cicūta, -ae. hemlock, hemlock plant

cingō, cingere, cinxī, cinctus. to bind, to gird, to surround

cinis, cineris (m.). ashes [*of a dead body*]

circumdō, circumdāre, circumdedī, circumdatus. to surround

cithara, -ae. lyre

citus, -a, -um. fast, swift, rapid

clāmō, -āre, -āvī, -ātus. to shout, to cry out

Claros, Clarī (f.). [name: *a favorite Greek town of the god Apollo in Ionia, which is an area on the southwestern coast of modern-day Turkey*]

clārus, -a, -um. clear, loud, sharp

claudō, claudere, clausī, clausus. to close, to shut

clāvus, -ī. nail, spike

clīvus, -ī. slope, incline, progression

coctilis, -e (adj.). brick, baked, made of fired bricks

coeō, coīre, coiī / coivī, coitus. to come together [*both in a literal sense and in a figurative sense, i.e. in a group or in marriage*]; to assemble

coepī, coepisse, coeptus (defec.). to begin

coeptum, -ī. undertaking

coerceo, coercere, coercui, coercitus. to hold in place, to restrain, to bind

cognitor, cognitōris (m.). lawyer, representative

cognoscō, cognoscere, cognōvī, cognotus. to recognize, to learn; [*in the perfect tense*] to know

cōgō, cōgere, coēgī, coāctus. to force, to compel

colligō, colligere, collēgī, collectus. to assemble, to gather, to collect

collis, collis (m.). hill

collocō, -āre, -āvī, -ātus. to establish, to set up, to place

collum, -ī. neck

colō, colere, coluī, cultus. to cultivate, to worship; to till, to farm

color, colōris (m.). color

columba, -ae. dove

columna, -ae. column

coma, -ae. hair

comes, comitis (m./f.). companion

comitō, -āre, -āvī, -ātus. to go with, to accompany

commendō, -āre, -āvī, -ātus. to recommend

committō, committere, commīsī, commissus. to entrust

commūnis, -e. common, shared

cōmō, cōmere, compsī, comptus. to make beautiful, to adorn, to arrange attractively

compescō, compescere, compescuī, -. to quench, to satisfy

complector, complectī, complexus. to embrace, to hug

complexus, -ūs. embrace, hug

compōnō, compōnere, composuī, compositus. to assemble, to put together

comprendō, comprendere, comprendī, comprensus. to seize, to catch, to capture, to hold

comprimō, comprimere, compressī, compressus. to compress, to condense

concha, -ae. conch, conch shell, shellfish; pearl [*i.e. that which is found in a shell*]

concīdo, concidere, concīdī, concīsus. to fall down; to strike, to impact

concipiō, concipere, concēpī, conceptus. to develop, to worship, to speak with respect

concordō, -āre, -āvī, -āturus. to be in synch, to be in harmony, to be in agreement

concors, concordis (adj.). in agreement, agreeing, of like mind

concutiō, concutere, concussī, concussus. to shake, to cause to vibrate, to fluff

condō, condere, condidī, conditus. to found, to establish, to set up

confugiō, confugere, confūgī, confugiturus. to flee, to leave

congestus, -a, -um. accumulated, piled up

coniugium, -ī. marriage

coniunx, coniugis (m./f.). spouse

conscius, -ī. accomplice, witness

consenescō, consenescere, consenuī, -. to become old, to achieve old age

consistō, consistere, constitī, constitus. to stand still, to stop, to establish oneself

consors, consortis (m./f.). consort, spouse

conspiciō, conspicere, conspexī, conspectus. to catch sight of, to see, to view

constō, constāre, constitī, constatūrus. to stand, to stand on, to exist, to establish, to be established

consuescō, consuescere, consuēvī, consuētus. to be accustomed to, to be used to

consūmō, consumere, consumpsī, consumptus. to devour, to consume

contentus, -a, -um. happy, content

conterminus, -a, -um (+ dat.). bordering, next to, near

contiguus, -a, -um. connected

contingō, contingere, contigī, contactus. to touch, to contact, to come into contact with; [*when used with an infinitive, impersonal:*] it is granted (to…)

continuō (adv.). immediately

contrā (adv.). in return, in response, opposite, facing

cōnūbium, -ī. marriage, wedding

conveniō, convenīre, convēnī, conventurus. to come together, to meet; to be convenient, to be useful

convincō, convincere, convīcī, convictus. to overcome; [*when used with an infinitive*] to prove

Corinna, -ae. [name: *the name of Ovid's love and the subject of his love poetry*]

corniger, cornigera, cornigerum. horned, horn-bearing

cornū, -ūs (n.). horn, ivory, something made of ivory, tip

cornum, -ī. (cornelian) cherry, (cornal) berry

corpus, corporis (n.). body

Corsicus, -a, -um. of or belonging to Corsica, Corsican [*the northernmost of two large islands off of Italy's west coast, Corsica belonging to France, and Sardinia, to its south, belonging to Italy*]

cortex, corticis (m.). bark (of a tree), covering

crātēr, crātēris (m.; acc. = crātēra). [name: *the crater was a deep, wide-mouthed Greek vase which was used to mix wine and water*]

crēdibilis, -e. believable, credible

crēdō, credere, credidī, creditus (+ dat.). to believe, to trust

crescō, crescere, crēvī, crētus. to increase, to develop, to grow

Crētē, Crētēs (f.). [name: *large island in the Mediterranean that lies due south of mainland Greece; its capital city was Knossos, home to King Minos, the Minotaur, and the Labyrinth*]

crīmen, criminis (n.). crime, mistake, oversight, sin, transgression

crīnis, crīnis (m.). hair

cruentō, -āre, -āvī, -ātus. to stain with blood, to pollute

cruentus, -a, -um. bloody

cruor, -ōris (m.). blood, gore

crūs, crūris (n.). (lower) leg, shin

crux, crucis (f.). cross

cultus, -a, -um. cultivated, elegant, refined

cum (conj.). when, because, although

cum (prep.). with, along with

cunctus, -a, -um. whole, all, entire

cupīdō, cupidinis (m./f.). desire, want, longing

Cupīdō, Cupidinis (m.). [name: *the Roman god of love, son of Venus*]

cupiō, cupere, cupīvī, cupītus. to desire, to want

cūr. why

cūra, -ae. care, concern

cūrō, -āre, -āvī, -ātus. to care for, to care about

currō, currere, cucurrī, cursurus. to run, to move, to fly

cursus, -ūs. course, route, path

curvāmen, curvaminis (n.). curve, arc, bent shape

cuspis, cuspidis (f.). tip, (sharp) point

custōdia, -ae. protection, guard, custody

custōs, custōdis (m./f.). guard

Cyprus, -ī (f.). [name: *a large island in the northeastern corner of the Mediterranean, south of Turkey*]

Cytherēa, -ae. [name] Cytherean one, Venus

Daedalus, -ī (m.). [name: *famous artisan and architect; originally an Athenian but eventually exiled to Crete where he designed the Labyrinth*]

damnōsus, -a, -um. destructive, awful

Daphnē, Daphnēs (Gr. f.). [name: *a nymph, the daughter of the river god Peneus, who was loved and chased by Apollo and whose father eventually turned her into the laurel tree so that she could escape Apollo*]

daps, dapis (f.). feast

dē (prep. + abl.). from, down from, concerning, about

dea, -ae. goddess

dēbeō, dēbēre, dēbuī, dēbitus. to owe; [*with infin.*] ought

decens, decentis. fitting, right, appropriate

decet, decēre, decuit, - (impers.). it is fitting, it is right, it is appropriate

decor, decōris (m.). grace, beauty, charm

dēdecet, dēdecēre, dēdecuit, - (impers.). it is not fitting, it is inappropriate

dēdicō, -āre, -āvī, -ātus. to dedicate, to devote, to consecrate

dēferō, dēferre, dētulī, dēlātus. to bring down, to get

dēfleō, dēflēre, dēflēvī, dēflētus. to weep (for), to mourn

dēlicia, -ae. pleasure, enjoyment, delight

Dēlius, -a, -um. Delian, of or belonging to Delos [*an epithet for Apollo because of his close association with this island in the Aegean where supposedly his mother Latona gave birth to him*]

Dēlos, Dēlī (f.). [name: *an island; one of the larger of the Cyclades, a group of islands off the east coast of mainland Greece*]

Delphicus, -a, -um. Delphic, of or belonging to Delphi [*Delphi was a site sacred to Apollo; his oracle, the most famous in the ancient world, was located there*]

dēlūbrum, -ī. temple, shrine, small place of worship or devotion

dēmittō, demittere, dēmīsī, demissus. to thrust, to send into, to lower; [*with* animum:] to put one's mind to

dēmō, dēmere, dempsī, demptus. to cut (off), to slice, to remove densus, -a, -um. dense, thick

dēpōnō, dēpōnere, dēposuī, dēpositus. to satisfy, to quench

dēprendo, dēprendere, dēprendī, dēprensus. to seize, to catch

dēserō, dēserere, dēseruī, dēsertus. to desert, to leave

dēserviō, dēservīre, -, -. to serve, to be a servant

dēsidia, -ae. laziness, sloth, leisure, idleness

dēsidiōsus, -a, -um. idle, lazy

dēsinō, dēsinere, dēsivī, dēsitus. to stop, to cease

dēsultor, dēsultōris (m.). horse-jumper

deus, -ī [nom. pl., voc. pl. = dī; dat. / abl. pl. = dīs]. god

dēvoveō, dēvovēre, dēvōvī, dēvōtus. to curse, to damn

dexter, dextra, dextrum. right [not as in "correct" but as in "right" vs. "left"]

dī. [see deus]

Diāna, -ae. [name: the virginal goddess of the hunt; she foreswore marriage or any attachment to men]

dīcō, dīcere, dixī, dictus. to say, to speak; [when used in the passive, often accompanied by an infintive with the sense of "to be said to…"]

diēs, -ēī. day

difficilis, -e. difficult, hard, troublesome, meddlesome, useless

digitus, -ī. finger, toe

dignus, -a, -um (+ abl.). worthy (of)

dīmittō, dimittere, dimīsī, dimissus. to apply, to send to

dīmoveō, dīmovēre, dīmōvī, dīmōtus. to stir, to move around

dīrus, -a, -um. grim, awful, dire, horrible

dīs = [see deus]

discēdō, discēdere, discessī, discessūrus. to depart, to leave

discinctus, -a, -um. relaxed, easy-going, unbound, loosely-fitting

discrīmen, discriminis (n.). difference, distinction

dispār, disparis. unequal, disparate, uneven

diū (adv.). for a long time

dīvellō, dīvellere, dīvellī, dīvulsus. to tear apart, to tear to pieces

dīversus, -a, -um. different, opposite

dō, dare, dedī, datus. to give; [with an infinitive:] to allow

doceō, docēre, docuī, doctus. to teach

doleō, dolēre, doluī, doliturus. to be sad, to regret

dolor, dolōris (m.). grief, suffering, pain

domina, -ae. mistress

dominus, -ī. master, lord, ruler

domō, domāre, domuī, domitus. to tame, to overcome, to temper

domus, -ūs (-ī) (f.) [can be alternately 2nd or 4th declension]. house, home

dōnec (conj.). until, as long as

donō, -āre, -āvī, -ātus. to give, to grant

dubitō, -āre, -āvī, -ātus. to doubt, to be uncertain

dubius, -a, -um. doubtful

dūcō, ducere, duxī, ductus. to lead, to develop

dum (conj.). while

duo, duae, duo [dat. & abl. pl. = duobus]. two

duplex, duplicis (adj.). double, deceiving, two-faced, folded over

duplicātus, -a, -um. doubled, double in size, increased, swollen

dūrus, -a, -um. hard, harsh

dux, ducis (m.). leader

ē, ex (prep. + abl.). from, out of

ebur, eboris (n.). ivory, something made of ivory

eburneus, -a, -um. ivory, made of ivory

eburnus, -a, -um. ivory, made of ivory

ecce (interj.). look!

ēdō, ēdere, ēdidī, ēditus. to say, to narrate, to tell, to give forth, to produce

efficiō, efficere, effēcī, effectus. to make happen, to create, to produce

effūsus, -a, -um. flowing, undone, spread out

ēg-. [see ago]

ego, meī, mihi, mē, mē (pron.). I, me

ēgredior, ēgredī, ēgressus. to depart, to leave

ei (interj.). woe, miserable [an exclamation of grief or sadness]

ēiaculor, ēiaculārī, ēiaculātus. to shoot out, to discharge

elegī, -ōrum (m. pl.). elegiac verses, elegiac poetry

ēlīdō, ēlīdere, ēlīsī, ēlīsus. to crash, to break through, to shatter

ēlūdō, ēlūdere, ēlūdī, ēlūsus. to elude, to escape, to avoid

ēmicō, -āre, -uī, -ātus. to spurt out, to spurt upward

ēmodulor, -ārī, -ātus. to measure numerically, to put into meter, to control, to regulate

enim. for

ensis, ensis (m.). sword

eō, īre, iī / īvī, iturus. to go

eōdem. [see īdem]

ephēmeris, ephēmeridis (f.; acc. pl. = ephēmeridās). date book, account book

epulae, -ārum. feast, banquet

eques, equitis (m.). horseman, cavalryman

equidem. indeed

equus, -ī. horse

eram, eras, etc. [see sum]

ergō. therefore

ērigō, ērigere, ērexī, ērectus. to raise, to lift up

ēripiō, ēripere, ēripuī, ēreptus. to grab, to take away, to snatch, to steal

erō, eris, etc. [see sum]

errō, -āre, -āvī, -ātus. to wander aimlessly, to go astray

ērubēscō, ērubēscere, ērubuī, -. to blush, to turn red, to feel shame

ērudiō, ērudīre, ērudīvī, ērudītus. to teach, to pass on

erunt. [see sum]

es, esse, est. [see sum]

et (conj.). and

etiam. also, even

Eurus, -ī. east wind

ex (prep. + abl.). from, (out) of

exaudiō, exaudīre, exaudīvī, exaudītus. to hear, to listen to

excēdō, excēdere, excessī, excessūrus. to go out, to leave

excipiō, excipere, excēpī, exceptus. to consume, to devour, to capture

exeō, exīre, exiī / -īvī, exitus. to exit, to leave

exhorrēscō, exhorrēscere, exhorruī, -. to shudder (with fear)

exiguus, -a, -um. slight, paltry, minimal, small, barely noticeable

exilium, -ī. exile

eximō, eximere, exēmī, exemptus. to remove, to take away

exitium, -ī. outcome, end, death

exōsus, -a, -um (+ acc.). hateful (of), hating, detesting, despising

expallēscō, expallēscere, expalluī, -. to grow pale, to grow white

experiēns, experientis. active

expers, expertis (+ gen.). ignorant (of), inexperienced (with)

exstinguō, exstinguere, exstinxī, exstinctus. to extinguish [in both a literal and a figurative sense, i.e. a fire or a life]

extendō, extendere, extendī, extentus. to stretch (out), to reach, to hold (out)

exterō, exterere, extrīvī, extrītus. to crush, to wear down, to compress

exterreō, exterrēre, exterruī, exterritus. to scare, to terrify

extrēmus, -a, -um. outer edge, side

exuviae, exuviārum (f. pl.). spoils, pelt, skin, hide

fabricō, -āre, -āvī, -ātus. to fashion, to create, to make

fabrīlis, -e. of or belonging to a craftsman; craftsman's, blacksmith's

fābula, -ae. story

faciēs, -ēī. face, appearance

faciō, facere, fēcī, factus. to make, to do

faex, faecis (f.). dregs, solids, leftovers

fāgineus, -a, -um. of or belonging to the beech tree; made of beech wood

fāgus, -ī (f.). beech tree

fallō, fallere, fefellī, falsus. to deceive, to trick

falsus, -a, -um. false, untrue, misleading

famulus, -ī. slave, servant

fateor, fatērī, fassus. to admit, to acknowledge, to confess

fatigō, -āre, -āvī, -ātus. to tire, to fatigue, to weary

fatum, -ī. fate

favilla, -ae. ashes (of a fire)

favus, -ī. honeycomb

fax, facis (f.). torch, fire, wedding [because of the torches that burned at weddings]; wood

fēcundus, -a, -um. fertile, rich (in)

fēlix, fēlīcis. happy, fortunate, lucky

fēmina, -ae. woman

fēmineus, -a, -um. womanly, of or belonging to a woman

ferō, ferre, tulī, lātus. to bring, to bear, to carry, to endure; fertur: "it is said" [used with an infinitive]

ferreus, -a, -um. (made of) iron

ferrum, -ī. iron, sword

ferus, -a, -um. wild; [often used substantively as:] wild beast, wild animal

fervēns, ferventis. warm, hot, boiling, fervent, steaming

festus, -a, -um. of or belonging to a party or a festival

fētus, -ūs. fruit, offspring

fictile, fictilis (n.). earthenware, (terracotta) vase or pitcher

fidēs, -ēī. faith, trust, loyalty

fīdus, -a, -um. faithful, trustworthy, loyal, devoted

fīgō, fīgere, fīxī, fixus. to drive in, to insert, to fix, to affix, to attach

figūra, -ae. figure, shape, body, form

fīlia, -ae. daughter

fīlius, -ī. son

fīlum, -ī. thread

findō, findere, fidī, fissus. to split apart, to open

fīniō, -īre, -īvī, -ītus. to finish

fīnis, fīnis (m.). limit, boundary, border, end

fīō, fīerī, factus. to become, to happen, to be made, to be done [equivalent in meaning to the passive of facio, -ere, and shares the form factus with facio as its perfect passive participle]

fistula, -ae. pipe, tube; syrinx, pan-pipe [an ancient flute-type instrument that was made of reed pipes of differing lengths]

fīxī, fīxistī, etc. [see figo]

flāmen, flāminis (n.). wind, gust, sharp blast of air

flamma, -ae. flame, fire

flāvēns, flāventis. golden, blonde, yellow

flāvēscō, flāvēscere, -, -. to become blond, to turn yellow

flāvus, -a, -um. blonde, yellow

flectō, flectere, flexī, flexus. to bend, to curve

fleō, flēre, flēvī, flētus. to weep

flētus, -ūs. lamentation, sorrow, weeping

flōs, flōris (m.). flower

flūmen, fluminis (n.). river

flūmineus, -a, -um. of or belonging to a river; river [*as an adjective*]

focus, -ī. hearth, fireplace

folium, -ī. leaf

fons, fontis (m.). fountain, spring

forāmen, foraminis (n.). hole, crack, break, aperture

foras (adv.). outside

foris, foris (f.). door, door post

forma, -ae. shape, form, external appearance, body

formōsus, -a, -um. handsome, beautiful

fors, fortis (f.). chance

forte (adv.). by chance

fortis, -e. brave

fortiter (adv). bravely, strongly

foveō, fovēre, fōvī, fōtus. to be warm, to warm, to keep warm; to cherish

frangō, frangere, frēgī, fractus. to break, to shatter

fretum, -ī. water, sea, strait, channel

frīgor, frigoris (n.). cold, chill, frost

frondeō, frondēre, -, -. to become leafy, to sprout leaves

frons, frondis (f.). foliage, leafy part of a tree

frons, frontis (f.). forehead

fruor, fruī, fructus (+ abl) to enjoy, to take advantage of

frutex, fruticis (f.). shrub, bush, greenery, hedge

fuga, -ae. flight

fugax, fugācis. evasive, fleeing [*also used substantively to mean "one fleeing" or "the evasive one"*]

fugiō, fugere, fūgī, fugiturus. to flee, to run away, to escape

fugō, -āre, -āvī, -ātus. to make flee, to put to flight

fuī, fuistī, etc. [*see* sum]

fulgeō, fulgēre, fulsī, fulsurus. to gleam, to shine (brightly), to glow

fulica, -ae. water bird, water fowl

fūmō, -āre, -āvī, -. to smoke, to give off smoke

fūnebris, -e. of or belonging to a funeral, funeral

fungor, fungī, functus. to experience, to utilize, to incorporate

furca, -ae. fork

furtīvus, -a, -um. furtive, secret

futūr-. [*see* sum]

galea, -ae. helmet

Gallicus, -a, -um. Gallic, of or belonging to Gaul

garrulus, -a, -um. talkative, garrulous, chatty

gaudeō, gaudēre, gāvīsus (semi-dep.). to rejoice, to exult

gelidus, -a, -um. cool, chilled

geminus, -i. twin, double

gemma, -ae. gem, jewel

gena, -ae. cheek

gener, generī. son-in-law

geniālis, -e. genial, friendly, appealing, jovial

genitor, genitōris (m.). father, parent, creator

gens, gentis (f.). family, tribe, clan

genu, genūs (n.). knee

gerō, gerere, gessī, gestus. to bear, to carry, to wear, to reveal, to show, to indicate

gestāmen, gestaminis (n.). equipment, implement, something worn

gestiō, gestīre, gestīvī, -. to really want, to desire

gignō, gignere, genuī, genitus. to give birth to, to create

glōria, -ae. glory

gradus, -ūs. slope, grade, step, footstep

graphium, -ī. stylus, writing implement, "pencil"

grātēs (defec. f. pl.). thanks

grātus, -a, -um. pleasing

gravis, -e. heavy, serious

gravō, -āre, -āvī, -ātus. to be heavy, to be weighed down, to oppress

grex, gregis (m.). herd, flock, group

habeō, habēre, habuī, habitus. to have, to hold, to keep

habilis, -e. useful

habitābilis, -e. livable, habitable

habitō, -āre, -āvī, -ātus. to live, to dwell, to reside

haereō, haerēre, haesī, haesus. to stick, to be stuck, to cling, to be uncertain

harundō, harundinis (f.). reed, something made of reed, shaft; long, slender pole [*as in a fishing rod*]

haud (adv.). hardly, not, not at all

hauriō, haurīre, hausī, haustus. to drain, to empty, to drink

haustus, -ūs. a drink, a helping

Hector, Hectoris (m.). [name: *the most famous Trojan warrior, who is eventually killed by Achilles*]

Hēliades, Hēliadum (f. pl.). [name: *daughters of the sun god and sisters to Phaeton; when their brother died after unsuccessfully driving the chariot of the sun, they were changed into poplar trees, from which amber is "wept"*]

Helicē, Helicēs (acc. = Helicen). [name: *the constellation Ursa Major*]

Helicōnius, -a, -um. of or belonging to Mt. Helicon [*a mountain in Boeotia, a region of central Greece, that is sacred to Apollo and the Muses*]

herba, -ae. grass, herb, small plant or flower

hērēs, herēdis (m.). heir

hērōs, hēroidis (m.). hero

hesternus, -a, -um. of or belonging to yesterday, yesterday's

heu (interj.). alas! oh no!

hic, haec, hoc. this

hinc (adv.). from here, next; [*with* illinc] on this side

hisco, hiscere, -, -. to open, to yawn

hodiē (adv.). today

holus, holeris (n.). vegetable

honestus, -a, -um. honorable, forthright, upstanding

honor, honōris (m.). honor, glory, distinction, beauty

hōra, -ae. hour, time

horridus, -a, -um. horrid, horrible, awful, terrible

hortor, hortārī, hortātus. to encourage

hortus, -ī. garden

hospes, hospitis (m.). guest, host, friend, visitor

hostis, -is (m.). enemy

hūc (adv.). to this place, here

humilis, -e. humble, lowly

humus, -ī (f.). earth, dirt, soil

Hymēn, Hymenis (m.). [name: *god of marriage*]

Hymettius, -a, -um. Hymettian; of or belonging to Mt. Hymettius [*a mountain near Athens noted for its honey*]

iaceō, iacēre, iacuī, iaciturus. to lie down, to lie still, to lie motionless

iam (adv.). now, already

iamque (adv.). and now, at this point

ib-. [*see* eō]

ibi (adv.). there

Īcarus, -ī. [name: *the son of Daedalus*]

īciō, īcere, īcī, ictus. to strike, to beat

ictus, -ūs. a blow, a strike, a pounding

id. [*see* is, ea, id]

īdem, eadem, idem. same, the same, unchanged, constant

ideo (adv.). still, therefore, for that reason

ignārus, -a, -um. ignorant, unaware

ignāvus, -a, -um. cowardly, lazy

ignis, -is (m.). fire, flame

ignōtus, -a, -um. unfamiliar, strange

īlium, -ī. groin [*often used in the plural*]

illāc (adv.). there

ille, illa, illud. that

illic (adv.). to that place, there

illinc (adv.). from that side; [*with* hinc] on that side

illinō, illinere, illēvī, illitus. to cover, to smear, to wipe, to coat

imbellis, -e. not warlike, unsuited to war

imber, imbris (m.). rain

imitor, imitārī, imitātus. to appear as, to imitate, to resemble

immensus, -a, -um. immense, huge

immineō, imminēre, -. - (+ dat.). to hang over, to threaten, to press upon

immundus, -a, -um. unclean, sordid, dirty

immūnis, -e. immune, free (from), free (of), exempt (from)

impār, imparis. unequal, uneven

impatiens, impatientis (+ gen.). impatient, intolerant (of)

impediō, impedīre, impedīvī, impedītus. to hinder, to get in the way of, to impede

impellō, impellere, impuli, impulsus. to strike against, to beat, to compel

imperfectus, -a, -um. incomplete, unfinished

impiger, impigra, impigrum. swift, quick, fast

impius, -a, -um. disloyal, impious, lacking religious devotion

impleō, implēre, implēvī, implētus. to fill, to fill up

impōnō, impōnere, imposuī, impositus. to put on, to place on, to cover

īmus, -a, -um. the lowest (part of)

in (prep. w/ acc.). into, onto

in (prep. w/ abl.). in, on

incertus, -a, -um. uncertain

incola, -ae (m.). inhabitant, resident

increpō, increpāre, increpuī, increpitus. to beat loudly, to strike loudly; to make noise, to make a loud noise

incumbō, incumbere, incubuī, - (+ dat.). to fall (on), to lie down (on), to thrust oneself (on)

inde (adv.). from there, next

indignor, indignārī, indignātus. to view as inappropriate, to view as unworthy

indignus, -a, -um (+ abl.). unworthy, undeserving

indūcō, indūcere, induxī, inductus. to lead up, to lead in, to lead into; to cover

indūrescō, indūrescere, indūruī, -. to harden, to grow hard, to stiffen

inermis, -e. unharmed

iners, inertis. lazy, slow, lifeless

infāmis, -e. infamous, notorious, of ill repute

infēlix, infelīcis. unhappy, unfortunate, unlucky

inferior, inferius (gen.: inferioris). lower, inferior, following, next

infestus, -a, -um. savage, violent

ingeniōsus, -a, -um. clever, gifted

ingenium, -ī. genius, innate nature

ingrātus, -a, -um. ungrateful

inhaereō, inhaerēre, inhaesī, inhaesurus. to cling to, to stick to, to hold on to, to remain attached

inhibeō, inhibēre, inhibuī, inhibitus. to restrain, to hold back, to inhibit

inīquus, -a, -um. hated, detested; unequal, uneven

innīxus, -a, -um (+ abl.). leaning on

innumerus, -a, -um. countless, innumerable, uncountable

innuptus, -a, -um. unwed, virginal, maiden-like

inornātus, -a, -um. unadorned, simple, undecorated, disheveled

inquīro, inquirere, inquisīvi, inquisītus. to ask, to inquire

inquit (defec.). he/she said [*a verb that only occurs in a few forms, this being one of the most common; it is often used to quote directly somebody's words*]

insānus, -a, -um. insane, crazy, undone

insequor, insequī, insecūtus. to pursue, to follow

insīdō, insīdere, insēdī, insessus. to sink into, to press into

insignis, -e. distinguished, noted, important

instar (indecl.). the equivalent (of) [*sometimes used with a genitive noun to draw comparisons, i.e. something is the equivalent [instar] of [gen.] something else*]

instruō, instruere, instruxī, instructus. to build, to construct; (+ abl.) to equip, to furnish

insula, -ae. island

inter (prep. + acc.). between, among

intereā (adv.). meanwhile

interim (adv.). meanwhile

intibum, -ī. chicory, endive [*a lettuce-like leafy vegetable often used in salads*]

intonsus, -a, -um. uncut, untamed, wild, not trimmed

intrō, -āre, -āvī, -ātus. to enter

inūtilis, -e. useless

invādō, invadere, invasī, invasus. to invade, to attack

inveniō, invenīre, invēnī, inventus. to find, to discover

inventum, -ī. discovery, invention

invideō, invidēre, invīdī, invīsus. to refuse, to begrudge, to be resentful that

invidus, -a, -um. hateful, spiteful, malevolent

Īō (acc. = Io; f.). [name: *a lover of Jupiter whom he changed into a cow to hide her identity from his wife Juno*]

ipse, ipsa, ipsum. himself, herself, itself, themselves [*the intensive, not to be confused with the reflexive, both of which in English have the same forms; this word emphasizes or intensifies, i.e. "Daedalus himself is here" rather than "Daedalus sees himself in the mirror"; the latter is the reflexive*]

īra, -ae. anger

īrātus, -a, -um. angry, irate

īre. [*see* eo]

irrītō, -āre, -āvī, -ātus. to incite, to fire up, to provoke

is, ea, id (adj. / pron.). this, that; he, she, it, they [*a demonstrative adjective often used substantively, i.e. without a noun to modify, in which case it is translated as a personal pronoun: "he," "she," "it," "they," depending on number and gender*]

iste, ista, istud. this, that [*often but not always carries a negative connotation*]

ita (adv.). thus, so

īte. [*see* eo]

iter, itineris (n.). passage, path, journey, trip

iterum (adv.). again and again, over and over, repeatedly

iubeō, iubēre, iussī, iussus. to order

iūdicium, -ī. decision, judgment

iugālis, -e. nuptial, of or belonging to marriage

iūgerum, -ī. measure of land, acre, acreage

iugōsus, -a, -um. hilly, mountainous

iungō, iungere, iunxī, iunctus. to join

Iūnōnius, -a, -um. of or belonging to Juno, Juno's

Iuppiter, Iovis (m.). [name: *the sky god, the king of the gods*]

iūs, iūris (n.). law, rule, precept, guide, legal sanction, legal authority, control [*sometimes used in the ablative to mean "by law," "under the law," or "with legal authority"*]

iussī. [*see* iubeō]

iustus, -a, -um. just, lawful, right, appropriate

iuvenālis, -e. youthful, of or belonging to youth

iuvenca, -ae. young female cow

iuvencus, -ī. young bull

iuvenis, iuvenis (m.). youth, young man

lābor, labī, lapsus. to slip, to fall (off *or* from)

labor, labōris (m.). work, toil, labor

laborō, -āre, -āvī, -ātus. to work

lac, lactis (n.). milk

lacertus, -ī. arm, upper part of the arm

lacrima, -ae. tear

laedō, laedere, laesī, laesus. to harm, to hurt, to injure, to wound

laetus, -a, -um. happy

laevus, -a, -um. left

laniō, -āre, -āvī, -ātus. to tear, to shred, to mutilate

lapillus, -ī. small stone, gem

lascīvus, -a, -um. naughty, troublesome, playful

lassō, -āre, -āvī, -ātus. to fatigue, to wear out, to tire

lātē (adv.). far and wide, all over

latebra, -ae. hiding place, lair, refuge, escape

lateō, latēre, latuī, -. to take shelter, to hide, to lie in hiding, to be hiding

Latius, -a, -um. Latin, of or belonging to the Latins [*the Latins were, according to the Romans at least, the people who preceded the Romans at the site of Rome*]

lātus, -a, -um. wide, sprawling, far-reaching

laudō, -āre, -āvī, -ātus. to praise

laureus, -a, -um. laurel, of or belonging to the laurel tree

laurus, -ī (f.). laurel tree, laurel branch, sprig of laurel

laus, laudis (f.). praise, honor, glory

lea, -ae. lioness

leaena, -ae. lioness

Lebinthos, Lebinthī (f.). [name: *one of the Sporades islands, located off of the southwest coast of Asia Minor (modern-day Turkey)*]

lectus, -ī. bed, couch, bench

legō, legere, lēgī, lectus. to choose, to read

Lelex, Lelegis (m.). [name: *a Greek who participated in the Calydonian Boar Hunt, and who is Ovid's narrator for the Baucis and Philemon story*]

leō, -ōnis (m.). lion

lepus, leporis (m.). rabbit

lētum, -ī. death

levis, -e. light, slight, fine, delicate

levō, -āre, -āvī, -ātus. to lift, to raise up, to elevate, to hold up, to support

lex, legis (f.). law, rule

liber, librī (m). book, bark of a tree [*from which a book is made*]

lībertas, libertātis (f.). freedom, liberty

librō, -āre, -āvī, -ātus. to balance, to position

licet, licēre, licuit, - (impers.). it is permitted (+ dat.); [*when used with a subjunctive verb*] although

lignum, -ī. wood, bark

lilium, -ī. lily [*a flower*]

līmen, liminis (n.). door, threshold

līmes, limitis (m.). route, limit, path, boundary, course

līnum, -ī. thread, string

liquidus, -a, -um. liquid, fluid

lītoreus, -a, -um. of or belonging to the (sea)shore

littera, -ae. letter

līvor, livōris (m.). bruise

locus, -ī. place, location [*this noun becomes neuter in its plural forms:* loca, -orum]

longē (adv.). far, by far, far away

longus, -a, -um. long, far, far-reaching

loquor, loquī, locūtus. to speak, to say

luctus, -ūs. grief, lamentation

lūdō, lūdere, lūsī, lūsus. to play

lūmen, luminis (n.). light, eye

lūna, -ae. moon

lūnāris, -e. of or belonging to the moon

lunō, -āre, -āvī, -ātus. to bend into a curve, to shape, to bend back

luō, luere, luī, -. to suffer (a punishment), to endure (a punishment)

lupus, -ī. wolf

lūsus, -ūs. game, play, fooling around

lustrō, -āre, -āvī, -ātus. to wander, to roam

lux, lūcis (f.). light

Lyaeus, -ī. [name: *an alternate name for Bacchus, the god of wine*]

lyra, -ae. lyre [*an ancient stringed instrument*]

mactō, -āre, -āvī, -ātus. to sacrifice, to offer as a sacrifice, to slay as part of a sacrifice

madefaciō, madefacere, madefēcī, madefactus. to drench, to soak

madescō, madescere, maduī, -. to grow wet, to grow moist

Maenas, Maenadis (f.). Maenad [*female follower, characterized by her crazed devotion, to the god of wine Bacchus or Dionysius*]

maestus, -a, -um. sad, weary

magis (adv.). more

magnus, -a, -um. big, large, great

maior, maius (adj.; gen. = maioris). more

mālum, -ī. apple

mandō, -āre, -āvī, -ātus. to entrust, to hand over; [*with* ut:] to request, to demand

māne (adv.). in the morning, early

maneō, manēre, mansī, mansurus. to remain, to stay, to wait, to pause

Mantua, -ae. [name: *a town in northern Italy where the Roman poet Vergil was born*]

manus, -ūs (f.). hand

margō, marginis (m.). edge, border, margin

marītus, -ī. husband

marmor, marmoris (n.). marble

Mars, Martis (m.). [name: *the Roman god of war*]

massa, -ae. lump, mass

māter, matris (f.). mother

māteria, -ae. material, subject matter, topic

māteriēs, -ēī. material, subject matter

mātūrus, -a, -um. mature, developed

mē. [*see* ego]

medicātus, -a, -um. medicated, treated; dyed [*as in a color*]

medicīna, -ae. medicine

medius, -a, -um. middle, the middle of

medulla, -ae. bone, bone marrow, marrow

mel, mellis (n.). honey

melior, melius (adj.; gen. = melioris). more, better

membrum, -ī. limb, part of the body

meminī, meminisse (defec.). to remember

mens, mentis (f.). mind

mensa, -ae. table, course, food [*i.e. what's on the table*]

menta, -ae. mint, mint-leaf

mereō, merēre, meruī, meritus. to deserve, to earn

mergō, mergere, mersī, mersus. to submerge, to flood, to inundate

mergus, -ī. sea gull, sea bird

meritus, -a, -um. deserved, merited, earned

mēta, -ae. turning-point; turning post [*the post around which chariots turned in Roman chariot races; often used metaphorically to refer to a turning point or shift in events*]

metuō, metuere, metuī, metutus. to fear, to be afraid

metus, -ūs. fear

meus, -a, -um. my, mine

micō, micāre, micuī, -. to shine, to flash, to gleam

mihi. [*see* ego]

mīles, militis (m.). soldier

mīlitia, -ae. military service

mīlitō, -āre, -āvī, -āturus. to be a soldier, to serve as a soldier

mille (indecl.). one thousand

Minerva, -ae. [name: *the Roman goddess of wisdom, akin to the Greek goddess Athena*]

minimus, -a, -um. least, smallest, slightest

ministerium, -ī. activity, duty

ministra, -ae. maid, female servant

minium, -ī. cinnabar [*a vibrant reddish-orange mineral that was used as both a dye and a medicine*]

minor, minus (adj.; gen. = minoris). less

Mīnōs, Minōis (m.). [name: *legendary king of Crete*]

minuō, minuere, minuī, minūtus. to decrease, to lessen, to diminish

mīrābilis, -e. wondrous, amazing, shocking

mīror, mirārī, mirātus. to wonder, to be amazed

mīrus, -a, -um. wondrous, amazing, wonderful

misceō, miscēre, miscuī, mixtus. to mix, to blend, to mingle

miser, misera, miserum. miserable, wretched, sad, pitiable, awful

miserābilis, -e. miserable, distraught

miserandus, -a, -um. to be pitied; miserable, wretched

mittō, mittere, mīsī, missus. to send

moderātus, -a, -um. moderated, slow, restrained, held back

modo (adv.). now...now; at this point...at this point [*shows actions that are happening in quick succession*]

modus, -ī. way, type, sort

moenia, -ium (n. pl.). wall

mollescō, mollescere, -, -. to grow soft, to soften

molliō, mollīre, mollīvī, mollītus. to make soft, to grow soft, to soften, to make pliable

mollis, -e. soft, pleasant

moneō, -ēre, -uī, -itus. to warn

monīle, monīlis (n.). necklace

monimentum, -ī. monument, memorial

mons, montis (m.). mountain

mora, -ae. delay, wait, pause; [*sometimes used with a negative to mean:*] without delay

morior, morī, mortuus. to die

moror, morārī, morātus. to delay, to wait, to remain

mors, mortis (f.). death

morsus, -ūs. jaws, mouth, bite, morsel, nibble

mortālis, -e. mortal, human

mōrum, -ī. mulberry, the fruit of the mulberry tree

mōrus, -ī (f.). the mulberry tree

mōs, mōris (m.). custom, character

moveō, movēre, mōvī, mōtus. to move

mox (adv.). soon

mucrō, mucrōnis (m.). the sharp end of a sword, the point, the tip

multifidus, -a, -um. split, split into pieces, splintered

multus, -a, -um. many

mūnus, muneris (n.). gift

murmur, murmuris (n.). murmur, whisper

mūrus, -ī. wall

Mūsa, -ae. Muse [*nine divine sisters who oversaw the arts*]

mūtō, -āre, -āvī, -ātus. to change, to shift

mūtuus, -a, -um. mutual, common

myrtus, -ī (f.). myrtle tree, myrtle leaf

nam. for

Napē, Napēs (f.). [name: *the servant of Ovid's girlfriend Corinna*]

narrō, -āre, -āvī, -ātus. to tell, to narrate, to say

nascor, nascī, nātus. to be born

Nāsō, Nasōnis (m.). [name: *Ovid's cognomen*]

nāta, -ae. daughter

nātālis, -e. of or related to birth, birth

nātūra, -ae. nature, natural order, essence

nātus, -i. son

-ne. [*indicates a direct yes / no question when attached to the first word of the question; or, when used in an indirect question:*] whether, or

nē (conj.). lest, so that...not [*the introductory word to a negative purpose or noun clause, or indirect command*]

nec (conj.). and...not [*equivalent to* et...non; *used with another* nec:] neither...nor

necō, -āre, -āvī, -ātus. to kill, to slay

negō, -āre, -āvī, -ātus. to deny, to refuse

nempe (adv.). of course, certainly

nemus, nemoris (n.). grove, forest, woods

nepōs, nepōtis (m./f.). descendant, grandson / -daughter, grandchild

neque (conj.) [see nec]

nēquīquam (adv.). uselessly

nervus, -ī. sinew, cord, string (or anything else made out of sinew)

nesciō, nescīre, nescīvī, nescītus. to not know

nescioquis, nescioquid (adj.). some, any; someone, -thing; anyone, -thing [a combination of the verb nescio, "I don't know," and the interrogative, becoming literally "I don't know who" or "I don't know what"]

neu (conj.). and, so that…not [a negative conjunction often continuing a negative purpose clause or other subjunctive clause]

nēve = ne + -ve [see these words individually for definitions]

nex, necis (f.). death

nīdus, -ī. nest

niger, nigra, nigrum. black

nimbus, -ī. cloud

nimis (adv.). too much, excessively; too close

nimium (adv.). too much, excessively

Ninus, -ī. [name: king of Assyria, founder of Nineveh, husband of Semiramis]

nisi (conj.). until, if…not [the negative form of si]

nītor, nītī, nixus (+ infin.). to struggle (to do something)

nitor, nitōris (m.). brightness, light, glory, beauty

niveus, -a, -um. snowy white, white

nix, nivis (f.). snow

nocens, nocentis (adj.). guilty

nocturnus, -a, -um. nocturnal, of or belonging to night

nōlō, nolle, noluī, -. to not want

nōmen, nōminis (n.). name

nōminō, -āre, -āvī, -ātus. to call, to address, to name

nōn (adv.). not

nōndum (adv.). not yet

nōs, nostrī / nostrum, nōbīs, nōs, nōbīs. we, us

noscō, noscere, nōvī, nōtus. to know

noster, nostra, nostrum. our

nōtitia, -ae. acquaintance, notice, familiarity

notō, -āre, -āvī, -ātus. to note, to mark, to scribe, to mar; to recognize, to know

nōtus, -a, -um. known, recognized

novem (indecl.). nine

noviens (adv.). nine times

novitās, novitātis (f.). novelty, strange or new phenomenon

novō, -āre, -āvī, -ātus. to make new, to change, to revise

novus, -a, -um. new

nox, noctis (f.). night

nudō, -āre, -āvī, -ātus. to expose, to reveal, to strip bare or naked

nūdus, -a, -um. nude, naked, bare

nullus, -a, -um. none, no [an irregular adjective whose genitive singular ends in -ius and whose dative singular ends in -ī]

nūmen, numinis (n.). power, divine power

numerus, -ī. number

nunc (adv.). now

nūper. recently

nūtriō, nutrīre, nutrīvī, nutrītus. to nourish, to cultivate, to feed at the breast

nūtus, -ūs. nod [especially one that indicates familiarity or assent]

nux, nucis (f.). nut

nympha, -ae. nymph

ō! (interj.). oh! [often signals the vocative case in Latin; does not need to be included in English, but sometimes helps if it is]

oblinō, oblinere, oblēvī, oblitus. to smear, to cover

obscenus, -a, -um. awful, obscene, disgusting, inappropriate

obscūrus, -a, -um. dark, gloomy

obsequor, obsequī, obsecūtus. to agree, to comply, to obey

observō, -āre, -āvī, -ātus. to guard, to watch over

obsideō, obsidēre, obsēdī, obsessus. to besiege

obstipescō, obstipescere, obstipuī, -. to be amazed, to be (dumb)struck, to be (awe)struck, to be stunned

obstō, obstāre, obstitī, obstāturus (+ dat.). to obstruct, to be in the way of, to stand in the way of, to hinder, to prevent

obstruō, obstruere, obstruxī, obstructus. to be a barrier, to be in the way, to block

obtūsus, -a, -um. dull, blunt

obvius, -a, -um. facing, opposite, opposing

occupō, -āre, -āvī, -ātus. to occupy, to take over

ōcior, ōcius (comp. adj.; gen. = ōcioris). quicker, swifter

oculus, -ī. eye

ōdī, ōdisse, ōsus (defec.). to hate

odōrātus, -a, -um. fragrant

offensus, -a, -um. offended, shocked

officium, -ī. duty

ōlim (adv.). once

ōmen, ominis (n.). omen, sign

omnis, -e. all, every

onus, oneris (n.). burden, weight, preoccupation

opifer, opifera, opiferum. aid-bringing, help-bringing [literally a bringer (-fer = fero) of aid (op- = ops)] opifex, opificis (m.). craftsman, artisan [*literally a maker* (-fix = facio) *of stuff* (op- = opus)]

ops, opis (f.). power, ability, aid, assistance, wealth

optō, -āre, -āvī, -ātus. to choose, to want

opus, operis (n.). work, deed; [*often when used with a form of* sum, esse:] to be necessary

ōrāculum, -ī. oracle, prophet, ability to see the future

orbis, orbis (m.). orb, wheel, disc, world, sun [*or any other spherical object*]

ordō, ordinis (m.). order

Ōriōn, Oriōnis (m.). [name: *a constellation named after the great mythological hunter*]

orior, orīrī, ortus (dep.). to rise [*often used with reference to the sun and where the sun rises, the east*]

ornō, -āre, -āvī, -ātus. to decorate, to adorn, to embellish

orō, -āre, -āvī, -ātus. to beg, to plead, to pray [*when used as* oro, *"I beg," as an aside, often meaning "please"*]

ōs, ōris (n.). mouth, face

os, ossis (n.). bone

osculum, -ī. kiss

ostendō, ostendere, ostendī, ostentus. to show, to display, to indicate

ōtium, -ī. leisure

ōvum, -ī. egg

pactum, -ī. pact, agreement, plan [*Latin will sometimes use a plural where English will use a singular*]

pactus, -a, -um. agreed upon, predetermined, specified

Paeān, Paeanis (m.). [name: *an epithet for the god Apollo, stemming from his role as god of healers*]

Paelignus, -a, -um. Paelignian; of or belonging to the Paelignians [*an ancient tribe of central Italy*]

pāgina, -ae. page

pallidus, -a, -um. pale, colorless

palma, -ae. palm, palm tree, fruit of the palm tree, date [*the date is the fruit of the palm tree*]

palūs, palūdis (f.). swamp, marsh

paluster, palustris, palustre. swampy, marshy

pandus, -a, -um. curving, curved, bent

Paphius, -a, -um. Paphian; of or belonging to Paphos [*a city on the island of Cyprus, in the northeastern corner of the Mediterranean Sea*]

Paphos, -ī (m.; acc. sing. = Paphon). [name: *the child of Pygmalion and his statue-turned-woman*]

pār, paris. equal, same

parātus, -ūs. preparations, accoutrements, equipment, stuff

parcus, -a, -um. thrifty, frugal, parsimonious

parens, parentis (m./f.). parent

pāreō, pārēre, pāruī, - (+ dat.). to obey

pariēs, parietis (m.). wall [*an interior wall that divides*

houses or rooms, as opposed to a murus *that is an exterior fortification wall*]

parilis, -e. equal, similar

pariter (adv.). equally; at the same time as [*often used with the preposition* cum]

Parnāsus, -ī. [name: *a mountain in central Greece, near Delphi, just north of the Gulf of Corinth; it is sacred to Apollo and is associated with him and the Muses as overseers of poetry*]

parō, -āre, -āvi, -ātus. to prepare

Paros, Parī (f.). [name: *an island; one of the Cyclades, a group of islands off the east coast of mainland Greece*]

pars, partis (f.). part, side

parvus, -a, -um. small, slight, little

passus, -ūs. step, gait, stride

pastor, pastōris (m.). shepherd

Patarēus, -a, -um. of or belonging to Patara [*Patara is a city on the coast of Lycia, a region on the southern coast of Asia Minor, modern-day Turkey; Apollo had an oracle there*]

pateō, patēre, patuī, -. to lie open, to be open, to open

pater, patris (m.). father

patior, patī, passus. to endure, to allow

patrius, -a, -um. of or belonging to a father; father's

patulus, -a, -um. broad, gaping, (wide) open

pauci, paucae, pauca. few

paulātim (adv.). little by little, in stages, gradually

paulus, -a, -um. small, slight, little

pauper, pauperis. poor

paupertās, paupertātis (f.). poverty

paveō, pavēre, -, -. to be scared, to be terrified, to be apprehensive

pectus, pectoris (n.). heart, chest

pelagus, -ī. sea, water, ocean

pellō, pellere, pepulī, pulsus. to strike, to beat, to beat away, to banish

Pelopēius, -a, -um. of or belonging to Pelops [*the father of Pittheus, and the grandfather of Agamemnon and Menelaus, the principle Greek generals in the Trojan War*]

Penātēs, Penātium (m. pl.). [name: *the household gods: gods particular to each household that look over and protect the household; also by synecdoche:*] house

pendeō, pendēre, pependī, -. to hang

Pēnēis, Pēnēidos (m; abl. sing = Pēnēide; voc. sing. = Pēnēi; accusative plural = Pēnēidas.). Daphne [*patronymic; daughter of Peneus, a river god, the father of Daphne*]

Pēnēius, -a, -um. of or belonging to Peneus; daughter of Peneus

penitus (adv.). completely, thoroughly

penna, -ae. feather

per (prep. + acc.). through

peragō, peragere, perēgī, peractus. to do, to complete

perarō, -āre, -āvī, -ātus. to plow through, to inscribe, to write on

percipiō, percipere, percēpī, perceptus. to grab, to seize, to grab hold of

percutiō, percutere, percussī, percussus. to shake violently, to scratch, to tear at, to strike, to beat, to hit

perdō, perdere, perdidī, perditus. to destroy, to ruin

perennis, -e. eternal

perferō, perferre, pertulī, perlātus. to carry through, to deliver

perīculum, -ī. danger

perimō, perimere, perēmī, peremptus. to ruin, to destroy, to kill

perlegō, perlegere, perlēgī, perlectus. to read completely, to read through

permātūrescō, permātūrescere, permātūruī, -. to become fully ripe, to ripen

perōsus, -a, -um. hating, detesting, hateful of

perpetuus, -a, -um. perpetual, eternal

persequor, persequī, persecūtus. to follow completely, to pursue

perveniō, pervenīre, pervēnī, perventurus (+ ad + acc.). to arrive at, to reach

pervigilō, -āre, -āvī, -ātus. to keep guard all night, to keep watch all night

pēs, pedis (m.). foot

pestifer, -a, -um. disease-bearing, deadly [a compound word: pest- = pestis, meaning "disease" and fer- = fero, meaning "to bear"]

petō, petere, petīvī, petītus. to seek

pharetra, -ae. quiver [holder for arrows]

pharetrātus, -a, -um. quiver-bearing, wearing or having a quiver

Philēmōn, Philēmonis (m.; acc sing. = Philēmona). [name]

Phoebē, Phoebēs (Gr. f.). [name: the goddess Diana]

Phoebus, -ī. [name: epithet for Apollo]

Phrygius, -a, -um. Phrygian, of or belonging to Phrygia [Phrygia is a region along the northeastern border of what is modern-day Turkey; also where the ancient city of Troy was likely located]

pictus, -a, -um. painted, colored

Pīeris, Pīeridos. Muse [a patronymic from the identification of the Muses as the daughters of Pierus]

piger, pigra, pigrum. sluggish, slow, inert, still

pila, -ae. ball, bauble

piscis, piscis (m.). fish

Pittheus, -i (disyll.). [name: son of Pelops]

pius, -a, -um. loyal, faithful, respectful, pious

placeō, placēre, placuī, placitus (+ dat.). to please

placidus, -a, -um. placid, peaceful, calm

plangor, plangōris (m.). lamentation, wailing, beating of the breast [as a sign of distress or mourning]

plēnus, -a, -um. full, complete

plūma, -ae. feather

plumbum, -ī. lead

plūrimus, -a, -um. most

plūs, pluris (comp. adj.). more

pōculum, -ī. cup

poena, -ae. punishment

poēta, -ae (m.). poet

pollex, pollicis (m.). thumb

pompa, -ae. parade, ceremony, ceremonial procession

pōmum, -i. fruit

pōnō, pōnere, pōsuī, pōsitus. to put, to place

pontus, -ī. sea, water, ocean

porta, -ae. gate, door

poscō, poscere, poposcī, -. to demand, to ask for

possideō, possidēre, possēdī, possessus. to possess, to have, to control

possum posse, potuī, -. to be able

post (adv.). after, afterwards

post (prep. + acc.). after

posterus, -a, -um. next, following

postis, postis (m.). doorway, door-frame, door-post

postquam (conj.). after

potentia, -ae. power

praebeō, praebēre, praebuī, praebitus. to offer, to furnish, to show, to display

praeceptum, -ī. advice, wisdom, rule, suggestion

praecipitō, -āre, -āvī, -ātus. to plunge, to sink, to hurl downward

praecordia, praecordiōrum (n. pl.). chest, breast

praeda, -ae. booty, prey, loot

praedor, praedārī, praedātus. to conquer, to plunder, to take as plunder

praeeō, praeīre, praeiī / -īvī, praeiturus. to approve, to commend

praeferō, praeferre, praetulī, praelātus. to prefer; to carry in front of, to bear in front of

praelātus, -a, -um. distinguished, preferred

praeripiō, praeripere, praeripuī, praereptus. to take away, to steal, to snatch away

praetereō, praeterīre, praeteriī / -īvī, praeteritus. to move past, to go beyond, to go ahead, to transcend

precor, precārī, precātus. to beg, to pray, to ask for

premō, premere, pressī, pressus. to press down, to compress, to touch

prex, precis (f.). entreaty, prayer

Priamēis, Priamēidos (f. patron.; abl. = Priamēide). daughter of Priam

prīmus, -a, -um. first

prior, prius. first (of two), previous

prō (prep. + abl.). for, on behalf of, instead of

proavus, -ī. ancestor, forefather

probō, -āre, -āvī, -ātus. to test, to try, to approve, to prove

procul (adv.). far away, from afar

prōdūcō, prōdūcere, prōduxī, prōductus. to produce, to lead forth, to bring forth, to create, to encourage, to give birth to

prohibeō, prohibēre, prohibuī, prohibitus. to prohibit, to forbid

prōiciō, prōicere, prōiēcī, prōiectus. to eject, to throw out, to expel

prōlēs, prōlis (f.). offspring, child

prōmō, prōmere, prompsī, promptus. to bring forth, to draw, to remove, to pull out

prōnus, -a, -um. prone, face-down

properō, -āre, -āvī, -ātus. to hasten, to hurry

Prōpoetides, Prōpoetidum (f. pl.). [name: *the daughters of Propoetus of Cyprus; they were considered the first prostitutes*]

prospiciō, prospicere, prospexī, prospectus. to see (something) in front, to look at, to gaze at, to stare at

prōsum, prōdesse, prōfuī, - (+ dat.). to be useful

prōtinus (adv.). immediately, at once

prōveniō, prōvenīre, prōvenī, prōventurus. to come forth, to come out

proximus, -a, -um. nearest, next

pruīnōsus, -a, -um. frosty, dewy

prūnum, -ī. plum

pudor, pudōris (m). decency, chastity, shame, embarassment, virtue

puella, -ae. girl

puer, puerī. boy

pulcher, pulchra, pulcrhum. beautiful

pullus, -a, -um. dark, dreary-colored

pulsō, -āre, -āvī, -ātus. to beat, to strike

pulvis, pulveris (m.). dust

purpureus, -a, -um. purple, dark blue

pūrus, -a, -um. pure, unsullied, uncorrupted

putō, -āre, -āvī, -atus. to think

Pygmalion, Pygmaliōnis (m.). [name: *a legendary king of Cyprus*]

Pȳramus, -ī. [name]

Python, Pythōnis (m.; acc. sing. = Pythona). Python [*the legendary snake whom Apollo killed to assume control of the oracle at Delphi*]

quā (adv.). where [*from the ablative of the relative pronoun*]

quaerō, quaerere, quaesīvī, quaesītus. to seek, to look for, to ask for

quantuluscumque, quantulacumque, quantulumcumque. however small

quantus, -a, -um. how much, how many; [*when used with a form of* tantus, -a, -um:] as much

quatiō, quatere, -, quassus. to shake, to flap

-que (conj. encl.). and [*attached to the second word of the pair it connects, i.e.* puer puellaque = *"the boy and the girl"*]

quercus, -ūs (f.). oak tree, oak leaf

queror, querī, questus (dep.). to complain, to protest

quia. because

quī, quae, quod. who, whom, which, that, whose, what [*the relative pronoun or the interrogative adjective, many of whose forms are identical to those of the interrogative pronoun; the relative will have an identifiable antecedent to which it refers, and the interrogative adjective will agree with a noun used in a question*]

quīcumque, quaecumque, quodcumque. whoever, whatever

quidem (adv.). indeed

quinque. five

quis, quid. who, what [*the interrogative pronoun, many of whose forms are identical to the relative pronoun; the interrogative must be used in a question, either direct or indirect*]

quisque, quaeque, quodque. each [*declined like* qui, quae, quod, *with -que as a suffix; the -que is not here a conjunction*]

quisquis, quidquid. whoever, whatever

quod (conj.). because

quondam (adv.). once

quoniam (conj.). since, because

quoque. also, still

radius, -ī. ray (of light / from the sun)

rādix, rādīcis (f.). root (of a tree or plant)

rādō, rādere, rāsī, rāsus. to scrape, to wipe; to pass closely, to sneak around

rāmāle, rāmālis (n.). branch, twig [*of a tree*]

rāmus, -ī. branch

rapidus, -a, -um. rapid, quick, swift

raucus, -a, -um. loud, raucous, noisy, noticeable

recens, recentis. new, recent, recently plucked or picked

recipiō, recipere, recēpī, receptus. to receive, to accept, to take in

recondō, recondere, recondidī, reconditus. to put away, to close

reddō, reddere, redidī, redditus. to return, to reflect, to mirror

redeō, redīre, rediī / -īvī, reditus. to return, to go back

redimīculum, -ī. garland, wreath

redimiō, redimīre, redimiī, redimītus. to wreathe, to encircle

redoleō, redolēre, -, -. to be odiferous, to give off a pleasant smell

referō, referre, retulī, relātus. to bring back, to return, to serve again; [*used impersonally:*] it makes a difference, it matters

refertus, -a, -um. packed (with), stuffed (with)

refugiō, refugere, refūgī, -. to flee, to flee from, to shrink back

rēgia, -ae. kingdom, palace, shrine

regiō, regiōnis (f). direction, spot, place

regnō, -āre, -āvī, -ātus. to rule, to reign, to wield power

regnum, -ī. kingdom, rule, power

relevō, -āre, -āvī, -ātus. to lighten, to rest, to ease

relinquō, relinquere, relīquī, relictus. to leave behind

remaneō, remanēre, remansī, -. to remain, to last, to endure

rēmigium, -ī. means of propulsion

remollescō, remollescere, -, -. to resoften, to become soft again

remoror, remorārī, remorātus. to delay, to pause

removeō, removēre, remōvī, remōtus. to remove, to take away

renīdeō, renidēre, -, -. to glow, to shine, to smile

renovō, -āre, -āvī, -ātus. to make new, to revive

reperiō, reperīre, repperī, repertus. to find, to discover, to come upon

repertor, repertōris (m.). discoverer, inventor

repetō, repetere, repetīvī, repetītus. to seek (repeatedly), to ask for

repleō, replēre, replēvī, replētus. to refill, to replenish, to fill again

repōnō, repōnere, repōsuī, repōsitus. to put back, to lay back, to put down; to do again; to put back in a former position

repugnō, -āre, -āvī, -ātus. to fight back, to resist

requiēs, requiētis (f.; acc. = requiem). rest, respite

requiescō, requiescere, requiēvī, requiētus. to rest, to lie at rest

requīrō, requirere, requisīvī, requisītus. to seek, to look for, to search for; to ask, to inquire

rēs, reī. thing, matter, situation, circumstance

rescrībō, rescrībere, rescripsī, rescriptus. to write back, to write again

resecō, -āre, -āvī, -ātus. to trim, to slice, to cut off

resīdō, resīdere, resīdī, -. to sit down, to go down, to fall

resistō, resistere, restitī, -. to stop, to pause, to halt, to cause to stop

respiciō, respicere, respexī, respectus. to look back

respondeō, respondēre, respondī, responsus. to respond

resupīnus, -a, -um. flat on one's back, lying flat on one's back

resurgō, resurgere, resurrexī, resurrecturus. to rise again

retractō, -āre, -āvī, -ātus. to handle repeatedly, to feel over and over, to touch again and again

retrō (adv.). back, backwards

revellō, revellere, revellī, revulsus. to tear away, to remove with force

reverentia, -ae. reverence, respect

revocō, -āre, -āvī, -ātus. to call back, to call out, to summon

Rhēsus, -ī (m.). [name: *a Thracian who was an ally of Priam, the king of the Trojans, in the Trojan War; he was killed by Odysseus and Diomedes during their night raid on the Trojan camp*]

rictus, -ūs. jaws, open mouth

rideō, ridēre, risī, risus. to laugh, to joke

rigidus, -a, -um. rigid, hard

rigor, rigōris (m.). rigor, stiffness

riguus, -a, -um. well-watered, well-irrigated

rīma, -ae. crack, opening

rīvālis, -is (m.). a rival [*with the connotation of a rival for someone's affection*]

rōdō, rōdere, rōsī, rōsus. to erode, to waste away, to nibble (at)

rogō, -āre, -āvī, -ātus. to ask

rogus, -ī. funeral pyre

Rōma, -ae. Rome

rostrum, -ī. beak, nose, snout

rota, -ae. wheel, revolution, circle

rubeō, rubēre, -, -. to become red, to redden, to turn red

rubor, rubōris (m.). red coloring, blush

rudis, -e. coarse, simple, rudely-fashioned

rūgōsus, -a, -um. wrinkled, shriveled

rumpō, rumpere, rūpī, ruptus. to break, to burst (under pressure)

rūpēs, rūpis (f.). rocky cliff, crag

rursus (adv.). back, in return, again and again, over and over

rūs, rūris (n.). country, countryside

rusticus, -a, -um. rustic, old, ancient, archaic

sacerdōs, sacerdōtis (m./f.). priest, priestess

sacer, sacra, sacrum. sacred, holy

saeculum, -ī. age, generation; **per saecula** [*expr.*]: through the generations, through the ages

saepe. often

saepēs, saepis (f.). hedge

saevus, -a, -um. harsh, rough, wild

sagitta, -ae. arrow

sagittaferus, -a, -um. arrow-bearing [*a compound of*

sagitta, *"arrow" and* fero, *"to bear"*]

salignus, -a, -um. made of willow-wood, willow

saliō, salīre, saluī, saltus. to jump, to pulse, to beat

salūs, salūtis (f.). health, well-being, safety

Samos, -ī (f.). [name: *a large island just off the southwest coast of Asia Minor, modern-day Turkey*]

sānābilis, -e. treatable, curable

sanguinulentus, -a, -um. bloody, red

sanguis, sanguinis (n.). blood, family

satis (adv.). enough

Sāturnius, -a, -um. of or belonging to Saturn, Saturnian [*in the Roman tradition, Saturn was the father of Jupiter*]

scelerātus, -a, -um. sinful, wretched

scindō, scindere, scidī, scissus. to cut, to construct, to make

sciō, scīre, scīvī, scītus. to know, to recognize, to understand

scrībō, scrībere, scripsī, scriptus. to write

sculpō, sculpere, sculpsī, sculptus. to sculpt, to carve

sē. [*see* suī]

secō, secāre, secuī, sectus. to cut, to slice, to carve

sēcum = cum sē

secundus, -a, -um. second, favorable

sed (conj.). but

sedeō, sedēre, sēdī, sessurus. to sit

sēdēs, sēdis (f.). seat, location, spot

sedīle, sedīlis (n.). chair, seat, bench

sēdūcō, sēdūcere, sēduxī, sēductus. to take away, to clear away

sēdulus, -a, -um. deliberate, painstaking, attentive, focused

segnis, -e. lazy, sluggish

semel. once, a single time

Semīramis, Semīramidis (f.). [name: *legendary queen of Assyria, wife of Ninus, founder of Babylon*]

semper (adv.). always

senecta, -ae. old age

senectūs, senectūtis (f.). old age

senex, senis (adj.). old; [*often used substantively as:*] old man, old woman

senīlis, -e. of or belonging to an old person; old man's, old woman's

senior, seniōris. [*comparative of* senex, senis]

sentes, sentium (m. pl.). thorns, bushes, brambles, shrubbery

sentiō, sentīre, sensī, sensus. to sense, to feel, to understand

sepeliō, sepelīre, sepelīvī, sepultum. to bury, to entomb

sepulchrum, -ī. tomb

sequor, sequī, secūtus. to follow, to pursue

sera, -ae. lock, bolt, bar (of a door)

sermō, sermōnis (m.). speech, conversation, speaking

sērō (adv.). late (comparative = serius)

serpens, serpentis (m./f.). serpent, snake

serta, -ōrum (n. pl.). garland (of flowers), wreath (of flowers)

serus, -a, -um. late

serviō, servīre, servīvī, servīturus (+ dat.). to serve, to be a servant to

servō, -āre, -āvī, -ātus. to save, to protect, to safeguard

sex. six

sī (conj.). if

sīc (adv.). thus, so, in this way [*often used at the conclusion of an epic simile to return or reconnect to the text*]

siccō, -āre, -āvī, -ātus. to dry

siccus, -a, -um. dry

Sīdonis, Sīdonidis. Sidonian; of or belonging to Sidon [*a city on the Phoenician coast famous for its production of purple dye taken from the* murex, *the conch shell*]

sīdus, sideris (n.). star

signum, -ī. sign, signal, mark, indicator; standard [*the symbol of a Roman army carried into battle*]

silens, silentis (adj.). silent, quiet, calm

silex, silicis (m.). hard rock, stone

silva, -ae. forest

sim, sis, etc. [*present subjunctive of* sum]

similis, -e. similar

simplicitās, simplicitātis (f.). simplicity, unity, sincerity

simul. at the same time

simulācrum, -ī. statue, likeness, representation

simulō, -āre, -āvī, -ātus. to simulate, to pretend, to fabricate, to create

sincērus, -a, -um. pure, unsullied, unadulterated, unblemished

sine (prep. + abl.). without

sīnō, sinere, sīvī, situs. to allow

sinuōsus, -a, -um. curvy, bent, curved

sistō, sistere, stetī, status. to set up, to set down, to establish, to place

sitis, sitis (f.; acc. = sitim). thirst

situs, -ūs. site, location

sōbrius, -a, -um. sober

socia, -ae. associate, friend, partner

socius, -a, -um. of or belonging to a companion

socius, -ī. associate, companion

sōl, sōlis (m.). the sun

soleō, solēre, solitus. to be accustomed, to be used (to do something) [*often followed by an infinitive*]

solitus, -a, -um. usual, accustomed

solum, -ī. earth, ground, land

sōlus, -a, -um. alone, lone [*an irregular adjective whose genitive singular ends in -ius and whose dative singular ends in -ī*]

solvō, solvere, solvī, solūtus. to loosen, to open, to unravel, to unbind, to release

somnus, -ī. sleep

sōpītus, -a, -um. sleeping, asleep

sopōrātus, -a, -um. asleep, put to sleep

sordidus, -a, -um. sordid, dirty, imperfect

soror, sorōris (f.). sister

spargō, spargere, sparsī, sparsus. to splatter, to spray, to stream, to strew

spatior, spatiārī, spatiātus. to walk about, to wander

speciēs, -ēī. appearance, guise, sight

spectō, -āre, -āvī, -ātus. to look at, to watch

speculātor, speculātōris (m.). spy, scout

speculum, -ī. mirror

spērō, -āre, -āvī, -ātus. to hope

spēs, speī. hope

spiculum, -ī. sharp point, arrow

splendidus, -a, -um. bright, shiny, gleaming, brilliant

sponda, -ae. bed, bed frame

sponte (defec.). [*used often with* sua] sua sponte = "of one's own volition" or "of one's own choice"

spūmō, -āre, -āvī, -ātus. to foam, to be covered with foam

stāgnum, -ī. marsh, swamp

statuō, statuere, statuī, statūtus. to decide; [*often accompanied by* ut + *a subjunctive verb:*] to decide (that)

sterilis, -e. barren, empty, sterile

sternō, sternere, strāvī, strātus. to lay low, to lay out, to kill, to slay

stīpes, stipitis (m.). trunk (of a tree)

stipula, -ae. grain, stalk of grain

stīva, -ae. plow-handle

stō, stāre, stetī, staturus. to stand

strāmen, straminis (n.). straw, hay, thatch [*as in a thatched roof*]

strātum, -ī. cover, quilt; [*in pl.*] bed

strēnuus, -a, -um. energetic, enthusiastic

strīdō, strīdere, strīdī, -. to hiss

stringō, stringere, strinxī, strictus. to bind, to draw near, to draw (a sword)

strix, strigis (f.). screech owl [*a bird often associated with bad omens*]

stupeō, stupēre, stupuī, -. to be amazed, to gape

sub (prep. + acc. *or* abl.). under

subeō, subīre, subiī / -īvī, subditus. to place under, to support; to replace

sūbiciō, sūbicere, sūbiēcī, sūbiectus (+ dat.). to control, to

put under the control of

subscribō, subscribere, subscripsī, subscriptus. to write underneath, to append

subsīdō, subsīdere, subsēdī, - (+ dat.). to yield (to), to give way (to)

succingō, succingere, succinxī, succinctus. to gird up, to gather up

succrescō, succrescere, succrēvī, -. to rise up

sufferō, sufferre, sustulī, sublātus. to hold up, to raise up

suffundō, suffundere, suffūdī, suffūsus. to cover, to suffuse, to pour throughout

suī, sibi, sē / sēsē, sē / sēsē. himself, herself, itself, themselves [*reflexive pronoun, not to be confused with the intensive* ipse, ipsa, ipsum, *which has the same forms in English; the reflexive's definition will depend on its antecedent, i.e. he sees himself, she sees herself, etc., & the reflexive has no nominative, which is why it is listed under its genitive*]

Sulmō, Sulmōnis (m.). [name: *modern Sulmona, a town just east of Rome over the mountains where Ovid was born*]

sum, esse, fuī, futūrus. to be

summittō, summittere, summīsī, summissus. to send down, to bend low, to lower

summus, -a, -um. highest, the topmost (part of); [*as a substantive:*] the top, surface [*i.e.* summum montis = *the peak of a mountain,* summum aequoris = *the surface of the sea*]

sumptus, -ūs. the act of spending money; expenditure

super (adv.). above, over

super (prep. + acc. *or* abl.). above, over

superbus, -a, -um. proud, haughty

superiniciō, superinicere, superiniēcī, superiniectus. to throw over, to cover

superstes, superstitis (adj.). surviving, living, alive

supersum, superesse, superfuī, -. to remain, to be left over

superus, -a, -um. high, upper; [*as a substantive:*] those above, the gods

supīnus, -a, -um. lying on the back, supine, backwards, upturned

suppleō, supplēre, supplēvī, supplētus. to fill (with a liquid)

surgō, surgere, surrexī, surrecturus. to rise (up), to get up

surripiō, surripere, surripuī, surreptus. to steal, to take away

sūs, suis (n.). pig, sow

suscitō, -āre, -āvī, -ātus. to stir up

suspendium, -ī. the act of hanging [*referring specifically to suicide*]

suspensus, -a, -um. hanging, hung

sustineō, sustinēre, sustinuī, -. to sustain, to maintain, to do something continuously or consistently

suus, -a, -um. his, her, its, their [*the reflexive adjective; its translation depends on the gender of its antecedent, rather than the word that it's modifying*]

tabella, -ae. tablet, writing tablet

tābescō, tābescere, tābuī, -. to melt, to dwindle, to diminish, to disappear

tabula, -ae. account book, financial record

tacitus, -a, -um. quiet

taeda, -ae. wedding torch, wedding, marriage

tālis, -e. such, of such a sort, of such a type

tam (adv.). so

tamen (adv.). nevertheless

tamquam. as if

tandem (adv.). finally, at last

tangō, tangere, tetigī, tactus. to touch, to reach

tantum (adv.). only

tantus, -a, -um. so great, so much

tardus, -a, -um. slow, late, sluggish

tē. [*see* tū]

tectum, -ī. roof, house

tēcum = cum tē

tegō, tegere, texī, tectus. to cover, to hide

tellūs, tellūris (f.). earth, ground

tēlum, -ī. dart, weapon

temerārius, -a, -um. rash, unthinking, impulsive, bold

tempē (n. pl. nom. *and* acc). valley [*a Greek form*]

temperō, -āre, -āvī, -ātus. to control, to temper, to moderate

templum, -ī. temple

temptō, -āre, -āvī, -ātus. to try, to attempt

tempus, temporis (n.). time; the side of the head, the temple, the forehead

tenebrae, -ārum. darkness, shadows

Tenedos, -ī (Gr. f.). [name: *an island off the western coast of Asia Minor, modern-day Turkey, where there is located a temple to Apollo*]

teneō, tenēre, tenuī, tentus. to have, to hold, to keep

tener, tenera, tenerum. tender, soft, kind, loving

tenuis, -e. thin, slight

tepeō, tepēre, -, -. to be warm, to have warmth, to grow warm, to heat up

tepidus, -a, -um. warm, tepid

ter. three times

teres, teretis. smooth, polished, rounded

tergeō, tergēre, tersī, tersus. to wipe, to dry

tergum, -ī. back

tergus, tergoris (n.). back [*specifically of an animal*]

terra, -ae. land, ground, earth

tertius, -a, -um. third

testa, -ae. sherd, terracotta piece, piece of baked clay

tetigī, etc. [*see* tango]

texi, etc. [*see* tego]

texō, texere, texuī, textus. to weave

thalamus, -ī. bed

Thisbē, Thisbēs (acc. sing. = Thisben). [name]

Thrēcius, -a, -um. Thracian, of or belonging to Thrace [*a region in the northeastern corner of Greece, on the northern coast of the Aegean Sea*]

Thȳnēius, -a, -um. Bithynian, of or belonging to Bithynia [*a region in Asia Minor, modern-day Turkey, that stretches along its northern coast, where it borders the Black Sea*]

thyrsus, -ī. thyrsus [*the staff carried by Bacchus and his retinue; it was topped with some sort of vegetation, often a pine cone*]

tibī. [see tū]

tignum, -ī. piece of wood, plank (of wood), beam

tilia, -ae. linden tree

timeō, timēre, timuī, -. to fear, to be afraid of

timidus, -a, -um. timid, afraid, apprehensive, hesitant

timor, timoris (m.). fear

tingō, tingere, tinxī, tinctus. to stain, to soak, to color, to dye, to paint

tollō, tollere, sustulī, sublātus. to lift up, to raise

torpor, torpōris (m.). sluggishness, numbness, paralysis

torus, -ī. bed, bench, couch, cushion

tot (indecl.). so many

tōtus, -a, -um. whole, all, every

totiēns (adv.). whenever, as often as

tractō, -āre, -āvī, -ātus. to tug, to keep pulling, to keep dragging, to keep rubbing, to handle repeatedly, to work over and over

trādō, trādere, trādidī, trāditus. to pass down, to hand down

trahō, trahere, traxī, tractus. to drag, to pull

trāiciō, trāicere, trāiēcī, trāiectus. to throw to, to throw into, to throw across, to strike, to pierce, to transfix

transeō, transīre, transiī / -īvī, transitus. to cross, to go over

transitus, -ūs. passage, path, way

tremebundus, -a, -um. trembling, quivering

tremō, tremere, tremuī, -. to tremble, to shake, to vibrate, to shiver, to shudder, to ripple

tremulus, -a, -um. trembling, shaking, shivering

trepidō, -āre, -āvī, -ātus. to tremble, to quiver, to shiver, to shake

tristis, -e. sad

trivium, -ī. crossroad

Triumphus, -ī. triumph, triumphal procession

Trōs, Trōis (m.; nom. & voc. pl. = Troēs). Trojan

truncō, -āre, -āvī, -ātus. to split, to break; (+ abl.) to strip (of)

truncus, -ī. trunk [*either of a tree or a person, i.e. the torso*]

tū, tuī, tibi, tē, tē. you

tueor, tuērī, tuitus. to look at, to gaze at, to protect, to defend

tulī, tulistī, etc. [*see* ferō]

tum (adv.). then

tumidus, -a, -um. swollen, grown, expanded

tumulō, -āre, -āvī, -ātus. to bury, to cover with a burial mound

tumulus, -ī. grave, grave mound, tomb

turba, -ae. crowd, mob

turbō, turbinis (m.). something spinning; whirlpool, whirlwind

turpis, -e. foul, disgusting, offensive

tūs, tūris (n.). frankincense

tūtēla, -ae. defense, protection, guard

tūtus, -a, -um. safe

tuus, -a, -um. your

ūber, ūberis (adj. + abl.). copious, abundant, rich (in)

ubī (conj.). where, when

ubīque. everywhere

ullus, -a, -um. any

ultimus, -a, -um. last, ultimate, final

ultrā (adv.). beyond, further

ulva, -ae. water grass

umbra, -ae. shade, ghost

umbrōsus, -a, -um. shady

umquam (adv.). ever

umerus, -ī. shoulder

ūnā (adv.). together (with someone)

unda, -ae. wave, water

undēnī, -ae, -a. eleven (at a time)

ūnicus, -a, -um. lone, sole, single

ūnus, -a, -um. one, lone, alone [*an irregular adjective whose genitive singular ends in* -ius *and whose dative singular ends in* -ī]

urbs, urbis (f.). city

urna, -ae. vase, (funerary) urn [*for holding the remains of a cremation*]

ūrō, urere, ussī, ustus. to burn, to smolder [*can have both the literal and figurative meaning, i.e. to burn with passion*]

usque. continuously

ūsus, -ūs. use, something useful

ut¹ (conj.). so that, that [*the introductory word to a purpose clause, result clause, noun clause, or indirect command*]

ut² (conj.). as, just as [*used with an indicative verb, often indtroducing a simile or a temporal clause*]

uterque, utraque, utrumque. each (of two), both [*an irregular adjective whose genitive singular ends in* -ius *and whose dative singular ends in* -ī]

ūtilis, -e. useful

ūtor, ūtī, ūsus (+ abl.). to use, to take advantage of [*one of the so-called VPUFF verbs: deponents who take their object in the ablative; the term VPUFF comes from the first letters of the verbs:* vescor, potior, utor, fungor *and* fruor *(including their compounds)*]

ūva, -ae. grape, bunch of grapes

uxor, uxōris (f.). wife

vacō, -āre, -āvī, -ātus. to be empty, to be free, to be vacant

vacuus, -a, -um. empty, hollow; alone, without company; devoid of (+ abl.)

vadimōnium, -ī. bond, summons [*in the sense of a legal obligation to appear in court*]

vagus, -a, -um. wandering, shifting

valē (s.); valēte (pl.). goodbye, farewell

vānus, -a, -um. empty, foolish, silly, unreliable

vārus, -a, -um. curving, bent

vātēs, vatis (m.). poet, prophet, seer

-ve (encl. conj.). or; and

vehō, vehere, vexī, vectus. to carry, to convey

vel. or; [*when used in conjunction with another* vel:] either…or

vēlāmen, vēlāminis (n.). cloak, shawl

vellō, vellere, vulsī, vulsus. to pull out, to remove, to pull up; [*with* signa]: to remove an army's standards [*to indicate the departure of the army from that place*]

vēlō, -āre, -āvī, -ātus. to cover, to hide

vēlox, vēlōcis. swift, quick

velut (conj.). just as [*introducing a simile*]

vēna, -ae. vein, blood-vessel, blood

venia, -ae. grace, thanks, favor, kindness

veniō, venīre, vēnī, ventus. to come

venter, ventris (m.). stomach, belly

ventilō, -āre, -āvī, -ātus. to fan

ventus, -ī. wind

Venus, Veneris (f.). [name: *the Roman goddess of love, also used by metonymy for love itself*]

verbum, -ī. word

vērē (adv.). truly

verēcundus, -a, -um. modest, chaste

vereor, verērī, veritus. to fear, to be afraid

Vergilius, -ī. [name: *Vergil, the Roman poet of the* Aeneid *and a poetic influence on Ovid*]

vērō (adv.). truly, indeed, for certain

Vērōna, -ae. [name: *a city in northern Italy where the poet Catullus was born*]

verrō, verrere, versūrus. to dust, to sweep, to cut across, to skim

versō, -āre, -āvī, -ātus. to turn, to spin

versus, -ūs. verse (of poetry), line

vertex, verticis (m). whirlpool, head

vertō, vertere, vertī, versus. to turn, to spin

vērum (conj.). but

vērus, -a, -um. true, actual, real

vester, vestra, vestrum. your

vestigium, -ī. vestige, trace, footprint, sign, remnant

vestis, vestis (f.). clothes, clothing, garment

vetō, vetāre, vetuī, vetitus. to forbid, to deny

vetus, veteris. old

via, -ae. road, way, path

viātor, viatōris (m.). wanderer, journeyman, traveller

vibrō, -āre, -āvī, -ātus. to shudder, to shake, to quiver, to make shake

(in) vicēs (expr.). each in turn, alternately, back and forth

vīcīnia, -ae. neighborhood, area nearby, vicinity, proximity

vīcīnus, -a, -um. neighboring, nearby, near, next to

victrix, victrīcis (f.). female victor

videō, -ēre, vīdī, vīsus. to see

vigil, vigilis (m.). guard, watchman

vīlis, -e. cheap, inferior, lowly

villa, -ae. country home

vincō, vincere, vīcī, victus. to conquer, to overcome

vinculum, -ī. chain, fetter

vīnum, -ī. wine

violentus, -a, -um. violent, savage, fierce, aggressive

vir, virī. man, husband

vireō, virēre, viruī, -. to grow green, to be fresh, to sprout

virgineus, -a, -um. of or belonging to a maiden; maiden's

virginitās, virginitātis (f.). maidenhood, virginity, the state of being a maiden or unmarried woman

virgō, virginis (f.). maiden, virgin, unmarried woman

vīs, - (f.; defec.; nom. *and* acc. pl. = vīrēs). strength, power, force

viscus, visceris (n.). entrails, innards, guts [*often used in the plural, as in English, i.e. you can't have one gut or one innard*]

vīsō, visere, visī, -. to look at, to behold, to view

vīta, -ae. life

vitiātus, -a, -um. faulty, defective

vitiō, -āre, -āvī, -ātus. to make faulty, to corrupt, to weaken

vītis, vītis (f.). grapevine

vitium, -ī. fault, crack, imperfection, blame

vītō, -āre, -āvī, -ātus. to avoid

vitta, -ae. garland, headband, ribbon

vīvō, vīvere, vixī, victūrus. to live

vix (adv.). scarcely, hardly

vocō, -āre, -āvī, -ātus. to call

volātus, -ūs. flying, the act of flying, flight

volō, velle, voluī, -. to want, to wish

volō, -āre, -āvī, -ātus. to fly

volucris, volucris (f.). bird

voluntās, voluntātis (f.). wish, desire

vōs, vestrī / vestrum, vōbīs, vōs, vōbīs. you (pl.)

vōtum, -ī. prayer

vox, vōcis (f.). voice

vulgō, -āre, -āvī, -ātus. to prostitute, to corrupt

vulgus, vulgī (n.). crowd, multititude, throng

vulnus, vulneris (n.). wound

vultur, vulturis (m.). vulture

vultus, -ūs. face, countenance, appearance, expression